State-Society Relations and Confucian Revivalism in Contemporary China

Qin Pang

State-Society Relations and Confucian Revivalism in Contemporary China

palgrave
macmillan

Qin Pang
Sun Yat-Sen University
Guangzhou, Guangdong, China

ISBN 978-981-10-8311-2   ISBN 978-981-10-8312-9   (eBook)
https://doi.org/10.1007/978-981-10-8312-9

Library of Congress Control Number: 2018935194

Cover illustration: © Photos.com / Getty Images and © drk1234 / Getty Images

Printed on acid-free paper

This Palgrave Macmillan imprint is published by the registered company Springer Nature Singapore Pte Ltd. part of Springer Nature.
The registered company address is: 152 Beach Road, #21-01/04 Gateway East, Singapore 189721, Singapore

PREFACE

Whether the Chinese state can effectively control an increasingly powerful and autonomous society produced by China's rapid economic modernization remains a major debate of Chinese politics. This book contributes to a crucial but often neglected aspect of the debate, specifically whether the Chinese state can properly structure different ideologies and beliefs generated amid a modernizing society. This is significant in that the Chinese Communist Party (hereafter CCP) remains a Leninist party which still relies on its official ideology to energize the loyalty of its rank-and-file members. The state, moreover, as a post-totalitarian regime, still resorts to the official ideology to win at least part of its ruling legitimacy with the public. Hence, whether the Chinese state can keep non-official ideologies and beliefs within its grip remains critical for its control over society.

This book explores the issue by examining an important case, specifically, the state's engagement with the revival of Confucianism in China's urban society. During the early twenty-first century, Confucianism has undergone a revival among China's urban citizens, particularly intellectuals, private entrepreneurs, and the urban middle class. Together with Liberalism and Socialism, it has now become the most influential ideological current in contemporary China (Tu 2011). Why has Confucianism experienced such a rapid rejuvenation? What is the role of the state in the Confucian revival? What does the state's involvement in the Confucian revival tell us about its capacity in structuring China's symbolic environment? After all, Confucianism, as a non-official ideology, maintains controversial and even strained relations with the CCP, though some of its tenets are arguably compatible with its authoritarian rule. This book, by exploring the state's interactions with urban intellectuals, private entrepreneurs, and the middle class who are interested in Confucianism, reaches the following conclusions.

The Confucian resurgence has been mainly brought about by an increasingly activated and strong society, which has experienced rapid socio-economic transitions and intended to rebuild part of the social order wrecked by accelerated modernization through promulgating Confucianism. It is true that the Chinese state's softened attitudes towards and even tacit acceptance of Confucianism since the early 1990s is a contributing factor in the current Confucian renaissance, but it is *not* the decisive determinant. This argument challenges existing research which views the Chinese state as the main orchestrator for the Confucian resurgence.

The Chinese state has regulated the Confucian revival through a decentralized response mechanism. While the central government has only set broad policy parameters as regulations, it is the local authorities that make most of the decisions concerning how to handle the Confucian revival. Local authorities, therefore, have considerable room to maneuver. But interestingly, central and local government policies are seen as distinctive from and even contradictory to each other. The central government's policy parameters are coercive in nature and tend to suppress the rapid growth of Confucianism. Local authorities, however, guided by a strong instrumental mentality, are inclined to promote the Confucian revival in order to manipulate it for their own advantage. Their policies, however, vary for different social constituencies, namely, intellectuals, private entrepreneurs, and the urban middle class.

A decentralized response mechanism enables the state's control over the Confucian revival to be flexible and balanced. Local authorities are given substantial authority in dealing with the Confucian revival, thus allowing local authorities' experiments with Confucianism in their local policies. Furthermore, the central government's coercive policies and local authorities' co-opting stance, to some extent, both preserve the stability of the official ideology and accommodate the growth of the Confucian revival. On this score, they have enabled the state to reach a somewhat delicate balance of keeping ideological stability and extending ideological freedom, two seemingly paradoxical trends that in combination serve as the very basis for the CCP's ideological policies.

The state's decentralized response is largely shaped by its institutions. Local authorities' active responses are underpinned by decentralized political institutions. In parallel, the central government's conservative attitude towards Confucianism also has institutional reasons. As a Leninist party-state, the central government has to insist on its official ideology, as the official ideology remains essential to its organizational coherence and solidarity, especially given the historical institutional legacies of the official ideology.

While reaching these conclusions, this book provides a fresh perspective on the existing understanding of the Chinese state, its authoritarian resilience, and its relations with society. It refutes the common myth that the Chinese state is ossified in its ideological world, by revealing the ideological reforms and renovations made by subnational Chinese governments. Accordingly, it offers a new understanding of the local governments' increasing importance in China's ideological development. Second, through the decentralized response model, this study shows that the Chinese state's balanced approach to both sustaining its ideological stability and responding to social pressures is a key for its durability. Third, it reveals a new dimension of Chinese state and society relations by demonstrating that the Chinese state is not an integrated power entity as described by most existing theoretical models, but a set of scattered power entities which conduct multilevel and multidirectional interactions with society.

Guangzhou, Guangdong, China   Qin Pang

Reference

Tu, WM 2011, 'Confucian Spirituality in Contemporary China', In Yang, FG & Tamney, J (eds.), *Confucianism and spiritual traditions in modern China and beyond*, Brill.

ACKNOWLEDGMENTS

Writing a book has always been my dream since I was young. When I finally finished the book, I found it a tortuous yet exciting journey. During such journey, many people accompanied and assisted me. They include William Case, Mark Thompson, Jonathan London, Nick Thomas, and Justin Robertson. I am in great debt for their sound suggestions, thoughtful comments, inspiring questions, and even harsh criticisms. Besides, this book also benefits from suggestions and comments from Gerome Barme, John Makeham, Paul Commack, Brad Williams, Kang Xiaoguang, Xiao Bin, and Peng Guoxiang.

My gratitude extends to City University of Hong Kong, which has kindly funded my two field trips in different regions of China and two overseas stays in the University of California in Los Angeles, USA, and Australian National University (ANU) in Canberra, Australia. The China in the World Center in ANU has graciously hosted me, enabling me to communicate parts of my research with its academic staff and research fellows. Paul Farrelly, Lu Peng, and Zhu Yayun were particularly supportive of my life and writing in Australia.

Above all, I acknowledge the unreciprocated generosity of my interviewees. Some of them were quoted anonymously in my thesis. Others were not. But all of them have assisted me by spending precious time from their busy schedules. Without their sincere help, I could hardly have completed my book. Special thanks go to Jiang Huifeng whose enthusiastic support greatly facilitated my field trip in Qingdao.

Special thanks go to Palgrave editor Jacob Dreyer and Anushangi Weerakoon who have been very supportive throughout the whole process of manuscript revision and production. My research assistant Luo Yifu turned out to be an angel in helping me out in the painful work of collecting and sorting numerous online data. I really appreciate their help.

The best part of any discovery is often the companionship. My husband, Chen Rui, has always been the first reader of my work. His insightful comments and sometimes merciless criticisms have greatly improved my book and research skills. I would also like to thank him for sharing all my successes and failures, happiness and frustrations in life. Every bit of my progress is owed to his support. My parents have unselfishly assisted me by their constant encouragement and care. My lovely and naughty daughter, Pudding, has always been the source of my inspiration. Had it not for her, I would not been able to write for long hours with strong sense of guilty. It is to her that I dedicate this book with love.

East Asian Institute, National University of Singapore, National University of Singapore Press, has kindly agreed to use part of the materials published in "Confucian Education in Urban Public Schools: An Ideological Solution to Social Disorder in China's Cities?" in *China: An International Journal*, vol. 14, no. 4, 2016.

Institute of China Studies, University of Malaya, has kindly agreed to use part of the materials published in "The 'Two Lines Control Model' in China's State and Society Relations: Central State's Management of Confucian Revival in the New Century" in the *International Journal of China Studies*, vol. 5, no. 3, 2014.

CONTENTS

NOTE ON ROMANIZATION

PINYIN is used as the primary Romanization system for Chinese characters throughout this book; however, some names and organizations in the Wade-Giles system of Romanization remain unchanged, because they have long been familiar among the West. For example, Kuomintang (Guomindang in the pinyin system), Sun Yat-sen (Sun Zhongshan), and Chiang Kai-shek (Jiang Jieshi).

ABBREVIATIONS

BMG   Beijing Municipal Government
CCP   Chinese Communist Party
CEC   Confucian Entrepreneur conference *(rushang dahui)*
CEP   Confucian Entrepreneur pageant *(rushang pingxuan)*
CES   Cadre Evaluation System *(ganbu kaohe)*
CPSU   Communist Party of the Soviet Union
CRS   Cadre Responsibility System *(gangwei zerenzhi)*
CSA   Confucian Studies Association
ICEC   International Confucian Entrepreneurs Conference *(guoji rushang dahui)*
KMT   Kuomintang
NCWC   National Children's Work Committee
NFSS   National Fund for Social Sciences *(guojia shehui kexue jijin)*
NSC   National Studies College
OMRI   Oriental Morality Research Institute *(dongfang daode yanjiusuo)*
PRC   People's Republic of China
PRS   President Responsibility System
PUC   People's University of China *(zhongguo renmin daxue)*
SCHD   Socialist Concepts on Honours and Disgraces *(shehui zhuyi rongruguan)*
SCV   Socialist Core Values
SOE   State-Owned Enterprise

LIST OF FIGURES

LIST OF TABLES

CHAPTER 1

Introduction

The revival of Confucianism in contemporary China is puzzling. In the midst of the 1960s Cultural Revolution in China, Levenson (1968), after observing Communist iconoclasts' massive depredations of Confucian legacies, lamented that Confucianism had passed forever into the museum of Chinese history. He wrote, "as the Communists claimed to stand for the whole nation, the ancient mentor of a high, once mighty part (Confucius) was quietly taken over, and given his quietus" (Levenson 1968, p. 77). However, since the beginning of the new millennium, Confucianism, in defiance of Levenson's declaration, has been resurrected and even steadily restored as a living tradition in Chinese society. The revival of Confucianism is evident everywhere, from the unprecedented enthusiasm for Professor Yu Dan's TV lectures on Confucianism to the springing up of Confucian academies (*shuyuan*) across the country. In less than a decade, Confucianism has rapidly become one of the most powerful ideological trends in contemporary China (Xiao 2008; Yang and Tamney 2011; Tu 2011; Pang 2014, 2016; Wu 2015; Xu 2017). More importantly, the Confucian revival, compared with the transient revival of Confucian scholarship in the early 1990s,[1] has gone far beyond academic circles and received extensive popular support.

Why has Confucianism suddenly gathered great momentum in contemporary Chinese society? What is the role of the Chinese state in its rise? Is the state really the orchestrator of the Confucian revival as has been widely assumed by Western media and scholars? One needs to understand

© The Author(s) 2019
Q. Pang, *State-Society Relations and Confucian Revivalism in Contemporary China*,
https://doi.org/10.1007/978-981-10-8312-9_1

that in China's post-totalitarian political system, the domination of the official ideology is still an essential means for the ruling Chinese Communist Party (CCP) to assert its organizational control within the party and political legitimacy over society. The CCP may be interested in exploiting certain Confucian elements to supplement its official ideology. However, it would not be so shortsighted as to uphold a once antagonistic ideology to compete with its own orthodoxy, unless the CCP intends to forgo its current official ideology or its position as the sole center of power in China. Neither of the two, however, is likely.

How, then, does the Chinese state cope with the society's interest in Confucianism? How should we evaluate the state's coping strategies? Are these strategies helpful for perpetuating the state's authoritarian rule? China has been experiencing rapid modernization, and modernization has brought about a pluralistic society with multiple ideologies, which have presented unprecedented challenges to the current authoritarian regime. How the state engages with society to control these competing ideologies (such as Confucianism in this study) will determine, to a significant extent, whether the state can endure the proliferation of various ideologies arising out of society amid modernization.

The previous questions are the focus of my book. This book is not about the nature of Confucianism but a study of the causes of the Confucian revival and the party-state's response in China today. It concentrates on the interactions between state and society, and the implications for the Chinese state's control over society, or in other words, its survival over a rapidly modernizing society. This chapter will first discuss the revival of Confucianism in contemporary China, present research puzzles, and define key terms. It will then point out the significance of the study. Next, it will provide background for the study by showing how Confucianism has changed over time, and its controversial relationship with the CCP. Finally, it will detail the research methodology and preview the content of the following chapters.

1.1   THE PUZZLING CONFUCIAN REVIVAL IN CONTEMPORARY URBAN CHINA

1.1.1   Background

Historian Yu Yingshi (1987) once used the term "wandering soul" (*you-hun*) as a metaphor to describe Confucianism in China. He pointed out that Confucianism, due to the uprooting of China's pre-modern political and social institutions to which Confucianism had been closely tied, had lost its institutional base and had therefore become a soul without a body. Indeed, after the CCP's eradication of the rural clan structure through its "social reconstruction" movement in the 1950s, Confucianism lost all institutional strongholds and narrowly retreated to the spiritual world of ordinary Chinese people. However, half a century later, the wandering soul, surprisingly, has begun to find a body and home back in China. Since early in the twenty-first century, there has been a robust revival of Confucianism in China's urban population. Participants of this social phenomenon are mostly highly educated, well-off urban middle-class citizens; their aim is to apply Confucianism in their daily lives or, more broadly speaking, to make Confucianism regain its relevance in Chinese society.

The Confucian revival has been most evident in the area of academia, business, and urban groups. Confucianist academic discourses have proliferated in scholarly conferences, journals, and books since the mid-1990s (Ai 2008; Makeham 2008). Confucian academic associations formed by intellectuals have proliferated across the country. According to one account, before 1990, there were only 14 Confucianism-related organizations established in China, and the number had soared to approximately 100 by 2000 (Zhang 2003 cited in Makeham 2008). Some intellectuals have publicly issued manifestos appealing for the adoption of Confucianism in wider society. Some have even submitted related policy proposals to the National People's Congress or Chinese People's Political Consultative Conference (Kang 2008). In business, growing numbers of enterprises began to promote the learning of Confucianism, particularly *Dizigui* (*Standards for Students*), a simple manual of Confucian morality, among their employees. Moreover, an increasing number of entrepreneurs began attending Confucian lectures, spending considerable money and time to take Confucianism-related courses at China's most prestigious universities (Kang et al. 2010). In some urban areas, rising numbers of citizens send their children to attend after-school Confucian courses which teach basic Confucian texts (*dujingban*) or to full-time private Confucian academies which replace the state-run orthodoxy by instruction in the Confucian canons (*shuyuan*). According to one report from the International Confucius Studies Association, children learning the Confucian canons have amounted to over 10 million in 2006 (Chen 2007), and the number has been increasing steadily. Confucian associations organized by urban residents have also increased dramatically. Many have their own websites and online forums for discussing Confucianism-related topics. These associations have organized non-official "traditional Confucian rites" such as the worship ceremony of Confucius, Confucian weddings, and "pen-opening" ceremonies for those starting school for the first time (Chen 2012; Sun 2011).

Interestingly, the Confucian revival is promoted *not* by the relatively isolated, poor, conservative rural peasants or laborers, *but* rather the educated, well-off, cosmopolitan urban middle-class citizens and professionals. These people are the outgrowth of China's modernization and a "new" social force rapidly transforming Chinese society. For instance, according to a survey of over 1200 respondents conducted by Kang Xiaoguang and his team in ten Chinese cities in 2007,[2] participants in the Confucian revival have the following characteristics ("participants" in Kang's survey are defined as those who are identified with Confucianism or Confucian culture and participate in at least one Confucian social activity). In terms of occupation, 13.3% of participants are government bureaucrats; 14% are entrepreneurs or managerial staff in business enterprises; 52% are the so-called "white collar" workers such as professionals, accountants, teachers, lawyers, and clerks; 7.5% are university students who are potentially middle class. Only 1.5% of those surveyed are workers, laborers, or peasants.[3] With regard to individual and family income, participants' average income level is significantly higher than that of non-participants or the national average.[4] A striking characteristic of the participants is their high education level: 89.6% of participants have at least associate degrees, while the rate of non-participants is only 24.3% (Kang 2008).

Some participants' political and social attitudes also confirm that they are the informed urban social groups produced by China's modernization, rather than those who live in areas basically untouched by modernization. For example, as far as political attitudes are concerned, most participants, according to Kang's research, are conscious of their political freedom and willing to protect their rights through "rightful resistance" (Kang 2008). Of them, 56.2% had resorted to methods like filing complaints to various levels of government, protesting, and seeking help from the media when they believed they had been unfairly treated. The rate of non-participants who undertook these activities to protect their rights is significantly lower. Confucian participants also tend to be politically attentive, spending more time reading newspapers and magazines concerning domestic and international politic affairs than non-participants. In terms of social life, participants are likely to be cosmopolitan in outlook. 83.5% participants had traveled around China or had worked in other Chinese cities in the previous year. Around 35.1% have had overseas work or traveling experience. Kang's survey results are largely in line with most of the academic literature and media reports in showing that the various manifestations of the Confucian resurgence mostly occur among the informed urban public rather than in the rural population (Chen 2007, 2012; Billioud 2007a, b; Billioud and Thoraval 2008).

The Confucian revival brought about by contemporary urban Chinese society is the background and starting point for this book. It needs to be made clear that the Confucian revival, strictly speaking, is not an organized social movement.[5] This is because it does not meet some of the basic requirements for social movements. For example, participants in the Confucian revival do not make collective claims nor do they show concerted coordination in their activities. Rather, most of them are independent of each other and even without consciousness of each other. Moreover, they do not have clear target groups such as elites, authorities, dominant groups, or cultural codes on whom they make their claims, though they do share some common aims (for details concerning definitions of social movements, see Tarrow 1994; Tilly 2004). Thus, the Confucian revival is a wide-ranging social phenomenon seeking to regenerate Confucianism simultaneously by different individuals and social groups. My research questions regarding this Confucian revival will be elaborated in the following section.

1.1.2   The Puzzles

This study aims to explore the Chinese state's interactions with society in the Confucian revival and examine how the state's response affects its control over society. Specifically, it tries to answer the three following questions:

1. Why has Confucianism undergone a revival in contemporary urban Chinese society?

   Is the Confucian revival, as suggested by some in the media and academia, mainly orchestrated by the CCP? Or has it gained its momentum mainly from Chinese society?

2. What is the role of the Chinese state in the Confucian revival?

   How is the Chinese state involved in the revival? What strategies have Chinese officials adopted to bring the Confucian revival within its control? In particular, how have they responded to social forces interested in Confucianism?

3. What does the state's involvement in the Confucian revival tell us about its capacity of shaping China's symbolic environment?

How should we evaluate the state's response to the Confucian revival? Are they, generally speaking, helpful for the authoritarian state's control of society in the ideological realm? China's modernization has given rise to a pluralized society with various ideologies ranging from the ultraleft, such as the recent attempts to resurrect Maoism, to the right, like radical Liberalism. Confucianism in this study is one of them. The various ideologies are produced and developed by different social forces formed during a time of rapid economic and social change. These ideologies are, in nature, symbolic resources that these social forces can command to acquire political influence and exert social control. Growing influence of these ideologies, in fact, will not only undermine the persuasive power of the official ideology, but also constitute major threats to the authoritarian state, which simply does not allow existence of powerful autonomous social forces. Hence, whether the state can bring these ideologies and their supporting social forces within control is vital for its management of an increasingly active society. Regulations of the state dealing with the Confucian revival, therefore, provide an important window for us to explore whether and how the state can meet these challenges.

Of the three research questions, the second and third question will be the focus of this study, as the first question concerning the origins of the Confucian revival has been widely addressed in quite a few academic studies.[6] This study, therefore, focuses on the Chinese state and its interactions with society in the Confucian revival, particularly the state's engagement with social forces that have brought about this revival, and its implications for the state's control over society.

1.1.3   Key Terms

Although this study is not about the nature of ideology, key terms used throughout this chapter such as "ideology", "official ideology", and the "state" need to be defined.

"Ideology" is arguably one of the most widely used but least agreed terms in the social sciences.[7] Ever since it was coined by Count Antoine

Destutt de Tracy in his *Elements d'Ideologie* in 1817 (Hart 2002 cited in Knight 2006), it has occasioned numerous debates about what it means and been endowed with numerous definitions. In this book, ideology refers to a system of ideas, thoughts, beliefs, and values that are shared by people of a certain social, economic, and cultural background. Ideology helps people to explain the world around them (North 1991). More importantly, it is value-laden and contains normative views of how the world should be organized (Roucek 1944). Thus, it has strong implications for human actions.

Ideology as a concept as used in this book is neutral and does not contain a negative connotation. It needs to be pointed out that an ideology has been frequently viewed as carrying connotations of political sophistication including concealed interests and power orientation. For example, Lasswell and Kaplan (1950, p. 117) believe that "ideology is the political myth functioning to preserve the social structure". Metzger (1949, p. 125) defines ideology as "a system of beliefs that presents value-judgments as empirical truths in order to justify, with or without conscious intent, a particular socio-economic group's claim to material and prestigial rewards". Mannheim (1943, p. 83), similarly, claims that "by ideologies we understand those interpretations of situations which are not the outcome of concrete experiences but are a kind of distorted knowledge of them, and which serve to cover up the real situation and work upon the individual like a compulsion". However, in this book, ideology is used neutrally, as it not only refers to the official ideology which is closely connected with power and authority but also various non-official ideologies which aim to challenge the current authority and change the status quo.

Ideology, though abstract and invisible, can be manifested in human actions and discourses. For this reason, scholars sometimes treat ideology primarily as a set of human practices including both verbal acts such as discourses and non-verbal acts like behavior (Thompson 1984). For example, Thompson claims that "the language of everyday life is the very locus of ideology and the very site of the meaning which sustains relations of domination" (1984, p. 89). Gerring (1997) also points out that it is impossible to isolate ideology from the real world. Accordingly, this book will also focus on various manifestations of Confucian ideology (rather than pure Confucian philosophy) in discourse and action.

"Official ideology" here refers to the ideologies that are sanctioned by the CCP as its guiding ideology. According to the Constitution of the Chinese Communist Party which was passed by the CCP's 18th National

Congress in 2012, CCP enshrines five theories as their (collective) guiding ideology: Marxism-Leninism, Mao Zedong Thought, Deng Xiaoping Theory, the "Three Represents" (*sange daibiao*), and "Scientific Development Outlook" (*kexue fazhanguan*). Among them, Marxism-Leninism is pure ideology, while the rest of them are "practical" ideologies. According to Schurmann (1966), pure ideology is a set of theories which are employed for the sole purpose of molding the thinking of individuals, while practical ideology means ideologies based on experiences and practices, which lead to formulation of a policy or an action. Therefore, while Marxism-Leninism is pure ideology which is supposed to have universal applications, the rest are practical ideologies which contain strong practical and policy implications for contemporary Chinese politics. But the two are closely connected as the practical ideologies lay their philosophical foundations on Marxism-Leninism. The official ideology is manifested mainly through official propaganda and also through official government policies and practices.

The "State" in this book is defined as a set of administrative, law enforcement, and security-military organizations under the centralized control of a supreme authority.[8] The state thus defined is a Weberian state which is fundamentally a bureaucracy developing according to an internal logic. It is different from a Marxist state which is an instrument of the domination wielded by the ruling classes (Weber et al. 1994). The state in this book, therefore, is seen as autonomous, in large measure, from society.[9] In addition, the Chinese state refers to the hybrid party-state due to the organizational penetration of and political hegemony by the CCP.[10] In this book, the party and state will not be conceptually distinguished, as in most cases, the two are merged and there is no need to differentiate the two (Pei 1994).

Although a state can be distinguished analytically from a regime, the Chinese state in this book is closely linked with the Chinese authoritarian regime. A "regime" can be understood as the formal and informal institutions of power which decide who has political clout and who does not (O'Donnell and Schmitter 1986; Fishman 1990). A regime can be further categorized as democratic, authoritarian, or totalitarian. Though, analytically, a regime is different from a state, the two are closely interwoven in empirical reality (Fishman 1990). In this book, the term "Chinese state" is also closely associated with the Chinese authoritarian regime, and the two are sometimes interchangeable.

1.2   Why Study It?

This book explores how the Chinese state deals with the Confucian revival as an important case showing how the state controls society in the ideological realm. Its research value mainly lies in its theoretical contributions to Chinese politics, especially with regard to state-society relations and authoritarian resilience in China. It addresses Chinese state-society interactions in structuring symbolic and belief systems, and their possible effect on the state's control over society. This has been under-analyzed in the past but is significant given the fundamental role of ideology in legitimacy building, especially within the context of China's post-totalitarian polity in which official ideology still features prominently in the CCP's ruling agenda.

1.2.1   Ideological Control as a Research Gap in Studying China's Authoritarian Resilience

Can the current Chinese political system endure China's rapid modernization? This is a core question in China's transitional politics giving rise to heated scholarly debate. The pessimists, for example, Pei (2006), contend that the Chinese Communist state is unable to overcome its absolutist origins, and the CCP's monopoly of political power will ultimately suffer some form of systemic paralysis or power transition (see also Gilley 2004; Cheng 2001; Hutton 2006). However, the optimists, represented by Yang (2004), argue that the CCP has shown a strong capacity to adapt, adjust, and innovate, and its authoritarian polity has become more responsive and more attentive to economic and social needs. Therefore, it will be durable, at least, for the near future (see also Nathan 2003; Fewsmith 2001; Dickson 2003, 2008).

This debate, in nature, is about whether the Chinese state has the capability to control an increasingly heterogeneous and strong society produced by China's modernization. Most of the existing discussion, however, has concentrated on the state's adaptations to the ever-increasing economic stresses from society. Only a handful of works deal with the ideological side of the question, that is, how the state has responded to the changing belief systems within society. This leaves a gap in our understanding, especially considering that the ruling CCP, as a Leninist party, still enshrines Marxism-Leninism as its guiding principle, at least officially, and that the party-state, as a post-totalitarian regime, still uses official orthodoxy as a benchmark for shaping public opinion. Even among the few works on the CCP's adaptations in ideology, the majority focus on the CCP's transformation of its own official ideologies of Marxism and Socialism, such as President Jiang Zemin's "Three Represents" and Hu Jintao's "Socialist Harmonious Society".[11] How the CCP has responded to the revival of "non-official ideologies" such as Confucianism and how such response may affect the CCP's control over society has been largely ignored.[12]

1.2.2   Ideology as a Basis for Building Political Legitimacy

This study's research value is also related with the fundamental role of ideology in political legitimacy, which constitutes "the core of any political organization" (Alagappa 1995, p. 3). Legitimacy can be broadly defined as "the capacity of the system to engender and maintain the belief that the existing political institutions are the most appropriate ones for the society" (Lipset 1981, p. 84). Although in authoritarian countries such as China, legitimacy will not be easily questioned due to the lack of counter-hegemony which can project collective political alternatives for the people (Prezworski 1991), legitimacy still has strong relevance to the authoritarian stability (Gilley 2006). Another problem about legitimacy in non-democratic countries is that it will be difficult to measure because of the limits on polling as well as fear of being trustful to pollster in these societies. But according to Tilly (2005), the factor of fearing giving honest answers had significantly declined in China since the beginning of the twenty-first century. Thus, the concept of legitimacy is applicable to the Chinese authoritarian regime.

According to Bruce Gilley (2006, p. 500), "a state is more legitimate the more that it is treated by its citizens as rightfully holding and exercising political power". The perception of "rightfulness", however, is heavily influenced and mediated by ideology, because it is the ideology that provides the expectations and evaluative norms on which the government' s "rightfulness" is judged and evaluated.

Specifically, ideology provides the normative benchmark against which the government's normative legitimacy is measured.[13] According to Beetham (1991), a political system's normative legitimacy can be generated by conforming to established rules and shared beliefs within society. According to Viviane Shue (2004), the Chinese state's normative legitimacy mainly comes from its endeavor to match the Chinese ideals of "truth, benevolence and glory", the three most important rules and beliefs relating to state power. The CCP now pursues the "truth" by insisting on modern scientific rationalism and pragmatic empiricism, and encouraging the learning of scientific knowledge and technological know-how. The CCP also bases its legitimacy by practicing humane "benevolence" such as massive government-led efforts at mobilizing charitable relief through nationwide foundations and emergency funds. In addition, it attains its legitimacy by associating itself with China's "glory" such as a vision of a "rising China" that will shine in the international community.

In addition, ideology also provides criteria for judging the government's performance legitimacy. Performance legitimacy is very close to "effectiveness", to use Lipset's term (1983). It involves actual performance, the extent to which the system satisfies the basic functions of government as most of the population within it (such as big business or the armed forces) sees them. The Chinese state, by linking its effectiveness with "economic growth" rather than other criteria such as "social equity", significantly enhances its performance legitimacy. For example, Deng Xiaoping, the CCP's former leader, repeatedly emphasized economic growth as the first criterion for the government's effectiveness. This belief was also widely accepted among the Chinese public. All four World Values Surveys in 1990, 1995, 2001, and 2005 show that ordinary Chinese citizens gave more priority to economic growth than to human rights, environmental protection, and national defense, when asked "what is the most important goal for the country".[14] Rapid Chinese economic growth in the past 30 years, therefore, has gained the Chinese state considerable performance legitimacy. However, had the Chinese public not been persuaded to believe that economic growth was more important than other social concerns such as social equity or human rights (or had they still been indoctrinated with Maoism), the economic performance would only bring a weak legitimacy for the Chinese government.

Ideology will be critical for the CCP's legitimacy in the event of China's economic slowdown. As has been mentioned, the CCP's legitimacy now draws heavily on its economic performance (Chen 1995; Pei 2011). However, after three decades' impressive growth, there have already been signs of an economic downturn since 2011 (Eichengreen et al. 2012; Bradsher 2012). A plethora of obstacles have been noted, such as an economic slump of major export markets, stalled economic reforms, institutional deficiencies, resource constraints, demographic aging, and environmental degradation, all of which have depressed China's growth and will continue to do so in the foreseeable future.[15] In 2008 and 2012,

over 70% and 60% of Chinese people claimed that "rising prices" (infla-
tion) were a very big problem for China (Pew Research Center 2012). It
is widely speculated that in case the "quick win" of rapid growth is
exhausted, the current regime's legitimacy will soon come under serious
attack. In such a scenario, ideology would become the last resort for the
state's legitimacy. In fact, to rebuild ruling legitimacy troubled by economic slowdown and widening corruption, President Xi Jinping has
launched the largest ideological campaign in post-Mao period since he
came to power in 2012 (Zhao 2016).

1.2.3   Ideology in Post-Totalitarian China

In addition to its importance for legitimacy, ideology has special relevance
for China's particular form of post-totalitarian rule. In contrast to more
ordinary forms of authoritarian rule, China perpetuates a post-totalitarian
regime operated by a Leninist party, the CCP (McCormick 1990; Dickson
1997). The ruling CCP has had a strong tradition of using ideological
orthodoxy to rally organizational coherence and test the loyalty of its
rank-and-file members ever since its establishment. More importantly, the
CCP practiced almost 30 years of totalitarian control over ideology from
1949 to 1978, which still has a lingering impact upon the contemporary
Chinese political system.

Historically, since the CCP's establishment in 1921, its leaders have
employed ideological indoctrination to enforce its control over party
members. In the early years of the CCP, all members had been indoctrinated with Marxism-Leninism through various means such as group study
and self-study. During the Yan'an period (1935–1945), Mao Zedong used
thought work (*sixiang gongzuo*), a way of ideological control, to "rectify"
the so-called "wrong" or "deviant" thoughts to his ideological orthodoxy
among CCP members. From Mao's point of view, "correct ideological
consciousness" is the ultimate decisive factor in determining success or
failure of revolutionary action (or to put it directly, the CCP's rule in
China) (Meisner 1999). Mao's intention of instilling correct ideologies in
cadres and members was to effect a "fundamental transformation" in the
way cadres viewed the world, so that his will or the central CCP's will
could be enacted by these local cadres and members (Lynch 1999).[16]

After the CCP seized power in 1949, it ruled the country by instilling
an official collective of ideologies including Marxism, Leninism, and
Maoism to not only CCP cadres but also the whole of society. It adopted

various means such as persuasive propaganda and study groups to indoc-trinate the public with the official orthodoxy (Schurmann 1968; Solomon 1971; Lifton 1961; Chang 1997). Prior to the 1978 economic reforms, the CCP relied heavily on the official orthodoxy to mobilize mass consent and gain legitimacy for its totalitarian rule (Starr 1986). During this period, Communist orthodoxy substituted the former ethos in Chinese society and became the axis by which the CCP and even the country had been united and shaped (Schurmann 1968).

After the 1978 economic reforms, China began its transition from a totalitarian to post-totalitarian regime, and the prominent role of ideology in China's political life has weakened. However, party-sanctioned official ideology still holds an important presence in at least the organizational life of the party-state and cannot be questioned or ignored.[17] All party cadres have to adhere to the official ideology, and their ideological commitment is still used as a test of their political loyalty to the regime (Holbig 2009; Brown 2012). Indeed, one of the primary requirements for local CCP's cadres is "to keep in line with the CCP central committee in mind" (*zai xixiang shang he dangzhongyang baochi yizhi*). Outside the party, official ideologies remain instrumental for CCP's ruling legitimacy over society. Besides providing sources of political authority and criteria for perfor-mance legitimacy, official ideologies are still used as benchmarks to shape public opinions and serve as a framework for which the social construction of reality is made (Wohlgemuth 2002 cited in Holbig 2009). According to Beetham (1991), legitimacy needs continuous reproduction through expressed consent. While in liberal democracies, consent is expressed through election (the so-called electoral mode of popular consent), for post-totalitarian regimes such as China, ideological campaigns and ideo-logical education are still important methods for mobilizing social consent (the so-called mobilization mode of popular consent).

However, the CCP has to face the fact that its official ideology has lost almost all of its appeal among the public and even its party members. Even though the party itself has endeavored to innovate official ideology in vari-ous ways (Kerry 2012; Shambaugh 2008), the official ideology is still widely deemed as decayed and makes the party-state vulnerable to chal-lenges from competing ideologies. This is shown from the downfall of former Eastern European Communist states in which loss of ideological conviction in both state and society led to not only diminished societal enthusiasm for punishing oppositions against the state but also defections from the ruling elites (Linz and Stepan 1996; Thompson 2002).

Thus, the CCP considers ideological control a top priority and spares no effort in reconstructing, reforming, and propagating its official ideology. This can be shown from the CCP's personnel arrangement for ideology management. It has always been the CCP's supreme leaders such as Jiang Zemin, Hu Jintao, and Xi Jinping who hold primary responsibility for the CCP's ideology, propaganda, and mobilization from 1987 to now. According to Nathan (2003), the CCP's ruling elites have already developed the separation of authority and responsibilities in their management of state affairs. It is usually the top CCP leader who is in charge of ideological control. During Jiang's era, ideological management was mainly controlled by several top CCP leaders such as Jiang himself, Li Ruihuan, Hu Jintao, and Zeng Qinghong, while economic policies which are considered vital to the CCP, in fact, fall within the bailiwick of deputy leaders such as Premier Zhu Rongji from 1998 to 2003, Wen Jiabao from 2003 until 2012, and Li Keqiang from 2013.

The CCP leaders have endeavored to restructure and reform the official ideologies to cover the growing disjunction between ideological claims and social realities. Both President Jiang Zemin and Hu Jintao invested much conceptual energy and large sums of money in reforming and renewing the party's ideology (Holbig and Gilley 2010). In 2001, Jiang came forward with his "Three Represents" which claims that the CCP embodies the development of advanced social productive forces, advanced culture, and the fundamental interests of the greatest majority of the people. Through the "Three Represents", the CCP clearly redefines its formerly proletarian social base and casts its lot with China's newly affluent segments (Lewis and Xue 2003). In 2004, Hu launched his "Scientific Development Outlook" and "Harmonious Socialist Society".[18] The two theories emphasize the necessity of balancing economic development and social development, acknowledging that the growth-only mentality of the previous two decades is lopsided and that there are strong social tensions within society which may cause social instability. Since 2013, President Xi Jinping has launched the largest campaign in post-Mao period to champion an official ideology mixing communism, nationalism, and Leninism in the name of "China Dream". He promoted his ideology by imbuing a call for great national rejuvenation for China, resorting to the nationalist sentiments in China. The point here is that all leaders including Jiang, Hu, and Xi show that they have realized the problems of existing official ideologies and decided to modify them for the purpose of enhancing their value in CCP's organizational control and legitimacy building.

The CCP also invests heavily in ideological campaigns and education to promote its official orthodoxy. In 2005, the CCP under Hu Jintao launched the campaign of "preserving the party's progressive nature" among the then 70 million party members. The campaign lasted for 18 months and mobilized party members to study the most recent party theories, particularly the "Scientific Development Outlook" and "Harmonious Socialist Society" (*People's Daily* 2005). It was probably the best-known and most intensive ideological educational campaign since the introduction of economic reforms (Holbig and Gilley 2010). To strengthen ideological education, the central committee of the CCP issued a document entitled "Opinions on Further Strengthening and Improving the University Students' Ideological and Political Education" in 2004, requesting that "intellectuals in the faculty of Philosophy and Social Sciences (in higher educational institutes) should insist on and consolidate the guiding position of 'Marxism' in the realm of ideology, and apply the latest theoretical developments of Sinicized Marxism (Marxism combined with the Chinese realities such as Deng Xiaoping Theory) in their teachings". Such control has been greatly strengthened during Xi's ideological campaign (Zhao 2016).

In addition, the CCP also selectively controls the information flow in China to avoid open opposition to its official ideologies. According to Shambaugh (2007), virtually every conceivable medium which transmits and conveys information in China falls under the bureaucratic purview of the CCP Propaganda Department. This means, for example, in 2010, the CCP, at least in theory, controls 3350 television stations, 1939 newspapers, and 9884 journals (National bureau of Statistics of China 2011).[19] During Jiang and Hu's period, while the CCP Propaganda Department may not control all information in all these outlets, it has the capacity to censor and to crack down when and where it sees fit (Esarey 2005; Shambaugh 2007). Since Xi came to power in 2012, the information environment has been further locked down by new Internet control technology and policies (Zhao 2016).

In a word, ideological control had been and continues to be indispensable for and even intrinsic to the CCP's exercise of power monopoly. The CCP insists on upholding its official ideologies by, for example, building, circulating, educating, and safeguarding its official ideologies among both party members and general public. However, with China's intensifying modernization and increasing contact with the outside world, various non-official ideologies have constantly been developed by different social forces and competed with the official ideology not only among citizens but also party members. If the CCP intends to maintain its domination over society, it has to keep its grip over these non-official ideologies and their attached social forces, because it cannot afford to lose control over ideology. How, then, would the CCP deal with them?

The forthcoming section will first elaborate the rationale for selecting Confucianism for the study and then explain what Confucianism is and its historical evolution. It will then analyze the intricate relations between Confucianism and the CCP as the broad context for the whole study.

1.3   CONFUCIANISM AND ITS HISTORICAL EVOLUTION

1.3.1   Rationale for Choosing the Confucian Revival as Object for Study

Since 1978 when the CCP began to lift totalitarian control over society, various ideological currents sprang up and attracted large numbers of intellectuals and common citizens. These ideologies range from the left such as Neo-Maoism and Neo-Conservatism to the right such as Liberalism (see Goldman and Lee 2001; Moody 2007; Sleeboom-Faulkner 2007).[20] The rationale for choosing the Confucian revival for this study is threefold.

First, Confucianism has a broader social base than most intellectual currents such as Liberalism or Neo-Conservatism whose audiences are usually narrowly confined within academic circles or elite intellectuals. For example, Neo-Conservatism, which favors centralization of state power and nationalist appeals, finds most of its supporters among intellectuals and the CCP elite. Such political ideologies are, to a large extent, outside the concerns of ordinary Chinese citizens. Confucianism, by contrast, is more closely related with the daily life of ordinary citizens because of its ethical and religious dimension, though it also contains political aims and pursuits. Thus, it enjoys a more intensive resonance from the public than do other ideologies. This fits in with this study's aim of examining the state and society's interactions in structuring beliefs and ideologies in contemporary China.

Second, the Confucian revival's social base is of particular importance for the persistence of the current authoritarian regime. As was shown at the beginning of this chapter, participants in the Confucian revival are largely comprised of educated, well-off, urban middle-class citizens who have become upwardly mobile by China's economic reform. It is these new social groups that test the current authoritarian state's capability to survive modernization. As modernization proceeds, according to Huntington (1968), new social forces emerge and constantly demand to participate in the political system to protect their interests, a dynamic that exerts considerable pressure on the authoritarian state. These new social forces may make use of their ideological resources such as certain Confucian beliefs to mobilize social members and organize autonomous associations against the state. Thus, whether the Chinese state can control the belief systems prevalent among these new social elements is closely linked with the state's durability amid modernization.

Lastly, given the controversial relations between Confucianism and the CCP (which will be analyzed in the following section), it is more challenging for the CCP to adopt appropriate response strategies to Confucianism than for radical Liberalism or Maoism. Confucianism, on the one hand, is compatible with the authoritarian power structure in some aspects, but on the other hand, is in conflict with the CCP's official orthodoxy in SOME fundamental ways. Thus, for the CCP, it is not to their advantage to simply promote or suppress Confucianism. There is no direct "yes" or "no" strategy in regard to Confucianism. The study of how the Chinese state responds to the Confucian revival, therefore, could better examine the complex dynamics involved in the state's control over non-official ideologies.

1.3.2   What Is Confucianism?

Although this study is not about the nature of Confucianism or its contemporary development, Confucianism remains vital for the whole book. The following part, therefore, will briefly introduce Confucianism and its historical development as an important background for the study. Karl Mannheim (1952) has pointed that there are two basic approaches to understanding ideologies: one is to interpret it "from within", as to its content taken in itself, and the other is "from without", the socio-economic context upon which the ideology was dependent. The following two sections will begin by elaborating Confucianism from within, that is, its main components and tenets, and then explore Confucianism from without, showing the social and historical conditions that have shaped the evolution of Confucianism in China.

Confucianism is a widely used but loosely defined term. In its most narrow sense, it refers to the traditions and doctrines of the literati of ancient

China. In this book, it means a set of ideas and beliefs that are developed and transmitted by Confucius (*Kong Zi*, 551–479 BC), his disciples, and the numerous later thinkers who regarded themselves as followers of his tradition (Goldin 2011). However, it needs to be clarified that there is, in fact, little consensus on the definition of "Confucianism" among the scholars. Some extremists such as Joseph Tamney (2011, p. 97) claim that there is no such thing as "Confucianism". The reason may be because after more than 2000 years of development, Confucianism has absorbed and integrated many different ideas and beliefs, and it is difficult for Confucianism to maintain coherence. As De Bary claims, "Confucianism itself is just a life-style, an attitude of mind, a type of character formation, and a spiritual ideal that eluded precise definition" (De Bary 1975, p. 24).

Though miscellaneous, Confucianism has some basic assumptions among which the most important is that humans are teachable and perfectible through personal endeavor, especially self-cultivation and self-creation (Tu 1989). For example, Confucianism believes that human beings are born with the capacity to develop morally, and that moral development begins with moral self-cultivation, that is, reflection on ones' own behavior and concerted improvement where it is found lacking (Goldin 2011). In this way, human beings can establish harmonious relations not only with each other but also with nature.

Confucianism has three major dimensions. The first and most fundamental one involves its ethical system, which is a set of behavior patterns revolving around social relations, especially family relations (Needham 1970; Tu 1992). Among the set of social virtues and ethics, the most basic are the "three guiding principles (*san gang*)" and the "five constant regulations" (*wu chang*). The three guiding principles refer to the subordination of a subject (minister) to his ruler, a son to his father and a wife to her husband. The five regulations are five basic virtues: humanity (*ren*), righteousness (*yi*), ritual/propriety (*li*), wisdom (*zhi*), and faithfulness (*xin*). These are believed to be as constant as natural laws, remaining the same for everyone and for all time. In fact, the "five regulations" are what attract most contemporary participants in the Confucian revival.

Confucianism's second dimension is its function as an official orthodoxy justifying the legitimacy of the Chinese dynastic rule for more than 2000 years, since the Han dynasty (206 BC–AD 220). According to Guo (2003a), the justification of political legitimacy in imperial China can be articulated by four Confucian concepts: the Mandate of Heaven (*tian ming*), rule by virtue (*ren zhi*), popular consent (*min ben*), and legality (*he fa*). The Mandate of Heaven means that the emperor's right as a ruler is granted by heaven, which is a supernatural force. "Rule by virtue" means the ruler should be virtuous. In the Confucian paradise of the Great Harmony (*da tong*), there was a system of moral hierarchy in which an emperor is perceived as the most virtuous man on earth. According to Mencius, the rule of a truly moral king is characterized by his benevolence towards his people. "Min ben" can be translated as "regarding the people as the roots of the state". This means that rulers must constantly seek popular approval (not by way of expressed public opinion but through winning the hearts and minds of the people). "Legality" means governing by established laws and regulations. But legality in Chinese context is more often based on family rules, clan norms, community customs, and social traditions than on common laws.

Confucianism's third dimension is its religious tradition. As a quasi-religion, Confucianism is characterized by its faith in Heaven (*tian*), the Mandate of Heaven, and the belief that humanity can achieve perfection and live up to heavenly principles (Yao 2000, p. 43). Confucianism also has practices like ancestral worship, patronage of Confucian sages, and sacrifices offered to heaven. Although Confucianism has some religious traditions, it is, on the whole, non-theistic and does not involve a belief in a personal god.

Confucianism, as an ideology, has a great variety of manifestations including both oral and behavioral. For more than 2000 years of history, numerous discourses relating to Confucianism have been produced. Large amounts of rituals and ceremonies were invented and reinvented according to Confucian principles such as ancestral worship and matrimonial ceremonies. The long-standing (605–1905 AD) institution of "civil examinations" (*keju*), which rigorously and rigidly examine the participants' knowledge of Confucian learning and therefore select proper candidates as state officials, can also be seen as an important manifestation of Confucianism. Some of the Confucian discourses and rituals began to reemerge and revive in modern Chinese society.

1.3.3   *The Historical Origins and Evolution of Confucianism*

Confucianism has a history of over 2000 years, during which it has experienced continuous change and development. To grasp the change, one needs to understand the particular social and economic background that had sustained the evolution. Marx contends that "the 'ideological superstructure' is ultimately determined by certain historical conditions and economic realities by way of various socioeconomic processes" (Volker and Stehr 1999, p. xiv). Mannheim (1952) also argues that ideologies are responses to crises at specific moments in history and serve to promote a particular social agenda. Much of the same is true of Confucianism. Its evolution during the previous two millennia is a history of intellectual efforts seeking to build and rebuild social order for Chinese society amid various social crises. The following part of the chapter will illustrate Confucianism's historical development by providing corresponding socio-economic background and introducing its confrontations with other competing ideologies.

1.3.3.1 The Emergence of the Confucian School

There is a common misperception that Confucius is the founder or creator of Confucianism. In fact, the relation between Confucius and Confucianism is not what Buddha was to Buddhism or Christ to Christianity. Confucius considered himself a transmitter or editor of a scholarly tradition called "*ru*", which had existed at least one millennium before he was born. The *ru* tradition had been closely associated with ancient religious rituals, rites, and ceremonies since the Shang dynasty (1600–1046 BC) and was involved with knowledge in history, poetry, music, astrology, archery, and mathematics (Yao 2000). According to Liu Xin (?–AD 23), a prominent scholar in Han dynasty, the *ru* tradition should have already covered the "Six Arts" (*liu yi*), or the "Six Learnings" (*liu xue*) embodied in the six classics, the *Classic of Poetry* (*shi jing*), the *Classic of History* (*shang shu*), the *Classic of Rites* (*li yi*), the *Classic of Music* (*yue jing*), the *Classic of Changes* (*zhou yi*), and the *Spring and Autumn Annals* (*chun qiu*), which later came to constitute the core of the Confucian thought until at least the Song dynasty (Yao 2000; Littlejohn 2011).

The Confucian school (*rujia sixiang*) emerged as a response to the political chaos and social transformations during the Spring and Autumn period (770–481 BC). Before this period, the preceding Zhou dynasty (1046–256 BC) had provided economic well-being, political stability, social order, and cultural development for several centuries. However, it later fell into rapid decline and disintegration. Even before Confucius was born in 551 BC, the Zhou dynasty's federal system had been so seriously undermined that its member states had generally ignored the central government's order and fought with each other for land and property (Littlejohn 2011; Oldstone-Moore 2002). At the same time, society had also undergone major social restructuring brought by unprecedented economic growth, for example, the use of iron for agricultural implements, the availability of metallic coinage, commercialization, and urbanization (Tu 1989). These social transformations had substantially diluted previous social order and moral establishment during the early Zhou dynasty.

Confucius's solution to the pressing political and social problems lay in the individual's self-cultivation of virtue, or learning to be a virtuous human. By transforming people's consciousness, Confucius hoped that the order for family, local community, and state could be reformulated and reestablished. According to the *Analects* (*lunyu*), a book recording Confucius's sayings by his disciples, Confucius attached special importance to the following virtues: filial piety (*xiao*), humanity (*ren*), ritual (*li*), and self-cultivation (*haoxue*). Filial piety was viewed by Confucius as the first step towards moral excellence. The recognition of and reverence for parents can enable people to move beyond self-centeredness, and it can be carried over to life in community and even state politics (*Analects*, Chap. 1). Humanity (*ren*) can also be understood as benevolence and goodness. Specifically, a person who is *ren* is the one who can endure hardship, identify right from wrong, and insist on doing good and stand out against evil (wrong) (*Analects*, Chap. 4). "Ritual" (*li*) means rites and morality. Confucius believed that observing rites was a way to develop *ren* (*Analects*, Chap. 3) and bring spiritual transformation. By performing and participating in rituals, one can elevate his/her inner being (*Analects*, Chap. 17). Self-cultivation (*haoxue*) refers to full dedication and commitment to cultivating one's learning and character. Confucius once said, "the failure to build virtue, to go deeply into my learning, to move up to what I heard to be right and to correct my defects is what makes me concerned most" (*Analects*, Chap. 7).

Confucianism, however, was only one of the competing schools of thought which aimed to bring order to social chaos. According to Tu Weiming, a leading expert in Chinese philosophy, there were four major schools during this period, the Taoist, Moist, Legalist, and Confucian schools. Tu (1989, p. 2) provided a thorough description differentiating these schools' main prescriptions for solving the pressing social problems of the time:

> The Taoists, who developed a philosophy of nature and spiritual freedom, advocated a total rejection of human civilization which they believed to be the source of suffering. The Moists were concerned about the aggressiveness of the newly arisen hegemonic states, the wastefulness of the aristocratic

style of life, and the pervasive injustice. They organized themselves into military units to bring about love and peace through self-sacrifice. The Legalists accepted the inevitable disintegration of the feudal ritual system (Zhou's political system) and allied themselves with the centers of power. The Confucians opted for a long-term solution to the collapse of the Zhou dynasty through education as character-building. They believed that one could attain true nobility though self-cultivation and inner enlightenment.

Confucianism was developed in confuting other schools of thoughts. It took several generations of concerted effort to establish the "scholar tradition" advocated by Confucius. Of his followers, Mencius (371–289 BC?) and Xun Zi (298–238 BC?) were the most influential and significantly developed Confucius's ideas. For example, Mencius's "populist" conception of politics and Xun Zi's naturalistic interpretation of heaven and his belief in progress and interest in political institutions have all added new dimension to Confucian thought (for details, see Goldin 2011; Yao 2000). All these subsequent developments shared the same concern as Confucius about perceived social ills. The Confucian school during this period was only one of many in China's world of thought at this time and its fate remained one of many until the establishment of the Han dynasty (206 BC–AD 220).

1.3.3.2 The Rise of Confucianism as the State Cult

An important milestone in the evolution of Confucianism is its ascendance as a state-sponsored political ideology since the Martial Emperor of the Han dynasty (*wudi*, 141–87 BC). This development should be attributed to the relative lack of social and political order during the early Han. Before the Han, there was a short-lived dictatorship of the Qin dynasty which practiced an unprecedented harsh rule according to Legalist principles.[21] The emperor commanded absolute power, total uniformity of thought, and ruthless enforcement of laws, which later evoked rebellions from peasants and the populace and eventually led to the downfall of the Qin Empire. The founding fathers of the following Han dynasty, learning from the Qin's failure, adopted the Taoist practice of non-interference in their rule over society (or the so-called *Huanglao* method of rule, see Tu 1989). Taoism emphasizes following the course of nature, and discouraged any willful human intervention in changing people or their surrounding environment. As *Daodejing*, one of the Taoist classics, writes, "those who try to do something with the world will lose it" (Chap. 29). Taoists also believed that practicing Confucian moral concepts such as humanity (*ren*) and ritual (*li*) would stand in the way of pursuing national development of oneself (Littlejohn 2011). Thus, a firm political and social order would be difficult to establish.

However, a sustained dynastic rule required a stable political and social system, which precipitated the later Han emperors to seek a new ideology which could stabilize society. This gave rise to the rapid ascendance of Confucianism, an ideology not only emphasizing social order but also calling for proactive action to create social order. The Martial Emperor, finally, took the advice of Dong Zhongshu (179–104 BC), a minister and influential Confucian philosopher, to announce that the Confucian school *alone* would receive state sponsorship. Confucianism, therefore, was promoted as an official imperial ideology. In consequence, all Confucian classics, mainly the Five Classics, were set up as the core curriculum for all levels of education (Tu 1989). The Martial Emperor also built some imperial institutes to develop and research the Confucian classics. The state also began to enroll its bureaucrats from those who had a Confucian education and routinized this practice by setting an imperial examination system wholly based on Confucian texts.

Meanwhile, Confucianism was reinterpreted and reshaped so as to suit its role as a state orthodoxy. Among scholars, Dong Zhongshu made the greatest contribution by not only continuing the Confucian tradition of emphasizing virtues and self-cultivation (including humane governance) but also attaching importance on a supernatural heaven which commands that Confucian virtues be preached by both commoners and the emperor (Yao 2000). Drawing on elements of Taoism, Yin-Yang cosmology, and other intellectual traditions, Dong built a nationalistic cosmology in which the unity of heaven, earth, and human forms the foundation of peace and harmony. Based on this cosmology, he believed that there was mutual responsiveness between heaven and human beings, in which heaven was the transcendental reality and human should follow the mandate of heaven (*tianming*). The emperor, according to Dong, is the Son of Heaven and the emperor's rule is the Mandate of Heaven, which is similar to "the divine rights of kings" in Christianity. However, Dong's theory did not merely provide "convincing" theological justifications for the imperial rule. The rulers, as Dong argued, should also follow the principles of Heaven by practicing Confucian virtues and they should make themselves Confucian moral exemplars for their subjects to follow.

1.3.3.3   The Rise of Neo-Confucianism During the Song Dynasty

Since the collapse of the Han dynasty in the third century, Confucianism had been in a relative decline until the eleventh century. Its dominance over Chinese political, social, and family life had been, at least partly, replaced by the Taoist and Buddhist persuasions, which had gradually gained prominence among both the cultural elites and the populace. Confucianism, to be sure, did not disappear. It still remained an essential part of the political order, but its relevance in social and family life significantly contracted.

During the Song dynasty (960–1279), social and economic conditions led to a revival of Confucianism, later termed Neo-Confucianism (*li xue*). The Song dynasty experienced rapid technological advances and a "commercial revolution", which produced new social patterns such as "flourishing markets, densely populated urban centers, elaborate communication networks, theatrical performances, literary groups and popular religions" (Tu 1989, p. 28). Society also underwent major restructuring and transformation involving the decline of the aristocracy and the rise of a new social class, the gentry, who were noted for their literary proficiency, social consciousness, and political precipitation (Tu 1989). The gentry, mainly comprising of Confucian scholars or people with a Confucian education, viewed the predominant Buddhist and Taoist persuasions as harmful for the strength and cohesion of Chinese society (Chen 2004). They attributed the Buddhist and Taoist influence to the major socio-economic ills of its day. Some of the outstanding Confucian scholars, therefore, began to reformulate the Confucian tradition in order to establish a new social and moral order.

However, it took several more generations of Confucian scholars to reshape and reinterpret the Confucian traditions to meet new intellectual and spiritual expectations. Finally, Zhu Xi (1130–1200) synthesized these different thoughts and set one dominant school of the Neo-Confucianism, namely, the School of Principle (*lixue*). Zhu Xi's philosophy, in one word, is a humanistic and rationalistic belief that all components of the universe are manifestations of a single "Principle" (*li*), and this Principle was the essence of morality. Humankind can understand the "Principle" through human reason, specifically the investigation of things and the extension of knowledge (*gewu zhizhi*). By understanding principle, people could grasp and practice the vital moral principles (that are embodied in the Principle) so that they achieve an ordered family, community, society, and even harmonious relations between people and nature (Hucker 1975; De Bary and

Bloom 1999). Later in the Ming dynasty, another branch of Neo-Confucianism, the School of Heart (*xinxue*) emerged. Its main difference from the school of *Li* is that it raised a different way to grasp the Principle, that is, other than investigating the outside world, one should look into one's own heart to search for the Principle. For example, one of its representatives, Wang Yangming (1472–1529), argued that since the Principle lay in every living thing, it should also be embodied in one's own heart or mind. Thus, one needs only to consult his/her own heart in order to understand the Principle (or the morality). Anyone who understands his or her true nature understands the Principle of the universe (Tu 1976).

Neo-Confucianism mainly developed as a reaction to the ideas of Buddhism and religious Taoism and raised strong critiques towards both. It stressed rationalism, emphasizing that reality existed, and that it could be grasped by humankind. This is in direct opposition to Buddhist mysticism which insists on the unreality of things and that existence came out of, and returned to, non-existence (Craig 1998).[22] More importantly, to confront the "disturbing" influence of Buddhism on Chinese social relations, especially family relations, Neo-Confucianism substantially developed the traditional Confucian concept of Ritual (*li*) and specified the various formalities in the domestic rites of birth, wedding, funerals, and memorial services. From the Neo-Confucianist point of view, Buddhism's de-emphasis on family life, especially the filial piety for parents by encouraging a monastic vocation was really troubling, heavily subverting the Confucian tradition on family order which was seen as the base for other social relations. To strengthen the family order, Neo-Confucianist scholars such as Zhu Xi wrote extensively on family rituals and morality in family conduct, which shows the Neo-Confucianists' active pursuit of social order.

Not surprisingly, imperial rulers in the Song and later dynasties found enormous value in Neo-Confucianism, especially the school of Principle, in stabilizing society, and thus actively promoted the belief system among society.[23] The Confucian canon codified by Zhu Xi, the Four Books (the *Great Learning*, the *Doctrine of the Mean*, the *Analects* of Confucius, and the *Mencius*), were set by the imperial state as the core of the official curriculum for the civil service examinations in the Ming and Qing dynasties (Elman 2000). The Neo-Confucianist (or Zhu Xi's) commentaries and interpretations of the Confucian classics became sole references for questions in the examination (Littlejohn 2011).[24] This continued throughout the Qing dynasty until the end of the civil service examinations in 1905.

In gaining imperial support, Neo-Confucianism heavily shaped almost every aspect of the Chinese social relations including government, education, family rituals and social ethics. It also exerted profound influence over other East Asian countries, notably, Korea and Japan. Since the fifteenth century, Neo-Confucian values have deeply penetrated in both court politics and social life among the populace in Korea. Although Japan was not as Confucianized as Korea, most of its educated persons were exposed to Neo-Confucian influence (Tu 1989).

1.3.3.4 The Modern Decline of Confucianism and Its Revival in Contemporary China

The power of Confucian doctrine in Chinese society remained dominant until the time of the Opium War (1839–1842), in which the Qing dynasty was heavily weakened by an expanding British Empire. Following the war, the swift and deep penetration of Western culture seriously undermined the power of Confucian as a doctrine, first among political and cultural elites and then the public in general. Many elite intellectuals such as Kang Youwei and Liang Qichao began to accept the superiority of Western civilization and questioned the viability of Confucian culture for modern China, calling for sweeping political and social reforms. This sentiment soon spread to middle- and lower-level intellectuals and common urban citizens. After experiencing the continuing and transforming Western impact upon Chinese society, they also began to doubt the legitimacy of Confucianism as a viable tradition in modern times. This finally cumulated in the May Fourth Movement in 1919 which later became a wide-scaled anti-Confucian social movement. The triumph of the CCP and its exclusive promotion of Marxism-Leninism hastened the decline of Confucianism in Chinese society. After the founding of the PRC, the CCP launched one social movement after another in order to smash the Confucian legacy, finally destroying most of the nation's Confucian heritage.

It needs to be acknowledged, however, that Confucianism still existed in the Chinese social and cultural life during this period of time, even though sometimes as unacknowledged. Confucianist doctrines struggled to exist in other parts of the world such as South Korea, Taiwan, Hong Kong, and Singapore. Some Chinese intellectuals creatively integrated Western philosophy such as rationalism and humanism with Confucian traditions, thus forming the New Confucianism (*xin ruxue*) (this is different from Neo-Confucianism since Song dynasty; for details, see Makeham 2003; Yu 2002). Among them, Xiong Shili's ontological reflections, Liang

Shuming's cultural analysis, Feng Youlan's reconstruction of the Learning of Principle, and Mou Zongsan's moral metaphysics are noteworthy examples (Tu 1989). However, these significant developments in philosophy failed to save the massive retreat of Confucianism from Chinese political, social, and family life in most of the twentieth century.

Beginning in the twenty-first century, however, Confucianism regained some of its vitality and experienced a revival in China's urban society. This revival, as will be analyzed later, involves renewed social efforts to rebuild the social and moral order shattered by political suppression and rapid modernization. Like their predecessors, contemporary Confucianist intellectuals and ordinary citizens have participated in the revival for the purpose of rebuilding relevant Confucian social and moral norms in contemporary Chinese society. The Chinese party-state, in order to control society, can never afford to lose its relevance or more specifically, control over such social efforts to reshape social order. How, then, would the state regulate or manage the Confucian revival? Or is it actually the CCP that has instigated this revival? Before providing an answer, the next section will analyze the complex and intricate relations between the CCP and Confucianism as further background to the study.

1.4   CONFUCIANISM AND THE CCP: AN ODD COUPLE

As has been analyzed previously, the CCP cannot afford to lose its control over ideology. How then would the CCP deal with the Confucian revival? A popular suggestion is that Confucianism is a proper supplement or backup for the CCP's official ideology. Confucian traditions, first of all, were argued to be the best foundation to build Chinese identity and strengthen national cohesion (Lee and Ho 2005). Moreover, as an ideology emphasizing authority and hierarchy, Confucianism is seen as being able to "quell growing dissent, maintain social stability and inspire new loyalty for the current Chinese government" (Baum cited in Robertson and Liu 2006; Lin 1938; Tu 1993). For example, Baum has stated that "the reason for CCP to promote a campaign to resurrect Confucianism in China today is because the party estimates that by embracing the paternalistic model of 'benevolent authoritarianism' promoted by the Great Sage, the party-state is able to preach the virtues of ethical behavior and a 'harmonious society' without requiring fundamental political reforms" (Baum cited in Robertson and Liu 2006; similar views in *Nanfang dushi bao*

2011).[25] Thus, the Chinese government was widely assumed as being enthusiastic in the promotion of Confucianism (Ho 2009).

These arguments do have some basis. Some Confucian concepts such as "rule of virtue" and "popular consent" could provide some rationale for the CCP's insistence on authoritarian control, because as long as the CCP could rule with virtue and constantly seek popular approval, there would be no need to democratize. However, these arguments neglect the challenges that Confucianism poses to the CCP, which may surpass the benefits that it provides for the CCP. First, Confucianism, as an ideology, diverges diametrically with the official ideology of Marxism-Socialism, in ontology and epistemology. The divergence is detrimental to the current Chinese government's political legitimacy. Second, given the Maoist and Liberalist's opposition to Confucianism, the CCP's support for Confucianism may easily exacerbate existing ideological gulfs between different ideological schools within both the party and society, which the CCP endeavors to avoid. Therefore, unless the CCP intends to forgo its official ideology completely, it will not uphold Confucianism in any obvious way. This is exemplified by the January 2011 erection of a statue of Confucius near Tiananmen Square. Its sudden disappearance four months later took place under cover of darkness.[26] This vividly suggests the underlying contradictions between Confucianism and the CCP beyond their "harmonious" surface.

1.4.1   Philosophical Conflicts Between Confucianism and the Official Ideology

There are clear oppositions between Confucianism and the official ideology in their ontology and epistemology. First, the official Marxism relies on materialism, especially historical materialism, which holds that the causes of a human society's development lie in its means of production. The non-economic aspects of a society such as the political structures and ideologies are only an outgrowth of economic activity.[27] It is based on such a materialist assumption that Marx's historical materialism is built, and by exploring the rules of social developments in human societies, historical materialism predicts the triumph of Socialism/Communism and justifies the rule of Communist Parties (Wolff 1987). Although after the 1978 opening and reform policy, there has been a public re-evaluation of Maoism and the Marxist theory of history, and some of the Marxist prescriptions and Maoist doctrines such as class struggles had to be discarded or heavily modified in order to accommodate the new official theory of "socialism with Chinese characteristics", the CCP has never been prepared to dispose of the materialist assumption, which, in their perception, is the foundation of the "truth" (Shue 2004).

More importantly, the CCP's version of "truth", as has been argued by Shue (2004), has long served as a cornerstone of the CCP's legitimacy, because it is the materialist "truth" that the CCP-led modernization process and its economic performance are built on. Economic performance, which the CCP strives to perpetuate in order to maintain its performance legitimacy, is also firmly grounded in the materialist assumption of truth. Without this materialist assumption, all the economic construction or modernization would be pointless. So too would be the CCP's recent "theoretical breakthroughs" such as the "Three Represents", as they are all founded on the CCP's claim to be in command of the "truth" of social development.

However, Confucianism, particularly Neo-Confucianism and New Confucianism,[28] by contrast, adheres to idealism or cultural determinism, which is diametrically opposed to Marxist materialism (Ai 2008). Confucianism does not stress the importance of the materialist base or economic development. It only focuses on moral development and treats it as the sole measure to achieve harmony among human beings or that between human beings and nature. In reality, Confucianism is widely seen as a quasi-religion. As has been pointed out previously, Confucianism has certain religious traditions which can be characterized by its faith in "Heaven" and "Heaven's Mandate". From the Marxist point of view, Confucianism directly contradicts materialism and therefore is a total negation of Marxism (Fang 1997; Yi 1994). As one of China's respected Marxist scholars, Fang Keli (1997, p. 238) has put it, "New Confucians (Confucianism) are resolutely against the Chinese Communist Party, socialism and proletarian dictatorship".

In parallel, there are fundamental differences between Confucianism and the official ideology in epistemology. Official Marxism holds modern scientific rationalism and pragmatic empiricism as its basic attitude towards "truth". In official Marxism, truth is verifiable and knowledge can be acquired by scientific methods; hence, we should "seek truth from facts", as Deng Xiaoping has famously put it. Scientific rationalism, along with materialist ontology, is believed to the real dominant official ideology of the CCP (Tu 2011). In fact, it is the scientific epistemology that has underpinned China's advances in science, technology and economy for which the CCP has taken great credit. Further, this scientific empiricism, in contemporary China, is the only epistemology that is accepted and promoted by the Chinese state (Anagnost 1997).

Confucianism, however, is grounded neither in the principles of scientific rationalism nor pragmatic empiricism, but instead on humanist beliefs and sentiments. It does not proceed along the path of science, nor does it subscribe to the principles of science. As a mode of thinking, Confucianism is not based on demonstrable proof or evidence (*lun zheng*), but rather it relies on human intuition (*zhijue*, Tang 1995). Thus, Confucianism, as an idealist ideology, is simply not compatible with the science-oriented official ideology. For this contradiction, Levenson comments (1968, p. 81), "A Chinese world in which science had to be owned was the very world in which Confucius could only be captured".

It is true that some argue that Confucianism is compatible with Marxism in some aspects, for example, some contend that both are committed to transformation of the world from within and that both stress economic well-being for all, especially the deprived (Tu 2011). Some even argue that Maoism itself is Sinicized Marxism (or Confucianized Marxism) because it contains strong Confucian ingredients (Fu 1993; Chan and King 2008). However, the compatibility is narrowly confined within the two ideologies' life-orientations, that is, emphasis on this-life, *not* after-life (Tu 2011). The two still diverge diametrically in their ontology and epistemology. Although there are some contemporary undertakings to combine the two together,[29] for example, it is argued that Confucian ideas of humanity and quality are supplements to Marxist ideas (Zhuang 1991). However, most Confucian scholars with liberal tendencies and the Confucian fundamentalists believe that the two are hardly compatible (see Ai 2008). Staunch Confucianists are firmly anti-Marxist and anti-Communist. In parallel, Marxist fundamentalists are also strongly against Confucianism.

Given the differences between Confucianism and the official ideology, Confucianism may easily dilute the CCP's social control. For many of the Chinese people, even though Confucianism and the CCP's official ideology may not be contradictory, they are *not* mutually reinforcing. This means societal members' interest in and commitment to Confucianism could be easily mobilized by certain social forces to form their own organizations, which would create competition with the CCP's efforts in party-building. Moreover, some powerful social forces, by claiming to represent the true meaning of Confucianism, could become a kind of autonomous authority which may endanger the CCP's rule, just as the *Falun Gong* organization.

Confucianism may also weaken some CCP members' ideological commitment and reduce the central CCP's organizational control. As has been emphasized previously, ideological control is one essential means for the central CCP to monitor the lower echelons of party members. For example, to strengthen the ideological cohesion, the central CCP has increased training for party cadres in ideology such as the Marxist-Leninist ideology and the latest party policy documents (Shambaugh 2008).[30] However, more and more CCP cadres have become followers of Confucianism. According to Kang's survey (2008), around 13.3% of active supporters of Confucianism are in fact CCP cadres. This poses potential threats to the central CCP, as these party members could be easily swung by other social forces that control the Confucian symbolic and belief systems to challenge the party.[31]

1.4.2   Confucianism: Challenges from Both the Left and the Right

In addition to its oppositions to the official ideology, Confucianism has another drawback which the CCP leaders cannot afford to ignore. Confucianism is severely criticized and challenged by both Maoists and Liberalists in and out of the party. Thus, if the Chinese state fully supported Confucianism, or incorporated it as backup for official ideology, there would be strong opposition from these elements. In fact, the central CCP itself has not come to a clear consensus concerning how to deal with Confucianism.

The rivalry between Maoism and Confucianism is intense. There are clear contradictions between Marxism to which the Maoists adhere to and Confucianism. Maoists generally follow Mao's class analysis which focuses on struggles between social classes (Joseph 2010). Confucianism, by contrast, emphasizes harmony among different classes. Thus, Maoists tend to view Confucianism as representatives of the established order and are therefore hostile to it. They condemn Confucianism as "feudal" and "unscientific". In fact, the removal of the Confucius statue from Tiananmen Square was said to be orchestrated by powerful "Leftists" in the Central Party School. After its removal, there were also celebrations among unrepentant Maoists on the Internet, notably the website of Maoflag.net (Jacobs 2011).

Liberals also oppose Confucianism. Liberals in China have long been anti-traditionalists. During the May Fourth Movement in 1919, they criticized Confucianism as "anti-democratic" and "anti-scientific" by holding the banners of "democracy" and "science". Even today, some of them also insist on its anti-Confucian stance. A case in point is their firm attacks against the ever-expanding Confucian education promoted by some Confucianists. In 2004, a classical textbook for youth, *A Reciting Text of Chinese Cultural Classics for Elementary Education* (*zhonghua wenhua jingdian jichu jiaoyu songben*) compiled by Jiang Qing, a well-known Confucian fundamentalist, provoked strong criticism from the Liberals.[32] The background is that after 1993 when Wang Caigui, a Taiwanese Confucianist, initiated the campaign for reciting Confucian classics among children in Mainland China, Confucian education has gained a robust revival among at least millions of children (Chen 2012). Jiang's work was to provide a textbook for children to recite the Confucian classics. Jiang (2004) himself also admitted that his purpose was to implant children with the seeds of the teachings of sages and worthies. Xue Yong (2004, 2007), a former PhD student at Yale, criticized Jiang's book as a "movement to stupefy the people" and "marching towards cultural obscurantism". In defense of Xue, some other Liberals also argued that the indoctrination of Confucian classics would rigidify or poison the souls of the children (Yuan 2006; Lin 2006).

The tension persists. Liberals continued to express their concern for the rapid expansion of Confucianism in Chinese education. In the gathering of National People's Congress in March 2011, Peng Fuchun, a representative from Hubei Province, proposed that the government control the overheated campaign of reciting Confucian classics among children (Sina. com 2011). He criticized having children recite Confucian classics such as *Dizigui* and *Sanzijing* (*Three-character Classics*) as being "anti-democracy" and "anti-science". Although he admitted that there was some value in studying the Confucian classics, he suggested government intervention in standardizing the text so as to make sure that only appropriate materials deemed "pro-science" and "pro-democracy" are included in the teaching of the Confucian classics.

Given that Maoists and Liberals have powerful presence in both the state and society (Fewsmith 2001; Feng 2010; Misra 2001), it is not in the interest of CCP leaders to promote Confucianism as this would surely arouse strong resistance and opposition from both leftists and rightists. The resultant ideological cleavages would endanger the CCP's internal stability for which the CCP has endeavored to maintain.

In a word, the relations between the CCP and Confucianism, underlying their harmonious surface, are intensively and intricately constrained.

How, then, could the CCP deal with the Confucian revival so that it can grasp some advantage from the revival but at the same time prevent it from being controlled by other social forces and posing threats to the current regime? This is a central question for this book. Before answering this question, the following will first introduce my research methodology.

1.5   METHODOLOGY AND DATA COLLECTION

This study aims primarily to analyze state-society interaction in the Confucian revival, especially the involvement of the state. Thus, it needs data from both the state and society. Data from the Chinese government (both central and local) is primarily used for this research. It includes both macro-level data such as public policies concerning Confucianism initiated at various levels of the Chinese government, and micro-level information concerning individual officials' motivations and calculations underlying their relevant policy decisions. Data from society, for example, information on how and why some social groups participate in Confucianist activities is indispensable. Their reports on the state's involvement in the Confucian revival are useful for this study, as these accounts help present a full picture of the state's role in the Confucian revival.

To obtain the data, I conducted six months' fieldwork in Beijing, Guangzhou, Shenzhen, Qingdao, and Yangzhou from December 2010 to May 2011 and also a single month-long trip from September 2011 to October 2011 in Yangzhou and Shenzhen. A second trip to Guangzhou and Shenzhen was made in June and July 2013 for the purposes of verifying and double-checking data collected during the first trip. During the fieldwork, I conducted in-depth interviews with governmental officials, intellectuals, staff in Confucianist NGOs, private entrepreneurs, and teachers in primary and middle schools. I also collected archival materials, made on-site observations, and obtained data from media reports and other secondary sources. The four data collection methods will be elaborated later.

The rationale for choosing qualitative rather than quantitative methods lies in the probing nature of this study. This research is a preliminary step for exploring the research question. Besides, it is difficult to conduct mass-scaled surveys of such a sensitive topic in current China. However, if future researchers would like to make rigorous quantitative testing of my research results by their own devising, and if time and conditions permit, they can use my models for their hypothesized theories.

As fieldwork sites, the reasons for selecting the five cities of Beijing, Guangzhou, Shenzhen, Qingdao, Yangzhou are as follows. First, the rationale for focusing on cities is that the urban sector is where the Confucian revival is most flourishing and at the same time the pressure of dealing with it is most intense. As has been shown earlier, the Confucian revival has its social base mainly among intellectuals, entrepreneurs, and middle-class citizens in urban areas. Thus, cities provide the best sites to observe state-society interaction in the Confucian revival, especially the state's involvement.

Second, Confucian revival in these cities are among the most relevant ones for this research. The criterion of "relevance" is primary for case selection (Yin 2004). After initial investigations of important events concerning the Confucian revival through the Internet, newspapers, and academic literature, I found around 20 representative cases of the recent Confucian resurgence in which the Chinese state has been involved. Based on accessibility to possible informants, 11 cases in those five cities were finally chosen. Among them, cases relevant to intellectuals and higher education institutes were mostly concentrated in Beijing. Cases concerning the urban population's participation in the Confucian revival are mainly in Qingdao, Guangzhou, and Shenzhen. Cases concerning private entrepreneurs' interest in the Confucian revival were located in Yangzhou and Guangzhou.

Third, selection of the five cities is also based on their spatial and developmental diversity. They are located in the North (Beijing), South (Guangzhou and Shenzhen), East (Qingdao), and Central (Yangzhou) parts of China, respectively (see Appendix 2, Map). Three (Beijing, Guangzhou, and Shenzhen) are first-tier cities, one (Qingdao) is a second-tier city, and one (Yangzhou) is a third-tier city. In China, the first-tier city usually has the highest economic development and the largest population size, while the second-tier city is less developed in economy and smaller in population, and the third tier is even lower in the rank of economy and population.[33] Thus, the five cities should be roughly representative of China's urban area where the main social base of contemporary Confucian revival is located.

The following part will introduce my four data collection methods in these cities in further detail.

1. In-Depth Interviews

In-depth interviews provide most of the data for the study. They have almost completely changed my previous understanding of the state's role in the Confucian revival. For choosing interviewees, I generally follow the principle of representativeness. By selectively interviewing people from different social sectors and with different positions, I was able to construct a sample of informants that represent the part of the Chinese state and urban society that have been involved in the Confucian revival. Altogether, I conducted 60 formal interviews and around 40 informal interviews with people from seven social sectors (Table 1.1). Among the formal interviewees, 18 of them were intellectuals in research organizations including universities and research institutes. Twelve worked in various levels of the Chinese government, and among them ten held leadership positions. Another 12 were from non-governmental organizations. The rest work in mass media (2), middle schools (5), primary schools (8), and private enterprises (3). The social sectors, positions, and geographical locations of 60 formal interviewees are listed in the Appendix.

The selection of interviewees was based on their representativeness. For governmental officials, I tried to contact those who were in charge of education and propaganda in the five cities (including those at the province (*sheng*), prefecture (*shi*), and district (*qu*) levels) and was able to gain interviews with ten bureaucrats with leadership positions and two bureaucratic staffs. Officials at lower levels of the bureaucracy such as the district level were more inclined to agree to be interviewed than those at the prefecture level or province level. The reason, as I later found out, was because of China's decentralized institutions in which most of the administrative responsibilities were actually taken up by the lowest level of bureaucrats. Higher-level officials, especially those at the province level, were usually not involved in making specific administrative decisions and therefore

Table 1.1 The sectors of formal informants

Sector	Number
Government	12
Non-governmental organizations (including those organized by intellectuals, private entrepreneurs, and urban middle class)	12
Mass media	2
Research organizations	18
Middle school	5
Primary school	8
Private enterprises	3
Total	60

could not provide me with much detail, though they would have known something about how lower officials dealt with Confucianism.[34] Despite my sample of officials not being evenly distributed among different levels, they should be representative of those who have participated in making decisions in the state's management of Confucianism.

As for intellectuals, selection was made according to their different ideological preferences. Most of the mainland-based intellectuals who specialized in Confucianism can be categorized into three different groups: Marxist Confucianists, Liberal Confucianists, and Fundamentalist Confucian scholars. Names of representative scholars in each camp have been specified in the existing literature (e.g. see Ai 2008). Based on these lists, I chose five or six scholars in each group for my interviews. Most of them agreed to be interviewed. Thus, the distribution of the scholars was roughly even among the three groups. Besides these scholars, I was also able to interview four intellectuals who specialized in Confucian entrepreneurism (which will be discussed in Chap. 5). A majority of the intellectual interviewees were based in Beijing, including Beijing University, Tsinghua University, the People's University of China, Beijing Normal University, and the Chinese Academy of Social Sciences. Some were from Sun Yat-sen University in Guangzhou and Yangzhou University in Yangzhou. One scholar who was based in Beijing but was visiting an overseas institute was interviewed online. Two from Beijing University and the People's University of China respectively were interviewed in Hong Kong while they attended a local conference in November 2011.

Schools, private enterprises, media organizations, and Confucianist associations were selected mainly by their connections with the government. They were divided into three groups: pro-government, neutral, and critical. For the pro-government group, they were usually recommended by local authorities (officials in local governments were often glad to provide such service, and sometimes they even arranged appointments with these organizations for me). The neutral and critical groups were found through news reports or recommendations by my informants. As I found out later, critical individuals (who held negative views of the state) usually knew each other quite well. Their personal connections enabled me to reach a few of my critical informants by recommendations, the so-called snowball technique. In fact, personal connections proved to be valuable, as I found directors and staff in associations that were recommended by personal connections tended to be more candid and willing to reveal what they thought than those without any connections. The reason, I assume, is that the interviewees would be less suspicious of my identity and purposes if I was introduced by one of their friends.

Interviews were based on semi-structured questions which had been prepared beforehand. Questions varied considerably in length and content for different interviewees. At first, a tentative interview schedule was used, but it was soon revised and expanded greatly during the field research. Informants often offered additional and even unexpected information, which not only changed my previous conceptual framework but also raised new questions. To search for answers, I sometimes had to hurriedly construct new follow-up questions about the unexpected dimensions they revealed. Questions in my list, therefore, evolved considerably in the course of my fieldwork. However, there were some focus questions that had been asked for almost all interviewees from the beginning. For example, as for government officials, they were all asked about how they viewed Confucianism and why they decided to (or not to) take measures to promote Confucianism. For intellectuals, the focus questions concentrated on their views of Confucianism and the government policies towards Confucianism. For directors and staff in Confucianist associations, schools, and universities, they were asked about how and why they launched Confucianist activities, and how the government reacted to their activities.

How could I ensure the reliability of the information provided by my informants? In other words, how did I know whether my informants were "telling the truth"? This is a common problem faced by field researchers. I assessed my informants' information by reflecting on whether he/she can be expected to know what they are reporting on, a widely acknowledged rule for testing one's reliability (Dean and Whyte 1969, pp. 110–112). For example, I constantly asked myself: "Is the informant reporting a setting or action in which she/he has experienced?" If not, their accounts could not be reliable. During my interview, one intellectual told me about how and why local officials made some policy decisions. I asked him whether he was present or had participated in the decisions. He acknowledged that his participation in policy-making was very limited. His accounts, therefore, could only be used for reference. Besides, when informants reported something that is novel, I would usually follow up with questions such as "how do you know" or "why do you think in this way?" Responses to these questions, their depth of detail, consistency, and clarity, could also help me to verify the trustworthiness of the informants' words (McCall 1969). In addition, it is usually possible to cross-check the informants' accounts with other sources such as almanacs, official websites, relevant media reports, and even other informants' words.

Another problem about reliability is that informants may only give self-serving interpretations of events and practices (Van Maanen 1983). For example, government officials' accounts may be distorted due to their position as policy-makers. Intellectuals and other interviewees' response may also contain their own personal biases. To compensate for this, I tried to interview people of different ranks and positions about the same event or institution, especially those with manifestly different viewpoints. For example, I interviewed both leaders and staff in governmental and non-governmental organizations, as they could provide different perspectives on the same event. I also gathered information from those who were either pro-government or anti-government to reduce bias. This method parallels the "triangulation" technique, and helps me come to well-grounded conclusions (Stake 2010; Merriam 2009).

It needs to be acknowledged that the total number of 60 formal interviews and approximately 40 informal discussions is relatively small for this study. The reasons are mainly twofold. First, it is difficult to secure informants from government officials, especially those higher-level ones. Second, some of the expected interviewees such as private entrepreneurs, refused to talk, worried about potential risks. To solve the problem, I spent considerable time in searching for and analyzing governmental and non-governmental documents as a way to compensate information missed in interviews. The following part will introduce how I collected these documents.

2. Governmental and Non-governmental Documents

They also provide important data for this study. They include a wide array of documents such as official policy documents, speeches by central leaders and local authorities, and internal reports (*neibu ziliao*) and publications in both governmental and non-governmental organizations. They can be roughly divided into two categories: governmental and non-governmental documents. Regarding governmental documents, both the central and local government issued large amounts of policy documents and directives concerning the management of the Confucian revival. Central leaders and local authorities also made public speeches relating to the state's policies towards Confucianism. Local governments also compiled internal reports documenting the Confucianist public activities which were initiated or sponsored by them. As for the non-governmental documents, they were usually event reports and internal publications compiled by universities, schools, and Confucianist associations. These documents record how they conducted Confucianism-related activities.

Governmental documents were mainly used for this study, especially policy documents. I had tried to systematically collect the central government's policy documents and directives online. Later during fieldwork, however, I found that some local governments' internal reports had already compiled the central documents in chronological order and classified them into different categories, for example, regulations concerning thought work in propaganda, civil education, and youth education. This really helps me as the internal reports provide systematic archives for the central policy documents. According to staff in local government, these central documents served as the basic guidelines for local authorities, though they were sometimes general in nature, and did not always contain sections concerning Confucianism.

As for local official documents, they were obtained mainly by three methods. First, some were collected during my interviews with officials at local governmental bureaus. Given that Confucianism is not very sensitive, local officials, especially those at the town (or district) level, were willing to share relevant policy documents with me. Among the five cities, the educational bureau at Baoan District, Shenzhen City provided the most systematic policy documents. Most of these documents appeared on their websites. However, some local officials, particularly those at the prefecture level or above, viewed opening their policy documents to those from overseas institutes as potentially troublesome and thus refused to provide some of the documents, even if those were not classified. But this could sometimes be overcome by the second method, turning to the archives of non-official associations. During my visits to these associations, some of them voluntarily showed me official documents which they had received from different levels of government authorities. These organizations, after receiving official documents or directives from their supervising governmental authorities, usually kept these files in order (some of these associations' internal publications also covered some public speeches made by central leaders and local authorities concerning Confucianism). The last method involved searching through the Internet. Some local policy documents can be found on the Internet. By these methods, I was able to secure most of the local policy documents concerning Confucianism in these five cities.

With regard to non-governmental documents, some were given to me during my interviews in non-official organizations, enterprises, schools, and universities. These organizations usually kept copies of all their internal publications and had spare ones for journalists or interviewers such as myself. Their purpose was, of course, to advertise themselves. To be sure, a few organizations believed it was not appropriate to offer me all their internal publications, so I only got some of the materials that were compiled or used by themselves and their staff. Thus, I had to obtain some of their publications through purchasing in bookstores or online.

3. Secondary Sources

Media reports were used to supplement this research. They covered large-scale or prominent Confucianism-related activities. These reports, though non-systematic, are good supplementary materials, because the reporters usually had better connections with government officials involved in the activities, and therefore could provide valuable "internal information" concerning the government's role in these activities. Furthermore, compared with local government internal reports, media reports were more balanced as they provide information from different perspectives, rather than the government's alone. However, media coverage of these Confucianist events was limited and often confined to high-profile occasions, and thus, they are not the major resources of data for the study.

In addition, there are other secondary sources including published academic papers and books that examine the Confucian revival. They also provide important first-hand data for the study. For example, some research papers contain a few rarely publicized government documents and national leaders' speeches. The existing literature also examines the Confucian revival from a sociological or anthropological perspective and contains data about participants in the Confucian revival, which is of auxiliary use for the study. Academic literature also provides a new perspective for this research and thus enriches the whole study.

4. Onsite Observation

During my fieldwork, I visited five higher educational institutes, six primary and secondary schools, five Confucian associations, and two companies which set up Confucian education for their employees. At each site, I observed closely how they conducted Confucian education and Confucianism-related activities, and also carefully read the documents and notices put on the "notice boards" in these institutes and organizations. These field observations enabled me to obtain information concerning how and why they began to introduce Confucianist education and events, and some evidence of local governments' involvement.

1.6   Précis of the Book

The book comprises seven chapters. This chapter is the introduction to the whole research. Chapter 2 aims to establish an analytical framework of state and society relations through which the state-society interaction in the Confucian revival can be carefully examined. It first reviews the existing literature concerning mutual engagement between state and society, and then builds a framework to explain how a state can maintain its grip over a growing society by tactically using coercion and co-optation of social forces. It also points out that the form and effect of a state's coercion and co-optation strategies are, to a large extent, determined by the state's institutions. It then provides a brief theoretical account of Chinese state-society relations in general for the purpose of locating the Confucian revival within a larger context of contemporary state-society interactions in China.

Chapter 3 narrows the theoretical inquiry to the Confucian revival and the state-society interaction within it. In the first part, it reviews existing literature and builds an analytical framework explaining the Confucian revival and the role of the Chinese state in this revival. It argues that the Confucian revival is mainly a bottom-up phenomenon bred by an increasing strong and autonomous society struggling for spiritual tranquility amid rapid socio-economic transitions. The Chinese state responds to the Confucian revival by a decentralized mechanism, that is, central and local authorities take distinctive response strategies in their management. It then moves on to illustrate China's decentralized political institutions which heavily shape the state's decentralized responses.

The subsequent three chapters systematically examine how the Chinese state has responded to the three social constituencies that have brought about the Confucian revival: intellectuals, private entrepreneurs, and urban middle class. Chapter 4 focuses on intellectuals and their rising interest in Confucianism and the state's responses. It first defines who are "intellectuals" and identifies their potential as both regime supporters and regime opposition, as well as the state's dilemma of extending intellectuals' freedom of speech while keeping it under control. All these serve as the context within which my analysis is situated. The chapter moves on to introduce the regeneration of Confucian academic discourses and its challenges towards the state. It then argues that the state copes with the Confucian revival by a decentralized strategy in which the central government acts as a conservative "ideological stabilizer" while the local governments as active "ideological reformers". It contends that this strategy enables the CCP to achieve the balance of expanding freedom to Confucian intellectuals and retaining firm grip over them, which is beneficial for stabilizing the CCP's rule.

Chapter 5 explores how the Chinese state handles the revival of Confucian entrepreneurism among China's capitalists and concludes that the state reacts to Confucian entrepreneurism by adopting a decentralized response pattern. It opens with an introduction to the history and socio-cultural implications of the so-called Confucian entrepreneur. It then elaborates the rise of Confucian entrepreneurism and explains that it is the private entrepreneurs' ambition for social status that has given rise to their enthusiasm to become such entrepreneurs. It argues that while local governments actively exploit Confucian entrepreneurs to satisfy the business elite's demand for social reputation, the central government takes a dampening attitude towards it. In this way, the official support for Confucian entrepreneurs is kept only at the local level, and therefore the Chinese state reaches its purpose of elevating the entrepreneurs' social status but keeping it within a certain level.

Chapter 6 examines how the Chinese state deals with the revival of Confucian education among the urban middle class, concluding that the state also reacts to it through decentralized means. It begins with an introduction of the rapid increase of the urban middle class, and their dependent as well as contentious relations with the state. It then explains the rise of Confucian education among the urban middle class and its challenges against the official ideology and the CCP's legitimacy. It contends that the state employs a decentralized response pattern to manage the revival. Specifically, the central government imposes rigid guidelines over Confucian education in order to avoid possible challenges to the education of the official ideology. Some local governments creatively promote Confucian education, due to their personal identification with Confucianism as well as possible opportunities for economic benefits and political promotions. It argues that the decentralized pattern has enabled the state to both divert the possible dangers of Confucianism and accommodate the urban middle class' interest in Confucian education.

The last chapter summarizes the major findings and points out the variations in the state's decentralized responses towards the three social groups, intellectuals, private entrepreneurs, and the urban middle class. It then elaborates the theoretical contributions of this study in the Chinese state's ideological reforms, its authoritarian resilience, and its relations with society. Finally, it points out possible directions for future studies.

NOTES

1. Confucian scholarship in the early 1990s is believed to be an integrated part of the new Conservatism which arose in the intellectual landscape as a response to revival of Liberalism in the 1980s (Goldman and Lee 2001; Chen 2012).
2. According to Kang, the ten cities are chosen from the eastern, middle, and western parts of China. In each part, at least one large city and one small town are selected. The three cities in Eastern China are Beijing, Shijiazhuang, and Baoding. The two in the central part are Taiyuan and Taigu; and the five in the western part are Chengdu, Luojiang, Mianyang, Shehong, and Ziyang.
3. Regarding the extreme low rate of peasants, workers, and laborers as participants, in addition to their lack of interest in Confucianism, another plausible explanation is that these particular social classes have insufficient understanding of Confucianism as an ideology, due to their limited education. Thus, even though they may also accept some Confucian values and enjoy some symbolic expressions of Confucianism such as celebrating traditional festivals and worshiping their ancestors, they are excluded from the category of "participants" in Kang's research.
4. "Non-participants" refer to those who do not meet the two requirements of "participants".
5. Although Kang (2008) defines the Confucian revival as a "cultural nationalist" social movement, Yang and Tamney (2011) believe that what Kang means by the movement is ambiguous.
6. Chapter 3 of this book will present a detailed review of the literature explaining the Confucian revival.
7. There are quite a few academic articles systematically summarizing different definitions of "ideology" in social science works, among which Gerring (1997) and Knight (2006) offer probably the most detailed and comprehensive summaries.
8. This definition is borrowed from Skocpol (1979).
9. In fact, the Chinese state, as a Leninist party-state, is seen as more autonomous than other forms of authoritarian state (McCormick 1990; Walder 1985).
10. The Chinese state only refers to the People's Republic of China.

11. Some representative works in this area include Shambaugh (2008), Holbig (2006, 2009, 2010), and Laliberte and Lanteigne (2008).
12. Even if there are some studies in this area, for example, how the Chinese state controls radical Liberalism, they tend to focus on how the Chinese state has controlled deviant intellectuals or activists. More importantly, how such responses affect China's authoritarian resilience has been seldom discussed. For details of the Chinese state's control of intellectuals, please refer to Goldman (1993, 1994, 1996).
13. The term "ideology" follows the previous definition, and refers to the subjective ideas in everyone's mind, not the official ideology per se.
14. For the surveys in 1990 and 1995, over 60% of all respondents chose "economic growth". For details, please visit www.wvsevsdb.com/wvs/WVSAnalizeQuestion.jsp
15. Among the pessimistic predictions of China's economic future, the argument of "unsustainable growth model" and "institutional deficiencies" are the most popular. For details of the "unsustainable growth model", see Betts and Devereux (2000), and Wheatley (2008). For "institutional deficiencies", see Nee (2006) and Liu (2006). Recently, Michael Petties considers that China suffers from an "unsustainable debt crisis" which would inevitably lead to economic recession (*The Wall Street Journal* 2012).
16. Ideological orthodoxy, accordingly, is essential for the CCP's coherence and solidarity. This can be shown in that ideological struggles within the party (elite) have often led to serious in-fighting within the CCP. For example, during the early 1930s, the ideological strife between Wang Ming and Mao Zedong led to the CCP's internal cleavages and resulted in serious military setbacks which forced the CCP and its Red Army to retreat and step out on the "Long March" (Kampen 2000). Even during the post-Mao period, power struggles and factional infighting among political elites often originated from ideological cleavages rather than the other way around (Sun 1995).
17. For details of ideology and post-totalitarian rule in former Communist East European countries, see Linz and Stepan (1996).
18. For a detailed discussion about the two theories, please refer to Holbig (2009).
19. For details, please refer to www.stats.gov.cn/tjsj/ndsj/2011/indexch.htm
20. All these ideologies have their own theoretical agendas and political aims, and raise challenges to the current government in different ways. While Liberalism advocates limiting government power through political reforms and eventually building a limited, responsive, and fair government based on popular consent, Maoism negates both the immediate need and ultimate value of Liberalism in contemporary China, though it also aims to restrain the power of the government and oppose some of the economic measures taken by the incumbent government, especially the full embrace of the free market. Maoism also decries the decentralization

which permits China's transition to a market economy and urges recentralized control over economic and cultural life (Goldman and Lee 2001). Other non-official ideologies such as Neo-Conservatism and Neo-Authoritarianism lie in between radical Liberalism and Maoism, but also challenge some of the incumbent government's political, economic, and cultural policies and practices.

21. Legalism was one of the four schools of thought introduced in earlier section. It emphasized the use of laws for political and social rule; specifically, laws should be strictly enforced so as to reward those who obey them and punish accordingly those who dare to break them. For details, see Cohen et al. (1980).

22. Neo-Confucianism, nevertheless, borrowed heavily from Taoist and Buddhist terminology and concepts to explain its doctrine (for details, see Huang 1999; Tu 1979, 1985). For example, as Arthur Wright contends, "the Neo-Confucian understanding of all under heaven as manifestations of a universal principle is a derivation of the Buddhist concept of all things as manifestations of a 'pan-absolute'" (1959, p. 91).

23. However, Neo-Confucianism was not officially recognized when Zhu Xi was alive.

24. However, as Elman (2000) has emphasized, though they were used as the orthodox interpretations in state examinations, this does not mean the bureaucrats and Chinese gentry actually believed those interpretations. He also pointed out that there were some very active schools such as the Han learning (*hanxue*) school that offered competing interpretations of Confucianism (see Elman 2000).

25. There are similar views in China. Only such views were expressed indirectly by commenting on Kuo Ming Tang (KMT)'s use of Confucian education as a way to promote its authoritarian rule in the early period of the Republic of China (ROC).

26. For details about the whole event, see Jacobs (2011).

27. This idea has been clearly put forth in the preface of Karl Marx's *A Contribution to the Critique of Political Economy* (1979).

28. For differences between the two, see Makeham (2003, 2008).

29. For details, see Fang (1997), Song (2001), and Li (1999). Makeham (2008) and Ai (2008) have detailed analysis on Chinese Confucian scholars' academic discourses that attempt to combine Confucianism and Marxism.

30. According to a 2006 central CCP's directive, all cadres, every five years, must have a minimum of three months' training, which is conducted principally through the nationwide networks of cadre management schools, and administrative management schools and party schools (Shambaugh 2008, p. 143). The textbooks used in party schools, for example, emphasize the "Three Basics (*Sange Jiben*) and Five Contemporaries (*Wuge Dangdai*)". The "Three Basics" are Marxism-Leninism, Mao Zedong

Thought, and Deng Xiaoping Theory. The Five Contemporaries are the contemporary world economy, world science and technology, the world legal system, the world military and China's national defense, and world ideational trends (Ibid, p. 146). According to the General Office of the CCP's Central Organization Department (2001), by the end of 2001, around half of party cadres had received one or several forms of mid-career training.

31. Though the central CCP does not forbid cadres to adopt Confucianism, it does not lend encouragement. It is true that some scholars in the Central Party School have publicly confirmed the value of Confucianism in contemporary Chinese society (Xiang 2008; Wang 2006, 2007a, b), but this does not mean that the CCP Central Committee intends to promote Confucianism among its rank-and-file members. According to Xing Bensi (2010), former vice president of the Central Party School, the CCP is open to integrating some "proper" Confucian elements into Marxism-Leninism, but the priority should be put on so-called Socialist core values (*shehuizhiyi hexin jiazhiguan*, hereafter SCV). Confucianism should only *supplement* rather than replace the SCV. In fact, none of the textbooks used in Party schools are relevant to Confucianism. The CCP is wary of possible erosion of its official ideology and, more importantly, its organizational control over its members, due to the growing influence of other ideologies including Confucianism.

32. It needs to be pointed out that not all Liberals opposed Confucian education. Some Liberals, for example, Qiu Feng, a well-known freelance scholar, showed his sympathy towards such education.

33. The Chinese cities are divided into different tiers according to their economic and population size. There is no agreed definition on what constitutes the first, second, and third tier of cities in China yet. But there is some consensus on which cities fall into the different categories. For details, please visit http://www.cnbc.com/id/41420632/ The_Rise_of_China_s_2nd_and_3rd_Tier_Cities

34. Besides, according to one of my informants, higher-level officials were more alert to my Hong Kong identity and my close connections with overseas institutes.

REFERENCES

Ai, J 2008, 'The re-functioning of Confucianism: the mainland Chinese intellectual response since the 1980s', *Issues & Studies*, vol. 44, no. 2, pp. 37–65.

Alagappa, M 1995, *Political legitimacy in Southeast Asia: The quest for moral authority*, Stanford University Press, Stanford, CA.

Anagnost, A 1997, *National past-times: narrative, representation, and power in modern China*, Duke University Press, Durham, NC.

Beetham, D 1991, *The legitimation of power*, Palgrave Macmillan, London.

Betts, C & Devereux, M 2000, 'International monetary policy coordination and competitive depreciation: a reevaluation', *Journal of Money Credit and Banking*, vol. 32, pp. 722–745.

Billioud, S & Thoraval, J 2008, 'The contemporary revival of Confucianism, Anshen liming or the religious dimension of Confucianism', *China Perspective*, no. 3.

Billioud, S 2007a, 'Confucianism, 'cultural tradition,' and official discourses at the start of the new century', *China Perspectives*, no. 3.

Billioud, S 2007b, 'Jiaohua: the Confucian revival today as an educative project', *China Perspectives*, no. 4.

Bradsher, K 2012, 'Construction and real estate reveal problems in China's economy', *The New York Times*, September 9th.

Brown, K 2012. 'The communist party of China and ideology,' *China: An International Journal*, vol. 10, no. 2, pp. 52–68.

Chan, H & King, YC 2008, 'Chinese Religion', In Gamer, R *Understanding Contemporary China*, Lynn Reinner, New York.

Chang J 1997, 'The mechanics of state propaganda: the People's Republic of China and the Soviet Union in the 1950s', In Cheek, T & Saich, T (eds.), *New perspectives on state socialism in China*, M. E. Sharpe, Armonk, 1997, pp. 76–124.

Chen, F 1995, *Economic transition and political legitimacy in post-Mao China: ideology and reform*, SUNY Press.

Chen, L 2004, *Song Ming li xue (Neo-Confucianism)*, Hua dong shi fan da xue chu ban she (Huadong Normal University Press), Shanghai.

Chen, L 2007, 'Kongzi yu Dangdai zhongguo' (Confucius and contemporary China), *Dushu (Reading)*, no. 11.

Chen, Y 2012, 'Renewing Confucianism as a living tradition in the 21st century China: reciting Classics, Reviving Academies and restoring rituals', In Giordan, G (ed.), *Mapping religion and spirituality in a post-secular world*, Brill Press.

Cheng, L 2001, 'The end of the CCP's resilient authoritarianism?' *The China Quarterly*, vol. 211, pp. 595–623.

Cohen, JA, Edwards, RR & Chen, CF (eds.) 1980, *Essays on China's legal tradition*, Princeton University Press, Princeton.

Craig, E 1998, *Routledge encyclopedia of philosophy*, volume 7, Taylor & Francis, London.

De Bary, WT 1975, *The unfolding of Neo-Confucianism*, Columbia University Press, New York.

De Bary, WT & Bloom, I 1999, *Sources of Chinese tradition second edition, volume I: from earliest times to 1600*, Columbia University Press, New York.

Dean, JP & Whyte, WF 1969, 'How do you know if the informant is telling the truth?', in McCall, GJ & Simmons JL (eds.), *Issues in participant observation*. Addison-Wesley, MA.

Dickson, B 1997, *Democratization in China and Taiwan: the adaptability of Leninist parties*, Oxford University Press, New York.

Dickson, B 2003, *Red Capitalists in China: the party, private entrepreneurs and prospects for political change*, Cambridge University Press, Cambridge.

Dickson, B 2008, *Wealth into power: the Communist Party's embrace of China's private sector*, Cambridge University Press, Cambridge.

Elman, B 2000, *A cultural history of civil examinations in late imperial China*, University of California Press, Berkeley and Los Angeles.

Esarey, A 2005, 'Cornering the market: state strategies for controlling China's commercial media', *Asian Perspective*, vol. 29, no. 4, pp. 37–83.

Fang, KL 1997, *Xiandai xin ruxue yu zhongguo xiandaihua (Contemporary new Confucianism and Chinese modernization)*, Tianjin renmin chubanshe (Tianjin People's Press), Tianjin.

Feng, CY 2010, 'Charter 08 and China's troubled liberalism', *Asian Times*, viewed on November 3rd, available at http://www.atimes.com/atimes/China/LB26Ad04.html

Fewsmith, J 2001, *China since Tiananmen: the politics of transition*, Cambridge University Press, Cambridge.

Fishman, RM 1990, 'Rethinking state and regime: Southern Europe's transition to democracy', *World Politics*, vol. 42, no. 3, pp. 422–440.

Fu, ZY 1993, *Autocratic tradition and Chinese politics*, Cambridge University Press, New York.

Gerring, J 1997, 'Ideology: a definitional analysis', *Political Research Quarterly*, vol. 50 (December), pp. 957–94.

Gilley, B 2004, *China's democratic future: how it will happen and where it will lead*, Columbia University Press.

Gilley, B 2006, 'The meaning and measure of state legitimacy: results for 72 countries', *European Journal of Political Research*, vol. 45, pp. 499–525.

Goldin, P 2011, *Confucianism*, Acumen Publishing House, Durham, UK.

Goldman, M & Lee, L (eds.) 2001, *An intellectual history of modern China*, Cambridge University Press, Cambridge.

Goldman, M 1993, 'The intellectuals in the Deng era', In Kau, MY & Marsh, SH (eds.), *China in the era of Deng Xiaoping: a decade of reform*, M.E. Sharpe, Armonk, pp. 285–326.

Goldman, M 1994, *Sowing the seeds of democracy in China: political reform in the Deng Xiaoping era*, Harvard University Press.

Goldman, M 1996, 'Politically-engaged intellectuals in the Deng-Jiang era: a changing relationship with the party-state', *The China Quarterly*, March, no. 145, pp. 35–52.

Guo, BG 2003a, 'Political legitimacy and China's transition', *Journal of Chinese Political Science*, vol. 8, no. 1–2, pp. 1–25.

Guo, X 2003b, *State and society in China's democratic transition: Confucianism, Leninism, and economic development*, Routledge, London.

Hart, D 2002, 'Antoine Louis Claude, Comte Destutt de Tracy (1754–1836): life and works', *The Library of Economics and Liberty*, Liberty Fund, viewed on December, 2012, available at http://www.econlib.org/library/Tracy/DestuttdeTracyBio.html

Ho, N 2009, 'Unlikely bedfellows? Confucius, the CCP and the resurgence of Guoxue', *Harvard International Review*, 26 October.

Holbig, H, & Gilley, B 2010, 'Reclaiming legitimacy in China', *Politics & Policy*, vol. 38, no. 3, pp. 395–422.

Holbig, H 2006, 'Ideological reform and political legitimacy in China: challenges in the post-Jiang Era', In Heberer, T & Schubert, G (eds.), *Regime legitimacy in contemporary China: institutional change and stability*, Routledge, London, pp. 13–34.

Holbig, H 2009, 'Remaking the CCP's ideology: determinants, progress, and limits under Hu Jintao', *Journal of Current Chinese Affairs*, vol. 38, no. 3, pp. 35–61.

Huang, SC 1999, *Essentials of neo-Confucianism: eight major philosophers of the song and Ming periods*, Greenwood Press, Westport.

Hucker, CO 1975, *China's imperial past: an introduction to Chinese history and culture*, Stanford University Press, Stanford CA.

Huntington, SP 1968, *Political order in changing societies*, Yale University Press, New Haven and London.

Hutton, W 2006, *The writing on the wall: why we must embrace China as a partner or face it as an enemy*, Free Press, New York.

Jacobs, A 2011, 'Confucius statue vanishes near Tiananmen square', *The New York Times*, April 22nd, viewed on May 1st, 2012, available at http://www.nytimes.com/2011/04/23/world/asia/23confucius.html

Jiang, Q 2004, 'Way of life and tradition of politics', available at website Confucius2000, http://www.confucius2000.com/admin/list.asp?id¼1269, accessed July 15, 2010.

Joseph, WA 2010, *Politics in China: an introduction*, Oxford University Press, Oxford & New York.

Kampen, T 2000, *Mao Zedong, Zhou Enlai and the Evolution of the Chinese Communist Leadership*, Nordic Institute of Asian Studies, Copenhagen.

Kang, XG 2008, *Zhongguo guilai—Dangdai zhongguo dalu wenhua minzuzhuyi yundong yanjiu (Back of China—research on the cultural nationalism movement in contemporary Chinese mainland)*, Global Publishing Company, Singapore.

Kang, XG, Wang, J & Liu, SL 2010, *Zhendizhan: Guan yu zhonghua wenhua fuxingde gelanxishi fenxi* (Struggle for cultural hegemony: Gramscian perspectives of revitalizing Chinese traditional culture), shehui kexue wenxian chubanshe (Social Science Literature Press), Beijing.

Kerry, B, 2012, 'The Communist Party of China and Ideology', *China: An International Journal*, vol. 10, no. 2, pp. 52–68.

Knight, K 2006, 'Transformations of the concept of ideology in the twentieth century', *American Political Science Review*, vol. 100, pp. 619–626.

Laliberte, A & Lanteigne, M (ed.) 2008, *The Chinese Party-State in the 21st century: adaptation and the reinvention of legitimacy*, Routledge.

Lasswell, HD & Kaplan, A 1950, *Power and society*, Yale University Press, New Haven.

Lee, WO & Ho, CH 2005, 'Ideological Shifts and Changes in Moral Education Policy in China', *Journal of Moral Education*, vol. 34, no. 4, p. 416.

Levenson, JR 1968, *Confucian China and its modern fate: a trilogy*, University of California Press, Berkley.

Lewis, JW & Xue, L 2003, 'Social change and political reform in China: meeting the challenge of success', *The China Quarterly*, vol. 176, pp. 926–942.

Li, CS 1999, 'Ruxue chuangxin yu Makesi zhuyi chuangxin (Innovation of Confucianism and innovation of Marxism)', *Zhexue dongtai (Contemporary Philosophy)*, no. 4, pp. 15–19.

Lifton, RJ 1961, *Thought reform and the psychology of totalism: a study of "Brainwashing" in China*, Norton, New York.

Lin, JX 2006, 'yetang suowei ertong dujing'(commentary on children reading the Classics), In Hu, XM (ed.), *Dujing: Qimeng haishi mengmei—laizi minjian de shengyin (Reading the Classics: Enlightenment or Obscurantism? Voices from Society)*, Huadong shifan daxue chubanshe (Huadong Normal University Press).

Lin, Y 1938, *The Wisdom of Confucius*, Random House, New York.

Linz, JJ & Stepan, A, 1996, *Problems of democratic transition and consolidation: Southern Europe, South America, and post-communist Europe*, John Hopkins University Press.

Lipset, SM 1981, *Political man* (expanded edition), Johns Hopkins University Press, Baltimore.

Lipset, MS 1983, *Political man: the social bases of politics*, Heinemann, London.

Littlejohn, RL 2011, *Confucianism: an introduction*, I.B. Tauris, London.

Liu, Q 2006, 'Corporate governance in China: current practices, economic effects and institutional determinants', *CESifo Economic Studies*, pp. 415–453

Lynch, DC 1999, *After the propaganda state: media, politics, and "thought work" in reformed China*, Stanford University Press.

Makeham, J 2003, *New Confucianism: a critical examination*, Palgrave, New York.

Makeham, J 2008, *Lost soul: Confucianism in contemporary Chinese academic discourse*, Harvard University Asia Center, Cambridge, MA and London, England.

Mannheim, K 1943, *Diagnosis of our time*, Routledge and Paul, London.

Mannheim, K 1952, *Essays on the sociology of knowledge*, Routledge & Kegan Paul, New York.

Marx, K 1979, *A contribution to the critique of political economy*, Progress Publisher.

McCall, GJ 1969, 'Data quality control in participant observation' In McCall, GJ & Simmons, JL (eds.), *Issues in participant observation*. Addison-Wesley, MA.

McCormick, BL 1990, *Political reform in post-Mao China: democracy and bureaucracy in a Leninist state*, University of California Press, Berkeley.

Meisner, M 1999, *Mao's China and after: a history of the People's Republic*, Simon and Schuster.

Merriam, SB 2009, *Qualitative research: a guide to design and implementation*, Jossey-Bass, San Francisco, CA.

Metzger, WP 1949, 'Ideology and the intellectual: a study of thorstein veblen', *Philosophy of Science*, vol. 16, no. 2, pp. 125–133.

Misra, K 2001, 'Curing the sickness and saving the Party: Neo-Maoism and Neo Conservatism in the 1990s', In Hua, S, (ed.), *Chinese political culture*, M. E. Sharpe, Armonk.

Moody, PR 2007, *Conservative thought in contemporary China*, Lanham, Rowman & Littlefield, MD.

Nathan, AJ 2003, 'Authoritarian resilience', *Journal of Democracy*, vol. 14, no. 1, pp. 6–17.

National Bureau of Statistics of China 2011, China statistical yearbook, Chapter 22, "Culture and Sports", http://www.stats.gov.cn/tjsj/ndsj/2011/indexch. htm, accessed on May 1st, 2013.

Nee, V 2006, *China's politicized Capitalism*, Cornell University Press, New York.

Needham, J 1970, *Clerks and craftsmen in China and the West: lectures and addresses on the history of science and technology*, Cambridge University Press, Cambridge.

North, D 1991, '*Institutions, ideology, and economic performance*', *Cato Journal*, vol. 11, no. 3, pp. 477–488.

O'Donnell, G & Schmitter, PC (eds.), 1986, *Transitions from authoritarian rule: comparative perspectives*, John Hopkins University Press.

Oldstone-Moore, J 2002, *Confucianism: origins, beliefs, practices, holy texts, sacred places*, Oxford University Press, New York.

Pang, Q 2014. 'The 'Two Lines Control Model' in China's State and Society Relations: Central State's Management of Confucian Revival in the New Century,' *International Journal of China Studies*, vol. 5, no. 3, p. 627.

Pang, Q 2016. 'Confucian Education in Urban Public Schools: An Ideological Solution to Social Disorder in China's Cities?' *China: An International Journal*, vol. 14, no. 4, pp. 70–94.

Pei, MX 1994, From reform to revolution: the demise of communism in China and the Soviet Union, Harvard University Press.

Pei, MX 2006, *China's trapped transition: the limits of developmental autocracy*, Harvard University Press, Cambridge, MA.

Pei, M 2011, 'China's bumpy ride ahead', *The Diplomat*.

People's Daily 2005, 'Hu Jintao delivered a speech on improving the ability of building a harmonious socialist society at the seminar for major leading cadres at the provincial and ministerial level', June 27th, 2005, Section 1, http:// www.people.com.cn/GB/paper39/15076/1337624.html, accessed on May 1st, 2013.

Pew Research Center 2012, 'Growing concerns in China about inequality, corruption', http://www.pewglobal.org/2012/10/16/growing-concerns-in-china-about-inequality-corruption/

Przeworski, A 1991, *Democracy and the market: political and economic reforms in Eastern Europe and Latin America*, Cambridge University Press.

Robertson, B & Liu, M 2006, 'Can the sage save China?', *Newsweek*, March 20.

Roucek, JS 1944, 'A history of the concept of ideology', *Journal of the History of Ideas*, vol. 5, no. 4, p. 279.

Schurmann, F 1966, *Ideology and Organization in Communist China*, University of California Press, Berkeley and Los Angeles.

Schurmann, F 1968, *Organization and ideology in communist China*, University of California, Berkeley.

Shambaugh, D 2007, 'China's propaganda system: institutions, processes and efficacy', *The China Journal*, vol. 57.

Shambaugh, D 2008, *China's Communist Party: atrophy and adaptation*, Woodrow Wilson Center Press & University of California Press, Washington DC & Berkeley.

Shue, V 2004, 'Legitimacy crisis in China?', In Gries, PH & Rosen, S (eds.), *State and society in 21st-century China: crisis, contention, and legitimation*, Routledge Curzon.

Sina.com 2011, 'zaopo buneng dang guoxue', viewed on October, 2012, available at http://news.sina.com.cn/c/2011-03-03/111622045558.shtml

Skocpol, T 1979, *States and social revolutions*, Cambridge University Press, Cambridge.

Sleeboom-Faulkner, M 2007, *The Chinese academy of social sciences (CASS): shaping the reforms, academia and China (1977–2003)*, Brill Academic Publishers.

Solomon, R 1971, *Mao's Revolution and the Chinese Political Culture*, University of California Press Berkeley.

Song, ZM 2001, 'Cong pi Kong dao shi Kong de zhuanzhe (From criticizing Confucianism to explaining Confucianism)', *Wen shi zhe (literature History and Philosophy)*, vol. 3, pp. 26–31.

Starr, CG 1986, *Individual and community: the rise of the polis, 800-500 BC*, Oxford University Press.

Stake, RE 2010, *Qualitative research: studying how things work*, Guilford Press, New York.

Sun, A 2011, 'The revival of Confucian rites in contemporary China', In Yang, FG & Tamney, J (eds.), *Confucianism and spiritual traditions in modern China and beyond*, Brill.

Sun, Y 1995, *The Chinese reassessment of socialism, 1976–1992*, Princeton University Press, Princeton, New Jersey.

Tarrow, S 1994, *Power in movement: collective action, social movements and politics*, Cambridge University Press, Cambridge.

The Wall Street Journal, 'Lardy vs. Pettis: Debating China's economic future', November 7th, 2012.

Thompson, JB 1984, *Studies in the theory of ideology*, University of California Press.

Thompson, MR 2002, 'Totalitarian and post-totalitarian regimes in transitions and non-transitions from communism', *Totalitarian Movements and Political Religions*, vol. 3, no. 1, pp. 79–106.

Tilly, C 2004, *Social movements, 1768–2004*, Paradigm Publishers, Boulder, CO.

Tilly, C 2005, *Trust and rule*, Cambridge University Press.

Tu, WM 1979, *Confucianism: symbol and substance in recent times. Value change in Chinese society*, Praeger, New York, pp. 23–25.

Tu, WM 1985, *Confucian thought: selfhood as creative transformation*, State University of New York Press, Albany.

Tu, WM 1976, *Neo-Confucian thought in action: Wang Yang-ming's youth (1472–1509)*, University of California Press, Berkeley and Los Angeles.

Tu, WM 1989, *Confucianism in historical perspective*, Institute of East Asian Philosophies, Singapore.

Tu, WM 1992, 'The exit from communism', *Daedalus*, vol. 121, no. 2, pp. 251–92.

Tu, WM 1993, *Way, learning, and politics: essays on the Confucian intellectual*, State University of New York Press, Albany.

Tu, WM 2011, 'Confucian Spirituality in Contemporary China', In Yang, FG & Tamney, J (eds.), *Confucianism and spiritual traditions in modern China and beyond*, Brill.

Van Maanen, J 1983, 'The fact and fiction in organizational ethnography', In: Van Maanen, J (ed.), *Qualitative methodology*, Sage, Beverly Hills.

Volker, M & Stehr, N (eds.) 1999, *The sociology of knowledge*, Edward Elgar, Cheltenham, UK.

Walder, A 1985, *communist neo-traditionalism: work and authority in Chinese industry*, University of California Press, Berkeley.

Wang, Jie, 2006, 'chongxin wajue ruxue de dangdai jiazhi' (Re-exploring the contemporary value of Confucianism), *People's Daily* (the theoretical edition), September 8th.

Wang, Jie, 2007a, 'rujia sixiang yu hexie guannian' (Confucian thoughts and the idea of Harmony), *zhongguo shekeyuan xuebao (The Journal of Chinese Academy of Social Science)*, June 26th.

Wang, Jie, 2007b, 'shidai xuyao hongyang he peiyu zhonghua minzu jinshen' (The need to carry forward and cultivate the Chinese national spirit during our age), *People's Daily*, March 21st.

Weber et al, 1994, *Weber: political writings*, Cambridge University Press.

Wheatley, A 2008, 'China cannot sustain its model of economic growth', *The New York Times*, February 4th.

Wohlgemuth, M 2002, 'Evolutionary approaches to politics', *Kyklos*, vol. 55, no. 2, pp. 2232–2246.

Wolff, J (ed.) 1987, *Stanford Encyclopedia of Philosophy*, Stanford University.

Wright, AF 1959, *Buddhism in Chinese history*, Stanford University Press, Stanford, CA.

Wu, S 2015. 'Politicisation and De-Politicisation of Confucianism in Contemporary China: A Review of Intellectuals,' *Issues and Studies*, vol. 51, no. 3, p. 165.

Xiang, CL 2008, *rujia wenhua de xiandai yiyi (The modern implications of Confucian culture)*, In Forum for Marxism and Confucianism, 2008, Beijing.

Xiao, GQ 2008, *zhongguo de da zhuanxing (The great transformation of China)*, Xinxin chubanshe (New Star publishing house).

Xing Bensi 2010, 'Dui Jianshe Makexi Xuexixing Zhengdao de Jidian Renshi (Some understandings about building a learning party with Marx doctrine)', *Qiushi (Seeking Truth)*, no. 5, pp. 16–19.

Xu, S 2017. 'Cultivating national identity with traditional culture: China's experiences and paradoxes,' *Discourse: Studies in the Cultural Politics of Education*, 2017, no. 4, pp. 1–14.

Xue, Y 2004, 'zouxiangmengmei de wenhua baoshou zhuyi' (Cultural Conservatism Marching forward to Cultural Obscurantism), *Nangfang Zhoumo (Nanfang Weekend)*, July 8th.

Xue, Y 2007, 'shenme shi mengmei? zaiping dujing' (what is Cultural Obscurantism? Commentary on Reading the Classics), *Lilun Cankao (Theory References)*, no. 7.

Yang, DL 2004, *Remaking the Chinese Leviathan: market transition and the politics of governance in China*, Stanford University Press, Stanford.

Yang, F & Tamney, J (eds.) 2011, *Confucianism and spiritual traditions in modern China and beyond*, Brill.

Yao, XZ 2000, *An introduction to Confucianism*, Cambridge University Press, Cambridge.

Yi, L 1994, *Zhongguo Makesi zhuyi yu xiandai xinrujia (China's Marxism and New Confucianism)*, Liaoning University Press, Shenyang.

Yin, RK 2004, *The case study anthology*, Sage, London.

Yu, JY 2002, *Contemporary Chinese philosophy*, Blackwell, Oxford.

Yu, YS 1987, *Zhongguo jinshi zongjiao lunli yu shangren jingshen (Modern Chinese religious philosophy and spirit of Merchantman)*, Lian jing chu ban shi ye gong si, Taipei.

Yuan, WS, 2006, 'ping dujing' (Commentary on Reading the Classics), In Hu, XM (ed.), *Dujing: Qimeng haishi mengmei—laizi minjian de shengyin (Reading the Classics: Enlightenment or Obscurantism? Voices from Society)*, Huadong shifan daxue chubanshe (Huadong Normal University Press).

Zhao, S 2016. 'The Ideological Campaign in Xi's China,' *Asian Survey*, vol. 56, no. 6, pp. 1168–1193.

Zhuang, Y 1991, 'Dui xiandai xin Ruxue jige wenti de zhenglun:'Xiandai xin Ruxue yu dangdai Zhongguo xueshu taolunhui' guandian jianjie (Debates on several questions of new Confucianism, Symposium on of new Confucianism and contemporary China)', *Xueshuyanjiu (Academic Research)*, no. 2, pp. 24–25, 60.

CHAPTER 2

China's Mutually Empowering State and Society Relations

This chapter aims to establish a theoretical framework for analyzing state-society interaction or, more specifically, state's control over society in the Confucian revival. The Confucian revival is an important aspect of contemporary Chinese social life, and the engagement between state and society in the revival is also a key aspect of Chinese state-society relations in general. The first part of the chapter will provide an analytical framework about state and society relations, focusing on how a state, with limited resources, can retain its control over a rapidly growing society. After explaining the predominance of power and resources in the struggles between state and society, the chapter then explains that a state can manage an increasingly strong society, by adroitly using coercion and co-optation. The state and society can even be mutually empowering during the process. The form and effect of mutual empowerment or the state's use of coercion and co-optation is, to a large degree, conditioned and even influenced by the state's own institutions, especially those governing internal power distribution within state and those shaping bureaucrats' policy orientations. In the second part, this chapter will draw a theoretical account about Chinese state-society interaction at large, as a backdrop for the elaborations of the mutual engagements between state and society in the Confucian revival in the next chapter.

© The Author(s) 2019   55
Q. Pang, *State-Society Relations and Confucian Revivalism in Contemporary China*,
https://doi.org/10.1007/978-981-10-8312-9_2

2.1   REVIEW OF STATE-SOCIETY RELATIONS: HOW STATES DEAL WITH SOCIETAL DEMAND

2.1.1   The Classical Debate Concerning State's Engagement with Society

2.1.1.1   Defining "Society" and "State"

Before coming to the theoretical debate of state and society interaction, this part will first specify how "society" and "state" are conceptualized in this book. Many social science scholars have defined "society" from different perspectives. For example, Mann describes society based on its boundary. He defines society as "a (human) unit with boundaries, and containing (human) interaction that is relatively dense and stable; that is, it is internally patterned when compared to interaction that crosses its boundaries" (Mann 1986, p. 13). Greenfeld and Martin (1988), however, define society by the common identity shared by the members of a group. They believe that society "is the outermost social structure for a certain group of individuals who, whatever might be their attitude toward it, view themselves as its members and experience their identity as being determined by it" (1988, p. iii).

This book combines the two perspectives together and defines society by adopting Giddens's four criteria for society (1981, pp. 44–46). Society has four basic characteristics: (1) "boundedness", a specifiable clustering of institutions across time and space; (2) "territory", an association between the social system and a specific locale or "territory of occupation"; (3) "legitimacy", the existence of normative elements that involve laying claim to the legitimate occupation of the locale; (4) "collective identity", the prevalence, among the members of the society, of feelings that they have some sort of common identity. Based on this definition, Chinese society refers to the people and their interactions within the boundary and territory of the Chinese nation-state. Persons or groups within Chinese society have at least some legitimate claims over the Chinese territory which they inhabit. They also share some level of collective identity manifest in Chinese-ness.

It needs to be emphasized that previous parameters for society, however, are not absolute, especially those concerning boundaries.[1] As Giddens (1984) has repeatedly insisted, boundaries of societies are permeable and that, in the modern world, all societies exist within the context of "inter-societal systems". In fact, the boundary of different societies are sometimes so blurred that some even argue that a unitary society simply does not exist. This book defines state as a set of administrative, law-enforcement, and security-military organizations under the centralized control of a supreme authority (Skocpol 1979; see also Chap. 1). The Chinese state refers to all the governmental organizations within Chinese territory and under the control of the political hegemony of the CCP.[2] However, it needs to be pointed out that such a unitary notion of state has sometimes been criticized and challenged.[3] Migdal (2001, pp. 15–22), for example, contends that though state has an image of "a coherent, controlling organization in a territory", it is, in practice, actually "a heap of loosely connected parts or fragments, frequently with ill-defined boundaries between them and other groupings inside and outside the official state borders and often promoting conflicting sets of rules with one another and with 'official' law".

Yet despite the elusive and diversified nature of the concept of the state, it still remains useful to identify a set of common organizational, administrative, legal, territorial, and socio-cultural attributes of public authority. Such an analytical definition, at least, can make the discussions concerning state and society less ambiguous. But it must be acknowledged that given that neither society nor state are clear-cut in their boundaries, and the two apparently share some common characteristics such as territory, and national identity (even overlapping in some important ways), the relationship between them is not straightforward.

2.1.1.2 The Society-Centered Paradigms

Concerning how states deal with societal demand, different theoretical schools have heated debates. One side is society-centered, and contends that society is the dominant part, shaping and even determining the nature of the state. The state, therefore, can only passively respond to rising demand from one social sector or conflicting demand from different social sectors, acting merely as "mediator, balancer and harmonizer of [differing societal] interests" (Dunleavy and O'Leary 1987, p. 46). The other side, by contrast, is state-centered and argues that the state is autonomous, acting in pursuit of its own interests and thus actively imposing changes upon society in order to resolve societal demand.[4]

The society-centered paradigm contains different theoretical schools among which pluralism and Marxism are the most representative. Both schools argue that societal members possess substantial power[5] and resources[6] to organize themselves, and hence are able to impose their preferences on the state whose role is mostly responsive.

Pluralism generally assumes that power and resources are mainly within society. For example, Dahl (1961, 1977) claims that power is not cumulative but dispersed in society. Social forces, by mobilizing means such as organizing interest groups, can usually advance their interests by exerting pressure upon public policy-making. Hence, society, particularly its organized members (interest groups) and their activities, can largely determine public policy and other political changes (Dryzek and Dunleavy 2009; Dahl 1961, 1963). For example, accounts of the American legislative process can usually find a pluralist universe of interest groups (Truman 1951, 1967) or an iron triangle between the legislature, the bureaucracy, and interest groups on public policy-making (McConnell 1966).

In addition, social forces' power in free organization is underpinned by their control of ideological resources for which the "civic culture" is a case in point. According to Almond and Verba (1989), civic culture emphasizes that every citizen have equal rights to organize themselves and they should also respect other's rights to do so.[7] Different groups should tolerate and reconcile differences of interests, and accept the compromises broken by the public authorities. Such civic culture, therefore, lends meaning and legitimacy for social forces' group activities. This pluralist approach, in fact, has largely drawn its resources from post-war American political and social experiences such as entrenchment of individual rights and the rise of various interest groups. In this approach, states are largely invisible or seen as "mainly inert recipients of pressure from interest groups" (MacPherson 1973, p. 188). They are often represented by individuals and groups in charge of public functions.

Marxism also contends that society determines the state's actions. Different from the pluralist approach, however, Marxism does not believe that power is dispersed in society or that all societal members have somewhat equal chances to influence the public policy. It introduces "social class" as its key variable, and argues that power and resources including ideological resources are concentrated in the dominant social class, namely, the capitalist class. It argues that capitalists use state as an instrument to realize their ambition; in other words, it emphasizes that the state's responses to social demand will be mostly oriented towards the capitalist's interests. The view has been fully developed in the early generation of Marxists. In the *Communist Manifesto*, for example, Marx (1973, p. 69) claims that "the executive of modern state is but a committee for managing the common affairs of the bourgeoisie". Lenin pushed the "instrument" view even further. He (1960, p. 392) maintained that the state is "a special force for the suppression of a particular class".

Later Marxists developed the argument by stressing that the capitalist class's rule of the subordinate class is maintained mainly through its ideological and cultural control, or the mobilization of consent, which Gramsci terms "hegemony" (1971). The state, as Gramsci has perceived, is the "entire complex political and theoretical activities with which the ruling class not only justifies and maintains its dominance, but manages to win the active consent of those over whom it rules" (Gramsci 1971, p. 244).

Other Marxist theorists have formulated some more subtle and nuanced propositions concerning the relations between the capitalist and state. They do *not* view the state as under the *direct* control of the capitalists who own the dominant power and resources; rather, they argue that the capitalists control states by allowing the existence of *the* state which can best protect and develop their overall interests. For example, Antonio Gramsci (1971) contends that the state is not the directive representative of the capital class, but the state perpetuates a capitalist social order in which the capitalist class benefits most. Poulantzas (1978) also argues that the state does not directly embody the will of the capitalist class but it serves the capitalists' long-term interests by holding together the capitalist society. In other words, the state does not act entirely according to the capitalists' wishes, but it still acts for the interests of the (some) capitalists in the negotiation of compromises among different classes (Jessop 1977, 1982).

2.1.1.3 The State-Centered Paradigms

On the other side of the debate, the state is seen as an independent entity with sufficient power and resources, and its own interests. Rather than being subject to the pressure of various social groups, the state itself pursues its own end and imposes its will upon society. In order to protect its interests, the state monopolizes coercive resources, controls key ideological persuasions, and exerts social control through means of coercion, co-optation, and legitimation.

Such a state-centered framework has been supported by several approaches in social sciences. One of the early approaches is elitism. It insists that a small group of political elites amass vast power and resources and thus are able to control or shape society. For example, it contends that political power will just *inevitably* concentrate in the hands of a small circle of elites who (will) govern whole society.[8] Mosca (1939), for instance, argues that there are two classes in any society, one is the class that rules and the other is the class to be ruled. The ruling class, though less in number, unavoidably monopolizes power and enjoys its benefits, whereas the ruled class is always under the control of the ruling. Similarly, Michels (1962) raises the infamous "iron law of oligarchy" which claims that effective decision-making power in any large organization will always ultimately rest with a small leadership group.[9]

In parallel, Marx Web's "democratic elitism" and Joseph Schumpeter's "competitive elitism" (1976) also confirm that power is monopolized in the hands of a few even in a democratic society. They maintain that power, especially which is involved in making and implementing collective decisions, narrowly resides in a small number of political elites. Another form of elitism, corporatism, argues that political elites would sometimes ally with elites in other social areas such as economics and religion, and these elites together deliver a kind of joint governance over a wider society (Schmitter 1974).

Although elitism accounts for the concentration of power within the state, it does not necessarily claim that the state is autonomous or it wields control over society. It is the New Statist literature that directly argues that the state, as an independent entity, holds central role in determining social relations and socio-economic changes.[10] Skocpol (1979), for example, emphasizes the fundamental role of states in social revolutions in her comparative study of social revolutions in China, France, and the United States. She argues that it is the form of the prior regime (state) that determines whether a society's "revolutionary situation" will happen (1979). This is because the prior regime's forms determine whether the regime will be able to respond to changes in the environment including domestic socio-economic issues and international economic and security competition. Evans et al. (1985) launched a well-known call for "bringing the state back in", highlighting the significant and even decisive influence of the state upon society. The large amount of literature on state and society relations later focuses on the unique place of the state in rule-making and effecting social changes (Hall and Ikenberry 1989; Weiss and Hobson 1995; Evans 1995; Kohli 2004). Evans's (1995) model of the state's embedded autonomy within society is a case in point. It accentuates the importance of the state over the economic development within society by explaining why developmental states such as Japan, South Korea, and Taiwan are more efficient in industrialization than other non-developmental states in the developing world.

Neoliberal theorists, based on their empirical observations of the welfare states in North America and Europe, view the modern state as advancing its own interests even at the expense of the wider society (Nordlinger 1981). The state, in their perspective, has extracted more and more resources from society and extended its policies into almost every corner of society, though it did this in order to promote a broadly social democratic and welfare agenda (Tullock 1976). The omnipresence of the state in society even suggested that the distinction between public and private had become meaningless (Kennedy 1982).

Besides, as an independent entity with substantial power and influence, the state is seen as *actively* dominating society by exercising social control. According to Migdal (1988), with high levels of social control, the state can mobilize its citizens to implement its preferences and protect its own interests. To realize social control, states build complex and coordinated apparatuses to manage society. Specifically speaking, Migdal (1989) argues that the state's control over society can be obtained in the three basic ways:

Compliance At the most elementary level, the state seeks to control society by gaining compliance from the population. Compliance is often achieved by the use of most basic sanction, force. For example, police are the essential instrument for the state to suppress the rebellion social forces. The state also employs other methods such as rewards to gain social compliance to its demands.

Participation To control society, the state needs not only compliance but also "participation". Participation means repeated voluntary use of state-run or state-authorized institutions, for instance, state-licensed clinics instead of unauthorized healers. In the Chinese case, the state encourages people to join state-affiliated unions (and groups) but restricts other society-organized NGOs. Participation, to some extent, is similar to "co-optation", which was defined by Philip Selznick (1949, p. 13) as "absorbing new elements into the leadership or policy-determining structure of an organization as a means of averting threats to its stability or existence".

Legitimation Legitimation is acceptance, approval, and even approbation of the state's rule as true and right. As Poggi (1978, p. 101 cited in Migdal 1989) has commented, "state leaders want citizens to comply with its authority not from the inertia of unreasoning routine or the utilitarian calculations of personal advantage, but from the conviction that compliance is right". The most potent method for the state to gain social control is legitimating its rule in society. Legitimation means the state needs to control the symbolic environment within society so that it could shape societal members' attitudes and actions towards itself.

2.1.2   State's Management with Societal Demand

2.1.2.1   Issues Areas and Power Resources

The two contrasting sets of state's management with social demand, namely, passive response towards society's pressure and active control over society, are present in any national setting, though their weighting varies across cases. For example, even for the United States, a country which Nettl (1968) describes as possessing low "state-ness", many accounts of its state-building highlight elements of state's imposition of its will upon society (Jensen 2008; King and Lieberman 2008). Conversely, in Communist political systems in which the state is perceived as the most autonomous among all types of authoritarian regimes (Walder 1985), elements of pluralist politics exist. Social groups still emerge amid the atomization of the totalitarian regime. They pursue their shared interests by subtly pressuring the bureaucracy which does submit to societal demand from time to time (Skilling 1983; Skilling and Griffiths 1970).

The question is: what determines the state's actions towards social demand? Two factors stand out. The first is the nature of social issues, that is, their importance and sensitivity for the state. The state and society operate in an environment with numerous social arenas and issues,[11] and every state has its own list of priority concerning social issues. For any state, its controlled material and human resources are not infinite, in most cases, very limited as far as satisfying all societal members' need and wishes. It has to selectively respond to issues according to its importance and sensitivity. Importance means generating vital effect upon the survival or development of the state and even the whole nation, and sensitivity refers to bringing urgent effect upon the state's security or development need. By establishing the two criteria, social issues can thus be divided into four types, as can be seen in Fig. 2.1. Type I refers to those important and sensitive issues such as national security threats, large-scale social protest, and economic development (stabilization), to which the state usually responds with high priority and often pre-emptive measures. Type II covers those issues with high importance level but weak sensitivity, for example, the ideological control issues in this study. Although such issues are often of considerable influence upon the state's security, their effects are not immediate and thus do not require swift or overwhelming responses (to be sure, ideological issues can sometimes become urgent). Type III refers to issues that are neither highly important nor urgent, and thus the state usually places them at the bottom of the priority list. Type IV refers to less important issues but with urgent effect, for example, diplomat formalities for visiting foreign heads.

The second factor is the relative distribution of power and resources between state and society. If social forces have the mobilizing capacity to organize formal or informal associations, able to extract or at least get access to the needed material resources, adroit in exploiting or even gen-

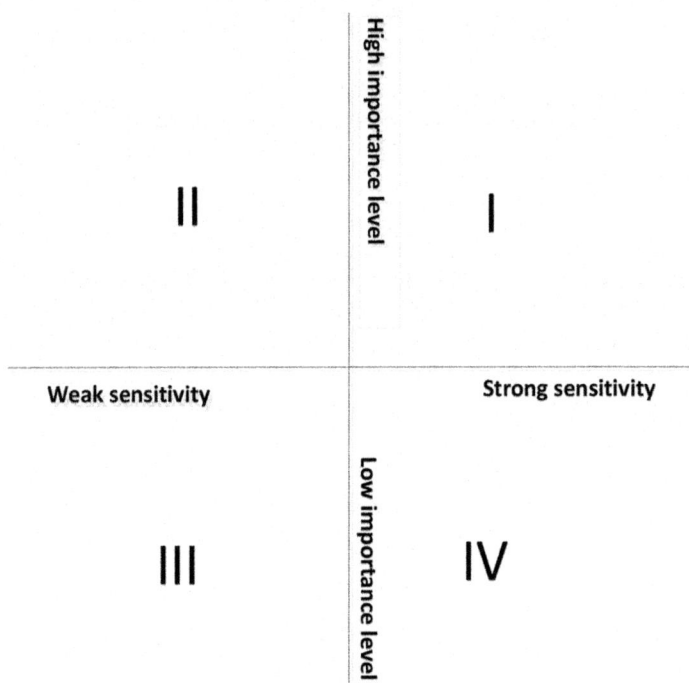

Fig. 2.1   Division of social issues by importance and sensitivity

erating normative symbols and beliefs, they will have a strong ability to lobby and even shape the state's decisions concerning their demand. However, if the state has the upper hand, possessing the capacity to penetrate relevant societal section and monopolizing substantial material and spiritual resources, it will have strong independence in its actions, pressing societal members accepting solutions to its advantage.

The significance of power and resources in determining state-society competition has also been echoed in previous literature exploring the state's failure to control society. Migdal (1989), for example, when explaining why some developing states are not able to change their societies in the ways political leaders intended, has pointed out that the real pressure comes from social elements who, by amassing material resources and effectively manipulating accepted beliefs and symbols, can successfully resist the state's initiatives. Evans (1995), for instance, through examining a range of states in developing and transitional countries, contends that the reason why some East Asian developmental states such as Japan, South Korea, and Taiwan could successfully implement industrialization projects within their societies while other states in Africa or South America failed, was because these developmental states had a set of formal and informal bureaucratic institutions which equipped them with substantial power and resources to penetrate into society while other states had only limited capability to do so.

2.1.2.2 State's Strategies: Co-optation and Coercion

This section focuses on the state's common strategies for dealing with Type II issues raised by social forces with increasing power and resources, as they can provide a highly relevant framework for analyzing the Chinese state's control over Confucian revival in a bourgeoning society. Such a framework is significant in that most of the issues in China's state and society struggles belong to this type, and whether the Chinese state can successfully manage similar cases is vital to its survival and development. While Type I issues are more related with the state's immediate security, Type II issues are highly relevant to the state's long-term regime duration. During China's transition from totalitarian to post-totalitarian regime, the Chinese society has been able to garner increasing material, human, and spiritual resources such as the Confucian revival, and their power in social organization has also been strengthened. How, then, could the Chinese state empower itself to bring this vibrant society's ideological demand within control?

The state, in general, has two main strategies to retain its control over a stronger society. First, it needs to build up its coercive power to deal with highly sensitive issues by appropriating more material resources, training more efficient forces such as armies and police. Coercive power is the basis for the state's capacity to subjugating dangerous social elements. If antagonistic social forces become more organized and possess more resources at hand, the state will have to increase its coercive force and use more draconian means to suppress them. In this way, the state can destroy or limit the resources that aim at weakening its control. As will be discussed later, the Chinese state during the post-Mao period has dramatically strengthened the security forces including the regular police, secret police, and armed forces to guard against the social threats and dissents (Guo 2012). An increasing amount of financial resources is being invested in the security forces. The government budget in this area (not including military spending) in 2012 has surged to an astonishing $111.4 billion, 11% higher than the previous year and hitting a new peak (Buckley 2012).

The state, however, does not use the same coercive power to sanction all hostile social forces, as this would drain its coercive resources. Coercion can be categorized into different levels according to the degree of liberty or freedom deprived from the coerced. These levels range from "total suppression" which means deprivation of all personal freedom to "bottomline control" referring to setting up forbidden zones. Along the spectrum, there are decreasing levels of coercion based on restrictions in freedom.[12] As for which level of coercion will be used to deal with hostile social elements, it depends primarily on how threatening the state perceives these social elements to be.[13] Generally speaking, the state adopts more draconian measures to repress those more threatening social forces. For example, the Chinese state chose to ban the Falun Gong but not other religions such as Christianity or Islam, because it viewed the Falun Gong as an organized social force which constituted impending threats to its rule while other religions were seen as less menacing in terms of their organizing capacity and intention to revolt against the state (Tong 2007). By adopting varied coercive strategies, the state increases its efficiency in using its coercive power to constrain adversary social forces and their resources.

The second strategy is the state's co-optation of existing social forces. State-society relations are not *always* a zero-sum conflict. They can also be mutually empowering. This means, if the state intends to retain its dominant position in its relations with an increasingly powerful society, it does not have to collect more resources than society has amassed. It can increase its own resources and power by coalition building, that is, by co-opting "cooperative" social forces. For example, it could incorporate powerful new social forces including their resources and symbols into the state system so that they tie their own fortunes to that of the state. This enables the state to appropriate these social elements' resources and capacity. The authoritarian military regime in Brazil, for instance, while implementing its social transformations, sought an implicit coalition with local traditional oligarchic elites who had strong ability to manipulate various resources (Hagopian 1994). But the state also needs to make changes and accommodations as it adapts to these social forces. In this way, the state and those social elements are, in fact, mutually empowering (Migdal et al. 1995). In such cases, a more powerful society, in turn, can provide more resources for the state to appropriate and exploit.

The state adopts different levels of co-optation with different social forces. According to Selznick (1949), co-optation can be viewed as responses to individuals or social groups who command necessary resources and are in a position to enforce demands.[14] During the co-option process, the state makes necessary accommodations, offering the co-opted party at least part of what they desire, and the co-opted side shows its loyalty for the state in return. Based on how much accommodations the state makes and the degree that the co-opted social forces' demand is satisfied, co-optation can be divided along a spectrum ranging from "complete co-optation" to "minimal co-optation" (see Fig. 2.2). In one extreme, complete co-optation, the state shares virtually all power with the co-opted forces and satisfies all of their demands. The two, therefore, tie their fortunes closely together. In the other extreme, minimal co-optation, the state makes very limited concessions and social forces' requirements are only marginally satisfied. Most of the state's co-optation strategies stand in between the two extremes but there are differences in degree in its co-optation with different social forces.

How would a state use the two strategies to deal with Type II issues? In general, the state should prefer to adopt less coercion but more co-optation, given that the Type II issue does impose urgent threats to the state but remains important for its long-term interests. It should refrain from frequently resorting to violence or imposing constraints, as this will not only waste its coercive resources for Type I issues but also arouse stronger public resistance, which will only create counter-effect for its grip over social members. Co-optation enables the state to obtain sufficient

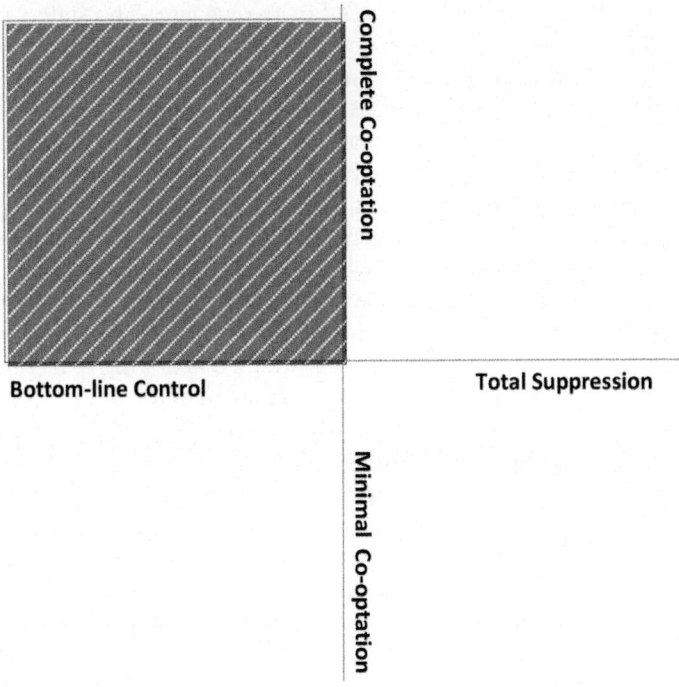

Fig. 2.2   Division of state's strategies in controlling society

resources to keep its control over these issues. However, it cannot make too many accommodations for co-opting social elements, because this may lead to the state's loss of its own autonomy in such important issues, not to mention its control over them. Thus, the state's strategies should lie between bottom-line control and complete co-optation (see the shadow area in Fig. 2.2).

Specifically, such low coercive and high co-opting strategies combination can also be used by states in dealing with social forces that produce and develop symbolic and belief systems which enjoy (wide) popularity among social members. On the one hand, the state uses coercive means to suppress those who dare to produce and circulate beliefs and ideas endangering its rule, by censoring their publications and heavily restricting their relevance in the symbolic environment; on the other hand, the state can actively co-opt those who at least do not directly challenge its rule, taking advantage of their symbolic sources for its own use. The state can also adopt different levels of coercion and co-optation to maximize its control over these social forces and their symbolic resources. The coercion ranges from "total suppression" in which the state strictly bans publications of ideas and beliefs to "bottom-line control" in which the state allows circulation of some ideas unless they step across the bottom line. The scope of this co-optation extends from "complete co-optation", in which the state fully accepts a group's ideas and actively promulgates their beliefs in society, to "minimal co-optation" in which the state just permits ideas to be circulated, offering some negligible (or even no) assistance. The state can make its decision about what kind of control to employ by judging the threats and benefits these different social forces could bring to its rule, and balance its use of coercing and co-opting strategies.

2.1.2.3   Effective Control and State Institutions

Whether the state can make efficient combination of coercion and co-optation strategies to deal with various types of issues (including Type II issues) is, to a large extent, determined by the state's institutions, particularly those arranging the internal power distribution and providing motivations. Institutions here refer to the formal or informal procedures, routines, norms, and conventions embedded in the organizational structure of the polity (Hall and Taylor 1996). The state's influence or control over society is exerted primarily through the state's institutions. Skocpol (1992) argues that political institutions and political processes (understood in non-economically determinist ways) heavily shape the state's actions including its interactions with society. Evans (1995) and Kohli (2004), for instance, through examining a range of developing and transitional countries, show that state institutions and policies have significantly affected these societies' economic development.

First, institutions distributing power resources such as the decision-making authority determine which state agencies carry out controlling strategies and how. This is because the allocation of power resources in a given political institution determines the strategy options that are available for political actors to pursue their interests (Kriesi et al. 1992; Mayntz and Scharpf 1995; Börzel 2002). As Hall (1986, p. 19) contends, "The organization of policy making affects the degree of power that any one set of actors has over policy outcomes". If the institutions can be more efficacious in assigning power resources to the proper level of bureaucrats who have the best information to make decisions, it can enhance the efficiency of the state's control over society. For example, in a highly centralized system in which the power and resources are concentrated in the central state, the center has the supreme authority over which social segment should be suppressed (or co-opted) and how. However, such an institution may not be efficient in dealing with a rapidly growing society as the central authorities may not have enough information to make proper decisions. A changing society will constantly generate new social forces and problems, and the central authorities cannot always possess so precise and sufficient information about these changes as local bureaucrats. Accordingly, institutions allocating power and resources to lower levels of the state apparatus that have more adequate information of these changes can improve the state's strategies, enhancing the effect of the state's control over local society.

Second, institutions can boost the efficiency of a state's control over society by providing sufficient motivations for proper co-optation and coercion actions. Institutions define appropriate actions and heavily influence political actors' perceptions of their roles and situations by generating motivations (March and Olsen 1989). Specifically, they influence actors' preferences by providing them with greater or lesser degrees of certainty about other actors' responses towards their actions (Hall and Taylor 1996). For example, institutions tell actors that they will be given awards for their compliance with superintendents but penalties for violations against rules. Hence, institutions may change actors' preferences over certain behaviors by providing motivations and constraints. Thus, if the institutions can be reformulated to provide clearer rules and routines that can motivate state bureaucrats to respond to social forces in a more sophisticated and timely way, it is helpful for maintaining the state's grip over a growing society. On the contrary, if the institutions do not provide proper impetuses, the effect can be less satisfactory.

In sum, this chapter so far has built a dynamic framework for explaining how a state can retain its control over a society with growing power (increasing material resources and associational power, and stronger capability to generate its own ideas, beliefs, and symbols) for Type II issues. The key is the state's adoption of correspondingly low coercing but high co-opting strategies, which can enable the state to suppress adversary social forces with limited coercive resources and maximize incorporation of cooperative social elements (and their resources). The effect of these strategies, however, is largely determined by the state's institutions, particularly those governing the state's internal power distribution and providing motivations for political actors' actions. Thus, a more efficient institution in assigning power resources to proper levels of bureaucrats (those who can make the best use of resources) and encouraging bureaucrats' motivations can strengthen the state's capacity to empower itself. This means though, from a static point of view, state and social forces can sometimes be viewed as a zero-sum conflict, due to the limited power and resources within a society, the two can also be mutually empowering in their constant struggles and accommodations. From a dynamic perspective, the evolution of state-society interactions can sometimes lead to a pattern of both a strong society and a strong state, in which a growing state maintains its grip over an increasingly strong society. The following section will use this framework to analyze Chinese state and society relations and the state's governance of Type II issue.

2.2   STATE-SOCIETY RELATIONS IN CHINA

This section aims to provide a general account of state-society relations in contemporary China, which can serve as the broad backdrop for understanding the finer dynamics between state and society amid the newly emerging Confucian revival. Before addressing contemporary Chinese state-society interaction, this section will first describe some dominant relational patterns in the state and society's mutual engagements in pre-modern and Mao's China (1949–1976), given the great continuities in the evolution of the Chinese state and society relations. This general account, however, is not a comprehensive discussion about the overall Chinese state-society relations in history given the limited space. The interactions between state and society in China have a historical span of at least 4000 years and cover a great variety of patterns. Few accounts, therefore, can fully grasp all the relational patterns of such a complex relationship. This account, instead, only focuses on several dominant and distinctive characteristics of Chinese state-society relations, which are relevant to the current Confucian revival. The second part will present the heated debate concerning contemporary Chinese state-society relations, that is, can the post-totalitarian state effectively control an increasingly vibrant and assertive society unleashed by marketization?

2.2.1   Chinese State and Society Relations in History

2.2.1.1   The Imperial State's Control over Society in Pre-Modern China

One of the defining characteristics of pre-modern Chinese state-society relations, compared with other ancient societies, is the imperial state's sophisticated control over society through its imperial bureaucratic system and Confucian indoctrination. Wittfogel's *Oriental Despotism* (1957), though has been questioned by many, provides a good starting point for understanding the aristocratic nature of pre-modern Chinese imperial states. According to Wittfogel (1957), by the time of Xia (2205–1766 BC), the Chinese civilization had already established an absolutist and centralized state based on a broad "hydraulic society". Hydraulic society refers to a society relying on water control and large-scale hydraulic systems to secure most of the food for that society. Due to the construction of large-scale water control projects, such as dredging rivers and building irrigation systems, hydraulic society bred a "total state" or "Oriental despotic state" which ruled in the name and authority of the emperor whose authority was absolute in the sense that no significant social forces could seriously challenge him (see also Reischauer and Fairbank 1962). Though many later studies challenged Wittfogel's model of hydraulic society, for example, Giddens (1987) believed that Wittfogel had exaggerated the amount of administrative centralization in building irrigation projects,[15] the model of "Oriental despotic state" remains useful for understanding the pre-modern Chinese state and society interactions. In 221 BC, after unifying the then Chinese territory, Emperor Qin built an even more despotic and centralized bureaucratic state. The basic institutions of this state stayed long after the dissolution of the Qin dynasty.[16]

The imperial state, represented by emperors and their families, amassed large amounts of resources and monopolized political power during much of Chinese history,[17] even though there was some obscure sharing of power within the state, for example, between the emperor and prime minister in the imperial court (Qian 2001). According to Wittfogel (1957), the state, in order to build massive irrigation systems such as dams, channels, and reservoirs, constantly extracted resources and recruited mass labor from society. It also controlled the division of labor, organizational planning, transportation, and other resources. Accordingly, the imperial state also held absolute political rule. There were virtually no independent societal forces equivalent to churches or nobles that could check and constrain the emperor as in the Western context (Fairbank and Feuerwerker

1986; Moody 1995; Guo 2012). One explanation for this offered by Francis Fukuyama (2011) is that the imperial state, due to its early maturation, had already consolidated itself before other social actors could institutionalize themselves, such actors as a hereditary, territorially based aristocracy, an organized peasantry, cities based on merchant class, churches, or other autonomous groups. In addition, the state's firm control of the military also prevented military coups like in ancient Rome from happening (Fukuyama 2011).

With resort to the monopoly of resources and power, the imperial state had developed a set of instruments to exert control over society among which the Confucian indoctrination and civil service examination system (*keju*) are the two most distinctive and important ones during much of imperial history. The two were closely intertwined and mutually reinforced. First, to legitimize its rule, most dynastic rulers enshrined a sanctioned Confucianism exclusively as the state ideology since the Han dynasty, except during short intervals. Confucianism has different branches, but the state-sanctioned version emphasized loyalty to the emperor, the Son of Heaven.[18] Second, the imperial monarch during the Sui dynasty had established a civil service examination to recruit bureaucratic elites which later became the main route to officialdom (Elman 2000). The examination was based on the Confucian classics, mainly the Four Books and Five Classics.[19] In order to sit for the examination, the candidates needed to master, or indeed memorize, all the Confucian texts, given that the competition was very keen (Ichisada 1981; Moody 1995).[20] Thus, the examination can also promote the indoctrination of state-sanctioned Confucianism. Wittfogel (1963, p. 63) regarded the competitive examination system as an excellent means for "thorough and comprehensive ideological training".

The civil service examination, more importantly, served as an essential means for the state to invite society's participation in state-authorized institutions, that is, the imperial bureaucratic system. It selected proper candidates for bureaucratic positions such as county magistrates from those who passed the examination.[21] The examination, theoretically speaking, was open to all male adults in society and was merit-based. Only those who excelled in Confucian literature and achieved exceptionally high grades would be chosen as bureaucratic officials and sent to different regions of the empire to manage local affairs. Thus, the examination recruited the most talented (male) members from society to participate in imperial rule.

The examination therefore produced a scholar-gentry class who assisted the state's penetration into society. These scholar-bureaucrats together with local gentry, who also obtained their status through the examination but nevertheless were not qualified as bureaucrats, ruled local society in accordance with the emperor's will.[22] Therefore, the scholar-gentry class, to some extent, served as the agents of the monarch in ruling local society, thus enabling the state's regimentation of society.[23] And, to make the scholar-gentry's rule more effective, the monarch entitled them with the highest social status and enormous social prestige (Weber 1963),[24] which, in turn, attracted more talent to take the civil examination and enter into the imperial bureaucratic institutions.

The examination also strengthened the monarch's monopoly on bureaucratic resources by reducing the aristocracy's power of assigning bureaucrats. This is distinctive to the imperial Chinese political system. Before the implementation of the examination, most appointments in the imperial bureaucracy were based on recommendations from prominent aristocrats (and ranking officials); and recommended candidates were often of aristocratic rank. The aristocratic families hence controlled considerable bureaucratic power, especially at the local level (Wittfogel 1963). However, after the examination, merit in Confucian attainment became the sole criterion for selecting officials. This means, any male adult, regardless of his wealth or social status, could become a high-ranking bureaucratic official, as long as he could pass the examination.[25] Since the examination was under direct and exclusive control of the emperor and his state, it heavily reduced the aristocracy's bureaucratic power.

The model of the imperial state's unrelenting hegemony over society through indoctrinating Confucianism and building a scholar-gentry class, to be sure, is but one relational pattern between the state and society in pre-modern China. Chinese history is full of accounts about social forces' active influence on the state's (or the emperor's) decisions. For example, influential landlords would often join together to block imperial reforms aiming to disaggregate their land or reduce their wealth. Social forces also actively exploited the imperial system to achieve their respective aims. In the case of the civil service examination, local gentry and merchants often brazenly used the examination to get their sons or grandsons political positions in order to sustain and enhance their social status and landed wealth (Elman 1990, 2000; Glahn 1996; Ho 1962). In addition, it needs to be pointed out that given the limitations of communication and transportation in traditional China, the state's reach over society was limited.

The state's command could only reach county magistrates and the local gentry. The state's capacity to extract resources from society was also limited and the bureaucracy it established was also comparatively small. Thus, large parts of society were, to some extent, autonomous in especially the economic and social arenas. However, the pattern of a strong central state ruling society by ideological and organizational control was dominant, with penetrating influence over the contemporary Chinese state and society relations, which will be discussed in the following section.

2.2.1.2 The Totalitarian State's Active Domination and Atomized Society's Silent Resistance in Mao's China (1949–1978)[26]

The pattern of a strong state exerting tight control over society grew most intense during the period from 1949 to 1978. The party-state thoroughly penetrated into every corner of society and controlled almost every aspect of social life (Lieberthal 1995; Walder 1985).[27] The base for totalitarian control is the party-state's absolute monopoly of the key economic resources and political power, through a series of fundamental social transformations. This pattern continued until 1978 when China began its economic reforms and still has strong hold over contemporary Chinese state-society relations.

After 1949 when the CCP took power, the party-state implemented nationwide socialist economic transformations such as "agricultural collectivization" (*nongye hezuohua*) and "industrial nationalization" (*gongye guojiahua*) and thus brought virtually all economic resources under its control. For example, by fall 1958, through large-scale agricultural collectivization movements, the party-state had incorporated around 117.5 million rural households and their land into 23,500 People's Communes (*renmin gongshe*), a basic administrative and economic apparatus of the state in rural China. By the early 1960s, the number of People's Communes increased to 74,000 (Worden et al. 1987). While in the urban areas, by the mid-1970s almost all private enterprises had been nationalized into state-owned enterprises (hereafter SOEs) or collective cooperatives that were run by central and local governments (Walder 1985).

Given its dominance of economic resources, the state established a work unit (*danwei*) system aiming to incorporate all adult social members into the state system. Work units are mass organizations such as schools, factories, business organizations, or any workplace where people are employed and they are directly controlled by the state. In rural areas, work units are the so-called production team or People's Communes. After the socialist transformation, almost every adult was associated with a work unit. This is, in essence, a strategy of co-optation, and compared with the civil service examination which only incorporated talented individuals into the imperial bureaucratic institution, the work unit system was far more comprehensive and intensive. First, it covered nearly all members of society while the civil service examination included only a tiny number of people. Second, the intensity of society's social members' dependency on the state in the work unit system was much higher than that of scholar-bureaucrats on the imperial state. According to Andrew Walder (1985), Chinese workers experienced "organized dependency" from their work units (the factories). "Organized dependency" refers to a situation in which workers are totally dependent upon their unit for every conceivable need and benefit and that they could not escape the control by seeking another work unit through a labor market, nor could they organize themselves autonomously in any possible way.[28]

Besides control through economic dependency, the state strengthened its political power by atomizing society. Societal members were deprived of all freedom to organize themselves. The party-state's grassroots apparatus in work units monitored its members. In addition, leadership in work units adopted "principled particularism" to control members' behavior. "Principled particularism" describes how the leadership exercised control over workers by building up networks of loyalists from among the workers, thus dividing the workers and creating antagonism which could split the workforce (Walder 1985). There were also other forms of bureaucratic control, for example, local cadres' routine and non-routine reports of and inspections over the members within a work unit, penalties and sanctions over "un-loyal" members in both material and non-material terms (Oi 1989). However, it needs to be emphasized that though the state had tight control over society though work units, it is also increasingly recognized that there were also wide self-management and individual participation in the work units, which, in effect, reduced the state's penetration over society. For example, (Lu & Perry 1997) claims that the economic and welfare functions of work units created a "small public" realm that became the institutional foundation for these work units to pursue their own interests (e.g. by concealing real profits and assets from the state), which was detrimental for the central state's management over society.[29]

Frequent ideological mobilization was the basic mechanism for legitimization during this period. Like the imperial state's indoctrination of Confucianism but much beyond its scope and intensity, the party-state conducted sweeping ideological campaigns to propagate its official ideologies among even common citizens (Schurmann 1966). This ideological control helped establish direct and impersonal ties between the totalitarian party (its elites) and the masses, which intensified the state's dominance over society (Kornhauser 1959; Arendt 1951). But the ideological control was not independent from other control mechanisms; rather, it was underpinned and greatly facilitated by the work unit system. For example, leadership in work units usually adopted "political study in small groups" and "mutual criticism" to carry out thorough-going indoctrination among members of the work unit. Individuals in small study groups were required to place their commitments to the Party and the official ideology over their personal interests and affections. They were even requested to report any errant word or behavior by themselves or others in the group (Schurmann 1966; Walder 1985; Guo 2012). These measures were usually very effective in creating ideological consensus among the members, because the leadership, by exercising comprehensive control over the members' conceivable need and benefit, could put heavy sanctions and penalties on members who dared to show disagreements with the ideology.

The state's pervasive power and seamless control, however, does not mean that society or the masses was entirely passive or defenseless against the state's demands. As Shue (1988, p. 19) writes, "the Chinese Party state, a self-described dictatorship, ... has provoked resistance, sometimes outright resistance, sometimes indirect or evasive resistance". State-society relations during this period were asymmetric but interactive. Societal members made efforts to influence cadres, affect policy implementations and pursue their interests, though they had only limited resources to achieve their aims. For example, workers, students, and peasants during this period, all had made demands on and participated in the political system (Oksenberg 1968; Burns 1978). As for individuals, though there were limited formal channels for meaningful participation and interest articulation, they could also pursue at least some of their interests through use of informal networks built upon personal ties with local leadership. Both individual worker and peasant, for instance, could influence the decisions of local leadership in the factories and production teams (a kind of work unit in rural areas) through some clientelist lines (Walder 1985; Oi 1985, 1989). But it needs to be acknowledged that the impact of society upon the state's policy-making and implementation was limited.

2.2.2   The Debate of Contemporary Chinese State-Society Relations: The Post-Totalitarian State Versus the Strengthening Society

The period after 1978 has initiated the state's comprehensive retreat from its totalitarian control over society. The state-led economic privatization and marketization have significantly reduced society's economic dependency on the party-state. For farmers and agricultural workers, the de-collectivization of farming including dismantling of the People's Commune system has allowed them much more independence in arranging their own economic activities and making extra money (Walker 1984; Oi 1992). For workers, the restructuring (privatization) of previous state-owned enterprises substantially diluted the economic and social welfare benefits formerly provided to them by the state. Workers now obtain most needs and benefits from the market rather than the state (Solinger 2004; Weston 2004).[30] Together with the weakening of economic control, the state's organizational control through such means as the work unit system has also been watered down. The ideological indoctrination and mobilization, which used to be frequent and pervasive in the organizational life of the work unit, has also dramatically declined with the attenuation of organizational control (Joseph 2010; Zhao 2001).

The Chinese state had gradually evolved into a "post-totalitarian" regime which can be largely characterized by "weakened faith in ideology, un-commitment to routine mobilization and loosened organizational control", but still "keeping rigid control over state bureaucracy and allowing limited socio-economic pluralism" (Linz and Stepan 1996). Can such a post-totalitarian state effectively control an increasingly vibrant and assertive society unleashed by marketization? This is a central debate in contemporary Chinese state-society relations.

2.2.2.1   The Pessimist Argument: Growing Societal Power and Possible Democratization

The pessimists of China's post-totalitarian state believe that the inflexible Chinese polity, with limited channels for meaningful societal participation and interest articulation, simply cannot answer burgeoning societal demand and will have to succumb to a transition to democracy. On the one hand, the economic privatization and marketization have brought about dramatic economic growth which gave rise to the emergence and growth of various new economic actors such as private entrepreneurs and the middle class who will press for greater freedom in order to protect their interests (Lu 2002; Li 2010a).[31] The middle class, particularly, will become the mainstream force for democratization, as the democratic transition experiences in South Korea and Taiwan have suggested. On the other hand, the economic reforms are not complete. The old state-owned economy has still been selectively retained, and these state-owned enterprises suffer heavily from the market-oriented reforms. Large numbers of laid-off workers and other "losers" in the market will demand decent social welfare and require sufficient political participation. The post-totalitarian system, however, may not be able to respond to the rising demand due to its limited socio-political pluralism.

Some scholars in this school adopt the "civil society" perspective, and claim that different segments of society, thanks to the state's relaxation of social control, form their own associations to advance the members' common interests (Gold 1990; Strand 1990; White 1993; Whyte 1992; Yang 1989). Since the early 1980s, various social organizations have been formed, especially the non-official (*minjian*) and semi-official social organizations such as the Individual Handicraftsman and Small Business Dealer Association. Official statistics reveals that in 2011 there were around 440,000 social organizations among which 195,000 were NGOs (National bureau of Statistics of China 2012). Though these organizations are still circumscribed, and in some cases tightly restrained by the state, they possess at least some autonomy in organizing their social activities, forming a kind of nascent "civil society" which links the state and individuals (Unger and Chan 1995, 1996; Brook and Frolick 1997). White (1993) believed that these social organizations can protect individuals' rights from the state's invasion (and also atomization and inequality brought by rapid marketization). Thus, Whyte (1992) also believed that the nascent "civil society" may produce societal pressure for political changes as their East European counterparts did.[32]

In line with the "civil society" argument, scholars in this side also posit that information technological advance facilitates the growth of "online activism" and thus strengthens social autonomy against the state. Owing to technological improvements combined with commercialization and globalization, the rapidly proliferating commercial newspapers, magazines, TV stations, and the Internet produce massive amounts of information and messages within China that can simply "drown out" the ideological messages that the CCP intends to impart (Kraus 2004). Social forces now have growing impact on the initiation and circulation of public information and messages within society, the building block of the "symbolic environment" from which people derive their worldviews, values, and action strategies. As Lynch has pointed out, millions of individuals and organizations now contribute to the construction of the symbolic environment, controlling more and more ideological resources and reducing the state's relevance in communication flows (1999). For the general citizenry, they also have a growing ability to voice their grievances through increasingly independent mass media, particularly the Internet (Perry and Selden 2003; Perry and Wasserstrom 1994; O'Brien 2008).[33]

2.2.2.2   The Optimist Argument: Strong Post-Totalitarian State and Authoritarian Resilience

Optimists of China's post-totalitarian state, however, argue that though the rapidly growing Chinese society poses unprecedented challenges, the Chinese state can still retain its control by actively adopting new institutions and adroitly adjusting the old. Some emphasize that the current Chinese state inherits its totalitarian predecessor's political resources such as a highly organized Leninist party system with deep penetration into society and the monopoly of bureaucratic power (Xiao 2002). Besides, the state appoints leadership personnel in major economic, social, and cultural organizations, for example, the remaining SOEs, universities, public schools, and publishing houses, and empowers them with considerable authority. The CCP's branches continue to be well-situated in these organizations and are active in re-socializing and monitoring their members (Zheng 2010).[34] Even in private enterprises and companies (including joint-venture enterprises), especially those of a large scale, party branches are also established, though their functions may be somewhat different (Dickson 2003, 2008). For urban and rural citizens, though they are allowed to elect their own "residential neighborhood committees" (*xiaoqu guanli weiyuanhui*) and "villager's committees" (*cun weihui*) to administer their local affairs, these committees are also under the direct control of local governments and party organs (Jennings 1997; Chan et al. 1992; Xu 2003). With these political resources, the state is well-positioned for effectively managing social crises that may put the regime in danger. Such comprehensive social penetration system offers the Chinese state extra advantages when comparing with Latin American and East Asian authoritarian regimes (Xiao 2002).

Besides political resources, the state maintains command of China's key economic resources. The enterprises it owns monopolize China's energy resources, telecommunications, traffic, and mass communications. According to the *Financial Times*' 2010 list of the 500 largest companies (in terms of market value) in the world, the 21 listed Chinese companies were all state-owned or state-controlled enterprises, covering areas such as finance, chemicals, construction, transport, and so on (*The Financial Times* 2010). The Chinese state's total revenue amounted to 10.37 trillion RMB in 2011, with a 24.8% increase over the year of 2010 (The Central People's Government of the People's Republic of China 2012). This large revenue provides financial expenditure for most official and semi-official organizations such as schools and academic institutes. Thus, employees in these organizations are still heavily reliant on the state for their incomes and welfare benefits (Guo 2012; Wright 2010).[35]

As for growing social organizations, scholars in this camp reject civil society or possible democratization argument, but view them from a quasi "state corporatism" perspective (Whiting 1991; Unger and Chan 1995, 2008; Dittmer 1987),[36] arguing that the state has been largely successful in preventing societal groups from unifying together and pressing threats to its power monopoly. The state, on the one hand, has created large numbers of semi-official intermediary functional organizations to resolve social need for organizations in newly developing social and economic areas (Yep 2000; Foster 2001, 2002; Unger 2008). Due to lack of internal cohesiveness for members (which are deliberately made by the state), these official organizations cannot effectively group their members or clearly express their collective interests. These organizations mainly transmit the state's order from above to their members.

For non-official organizations, the state refines its control by providing large amounts of resources in exchange for their submission for the state's control. For example, White (1993) shows that the more closely these organizations are related with local governments, the more political resources they can obtain, and the stronger influence they can have upon the government, but the more limitations they have in their autonomy. The state requires these organizations to be registered with the state authorities and imposes restrictions and monitoring measures such as requiring them to submit annual reports concerning their associational activities to the concerned state authorities. These non-official organizations may affect the state's decision in certain policy areas, but they do not hold sufficient autonomy to raise any threat to the state's rule (Kennedy 2005).

Scholars in this side also argue that the state has strengthened its suppression and incorporation of various social segments. It built up strong coercive power including its military and security forces. For example, its budget for domestic security covering the police, state security, militia, courts, and jails reached $111 billion in 2012, which is even higher than the publicly disclosed military expenditure (Lim 2012). The state's repression of opposition and popular resistance has become more strategic. Pei (2012) argues that the CCP has now shifted towards "smart repression". The regime has become more selective in using coercion as it has learned from the 1989 experience. It has narrowed the scope of repression by only targeting leading dissidents, so that it can avoid antagonizing the majority of the population while preventing organized opposition from emerging (Pei 2006; Dickson 2011; Shambaugh 2000). Analysts of "resistance politics" in China also maintain that the Chinese state has devised a set of strategies to avoid the escalation of parochial social unrest into national movements confronting the central government, therefore, effectively reducing threats to the political system (Cai 2008; O'Brien and Li 2006; Lee 2007).

The state undertakes tactical co-optation strategies for powerful social forces such as intellectual and economic elites. Dickson (2003, 2008) contends that the CCP, by forging corporatist links with various social organizations and co-opting economic elites (private entrepreneurs) into its organization, is largely successful in preventing their organized demands for political change (see also Chen and Dickson 2010). Pei (2006) argues that since the early 1990s, the CCP has launched a systematical campaign of co-optation to recruit intellectuals and professionals to its fold. For example, the CCP elevated their political status and raised their economic benefits such as assigning them strategic technocratic appointments and awarding them with salary increases. It also expanded the recruitment of intellectuals and professionals into the CCP organization (Cheng 2009). The co-optation has greatly eased the contentious relations between the CCP and the intelligentsia (and the professional classes) who had earlier challenged the CCP's authority and demanded political reforms.

The existing literature has greatly contributed to our understanding of China's contemporary state and society relations and the state's possible transitions. However, it still has left much to be unexplained. First, the current literature tends to focus on actor-specific state-society relations, for example, state's interactions with social segments such as intellectuals, private entrepreneurs, or laid-off workers, or its relations with social organizations; hence, it does not provide sufficient explanation over how the state strives to control the symbolic environment so that it can structure the systems of beliefs and ideas within society. It is easy to understand why the state wants to dominate the symbolic environment and not let it fall in the hands of social forces, given the importance of legitimacy for the state's rule.[37] But the current literature concerning China's ideology or religious development seldom explores the state-society interactions in these issues (Brown 2012; Williams 2010; Billioud 2011a, b; Sun 2013, 2017); thus, there is still a big gap in understanding the state-society relations in China's symbolic environment.

Moreover, the existing literature tends to concentrate on sector-specific and contextualized state-society relations, emphasizing their mutual influence, be it coordination or contestation. Only a small part has tried to build their analysis from an institutional perspective, particularly the state's internal institutions concerning power distribution and motivation. This is understandable given that the Chinese state's institutions and their functions are complicated, involving large numbers of "implicit rules". It is difficult to obtain their overall picture merely through outsiders' sociological fieldwork. But studies on institutions are of significant value as institutional evolution and function is critical in explaining various sector-specific state-society relational changes in contemporary China. Institutional studies have developed rapidly recently, especially with increasing relevant information released (Zhou 2000, 2010, 2014). This study, therefore, will adopt an institutional perspective and use the state's management of the Confucian revival as a window to explore the state's structuring of China's symbolic environment.

Notes

1. Jessop (1990, 2008), for example, believes that "society" as a generic expression, serves at best as an "indeterminate horizon" within which various "social projects" are situated.
2. The state thus defined can be traced back to Weber's (1958) concept of government bureaucracy which is "a compulsory association which organizes domination", and "a human community that (successfully) claims the monopoly of the legitimate use of physical force within a given territory". Such a view of the state is also based on empirical conceptions developed by Marx, Weber, and Hintze (Sellers 2010). It also has deep roots in the absolutist state that existed in the European continent during the Industrial Revolution.
3. For example, Sellers (2010) challenges the notion of a unitary state by showing that the actual modern state encompasses strong horizontal and

vertical diversity. Horizontally, it comprises of dozens of institutionally distinct policy sectors with highly diverse organizational architectures, from macroeconomic management to environmental regulations. Vertically, there is at least some amount of autonomy among different levels of the state organization.

4. It needs to be clarified that this book does not deliberately intend to treat the state and society in an undifferentiated manner. It is true that the image of the state (and also society) as a holistic entity pulling in single directions is sometimes misleading. Furthermore, the assumption is that the state and society as unitary actors acting strategically to maximize their interests is also oversimplified (Migdal 2001; Sellers 2010). However, a general pattern of state-society relations is still summarizable for this thesis. This is because even though different segments of states and societies do have distinctive patterns of interactions, this study only focuses on the key building blocks of states and societies, and their major interaction modes. Although my model will lose some delicacy and nuances in capturing the complexities in the state-society interactions, it still suffices to serve as a broad and general framework for a specific case, the Chinese state-society interactions in the Confucian revival.

5. As a core concept in social sciences, power has a long list of definitions given by numerous scholars from different perspectives (for some representative views, see Weber 1968; Thomson 1990; Nye 1990, 2004). For example, Weber (1968, p. 53) defined power as "the probability that one actor within a social relationship will be in a position to carry out his will despite resistance". In this book, it has a narrow focus on political activities and has different denotations for society and state. Specifically, for society, power means people's capacity to express and organize associations in order to affect the state's actions. For the state, it means the state's capability to *penetrate* society and *regulate* social relationships such as controlling the society's members' freedom of speech and association.

6. Resources refer to the economic, military, political, and ideological sources for social power (Mann 2012, p. 2). It does not only cover material resources such as money, manpower, service, and other assets but also spiritual ones such as accepted beliefs and symbols. According to Migdal (1988), systems of meaning and symbolic configuration, whether it is ideology or simple beliefs, are important resources for social power, especially when they are packed by powerful social forces together with material rewards and punishments. Power and resources are closely interconnected, as Giddens (1979, p. 91) has pointed out, "resources are the media through which power is exercised".

7. This is especially so in the "participant civil culture", one of the five types of civil culture listed by Almond and Verba (1989).

8. Such belief, in fact, is not new. It can be traced back all the way to Plato. It has regained its vigor in the early twentieth century particularly in continental Europe, where a few German and Italian political theorists developed the elitism argument while criticizing the idea that an extension of voting rights would mean a real, popular democratic decision-making (Pierson 2011).

9. Michels, in his 1911 book *Political Parties*, claims that any mass of citizens are psychologically not able to make complicated decisions, and thus they need powerful leaders to organize and lead them.

10. Statist literature remains a powerful part of some other social and political theories such as Structuralism, Neo-Realism, etc.

11. According to an arena is not necessarily spatially limited but a conceptual locus where significant struggles and accommodations occur among social forces.

12. To be sure, coercion can also mean stripping the coerced of other valuables such as social status or personal assets. However, constraint on freedom is fundamental because it limits social forces' exercise of power and resources and therefore averts possible threats to the state's rule (for details concerning the close relations between coercion and freedom, see Carr 1988; Anderson 2010; Pennock 2015).

13. But to be sure, there are also other factors affecting the state's use of different levels of coercion, for instance, how much resources the coerced element possesses, and how influential it is over other societal members. But the fundamental criterion is its perceived threat to state power.

14. According to Selznick (1949), there are two basic forms of co-optation. One is formal and the other informal. This part mainly talks about informal co-optation.

15. Eberhard (1970) and Huang (1985) also questioned Wittfogel's hydraulic society by showing that the irrigation systems in China were, more often than not, decentralized rather than centralized.

16. Fukuyama (2011) contends that the building of this centralized state by Qin should be attributed to the earlier warfare among different dukes, which had lasted for more than 500 years, because the warfare had greatly enhanced the state's capacity through facilitating the state's appropriation of economic resources and control of human power.

17. The imperial state was represented at different times by not only the emperor and his families, but also his court, eunuchs, and also high-ranking officials.

18. For details, see (Tu 1989).

19. The Four Books refer to *The Analects of Confucius* (*Lun Yu*), *The Mencius* (*Meng Zi*), *The Great Learning* (*Da Xue*) and *The Doctrine of the Golden Mean* (*Zhong Yong*); The Five Classics refer to *The Book of Songs* (*Shi Jing*),

The Classic of History (Shu Jing), The Classic of Rites (Li Ji), The Book of Changes (I Ching), and *The Spring and Autumn Annals (Chun Qiu),* all of which are said to be compiled or revised by Confucius.

20. There are different estimations of the ratio for passing the examination. Generally, there was less than 1.5% for even the lowest level of examination. Ichisada (1981) gives full accounts of the difficulties of preparing, participating, and passing the examination.

21. The examination has three levels, the county, provincial, and palace, with the county as the lowest and the palace as the highest. Those succeeding in the palace examination would be appointed a government official position and those passing the provincial examination, theoretically speaking, were eligible to become government officials, though no secure position could be guaranteed. Those who only received a degree at the lowest (county) examination level would not be awarded any official position. But they could become a member of the local gentry, who could help local officials in managing affairs and therefore be rewarded with social status and economic benefits such as tax exemption. Elman (2000) has a very detailed discussion of the appointment prospects for the holders of the different levels of degree.

22. "Scholar bureaucrats" here refer to those imperial officials who hold political power in the dynastic bureaucracy, including magistrates of counties or prefectures, and higher-ranking officials in imperial court. Gentry here mean local landlords who hold local social and economic power over local affairs, assisting bureaucrats for some administrative affairs. But they did not have official positions.

23. They remained loyal to the emperor, because the emperor was the only buyer of their talents (Elman 2000). Thus, they had a strong stake in the monarch's existence and prosperity. However, it needs to be pointed out that the scholar-gentry were not just an instrument of imperial rule. They had their own power, and sometimes evaded or even challenged the emperor's orders (Elman 1990; Glahn 1996).

24. This practice had an important side effect. It sustained strong social interest in and dedication for Confucian education, given the fact that Confucian learning could possibly lift one's social status and so therefore achieve upward social mobility.

25. But it needs to be made clear that those from low origins or poverty had very limited chances, given that the examination required long and money-consuming preparation (Ichisada 1981). Wittfogel (1963) provides detailed figures concerning the different percentages of bureaucrats from families of officials, the ruling house, and commoners respectively during China's Song, Yuan, Ming, and Qing dynasties. The general trend was that most of the recruited bureaucrats came from families of officials and the ruling house. Only 15–23% were commoners. But, the selection based on

the civil service examination did reduce the number of bureaucrats from aristocratic families.

26. The reason to omit state-society relations in modern China (1911–1949) is because this portion of history did not deeply affect the formation of contemporary Chinese state and society relations. As will be explained later, the Communist Party who later took power had implemented a series of social and economic transformations which had almost totally changed the pattern of state and society relations formed in this period.

27. The CCP's total control was, in many ways, in line with the "totalitarian" model formulated by Carl Friedrich and Zbigniew Brzezinski (1956), which highlights elite efforts to mobilize and control non-elites.

28. Walder's model, however, was also challenged by a few scholars. For example, Shue (1988) argues that the state's control over rural work unit was not that strict. She believes that rural work units suffered from "less direct and unmediated central penetration", as their strong parochialism had posed a serious obstacle to the state's control (Shue 1988, p. 54).

29. Lu and Perry (1997) and Warner (2000) provide detailed discussions about the previously ignored role of work units in the Chinese state-society relations.

30. Deborah S. Davis and Ezra Vogel's edited book, *Chinese Society on the Eve of Tiananmen*, has systematically captured the changes that the economic reforms had made upon the relationship between the Chinese state and society.

31. For details of contemporary social stratification, please refer to Lu (2010).

32. An often cited example is Hungary whose economic reforms in the 1970s led to the Solidarity trade union movement in the early 1980s; see Arato (1981) and Pelczynski (1988).

33. Perry and Selden (2003) have thoroughly examined the conflicts and "dominant modes of popular resistance" engendered by the economic reforms.

34. By using the concept of "economic reliance", I do not mean that the staff and employees are unsatisfied with the state. In fact, most of them are content with the "economic dependence" as the material benefits in these government bureaus and SOEs are often better than what can be obtained from the market. Hence, they are, more often than not, the staunchest supporters for the current regime. For details, see Wright (2010).

35. Zheng (2010) has a detailed discussion of the Party's domination of all state apparatus.

36. Many scholars contend that "state corporatism" may not be proper in examining China's state-society relations, because of China's Leninist Party system (Dickson 2000), weak social class cohesion (Yep 2000), and lack of interest intermediation between social groups and the state (Foster 2001, 2002).

37. The importance of legitimacy has been discussed in detail in Chap. 1.

REFERENCES

Almond, G & Verba, S 1989, *The civic culture: political attitudes and democracy in five nations*, Sage, Newbury Park, CA.

Anderson, SA 2010, 'The enforcement approach to coercion', *Journal of Ethics & Social Philosophy*, vol. 5, no. 1.

Arendt, H 1951, *The origins of totalitarianism*, Harcourt, Brace and Co., New York.

Arato, A 1981, 'Civil society against the state: Poland 1980–81', *Telos*, vol. 1981, no. 47, pp. 23–47.

Billioud, S 2011a, *Thinking through Confucian modernity: a study of Mou Zongsan's moral metaphysics* (Vol. 5), Brill.

Billioud, S 2011b, 'Confucian revival and the emergence of "Jiaohua Organizations": a case study of the Yidan Xuetang', *Modern China*, vol. 37, no. 3, pp. 286–314.

Börzel, TA 2002, *States and regions in the European Union: institutional adaptation in Germany and Spain*, Cambridge University Press, Cambridge.

Brown, K 2012. 'The communist party of China and ideology,' *China: An International Journal*, vol. 10, no. 2, pp. 52–68.

Brook, T & Frolic, BM 1997, *Civil society in China*, ME Sharpe, New York.

Buckley, C 2012, 'China domestic security spending rises to $111 billion', viewed on February 2nd, 2013, available at http://www.reuters.com/article/2012/03/05/us-china-parliament-security-idUSTRE82403J20120305

Burns, J 1978, 'Elections of production team cadres in rural china, 1958–1974,' *The China Quarterly*, vol. 74, pp. 273–296.

Cai, YS 2008, 'Power structure and regime resilience: contentious politics in China', *British Journal of Political Science*, vol. 38, no. 3.

Carr, CL 1988, 'Coercion and Freedom,' *American Philosophical Quarterly*, vol. 25, pp. 59–67.

Chan, A Madsen, R & Unger, J 1992, *Chen village under Mao and Deng*, University of California Press, Berkeley.

Chan, A & Unger, J 2008, *Associations and the Chinese state: contested spaces*, M.E. Sharpe.

Chen, J & Dickson, BJ 2010, *Allies of the state: China's private entrepreneurs and democratic change*, Harvard University Press.

Cheng, L (Ed.). 2009, *China's changing political landscape: prospects for democracy*, Brookings Institution Press.

Dahl, R 1961, *Who Governs? Democracy and Power in an American City*, Yale University Press, New Haven.

Dahl, R 1963, *Modern Political Analysis*, Prentice-Hall, Englewood Cliffs, NJ.

Dahl, RA 1977, 'On removing certain impediments to democracy in the United States'. *Political Science Quarterly*, vol. 92, no. 1, pp. 1–20.

Dickson, B 2003, *Red Capitalists in China: the party, private entrepreneurs and prospects for political change*, Cambridge University Press, Cambridge.

Dickson, B 2008, *Wealth into power: the Communist Party's embrace of China's private sector*, Cambridge University Press, Cambridge.

Dickson, B 2011, 'Sustaining party rule in China', In Brown, NJ (ed.), *The dynamics of democratization: dictatorship, development, and diffusion*, John Hopkins University Press, Baltimore.

Dickson, BJ 2000, 'Cooptation and corporatism in China: the logic of party adaptation', *Political Science Quarterly*, vol. 115, no. 4, pp. 517–540.

Dittmer, L 1987, "Public and Private Interests and the Participatory Ethic in China," in *Citizens and Groups in Contemporary China*, edited by Falkenheim V. C., pp. 18–23, Ann Arbor: Center for Chinese Studies, University of Michigan.

Dryzek, J & Dunleavy, P 2009, *Theories of the democratic state*, Palgrave Macmillan, London.

Dunleavy, P & O'leary, B 1987, *Theories of the state: the politics of liberal democracy*, Macmillan.

Eberhard, W 1970, *Conquerors and rulers: social forces in Medieval China*, Brill Archive.

Elman, B 2000, *A cultural history of civil examinations in late imperial China*, University of California Press, Berkeley and Los Angeles.

Elman, BA 1990, *Classicism, politics, and kinship: the Ch'ang-chou school of new text Confucianism in late imperial China*, University of California Press, Berkeley and Los Angeles.

Evans, P 1995, *Embedded autonomy: states and industrial transformation*, Princeton University Press, Princeton.

Evans, PB, Rueschemeyer, D, & Skocpol, T (eds.) 1985, *Bringing the state back in*, Cambridge University Press.

Fairbank, JK & Feuerwerker, A 1986, *The Cambridge history of China*, Cambridge University Press, Cambridge.

Foster, Kenneth W 2001, 'Associations in the embrace of an authoritarian state: state domination of society,' *Studies in Comparative International Development*, vol. 35, no. 4, pp. 84–109.

Foster, KW 2002, 'Embedded within state agencies: Business associations in Yantai', *The China Journal*, vol. 47, pp. 41–65.

Friedrich, C & Brzezinski, Z 1956, *Totalitarian dictatorship and autocracy*, Harvard University Press.

Fukuyama, F 2011, *The Origins of political order: from prehuman times to the French revolution*, Farrar, Straus and Giroux, New York.

Giddens, A 1979, *Central problems in social theory*, Macmillan, London.

Giddens, A 1981, *A contemporary critique of historical materialism*, Macmillan, London.

Giddens, A 1984, *The constitution of society: outline of the theory of structuration*, Polity Press, Cambridge.

Giddens, A 1987, *The nation-state and violence: volume 2 of a contemporary critique of historical materialism* (Vol. 2), University of California Press.

Glahn, RV 1996, *Fountain of fortune: money and monetary policy in China, 1000–1700*, University of California Press, Berkeley.

Gold, TB 1990, "Party-State versus Society in China." In *Building a Nation-State: China at Forty*, edited by Kallgren JK., pp. 125–151. Berkeley: Institute of East Asian Studies, University of California.

Gramsci, A 1971, *The prison notebooks*, Lawrence and Wishart, London.

Greenfeld, L & Martin, ML 1988, *Center: ideas and institutions*, University of Chicago Press, Chicago.

Guo, S 2012, *Chinese politics and government: power, ideology and organization*, Routledge, London and New York.

Hagopian, F 1994, 'Traditional Politics against State Transformation in Brazil', In Migdal, J, Kohli, A & Shue, V (eds.), *State power and social forces: domination and transformation in the Third World*, Cambridge University Press, Cambridge.

Hall, JA & Ikenberry, GJ 1989, *The state*, University of Minnesota Press, Minneapolis.

Hall, PA 1986, *Governing the Economy: The Politics of State Intervention in Britain and France*, Oxford University Press, New York.

Hall, PA & Taylor, RCR 1996, 'Political science and the three new institutionalisms', *Political Studies*, vol. XLIV, pp. 936–957.

Ho, PT 1962, *The ladder of success in imperial China: aspects of social mobility, 1368–1911*, Wiley & Sons, New York.

Huang, P 1985, *The peasant economy and social change in North China*, Stanford University Press.

Ichisada, M 1981, *China's examination hell: the civil service examinations of imperial China*, Yale University Press, New Haven.

Jennings, MK 1997, "Political participation in the Chinese countryside", *The American Political Science Review*, vol. 91, no. 2.

Jensen, L 2008, 'politics, history and the state of the States', *Polity*, vol. 40, no. 3.

Jessop, B 1977, "Recent theories of the capitalist state", *Cambridge Journal of Economics*, no. l, pp. 353–73.

Jessop, B 1982, *The capitalist state: Marxist theories and methods*, Blackwell, Oxford.

Jessop, B 1990, *State theory: putting the capitalist state in its place*, Polity, Cambridge.

Jessop, B 2008, *State power: a strategic-relational approach*, Polity, Cambridge.

Joel S Migdal 1989, 'Strong states, weak states: power and accommodation', in Myron Weiner and Samuel P Huntington, (eds.), *Understanding political development*, Little Brown, Boston, pp. 396–397.

Joseph, WA 2010, *Politics in China: an introduction*, Oxford University Press, Oxford & New York.

Kennedy, D 1982, "The States of Decline of the Public-Private Distinction", *University of Pennsylvania Law Review*, no. 130, pp. 1349–1357.

Kennedy, S 2005, *The business of lobbying in China*, Harvard University Press, Cambridge, MA.

King, D & Lieberman, RC 2008, 'Finding the American state: transcending the "statelessness" account'. *Polity*, vol. 40, no. 3, pp. 368–378.

Kohli, A 2004, *State-directed development: political power and industrialization in the global periphery*, Cambridge University Press.

Kornhauser, W 1959, *The politics of mass society*, Free Press, Glencoe.

Kraus, RC 2004, *The party and the arty in China: the new politics of culture*, Rowman & Littlefield Publishers.

Kriesi, H et al, 1992, 'New social movements and political opportunities in Western Europe', *European Journal of Political Research*, vol. 22, pp. 219–244.

Lee, CK 2007, *Against the law: labor protests in China's rustbelt and sunbelt*, University of California Press, Berkeley.

Lenin, VI 1960, 'The state and revolution', in *Collected Works* 25, Lawrence and Wishart, London.

Li, C 2010a, *China's emerging middle class: beyond economic transformation*, Brookings Institution Press, Washington, DC.

Li, S 2010b, 'Gaoshang daode: haizimen chengzhang de jinshen liliang' (The fine morality: the spiritual power for the children's growth), *Renmin Jiaoyu (People's Education)*, vol. 615, p. 33–37.

Lieberthal, K 1995, *Governing China: from revolution through reform*, W. W. Norton, New York.

Lim, L 2012, "In China, a ceaseless quest to silence dissent", viewed on November 30th, 2012, available at http://www.npr.org/2012/10/30/163658996/in-china-a-ceaseless-quest-to-silence-dissent

Linz, JJ & Stepan, A, 1996, *Problems of democratic transition and consolidation: Southern Europe, South America, and post-communist Europe*, John Hopkins University Press.

Lu, XB & Perry, EJ (ed.) 1997, *Danwei: The changing Chinese workplace in historical and comparative perspective*. M. E. Sharpe, Armonk and London.

Lu, X 2002, *Research report of the social strata in contemporary China*, Social Science Academic Press, China.

Lu, X 2010, *Dangdai zhongguo shehui jiegou (Contemporary Chinese social structure)*, Social Science Academic Press, China.

Lynch, DC 1999, *After the propaganda state: media, politics, and "thought work" in reformed China*, Stanford University Press.

MacPherson, CB, 1973, *Democratic Theory: Essays in Retrieval*, Oxford University Press, Oxford.

Mann, M 1986, *The sources of social power (Volume 1)*, Cambridge University Press, Cambridge.

Mann, M 2012, *The sources of social power: global empires and revolution, 1890–1945, (Volume 3)*, Cambridge University Press, Cambridge.

March, JG & Olsen, J 1989, *Rediscovering institutions: the organizational basis of politics*, Free Press, New York.

Marx, K 1973, 'Manifesto of the Communist Party', reprinted in *The revolutions of 1848*, Penguin Books, Harmondsworth.

Mayntz, R & Scharpf, FW 1995, 'Der Ansatz des akteurzentrierten institutionalismus', In Mayntz, R & Scharpf, FW (eds.), *Steuerung und selbstorganisation in staatsnahen sektoren*, Campus, Frankfurt am Main, pp. 39–72.

McConnell, G 1966, *Private power & American democracy*, Knopf.

Michels, R 1962, *Political parties: a sociological study of the oligarchic tendencies of modern democracy*, Free Press, New York.

Migdal, J 2001, *State in society: studying how states and societies transform and constitute one another*, Cambridge University Press, Cambridge.

Migdal, JS 1988, *Strong societies and weak states: state-society relations and state capabilities in the Third World*, Princeton University Press, Princeton.

Migdal, JS, Kohli, A, & Shue, V 1995, *State power and social forces. Domination and transformation in the Third World*, Cambridge University Press, Cambridge UK.

Moody, P 1995, Tradition and modernization in China and Japan, Wadsworth Pub. Co., Belmont.

Mosca, G 1939, *The ruling class*, Mcgraw Hill, New York.

National Bureau of Statistics of China 2012, China statistical yearbook, Chapter 23, "Culture and Sports", http://www.stats.gov.cn/tjsj/ndsj/2011/indexch.htm, accessed on June 1st, 2013.

Nettl, JP 1968, 'The state as a conceptual variable', *World Politics*, vol. 20, pp. 559–592.

Nordlinger, FA 1981, *On the autonomy of the democratic state*, Harvard University Press, Cambridge, MA.

Nye, JS 1990, 'Soft power', *Foreign Policy*, no. 80, pp. 153–171.

Nye, JS 2004, Soft power: the means to success in world politics. Public affairs.

O'Brien, KJ & Li, LJ 2006, *Rightful resistance in rural China*, Cambridge University Press.

O'Brien, KJ 2008, *Popular protest in China*, Harvard University Press, Cambridge.

Oi, J 1985, 'Communism and clientelism: rural politics in China', *World Politics*, vol. 37, pp. 238–266.

Oi, J 1989, State and peasant in contemporary China: the political economy of village government, University of California Press, Berkeley.

Oi, JC 1992, 'Fiscal reform and the economic foundations of local state corporatism in China', *World Politics*, vol. 45, no. 1, pp. 99–126.

Oi, JC 1995, 'Fiscal reform and the economic foundations of local state corporatism in China', *World politics*, 45(1), 99–126.

Oksenberg, M 1968, 'Occupational groups in Chinese society and the Cultural Revolution,' in Oksenberg, M, Riskin, C, Scalapino, R &Vogel, E (eds), *The Cultural Revolution: 1967 in review*, University of Michigan, Ann Arbor.

Pei, MX 2006, *China's trapped transition: the limits of developmental autocracy*, Harvard University Press, Cambridge, MA.

Pei, M 2012, 'Is CCP rule fragile or resilient?' *Journal of Democracy*, vol. 23, no. 1, pp. 27–41.

Pelczynski, ZA 1988, 'Solidarity and the rebirth of civil society', in *Civil society and the state*, pp. 361–380.

Pennock, JR 2015, *Democratic political theory*, Princeton University Press.

Perry, EJ & Selden, M (eds.) 2003, *Chinese society: change, conflict and resistance*, Routledge.

Pierson, C 2011, *The modern state*, Routledge, New York.

Poggi, G 1978, *The development of the modern state: a sociological introduction*. Stanford University Press, Stanford.

Poulantzas, N 1978, *State, power, Socialism*, Verso, London.

Qian, M 2001, *ZhongGuo Lidai Zhengzhi Deshi (Chinese political success and failure in past dynasties)*, Sanlian Chubanshe (Triad press).

Reischauer, EO & Fairbank, JK 1962, *East Asia: the great tradition*, Houghton Mifflin, Boston.

Schmitter, P 1974, 'Still the century of corporatism?' *Review of Politics*, vol. 36, no. 1.

Schumpeter, J 1976, *Capitalism, Socialism, and democracy*, Allen & Unwin, London.

Schurmann, F, 1966, *Ideology and Organization in Communist China*, University of California Press, Berkeley and Los Angeles.

Sellers, JM 2010, 'State-Society relations', In Bevir, M (ed.), *Sage handbook of governance*, Sage Publications, London.

Selznick, P 1949, *TVA and the grass roots: a study in the sociology of formal organization*. University of California Press, Berkeley.

Shambaugh, D 2000, *The Modern Chinese State*, Cambridge University Press, Cambridge.

Shue, V 1988, *The Reach of the State: Sketches of the Chinese Body Politics*, Stanford University Press, Stanford, CA.

Skilling, HG 1983, 'Interest groups and Communist politics revisited', *World Politics*, vol. 36, no. 1, pp. 1–27.

Skilling, HG & Griffiths, F (eds.) 1970, *Interest groups in Soviet politics*. Princeton University Press, Princeton.

Skocpol, T 1979, *States and social revolutions*, Cambridge University Press, Cambridge.

Skocpol, T 1992, 'State formation and social policy in the United States', *American Behavioral Scientist*, vol. 35, no. 4–5, pp. 559–584.

Solinger, D 2004, 'The new crowd of the dispossessed: the shift of the urban proletariat from master to mendicant', in Gries, PH & Rosen, S (eds.), *State and society in 21st century China: crisis, contention, and legitimation*, RoutledgeCurzon, New York.

Strand, D 1990. 'Protest in Beijing: Civil Society and Public Sphere in China,' *Problems of Communism*, vol. 39 (May–June), pp. 1–19.

Sun, Y 2013, 'Popular religion in Zhejiang: feminization, bifurcation, and Buddhification', *Modern China*, vol. 40, no. 5, pp. 455–487.

Sun, Y 2017. 'The Rise of Protestantism in Post-Mao China: State and Religion in Historical Perspective,' *American Journal of Sociology*, vol. 122, no. 6, pp. 1664–1725.

The Central People's Government of the People's Republic of China 2012, "The Chinese state's total revenue amounted to 10.37 trillion RMB in 2011, with a 24.8% increase over the year of 2010", it can be accessed via http://www.gov.cn/jrzg/2012-01/20/content_2050059.htm

Thomson, JJ 1990, *The realm of rights*, Harvard University Press, Cambridge, MA.

Tong, JW 2007, *Revenge of the Forbidden City: The suppression of the falungong in China, 1999–2005*, Oxford University Press.

Truman, DB 1951, *The governmental process: political interests and public opinion*, Alfred A. Knopf, New York.

Truman, DB (1967) 1951, *The governmental process: political interests and public opinion*.

Tu, WM 1989, *Confucianism in historical perspective*, Institute of East Asian Philosophies, Singapore.

Tullock, G 1976, *The vote motive*, Princeton University Press, Princeton.

Unger, J & Chan, A 1995, 'China, corporatism, and the East Asian model', *Australian Journal of Chinese Affairs*, vol. 33 (January 1995), pp. 29–53.

Unger, J & Chan, A 1996, 'Corporatism in China; a developmental state in an East Asian context', In McCormick, B & Unger, J (eds.), *China after socialism, In the footsteps of Eastern Europe or East Asia?* M.E. Sharpe, Armonk, NY, pp. 95–129.

Unger, J 2008, *Associations and the Chinese state: Contested spaces*, ME Sharpe.

Walker, KR 1984, 'Chinese agriculture during the period of the readjustment, 1978–83', *The China Quarterly*, vol. 100, pp. 783–812.

Walder, A 1985, *communist neo-traditionalism: work and authority in Chinese industry*, University of California Press, Berkeley.

Warner, M 2000, *Changing workplace relations in the Chinese economy*, Macmillan Press, Basingstoke and London.

Wasserstrom, J & Perry, E 1994, *Popular protest and political culture in China: lessons from 1989*, Westview Press, Boulder, CO.

Weber, M 1958, *From Max Weber: essays in sociology*, translated by Gerth HH & Mills CW, Routledge.

Weber, M 1963, 'Struggle of monarch & nobility: origin of the *career open to talent*', In Menzel, JM (ed.), *The Chinese civil service: career open to talent?* D.C. Heath, Boston.

Weber, M 1968, *Economy and society: an interpretative sociology*, Bedminster, New York.

Weiss, L & Hobson, J 1995, *States and economic development: a comparative historical analysis*, Polity Press, Cambridge.

Weston, TB 2004, 'Society's 'masters' struggle to survive: state workers, jobless-ness and contention in Post-Deng China', In Gries, PH & Rosen, S (eds.), *State and society in 21st century China: crisis, contention, and legitimation*, RoutledgeCurzon, New York.

White, G 1993. *Riding the Tiger: The Politics of Economic Reform in Post-Mao China*. Stanford: Stanford University Press.

Whiting, S 1991, 'The Politics of NGO Development in China,' *Voluntas*, vol. 2, no. 2 (November), pp. 16–48.

Whyte, MK 1992. 'Prospects for Democratization in China,' *Problems of Communism* (May–June), pp. 58–70.

Williams, J 2010. ''Attacking Queshan': Popular Culture and the Creation of a Revolutionary Folklore in Southern Henan,' *Modern China*, vol. 36, no. 6, pp. 644–675.

Wittfogel, K 1963 *"The hereditary privilege vs. merit"*, In Menzel, JM (ed.), *The Chinese Civil Service: Career Open to Talent?* D.C. Heath, Boston.

Wittfogel, KA 1957, *Oriental despotism, a comparative study of total power*, Yale University Press, New Haven.

Worden, RL, Savada, AM & Dolan, RE 1987, *China: a country study*, US Government Printing Office, Washington.

Wright, T 2010, *Accepting authoritarianism: state-society relations in China's reform era*, Stanford University Press, Stanford.

Xu, Y 2003, *Rural governance and Chinese politics*, China Social Sciences Publishing House Beijing.

Xiao, GQ 2002, 'Zhongguo xiandaihua zhuanxing zhong de defang bihuwang zhengzhi (The local asylum politics in China's modernization)', *Jingji guanli wenzhai (Economic Management Digest)*, no. 21, pp. 36–41.

Yang, MM 1989. 'Between State and Society: The Construction of Corporateness in a Chinese Socialist Factory,' *Australian Journal of Chinese Affairs*, vol. 22 (July), pp. 31–60.

Yep, R 2000. 'The Limitations of Corporatism for Understanding Reforming China: an empirical analysis in a rural county,' *Journal of Contemporary China*, vol. 9, no. 25, pp. 547–566.

Zhao, S 2001, 'Deadlock: Beijing's national reunification strategy after Lee Tenghui', *Problems of Post-Communism*, vol. 48, no. 2, pp. 42–53.

Zheng, YN 2010, *The Chinese Communist Party as organizational emperor: culture, reproduction, and transformation*, Routledge, London.

Zhou, L 2014. 'Administrative Subcontract (xingzheng fabaozhi),' *Society (shehui)*, vol. 34, no. 6, pp. 1–38.

Zhou, X 2000. 'Reply: Beyond the debate and toward substantive institutional analysis,' *American Journal of Sociology*, vol. 105, no. 4, pp. 1190–1195.

Zhou, X 2010. 'The institutional logic of collusion among local governments in China,' *Modern China*, vol. 36, no. 1, pp. 47–78.

CHAPTER 3

The Chinese State's Decentralized Response Towards the Confucian Revival and Its Institutional Base

This chapter aims to apply the theoretical framework constructed in the previous chapter to explore the state and society dynamics in the Confucian revival. It attempts to answer two key questions: why is Confucianism undergoing a revival in contemporary Chinese society, and what is the role of the Chinese state in this reemergence of Confucianism? Most existing literature explaining these questions bifurcates along two lines, namely, instrumentalist and primordialist. While the instrumentalists take a state-centered perspective and explain the Confucian revival as primarily driven through the state's top-down control over society (Meissner 1999; Barmé 2008; Min and Galikowski 2000; Ai 2008; Bell 2008), the primordialists, by contrast, adopt a society-centered perspective and view the revival as a bottom-up phenomenon originating from society's rising identification with Chinese traditional culture (Guo 2004; Makeham 2008; Billioud 2007a, b, 2008). The two approaches, however, exaggerate the state-society dichotomy and ignore the close and complex interactions between the two that have sustained the Confucian revival. The role of state institutions in the state and society interactions is also ignored by these two approaches.

This chapter builds a "decentralized response" model to explain the role of the state and society in the Confucian revival. This model proposes two sequenced but closely interconnected processes. Firstly, the revival of Confucianism is a bottom-up phenomenon bred by an increasing strong

© The Author(s) 2019
Q. Pang, *State-Society Relations and Confucian Revivalism in Contemporary China*,
https://doi.org/10.1007/978-981-10-8312-9_3

and activated society struggling for spiritual tranquility amid rapid socio-economic transitions. The state's tacit acquiescence, to be sure, is a necessary prerequisite. Second, the state responds to Confucian revivalism in a decentralized manner through which the central and local governments adopt different strategies. While central policies are flexible but coercive in nature, local responses are diversified and active in co-opting Confucian elements. The two processes in the Confucian revival are closely interrelated. Both state and society have strengthened their preferred symbolic resources and power during their mutual struggles and accommodations.

This chapter argues that the decentralized responses are largely shaped by the decentralized institutions which allocate sufficient decision-making authority and resources to local authorities. In the end, the chapter describes China's decentralized institutions and shows how these institutions shape the local authorities' policy approach towards the Confucian revival.

3.1   PREVIOUS RESEARCH APPROACHES
TO THE CONFUCIAN REVIVAL

3.1.1   *Instrumentalism and the Top-Down Control Model*

This paradigm takes a state-centered perspective in explaining the origins and perpetuations of political ideologies. Its core assumption is that the emergence of a political ideology within a society cannot be explained in terms of the ideology itself (or its cultural basis), but instead by structural forces involving political, economic, and social power. For example, the instrumentalists argue that nationalism is mainly created and manipulated by the state (or perhaps in conjunction with the intelligentsia) to justify the legitimacy of modern politics (Anderson 1991; Hobsbawn 1992; Spencer 2005; Breuilly 1985; Kedourie 1985). As Rousseau has illustrated, "a healthy political system needed citizens who took an active pride in their polity, and a sense of patriotism is needed to sustain the ties between citizens" (Spencer and Wollman 2005, p. 3).

This approach has also been frequently adopted in explaining the Confucian revival in China. Scholars in this camp believe that it is the Chinese government that has purposively created and manipulated the Confucian revival for its own political purposes. For example, Werner Meissner (1999, p. 18) contends that the Chinese government has funded large-scale research activities and programs for developing Neo-Confucianism in China with its purpose of deploying Confucianism as "an instrument to counter Western influence". Barmé (2009, p. 64) argues that the opening ceremony of the 29th Olympiad in Beijing, a full representation of Chinese traditional culture, was simply "created under Party fiat with the active collaboration of local and international arts figures". Similarly, also claim that "the Confucian tradition has been revived by the authorities as an important cultural source from which a new national identity can be constructed". Recent works concerning the new rise of Confucianism also accentuate the Chinese government's support of the Confucian revival among the Chinese scholars and general public (Ai 2008; Bell 2008).

The instrumentalist approach, by retaining much of its analytic focus on the state, builds a "top-down control" model to explain the Confucian revival (Fig. 3.1). In the model, the party-state is the one that initiates, manipulates, and imposes Confucianism on social groups. This model assumes that the Chinese state monopolizes power and resources within society, and therefore could freely mold societal attitudes.

The instrumentalist approach (and its "top-down control" model) is insightful in revealing the role of the state in the Confucian revival. However, it exaggerates the state's dominance over society, especially its capability to control thoughts and belief systems among the public. Indeed, its control has been seriously eroded by rapid commercialization, globalization, and technological advances since China's opening up to the outside world (Lynch 1999; Kraus 2004). There is a significant gap between the expressed intent of the party-state authorities and what can actually be enforced across the country (Saich 2000). In fact, the omnipotent image of the Chinese state only reinforces the old, outdated "totalitarian" image of the state's total domination over all power and resources

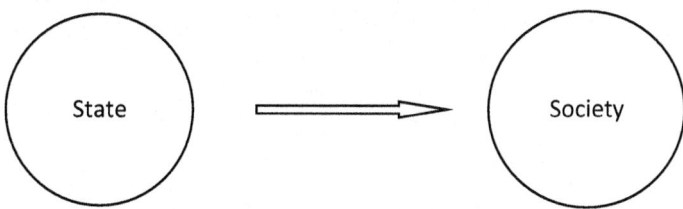

Fig. 3.1 The top-down control model by the instrumentalist approach

in society (Vogel 1989; Hinton 1968). Such an image may be true for Maoist China, but it is not in keeping with the autonomy and capacity possessed by the authoritarian regime during the post-Mao era.

Accordingly, this perspective underestimates autonomy and initiatives undertaken by society. It also assumes that Chinese society passively absorbs all policy aims that the state imposes on them. However, this view is no longer valid. The decline of official ideologies within Chinese society, in spite of the rigorous official efforts to promote them, demonstrates society's autonomy. Studies addressing contentious politics in China show that Chinese society is not passive but instead has shown strong willing-ness and power to resist the CCP's rule. Though much of the resistance is invisible and indirect (Friedman et al. 2005), some is quite confronta-tional, even violent (Perry and Selden 2010; O'Brien 2008; Lee 2007).

3.1.2   Primordialism and the Bottom-Up Model

Primordialism, by contrast, takes a society-centered perspective to account for the emergence of political ideologies. It stresses the role of society, rather than the state, in the initiation and circulation of political ideologies. For instance, scholars in this school, when explaining the origins of nation-alism, postulate that it is the society members' identification with their common ethnic ties and culture that has served as the base for modern nationalism (Van den Berghe 1978, 1995; Geertz 1963; Connor 1994; Hastings 1997). Johann von Herder (2010), one of the earliest primordial-ists, emphasizes the significance of language in differentiating nations. He believes that it is the different human languages that divide humanity into distinctive, discrete, and identifiable nations. Anthony Smith (1998, 1999) argues that the modern nation is built on what he terms *ethnie*, which refers to extensive groups whose members have already been tied to each other through sharing a particular history and operating within a common cul-tural framework, and with an enduring association with a particular place.

In tracing the origins of the Confucian revival, some scholars have adopted the primordialist approach, attributing the Confucian revival to a growing cultural identity of the national level within Chinese society. For instance, Guo (2004, p. 17) ascribes the rise of Confucianism to "identifi-cation with the nation, particularly national spirit or national essence". Makeham (2008, p. 9) also claims that "the idea that '*ruxue, rujia* thought, and *rujia* culture (Confucianism) constitute a form of cultural expression integral to Chinese identity' was pervasive among the discourse about Confucianism in contemporary China and covers a wide spectrum of participants—academic and official, mainland and overseas-based". Billioud (2007a, b, 2008) insists that though the Chinese government has been involved in the cultural revival, its role is only conducive and therefore limited. It is the rising interest over the Confucianism in Chinese society that has contributed to the Confucian revival in contemporary China. Zhao (1997, p. 738) also claims that the emergence of the cultural nationalistic discourse "was largely independent of ideological propaganda" or "repressive measures taken by the government".

The primordialists' society-based approach departs from the statist approach by focusing on agencies in society such as individuals and social groups as its main analytic focus. Its explanations can be summarized in a "bottom-up" model in which society takes the initiative, giving rise to the Confucian revival that challenges the state while the state is either not much involved or not powerful enough to make any meaningful responses (see Fig. 3.2).

The primordialists' views of the state as either the "bystander" or "crippled controller" are based on their assumption about the state's wariness about Confucianism. They doubt that the CCP elites favor Confucianism. As Guo (2004) has commented, the rising academic interest in New Confucianism is, in fact, against the CCP. Makeham (2008) also claims that at least part of the contemporary Chinese academic discourses about Confucianism is apparently anti-CCP and the emergence of these discourses makes it unconvincing that the Confucian revival has been brought about or encouraged by the state.

Although primordialist scholars, by carefully examining contemporary academic and public discourses about Confucianism, provide some valid arguments about the centrality of society's rising cultural identity in the Confucian revival, they underestimate the Chinese state's grip over society. The image of the "powerless" CCP in the bottom-up model (Fig. 3.2),

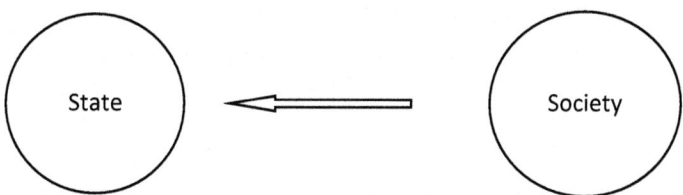

Fig. 3.2 The bottom-up model of the primordialist paradigm

apparently, does not accord with the CCP's actual control of Chinese society. Though the CCP has greatly loosened its totalistic control over society since the end of the Maoist era, it still retains a strong capacity in molding the symbolic environment within society. As Barme shows, the CCP still controls the ideological world of China by measures such as periodically circumscribing "deleterious" foreign ideas and censoring some of the "subversive" intellectuals' works which might undermine the officially approved values and ideologies (2010). In fact, the Chinese state's power can be seen from its near extermination of the Falun Gong during 1999 (Tong 2007). In addition, the party's control over society can also be seen from its restrictive policies towards popular religions, which have not only constrained religious activity but also religious content for its own purposes (Fallman 2010; Qu 2011).

3.2   The State's "Decentralized Response" to the Confucian Revival

For both the instrumentalist and primordialist approaches, there are two common problems when they are applied to explain the Confucian revival. First, they exaggerate the dichotomy of state and society. State-society relations in China are not unidirectional "top-down" or "bottom-up" processes; rather, they are mutually negotiated interactions between the state and society, with both sides devising strategies to negotiate and renegotiate with each other in order to maximize their own benefits and interests (Saich 2000; Friedman et al. 2005). Second, the literature associated with the two approaches, in its analysis of the Chinese state's role, ignores the impact of state institutions, which are significant in shaping and conditioning political actors' behavior. Indeed, the decentralized nature of institutions is often the key. The state power of the Chinese political system, after more than 30 years of decentralized reforms, has been heavily devolved from the central government to that at the local level (Landry 2008; Huang 1995; Edin 2003; Burns 1994). Because of the failure to fully assess the structure and functioning of political institutions, especially with respect to the decentralized ones, the two approaches tend to perceive the Chinese state as an integrated aggregation, without properly differentiating the central and local Chinese governments and their different roles in the Confucian revival.

This book, by drawing elements from the primordialist and instrumen-talist approaches, builds a dynamic and interactive model that addresses state and society interactions with respect to the Confucian revival. First, as the primordialists argue, the resurgence of Confucianism is, at least in its early phase, a bottom-up phenomenon. Reemerging Confucianism is a set of symbols and belief systems that the society has generated to address its social anomie amid rapid modernization. It is involved with society's efforts to rebuild part of the social order which has been destroyed by rapid social transformation. The state's acquiescence, to be sure, has accel-erated this revival, but its momentum derives more from society than the state. Second, the state, as the instrumentalists have contended, is heavily involved in the revival. But its role is more responsive than initiating. Further, this strategy is decentralized, that is, local authorities are the main agents in its developing response strategies. However, the two processes are closely interwoven, and both state and society have gained strength and resources from their mutual engagement (see Fig. 3.3).

3.2.1 Revival of Confucianism as a Bottom-Up Phenomenon

The Confucian revival originated more from contemporary Chinese soci-ety than the state. Contemporary Chinese society, as has been demon-strated in the previous chapter, has autonomy, however limited, to shape much of its belief system. Social forces now have increasing material resources and freedom to generate their preferred symbols and ideologies, especially so long as these beliefs are not in apparent conflict with the

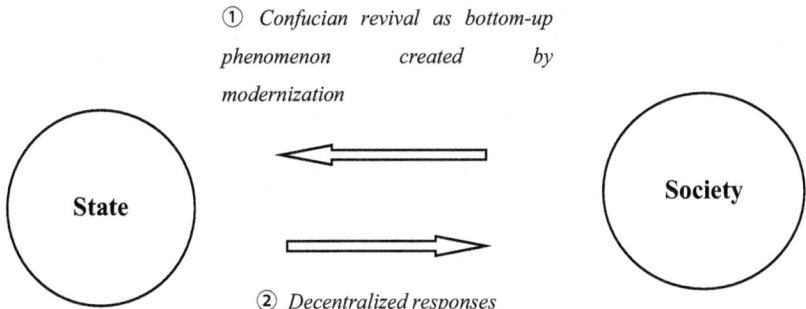

Fig. 3.3 The decentralized response model

official ideology, and social forces do not exploit the belief systems to launch collective anti-governmental activities.

Social forces, more importantly, have their own motivation to embrace Confucianism, which are not imposed by the state. This drive mainly comes from social transitions produced by China's economic modernization in the past several decades. To illustrate this, I will use Samuel Huntington's (1996) theory concerning "modernization and cultural resurgence". Huntington's theory posits that modernization in non-Western societies can contribute to the resurgence of indigenous culture such as Confucianism. In non-Western societies like China, Huntington argues that modernization, in its early phrase, promotes Westernization but later precipitates de-Westernization (the resurgence of indigenous culture). He explains the social and individual mechanisms that account for this change. First, at the societal level, modernization enhances the economic, military, and political power of society as a whole and encourages its people to develop confidence in their culture. Second, at the individual level, modernization generates feelings of anomie and leads to crises of identity, as traditional social bonds are broken. Traditional culture, therefore, provides a remedy for the anomie and identity loss. The causal relations are shown in Fig. 3.4.

China began its modernization process with its liberalizing in 1978. Over the next two decades, modernization led to sweeping Westernization at most levels of society, with Chinese society fervently worshipping and

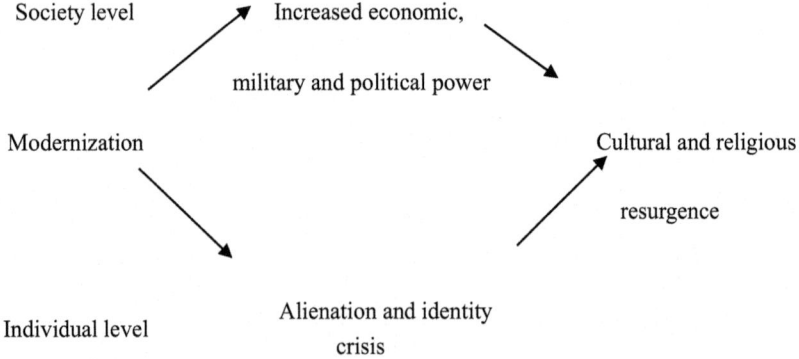

Fig. 3.4 Modernization and the indigenous cultural resurgence. (Source: Huntington 1996, p. 76)

absorbing Western culture (especially American culture). During this period, there were strong waves of "Western learning fever" (*xixue re*) among intellectuals, while traditional culture was widely blamed as the main impediment to China's modernization process (Zhao 1997).

However, after the turn of the twenty-first century, the rate of Westernization slowed and traditional culture underwent a revival in society. As modernization gained pace, public confidence in traditional culture mounted. In consequence, the "Western learning fever" has been overshadowed by "Chinese/Confucius learning fever" (*guoxue re*) (Zhao 1997). Some scholars ascribe this rise of Confucianism to growing confidence in indigenous culture. For example, Dirlik (1997, p. 225) relates the Confucian revival among the Chinese population to "resurgence in recent years of fundamentalistic nationalisms or culturalisms that are opposed to Euro-American ideological domination of the world". He also argues that "the Chinese success in capitalist development shows that the Confucian ethic is equal, if not superior to, the 'Protestant ethic' which Max Weber has credited with causative power in the emergence of capitalism in Europe. A 'Weberized' Confucianism in turn appears as a marker of Chineseness regardless of time or place" (1997, p. 226). Zhao (1997) contends that economic success transformed the nation's intellectual discourse and built up Chinese intellectuals' self-confidence in their tradition and awakened national pride and cultural identities. Kang (2005) also has similar arguments when explaining the rise of Confucianism among the general public.

At the same time, modernization, particularly urbanization, led to strong social anomie which gave rise to the public interest in Confucianism. "Social anomie" refers to an absence or diminution of standards or values (the so-called normlessness) within society (Durkheim 1997). One important contributing factor for rising anomie is that urbanization substantially undermines old social ties in rural societies, which had served as the basis for social values and norms. The last decade has witnessed accelerated urbanization in China, with urban population increasing from 39% in 2002 to 51% in 2011 (National bureau of Statistics of China 2012). Amid this rapid urbanization, people often feel the old rural social bonds that used to bind them have dissolved, but new urban social ties have not yet formed. Thus, many urban settlers began to experience different degrees of "social anomie".[1]

Because of this growing social anomie, many Chinese people began to seek new ideologies (or belief systems) to ease their anomie and build inner tranquility amid rapid social changes. Billioud (2008), for example, argues that the Confucianism has served as a "quasi-religion" for those who seek an "inner peace" in the face of rapid social and economic change. The revival of Confucianism as a "civil religion" echoes the concern for individual or collective destiny. Bell (2010) also emphasizes that the downside of modernization plays a role in the ascendance of Confucianism in current China. Modernity, as he conceives it, often leads to social atomization and psychological anxiety, because the competition for social status and material resources becomes fiercer and fiercer. Accordingly, social responsibility and concern for the other decline, and old communitarian ways of life and civility break down. Under these conditions, many ordinary persons begin to question the overriding value placed on materialist development.

In addition to social anomie, identity loss caused by modernization is another cause of the rise of Confucianism. Together with the intensification of China's globalization process, especially since China's entry into the World Trade Organization (WTO) in 2001, more and more Chinese have become confused about their Chinese identity. "What does it mean to be a 'Chinese'?" has become a common query raised through the public media. Along with the identity crisis, there has been a strong trend of cultural nostalgia among ordinary citizens (Billioud 2007a, b).

Last but not the least, the Confucian revival has also been driven by rampant commercialism, an important part of modernization in China. The popular interest in Confucianism has created lucrative business opportunities for cultural agencies and companies which, by providing large amounts of Confucianism-related books, courses, and even ceremonial costumes, have earned high profits. For example, some of China's prestigious universities offer extremely expensive courses on Confucianism (and also other traditional culture) to wealthy entrepreneurs (for details, see Kang et al. 2010; Billioud 2007b). Some educational companies have developed Confucian classes for children from urban middle-class families and have succeeded in achieving generous returns.[2] The accelerated marketization, therefore, gave rise to the boom in the production and supply of Confucian cultural products.

In short, the momentum for Confucian revival comes more from within Chinese society rather than through the imposition of the state. This revival is a rational search for spiritual peace and social order conducted by a society lost in the dislocations of rapid modernization. The revival itself shows an increasingly strong and autonomous society, with burgeoning resources, power, and mounting capacity to generate preferred symbols and beliefs to which many members of society attach themselves. This increasing social power and autonomy has posed a threat to the state which struggles to remain relevant in the symbolic environment, especially given that some social forces may deliberately drive and mold the Confucian revival along an anti-government vector. How, then, can the state control the social forces and the Confucian revival?

3.2.2   The State's Decentralized Response Towards the Confucian Revival

The Chinese state, as usual, adopts both coercion and co-optation strategies to regulate the Confucian revival. However, this coercion and co-optation are heavily influenced by decentralized institutions, which enable the state to carry out "decentralized responsiveness", that is, the central and local governments take different but mutually reinforcing responsibilities. Specifically, while the central government leans more to coercion, local governments are more interested in co-opting the local Confucian revival. The central government is flexible in establishing its guiding parameters about this coercion, thus leaving considerable room for local authorities' innovative co-optation. An important effect of the decentralized responsiveness is achieving a kind of balance and flexibility in managing the Confucian revival, thus maximizing the state's use of limited resources in controlling social forces and their symbolic systems. The following part of the chapter will first sketch the contours of central and local government, and define decentralization. It will then elaborate decentralized responses by mapping specific strategies deployed by the central and local governments in their regulations. Finally, it will analyze how this decentralized responsiveness entails a balance and flexibility for the state's contentions with, and accommodations of, social forces.

3.2.2.1   Defining Central Government, Local Government, and Decentralization

By adopting the concept of "decentralization", this book clearly differentiates the Chinese state into two interconnected power entities: the central and local governments. The contours of central and local governments are depicted in the diagram below (see Fig. 3.5). The central government in this book refers to the top-most level of the Chinese party-state which includes:

1. The Central Politburo of Chinese Communist Party and its constituent units
2. The State Council and its constituent ministries, commissions, bureaus, offices[3]
3. The National People's Congress, its Standing Committee and constituent Committees
4. The Supreme People's Court and Procuracy

The local government includes the following three tiers of the party-state: the "provincial (autonomous regions, municipalities, and prefecture-level cities)", "county", and "village and township" levels of the Chinese government (Fig. 3.5).

Decentralization, in this book, means the transfer of decision-making authority, responsibility, and tasks from the central level to local levels of Chinese government. According to Hanson (1998), there are three kinds of decentralization:

1. *De-concentration*: transfer of tasks and work without authority;
2. *Delegation*: transfer of decision-making authority from higher to lower levels, but authority can be withdrawn by the center;
3. *Devolution*: transfer of authority to an autonomous unit which can act independently with responsibility for the center.

The notion of "delegation" comes closest to the decentralization investigated in this book. The central government has shifted much of its authority to local authorities, but the center still retains the power to claim the authority back. In this way, both central government and local authorities can affect the Confucian revival, but in quite different ways. In fact, China's decentralized authoritarian system has also been described as "administrative subcontract" (*xingzheng fabaozhi*) (Zhou 2014). Specifically speaking, the allocation of authority between the principal (the central state) and agent (local authorities) functions as follows: the principal has the formal authority and residual control rights (such as the authority to appoint/remove, supervise, and monitor subcontractors and the option to intervene when necessary), and the agent, by way of subcontracting, enjoys considerable discretion and de facto power to do things in his own way.

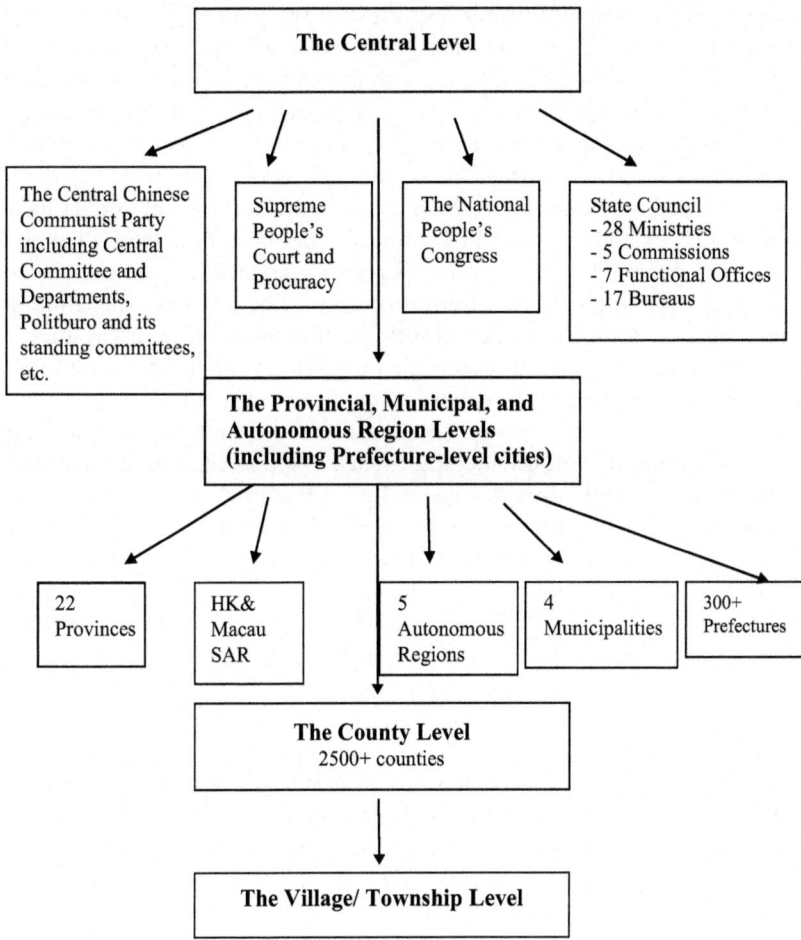

Fig. 3.5 The structure of the Chinese state. (Source: This diagram is based on chart entitled "The Chinese State in 2000", in David Shambaugh 2000, *The Modern Chinese State* (Cambridge University Press, 2000), p. 169)

3.2.2.2 The Role of the Central State in the Confucian Revival: Flexible Coercion

Flexibility and coerciveness are two defining characteristics of the central state's regulations concerning the Confucian revival, and involve the following three interconnected elements. First, the center has basic policy parameters for local authorities, but most of the guidelines are loose and general in nature. This allows local authorities a considerable degree of flexibility and discretion in dealing with the Confucian revival at the local level. Second, most of the center's policy parameters are coercive in nature. For example, central documents stipulate official limits for Confucian discourses and social activities to avoid direct challenges to the ruling party and its official ideology. The central propaganda department and its local branches check and even censor Confucian discourses or activities beyond the official limits. Third, the center's policy guidance has some nuanced differences for different social constituencies. For instance, the guiding parameters for Confucian educational activities among the urban middle class are often the strictest, those for intellectuals' discourses are looser, and those for private entrepreneurs are the least stringent.

The central state has relinquished its all-inclusive control over ideologies. Regarding non-official ideologies such as Confucianism in this study, the central state only provides general guidance in leading local governments' management. For example, the central state gives permission for promoting traditional culture in their policy documents, but it never clearly defines what traditional culture is nor does it stipulate how to promote traditional culture.[4] Thus, local officials have total discretion over whether to promote Confucianism or how to promote it.

The reason for the central state's retreat from controlling non-official ideologies lies in the difficulty and even the counterproductive nature of doing so. With rapid commercialization and globalization brought by the economic reforms, the central state's capacity to control information within the country has been seriously eroded (Lynch 1999; Kraus 2004; Shambaugh 2007). In addition, the decentralization of administrative power from the center to the local level, which will be explored in length in the next chapter, has left only inadequate power and resources to make specific responses to the bottom-up Confucian revival. In a word, the proliferation of information and ideologies within society has simply outgrown the center's bureaucratic capacity for overall control. The central state has had to narrow its focus to preserving the official ideology that sanctions and bolsters its rule.

However, a dominant theme of the central state's general policy parameters concerning Confucianism is to set a firm bottom line to prevent contraventions against the official ideology and the CCP's rule. The bottom line can be summarized as follows:

1. Inciting subversion of the regime of people's democratic dictatorship and the socialist system, national division, rebellion, or rioting;
2. Inciting opposition to the leadership of the Chinese Communist Party;
3. Inciting defiance or disruption to the implementation of the Constitution or laws;
4. Inciting ethnic or racial discrimination or hatred or disrupting national unity;
5. Propagating murder, obscenity, or pornography or instigating criminal activities.[5]

Local officials in ideology-related departments dealing with education and the mass media are required to familiarize themselves with the bottom line even during their pre-career training. The bottom line, to be certain, is not specifically designed for Confucianism but rather geared to all activities in the public media. The central state has an overarching and sprawling propaganda system penetrating its officialdom which exercises its censorship responsibilities for all information released to the public media, checking whether any public discourse of Confucianism contravenes the bottom line.[6]

The center's coercive measures are institutionally motivated. As head of the CCP organization and the state bureaucracy, central authorities still rely on the official ideology to mobilize the commitment and loyalty of the rank and file of the administrative staff at all levels, and to shape consensus and unity for the CCP's organizational life. In addition, the institutional legacies of Marxism and Maoism give the official ideology an important presence in at least the organizational life of the party-state that cannot be questioned or ignored.[7] Thus, the central authorities have a great stake in preserving the stability of the official ideology at least within the party. This also explains why official ideologies still feature prominently in the education of party members at various levels at party schools which aim at training the CCP's local cadres (Shambaugh 2007).

The central policy parameters are not uniformly structured for different social segments, therein allowing more flexibility for local decisions. Those applied to urban citizens are most stringent, containing detailed stipulations (both limitations and guidance) for the circulation of Confucian discourses and the organization of Confucian activities. Those regulating the intellectuals who produce Confucian academic discourses are less rigorous, given the state's intention of co-opting intellectuals and the limited impact of Confucian academic discourses in society. Those managing the Confucian revival among private entrepreneurs are loosely structured. This is, in part, driven by the state's incorporation of private entrepreneurs. At the same time, the Confucian revival among the new rich is seen as posing less threat to the regime's stability.

It, however, should be made clear that these policy differentiations are not purposively made by one or two central authorities. These policies are usually made separately by different departments in the central government. For example, those concerning the Confucian revival in education are decided by the Ministry of Education. Collective activities promoting Confucianism such as Confucius-revering ceremonies are generally (but not necessarily) managed by the Ministry of Culture. If a certain ministry regards the issue as significant, it will report it to the higher-leveled State Council (SC) or the CCP Central Committee (CCPCC) so that the SC or CCPCC will issue independent documents. The SC and CCPCC have developed explicit policy documents for the Confucian revival for the general public, and some implicit ones for intellectuals, but none for private entrepreneurs. This shows that the central authorities believe that the policies for the first two groups should be stricter than for the last group.

3.2.2.3 Local Authorities' Responses: Diversified and Creative Promotion

Given the center's loose parameters, local authorities, with their arbitrary power delegated by the decentralized political system, become the main agents in managing the Confucian revival. Not only can they decide whether to promote Confucianism but also in what ways, so long as they do not ignore the center's guidelines too flagrantly. Maintaining the relevance of official ideologies (and suppressing others) in the local symbolic setting, however, is not local officials' priority. This has created diversity in responses to the Confucian revival at the local level, which vary from one place to another. Local authorities' decisions are usually based on their own attitudes towards Confucianism (e.g. some have great personal interest in Confucianism while others dismiss or even disapprove of it) as well as their rational assessments of possible benefits and losses.

Though varied, most local authorities' responses towards the Confucian revival are at least neutral or mildly positive, aiming to incorporate relevant local social forces and Confucian symbols and beliefs. Rarely does any local government crack down on Confucian activities. Their response ranges from acquiescence to active promotion, varied for different social elements. Local officials generally provide greatest support to satisfy private entrepreneurs' interest in Confucianism, less accommodation to intellectuals and the least to the urban public. This is related to the fact that private entrepreneurs hold important economic resources which are most attractive for local authorities and that some intellectuals own Confucian symbolic resources which can be utilized for maintaining social/political stability, which also has its appeal. In the decentralized system, local officials are evaluated primarily through their performance in developing economy and perpetuating social/political stability (the details of the evaluation system will be discussed in later chapters). Thus, they are motivated to co-opt private entrepreneurs and intellectuals in different degrees.

The local autonomy in Confucian policies also allows some local authorities to adopt innovative measures in their responses, such as implementing authorized "Confucian education" in local primary and middle schools, or supporting the teaching and researching of their authorized Confucianism among intellectuals. These creative promotions of Confucianism, in fact, can be also attributed to the decentralized institutions which reward deft local administrative actions (the details of the causal mechanism will be introduced in the next section). Some local officials thus view strategically promoting the Confucian revival as a way to further build a political career.

In addition, the local authorities' promotion of Confucianism and the center's constraint form a balance between state coercion and co-optation, thus refining the use of the state's resources in controlling the belief system and relevant social forces. A balance of coercion and co-optation is crucial for the state's control, as excessive coercion will drain the state's material resources while extravagant promotion of Confucianism may also cause the loss of the official ideologies' relevance in the construction of the symbolic environment. By synthesizing local promotion and central restraint, the state can efficiently monitor and even make use of Confucian revivalism in China today.

Why does the state take the decentralized response? The response, in fact, is less a strategic choice made by political elites than a mechanism produced by the decentralization of political institutions that have shadowed the economic reforms begun in 1978. The following section will have a detailed analysis of the origins of the decentralization and its effect on the state's responses to Confucian revivalism.

3.3   THE INSTITUTIONAL BASE FOR DECENTRALIZED RESPONSIVENESS

In the decentralized responsiveness, there are two major questions that must be addressed. "Why are the local authorities empowered to make autonomous policies concerning Confucian revivalism?" "Why are some motivated to adopt varied and innovative strategies?" The "Cadre Responsibility System" (*gangwei zerenzhi*, hereafter CRS) heavily shapes these local authorities' behavior. First, it provides local authorities with enough power resources such as discretion to use financial revenue, to assign lower-level cadres, and other means of administrative authority. It also shapes local authorities' preferences over efficiency and innovation by evaluating their work performance through its "Cadre Evaluation System" (*ganbu kaohe*, hereafter CES). The local authorities' effective solutions to social problems and innovative performance may mean higher evaluations from higher-level officials, which are vital for local cadres, especially those with ambitions. The following part of the chapter will illustrate the two major aspects of the CRS and how it has changed over time.

3.3.1   Institutions Empowering Local Authorities

In the Chinese administrative system, authority over ideological control falls mainly to the Departments of Propaganda, Education, Mass Media, and Culture. Power in these related departments has been devolved to the local level through a series of reforms that began in the early 1980s, thus forming the institutional base for the local authorities to wield ideological control at the local level. This is one aspect of the CRS. This section will address why and how the state decentralized its power to the local level.

Before discussing the power decentralization in the ideological control agencies, it is necessary to review two fundamental decentralization reforms in the economic and cadre appointment system first, as these two have paved the way for the subsequent power devolution in the government agencies of ideological management such as in education and the mass media. Without economic reforms, local governments could not have gained independent revenue with which to finance their ideology-related departments. Without cadre appointment reforms, local governments could not have garnered the power to appoint leaders in their ideology control departments. These two reforms reduced local governments' deep subordination to the central government, enabling them to gain autonomous authority.

3.3.1.1 Decentralized Reform in the Economic System

China's decentralization reforms started in the area of economics with the Third Plenary Session of the 11th CPC Central Committee in 1978. Before these reforms, local governments were totally dependent on the central state for revenue and other financial expenditure. After the reforms, local authorities, however, were transformed into independent entities with their own revenues and responsibility for their own expenditures. This laid a solid foundation for other subsequent administrative reforms.

The economically decentralized reforms were designed to vitalize the Maoist economic system which had been seriously plagued by economic inefficiency, due to the highly centralized planned economy system borrowed from the Soviet Union in the early 1950s. The planned system led to a lack of incentives for local cadres to channel their talent into economic development. The rigid constraints of the central state plan and the Maoist fiscal system had seriously discouraged local cadres to produce more (Oi 1995). Additionally, the Maoist fiscal system required the local officials to turn over most or all of its revenue to the higher levels of government. Even if there were some surpluses, local authorities had no freedom to use these surpluses without approval from their superiors. Thus, local governments in the Maoist system simply had no incentives to improve economic performance beyond meeting the quota assigned by the central government.

To stimulate economic growth, the Chinese Communist Party under Deng Xiaoping had initiated a series of economic reforms which aimed to bring the initiative of the masses into play. These included the Contract Responsibility System (*chengbao zeren zhi*) and fiscal reforms, both of which transferred some of the center's economic administration to local government, especially at the "village and township" level (Oi 1995; Whiting 2000). Thanks to the institution of the "Contract Responsibility System", local authorities were empowered with the authority to make crucial decisions concerning all collectively owned enterprises like the township-owned and village-owned enterprises (*xiangzhen qiye*).

More importantly, fiscal reforms, especially tax responsibility reform empowered local governments with the right to share the revenue generated within their bailiwick (Oksenberg and Tong 1991; Wong 1991, 1992). After the reforms, provinces (and centrally controlled municipalities), prefectures, counties, and townships were no longer required to surrender nearly all of their revenue to the higher authorities as they had been under the Maoist system. Instead they were allowed to retain all, or most of the remaining revenue.[8] In this way, local governments had been turned into independent fiscal entities that had to be responsible for their own revenue and expenditures (Oi 1992). Together with the devolved power granted by the Contract Responsibility System, local Chinese governments have enjoyed a considerably higher degree of autonomy in local economic affairs.

3.3.1.2 Cadre Appointment System Reforms

The devolution of cadre appointment power is significant for China's decentralization, as the power of cadre appointment and dismissal (*ganbu renmian*) is fundamental to the Chinese political system.[9] Reforms in the appointment system transferred the power for appointing cadres which used to be monopolized by the central authorities to the lower levels of government. In consequence, local governments were granted with even greater authority in local affairs.

The devolution in appointment power was realized mainly through administrative reform carried out during 1983–1984 (see Manion 1995; Burns 1989; Lee 1991; Landry 2008). Prior to 1983, the central state, specifically the CCP Organization Department, not only oversaw appointments for its immediate lower level, the provinces, prefectures, and municipalities, but also the next lower level, bureau-level cadres. This was termed "two-level down" (*xialiangji*). The 1983–1984 reforms also devolved the center's appointment power for positions at the bureau level to the province. Hence, the center now is only responsible for appointments in the immediate lower level, the province. By the same token, each level of state, from the center to the local, only takes charge of cadre appointments at the level immediately below it. This is called "one-level down" (*xiayiji*).[10]

This appointment reform has significantly empowered local governments as the center's control over the level of county and village (township), the lowest level, has been substantially diluted. This amounts to a major step in the central state's retreat from local administration, allowing for local governments to respond autonomously to local society. After 1989, there were some moves towards recentralization, but the basic pattern has not been altered (Burns 1994).

3.3.1.3 Power Devolution in Education Agencies and Mass Media

Thanks to the economic and cadre appointment reforms, local governments now have their own revenue to finance their ideology and propaganda bureaus (such as education and the mass media) as well as their power to appoint leaders in these bureaus. However, in the early stages of reform, regarding departments of ideology, the center still retained great control. Only after a series of administrative reforms, was the authority in these functional agencies decentralized to the local level. The next section will show how power has been devolved in these two critical departments related to ideology control: education and the mass media.

3.3.1.4 Decentralization of Education

The Chinese education system in the Maoist era was highly centralized in terms of financing resources and school management, though a few decentralized measures had been taken such as establishing rural schools funded and run by rural communes (*minban xuexiao*) during this period (Hawkins 2006). Due to the economic and personnel reforms, however, the central educational authorities found themselves less and less able to serve as the sole provider of educational services, because, on the one hand, the fiscal reform had significantly reduced the central revenue, while, on the other, the personnel reform had weakened the center's ability to control local educational bureaus. Further, the fiscal reforms also created an unexpected effect, rising budget deficits for the central government. The deficit was exacerbated by the local governments' evasion of taxes (Whiting 2000). The central budget deficits, therefore, kept increasing during the first several years after fiscal reform, from 1.5 million RMB in 1982 to 3.5 million RMB in 1984 (Lynch 1999).

Since the early 1980s, the central government has gradually relaxed its stifling control and assigned more and more authority and responsibility for the management of education to the local level. This retreat is first seen in the area of higher education (Hawkins 1998; Mok 1997), later at the pre-collegiate level. The first step was *Decision of the Central Committee of the Communist Party of China on the Reform of the Educational Structure* (*zhonggong zhongyang guanyu jiaoyu tizhi gaige de jueding*) issued by the CCP's central Committee in May 1985.[11] In this document, it was clearly stated that the central government's control of schools was too rigid and its management was inefficient, and authority should be "devolved" to the lower levels of government (Hawkins 2000). These decentralized policies were restated in a 1993 document entitled *Guidelines for China's Educational Reform and Development* (*zhongguo jiaoyu gaige he fazhan gangyao*) issued by the State Council.[12] The 1993 document further specified the division between the central and local, re-emphasizing that the central educational agencies should devolve more power, authority, and responsibility to the local level, especially for the administrative and financial management of tertiary and pre-collegiate institutions. However, the central state should retain its authority for making fundamental rules and regulations. The center and local would collaborate through a "tiered" system in order to share their management of education, which resulted in further devolution of authority from the center to the local.

3.3.1.5 Decentralization of Mass Media

The decentralization of the mass media proceeded in similar ways as had the decentralization in education. During the Maoist era, the Chinese state had established a highly concentrated propaganda system to control the mass media throughout the country.[13] The center had absolute authority over not only the content but also the form of messages circulated by the mass media. However, after the economic reforms, the highly centralized system was found to be woefully inadequate for the building of a "socialist commodity economy" (later called "socialist market economy"), because limited information flows obstructed the economic growth. Together with economic and personnel reforms, Chinese leaders began to initiate a series of policies to shift the regulatory power over mass media from the center to the local.

Media reforms began with Zuo Hanye's call for more creativity and innovation among the subcentral-level radio and television stations in 1979. Zuo was then the director of the newly formed China Central Television (CCTV), and his intention was to encourage local media workers to cease merely copying CCTV's content. In 1983, during the All-China Radio and Television Work Conference, details of the decentralization process were declared. After this, the central authority over local radio and television was formally devolved to corresponding local authorities.[14]

Through similar policies, power in other agencies related to ideology has also been decentralized. Local governments, with newly delegated power, were now able to make their own decisions. We will now turn to the institutions that spur local cadres to make changes in their policies.

3.3.2 Institutions Motivating Local Cadres to Innovate

It is the CES which assesses local authorities' work performance and links this evaluation with economic and political rewards and shapes local cadres' desire to increase efficiency and innovate in their daily management. The CES is an integrated part of the CRS and is originally designed by the central government to monitor local cadres' behavior. The central state, ever since decentralization reforms began, has detailed rules and procedures for evaluating local cadres' performance. The aims are clearly specified. Since power has been delegated to the local level, the central state has strong motivation to monitor local agents in order to ensure the latter's compliance. During the Maoist era, there was little such need as local cadres simply did not have much incentive to deviate from strict central policies. The only evaluation was usually made at the time of appointment, that is, if one was ideologically unreliable, he or she could not pass the appointment process (Huang 1995). However, after the decentralization reforms, local officials developed strong incentives to evade the central government's rules. For example, as noted above, during the 1980s, township-level governments were well known for their tax evasion because they wanted to increase their share of revenue retained at the local level (Whiting 2000).

The CES has strong power in shaping the behavior of local cadres because the results of their evaluation determine their remuneration and heavily influence their political prospects such as "tenure in office and opportunities for promotion". In terms of remuneration, the CES results directly affect cadres' bonuses, which is the largest portion of their income (Whiting 2000; Edin 2003).[15] The cadres' tenure and promotions are also tightly linked with the results of their evaluation results. For example, only those who are assessed as "excellent" for two consecutive years or at least "competent" for three consecutive years are qualified for promotion. Those assessed as "incompetent" for two consecutive years are to be dismissed (Edin 2003). Moreover, these assessment results are important basis for selecting candidates at the same level who compete for the same higher position. Due to strong competition, these results could sometimes determine their career development. Thus, every local official who is ambitious is strongly motivated to achieve a rating of "excellent" in the exercise.

For a deeper explanation of how the CES has incentivized local cadres to be innovative in their administration, it is necessary to describe how local cadres are evaluated. The Chinese leadership started to establish the CES in 1979, but modified and institutionalized this system during the 1980s (Huang 1995).[16] According to the 1993 national regulations on the evaluations of civil servants, there are four primary criteria in assessing the local cadre's performance: political integrity (*de*), competence (*neng*), diligence (*qin*), and achievements (*ji*). Performances in the four criteria have different percentages. Usually "achievements" takes the largest share, around 60–70%, and the other three combined total around 30–40% (Edin 2003).[17] Achievements are closely related to job performance and any meaningful innovation could be helpful.

The CES assesses local cadres' work performance and arranges them into three different ranks: excellent (*youxiu*), competent (*chenzhi*), and incompetent (*bu chenzhi*). There is a strict quota for "excellent", which was stipulated to a limited percentage of the total cadre number in a particular work unit. The percentage was set at no more than 15% in the 1993 national regulations, but in some local regulations, the percentage can be higher. Cadres on the same hierarchical level were ranked according to the results of their evaluation, ensuring strong competition. Rankings are used as an important indicator for future promotion. In fact, "cadres were aware at all time of where they stood relative to leaders of other townships and villages in their areas" (Whiting 2000, p. 101). The competition can be very keen. In consequence, the CES provides strong institutional motivation for local officials to pursue effective and innovative policy-making.

However, it needs to be acknowledged that local officials' attitudes on efficacy and innovation are also mediated by their personal worldviews and values. Thus, even within the same CRS and CES system, there is still great variance in the behavior of local officials. As Sociological Institutionalism argues,[18] political actors do *not only* act instrumentally towards institutional incentives and disincentives in order to maximize their expected utilities. Political officials' decisions are guided by their understanding of "appropriate behavior" in specific situations, and thus also subject to their personal sets of values, some of which are exogenous to political institutions. Thus, the effect of the CES to motivate local authorities cannot be exaggerated, though it is strong.

In sum, this chapter has constructed a decentralized response model to elaborate the dynamics of the state-society interactions in the Confucian revival, especially the state and local authorities' distinctive responses towards different social elements in the Confucian revival. It also illustrates the decentralization of Chinese political institutions which sustains the decentralized response. The following chapter will apply the model to examine the Confucian revival among three different constituencies: intellectuals, private entrepreneurs, and urban middle-class citizens.

NOTES

1. For a detailed discussion of this point, see Chap. 6.
2. For a detailed discussion of the Confucian classes and courses, see Chap. 6.
3. For a clear description of the CCP and State Council's central organizations, please refer to Shambaugh (2000).

4. The central state's official documents have never explicitly claimed that it endorses Confucianism. What it claims to support is always for "traditional culture". In fact, this is an important tactic that the central state uses to control Confucianism. For details, please see Chap. 6. But due to the close relationship between Confucianism and traditional culture, at least some parts of Confucianism can be viewed as "traditional culture" and therefore can be promoted.

5. The five rules are included in the "Provisional Rules for the Administration of Periodicals". For detailed discussion of the rules, see Chang et al. (2003).

6. The Chinese propaganda system is mainly composed of two institutions: one is the Communist Party Propaganda system and the other is the state bureaucratic agencies concerning information control and propaganda like the General Administration of Press and Publications. In reality, as the party propaganda system usually leads the state functional agencies, the two can be viewed as merged. The central party propaganda department usually settles every detail of the newly developed party ideology, usually by party leaders. Local branches can only passively receive the edicts. Most of the CCPPD's work is concentrated on writing and disseminating official ideological propaganda information (Shambaugh 2007).

7. Such reasoning is supported by Historical Institutionalism which emphasizes the lingering impact of historical institutions or policies on the behavior of current political actors. Its sequencing approach supports "path dependent" theories and views contextual features of a given situation inherited from the past, as pushing current development along a set of "paths" (Collier and Collier 1991; Downing 1992; Krasner 1988). As North (1990, p. 112) explains, "Path dependence comes from the increasing returns mechanisms that reinforce the direction once on a given path". The self-reinforcing dynamics of path dependence can be illustrated through the case that political actors, during an early formative period of power consolidation, promote institutions that enable them to maintain their rule. During this period, once certain options are chosen, they would have strong influence over the sequencing of institutional development. Similarly, the Chinese state, during its early formative period, enshrined Marxism and Maoism as official ideologies and instilled them into the general public as a way of sustaining its rule. This practice has placed strong constraints upon the state's (especially the central state) subsequent policies concerning ideology, because it would incur immeasurable instability if the CCP went back on its current official ideologies.

8. For details, see Tong (1989); Wang (1989); Wang and Hu (2001).

9. The CCP adopts a method called *nomenklatura* in Soviet terminology to staff the party-state apparatus. Positions in the *nomenklatura* are under the full control of the Central politburo of the CCP. For details concerning the CCP's *nomenklatura* and its evolution, please refer to Burns (1987, 1989).

10. The details of the *nomenklatura* and its reforms are very complicated. The description here is only a brief outline of the complex party *nomenklatura* reforms from 1983 to 1984. Landry (2008) gives a detailed and insightful description of the reform as a whole, including its background and scope, etc.

11. For details, see Tsang (2003), Wong (1992), Fernanda et al. (2002).

12. For a full version of the document, please see www.eol.cn/guo-jia_3489/20060323/t20060323_49571.shtml

13. In fact, Lynch (1999) believes that the propaganda system during the Maoist period was decentralized at least in its form. However, he also acknowledged that the system was, in fact, highly centralized in terms of its propaganda content as the local cadres simply did not dare diverge from the center in any meaningful way.

14. For a detailed description of the whole process, please refer to Lynch (1999).

15. Whiting (2000) has a detailed description of the differences in bonuses due to different performances.

16. In 1986, 1988, and 1989, the Central Organization Department (*zhong-gong zhongyang zuozhibu*) has imposed and institutionalized several versions of the CES for the evaluations of local party and government officials.

17. However, in actual practice, there is great variance among different departments and localities in their local practices. But the general principle is that achievement is the primary indicator.

18. Sociological Institutionalism is one branch of New Institutionalism. It accentuates the intermediating impact of the socio-cultural context upon actors' behavior. While not denying that actors are purposeful or rational, Sociological Institutionalism stresses that political actors are more guided by their understandings of "appropriate behavior" in specific situations, the so-called social logic of appropriateness (March and Olsen 1989). It emphasizes that institutions work on actors through affecting their understanding of what is "appropriate behavior" within a given situation (Scharpf 1997). In other words, actors' behavior is mainly shaped by what they believe or interpret as socially and culturally appropriate, which, though heavily influenced by institutions, is also affected by the actors' personal worldviews or choices which are developed and transmitted through socialization and therefore exogenous to institutions. That is to say, institutions alone do *not* determine political actors' behavior.

REFERENCES

Ai, J 2008, 'The re-functioning of Confucianism: the mainland Chinese intellectual response since the 1980s', *Issues & Studies*, vol. 44, no. 2, pp. 37–65.

Anderson, B 1991, *Imagined communities: reflections on the origin and spread of nationalism*, Verso, London.

Barmé, GR 2008, 'China's flat earth: history and 8 August 2008', *The China Quarterly*, vol. 197, pp. 64–86.

Barmé, GR 2009, 'China's flat earth: history and 8 August 2008', *The China Quarterly*, vol. 197, pp. 64–86.

Barmé, G 2010, 'For truly great men, look to this age alone: was Mao Zedong a new emperor?', in Cheek, T (ed.) *A critical introduction to Mao*, Cambridge University Press.

Bell, DA 2008, *China's new Confucianism: Politics and everyday life in a changing society*, Princeton University Press, Princeton.

Bell, DA 2010, *China's new confucianism: politics and everyday life in a changing society*, Princeton University Press.

Billioud, S 2007a, 'Confucianism, 'cultural tradition,' and official discourses at the start of the new century', *China Perspectives*, no. 3.

Billioud, S 2007b, 'Jiaohua: the Confucian revival today as an educative project', *China Perspectives*, no. 4.

Billioud, S & Thoraval, J 2008, 'The contemporary revival of confucianism. Anshen liming or the religious dimension of confucianism', *China Perspectives*, vol. 2008, no. (2008/3), pp. 88–106.

Breuilly, J 1985, *Nationalism and the State*, University of Chicago Press, Chicago.

Burns, J 1987, 'China's nomenklatura system', *Problems of Communism*, vol. 36, no. 5, pp. 36–51.

Burns, J (ed.) 1989, *The Chinese Communist Party's nomenklatura system: a documentary study of Party control of leadership selection 1979–1984*, M.E. Sharpe, Armonk, NY.

Burns, JP 1994, 'Strengthening central CCP control of leadership selection: The 1990 Nomenklatura', *The China Quarterly*, vol. 138.

Chang, JTH et al, (eds.) 2003, *China's media and entertainment law* (Vol. I), TransAsia Publishing Ltd, Beijing.

Collier, RB & Collier, D 1991, *Shaping the political arena: critical junctures, the labor movement and regime dynamics in Latin America*, Princeton University Press, Princeton.

Connor, W 1994, *Ethno-nationalism: the quest for understanding*, Princeton University Press, Princeton.

Dirlik, A 1997, *The postcolonial aura: Third World criticism in the age of global capitalism*, Westview Press, Boulder, Colo.

Downing, BM 1992, *The military revolution and political change: origins of democracy and autocracy in early modern Europe*, Princeton University Press, Princeton.

Durkheim, E 1997, *Suicide: a study in sociology*, Free Press, New York.

Edin, M 2003, 'State capacity and local agent control in China: CCP cadre management from a township perspective', *The China Quarterly*, vol. 173, pp. 35–52.

Fällman, F 2010, 'Useful Opium? 'Adapted religion' and 'harmony' in contemporary China', *Journal of Contemporary China*, vol. 19, no. 67, pp. 949–969.

Fernanda, A et al, 2002, 'Slouching towards decentralization: consequences of globalization for curricular control in national education systems', *Comparative Educational Review*, vol. 46, no. 1, pp. 66–88.

Friedman, E et al, 2005, *Revolution, resistance, and reform in village China*, Yale University Press, New Haven.

Geertz, C 1963, 'The integrative revolution: primordial sentiments and civil politics in the new states' In Geertz (ed.), *Old societies and new states*, Free Press, Glencoe.

Guo, YJ 2004, *Cultural nationalism in contemporary China: the search for national identity*, RoutledgeCurzon.

Hanson, ME 1998, 'Strategies of educational decentralization: key questions and core issues', *Journal of Educational Administration*, vol. 36, no. 2.

Hastings, A 1997, *The construction of nationhood: ethnicity, religion and nationalism*, Cambridge University Press, Cambridge.

Hawkins, JN 1998, 'Higher education reform and science and technology in China', In Cummings, W & McGinn, N (eds.), *International Handbook of Education and development: Preparing Schools, Students and Nations for the Twenty-First Century*, Pergamon Press.

Hawkins, JN 2000, 'Centralization, decentralization, recentralization: educational reform in China', *Journal of Educational Administration*, vol. 38, no. 5, pp. 442–454.

Hawkins, JN 2006, 'Walking on three legs: centralization, decentralization, and recentralization in Chinese education', In Bjork C (ed.), *Education decentralization: Asian experience and conceptual contribution*, Springer, pp. 21–46.

Herder, J 2010, 'Essay on the origin of language', In Barnard, FM (ed.), *Herder on social & political culture*, Cambridge University Press, Cambridge.

Hinton, RW 1968, 'Husbands, fathers and conquerors', *Political Studies*, vol. 16, no. 1, pp. 55–67.

Hobsbawm, EJ 1992, 'Nationalism and ethnicity', *Intermedia*, vol. 20, no. 4–5, pp. 13–15.

Huang, YS 1995, 'Administrative monitoring in China', *The China Quarterly*, vol. 143.

Huntington, SP 1996, *The clash of civilizations and the remaking of world order*, Simon & Schuster, New York.

Kang, XG 2005, *Renzheng—Zhongguo zhengzhi fazhan de disantiao daolu (Benevolent politics—the third way for Chinese political development)*, World Science and Technology Press, Singapore.

Kang, XG, Wang, J & Liu, SL 2010, *Zhendizhan: Guan yu zhonghua wenhua fuxingde gelanxishi fenxi* (Struggle for cultural hegemony: Gramscian perspectives of revitalizing Chinese traditional culture), shehui kexue wenxian chubanshe (Social Science Literature Press), Beijing.

Kedourie, E 1985, *Nationalism*, Hutchinson, London.

Krasner, SD 1988, 'Sovereignty: an institutional perspective', *Comparative Political Studies*, vol. 21, no. 1, pp. 66–94.

Kraus, RC 2004, *The party and the arty in China: the new politics of culture*, Rowman & Littlefield Publishers.

Landry, P 2008, *Decentralized authoritarianism in China: the Communist Party's control of local elites in post-Mao China*, Cambridge University Press, Cambridge.

Lee, CK 2007, *Against the law: labor protests in China's rustbelt and sunbelt*, University of California Press, Berkeley.

Lee, HY 1991, *From revolutionary cadres to party technocrats in socialist China*, University of California Press, Berkeley.

Lin, M & Galikowski, M 2000, *The search for modernity: Chinese intellectuals and cultural discourse in the post-Mao era*, Macmillan.

Lynch, DC 1999, *After the propaganda state: media, politics, and "thought work" in reformed China*, Stanford University Press.

Makeham, J 2008, *Lost soul: Confucianism in contemporary Chinese academic discourse*, Harvard University Asia Center, Cambridge, MA and London, England.

Manion, M 1995, Ideological congruence in the Chinese countryside: village leaders and their electorates and selectorates (CAPS working paper series no. 18). Retrieved from Lingnan University website: http://commons.ln.edu.hk/capswp/79

March, JG & Olsen, J 1989, *Rediscovering institutions: the organizational basis of politics*, Free Press, New York.

Meissner, W 1999, 'New intellectual currents in the People's Republic of China', In Teather, D & Yee, H (eds.), *China in transition: issues and policies*, Palgrave Macmillan.

Mok, K 1997, 'Privatization or marketization: educational development in post-Mao China', *International Review of Education*, vol. 43, no. 5–6, pp. 547–567.

National Bureau of Statistics of China 2012, China statistical yearbook, Chapter 3, "Population", http://www.stats.gov.cn/tjsj/ndsj/2012/indexch.htm, accessed on June 1st, 2013.

North, D 1990, *Institutions, institutional change and economic performance*, Cambridge University Press, Cambridge.

O'Brien, KJ 2008, *Popular protest in China*, Harvard University Press, Cambridge.

Oi, JC 1992, 'Fiscal reform and the economic foundations of local state corporatism in China', *World Politics*, vol. 45, no. 1, pp. 99–126.

Oi, JC 1995, 'The role of the local state in China's transitional economy', *The China Quarterly*, vol. 144, pp. 1132–1149.

Oksenberg, M & Tong, J 1991, 'The evolution of central-provincial fiscal relations in China', *The China Quarterly*, vol. 125, pp. 1–32.

Perry, E & Selden, M 2010, 'Reform, Conflict and Resistance in Contemporary China', *Chinese Society: Change, Conflict and Resistance*, Routledge.

Qu, H 2011, 'Religious Policy in the People's Republic of China: an alternative perspective', *Journal of Contemporary China*, vol. 20, no. 70.

Saich, T 2000, 'Negotiating the state: the development of social organizations in China', *The China Quarterly*, vol. 161, pp. 124–141.

Scharpf, F 1997, *Games real actors play, actor-centered institutionalism in policy research*, Westview Press, Boulder/Cumnor Hill.

Shambaugh, D 2000, *The Modern Chinese State*, Cambridge University Press, Cambridge.

Shambaugh, D 2007, 'China's propaganda system: institutions, processes and efficacy', *The China Journal*, vol. 57.

Smith, A 1998, *Nationalism and modernism: a critical survey of recent theories of nations and nationalism*, Routledge, London.

Smith, A 1999, *Myths and memories of the nation*, Oxford University Press.

Spencer, P & Wollman, H (eds.) 2005, *Nations and nationalism: a reader*, Rutgers University Press, New Brunswick.

Spencer, P (eds.) 2005, *Nations and nationalism: a reader*, Rutgers University Press.

Tong, J 1989, 'Fiscal reform, elite turnover and central-provincial relations in post-Mao China', *Australian Journal of Chinese Affairs*, vol. 22, pp. 1–28.

Tong, JW 2007, *Revenge of the Forbidden City: The suppression of the falungong in China, 1999–2005*, Oxford University Press.

Tsang, MC 2003, "School choice in the People's Republic of China", In Plank, D & Sykes, G (eds.), *Choosing choice: school choices in international perspective*, Teachers College Press, New York.

Van den Berghe, PL 1978, *Race and racism: a comparative perspective*, John Wiley and Sons, New York.

Van Den Berghe, PL 1995, 'Does race matter?', *Nations and Nationalism*, vol. 39, no. 3.

Vogel, EF 1989, *One step ahead in China: Guangdong under reform*, Harvard University Press.

Wang, SG & Hu, AG 2001, *The Chinese economy in crisis: state capacity and tax reform*, M.E. Sharpe, Armonk, NY.

Wang, SG 1989, *From revolution to involution: state capacity, local power, and [Un]governability in China*, Manuscript, Yale University, n.d.

Whiting, S 2000, *Power and wealth in rural China: the political economy of institutional change*, Cambridge University Press, Cambridge.

Wong, C 1991, 'Central–local relations in an era of fiscal decline: the paradox of fiscal decentralization in post-Mao China', *China Quarterly*, vol. 128.

Wong, C 1992, 'Fiscal reform and local industrialization', *Modern China*, vol. 18, no. 2.

Zhao, SH 1997, 'Chinese intellectuals' quest for national greatness and nationalistic writing in the 1990s', *The China Quarterly*, vol. 152, no. 2.

Zhou, L 2014. 'Administrative Subcontract (xingzheng fabaozhi),' *Society (shehui)*, vol. 34, no. 6, pp. 1–38.

CHAPTER 4

The Confucian Revival Among Intellectuals and the State Responses

At the start of the new millennium, there has been growing interest in Confucianism among China's intellectuals. This brought about a genuine revival of intellectual discourses which intend to revive Confucianism and establish its relevance to contemporary Chinese political and social life. Although Chinese intellectuals' interest in Confucianism can be traced back to the early 1980s, this interest had been narrowly confined within a small circle of academics until the mid-1990s. The intellectual discourses during this period of time were also small in number and weak in influence. After the 2000s, however, the intellectual circle of Confucian studies has rapidly expanded, with Confucian intellectual discourses proliferating and increasingly influential in China's symbolic environment.

This chapter aims to explore how the Chinese state engaged with these "Confucian intellectuals" (those who produce discourses about Confucianism) and responded to the Confucian revival. It is crucial given the intrinsic closeness between ideology and intellectuals and the critical role that intellectuals have played on China's political stage. Intellectuals are the avant-garde in pushing ideological changes; and at the same time, they, by creating and transmitting culture, are also pivotal in maintaining or undermining the current regime's legitimacy. This is especially the case within the Chinese context given that the Chinese political power had relied on intellectuals (ancient Confucian scholars) to sustain its legitimacy for over 2000 years of history.

© The Author(s) 2019
Q. Pang, *State-Society Relations and Confucian
Revivalism in Contemporary China*,
https://doi.org/10.1007/978-981-10-8312-9_4

This chapter begins with an introduction of Chinese intellectuals' complex relations with the party-state to serve as the backdrop for the whole story. It then discusses the resurgence of Confucian intellectual discourses and its causes and analyzes how the Chinese state, including both central and local governments, responded towards these Confucian intellectuals and their discourses. It finally concludes that the state developed a "decentralized responsiveness" mechanism in its response, which effects flexible and balance control over the intellectuals and their Confucian discourses.

4.1   CHINESE INTELLECTUALS AND THEIR TANGLED RELATIONS WITH THE STATE

4.1.1   Who Are "Intellectuals"?

Intellectuals in this chapter are defined from a realist-structuralist approach, that is, they are delineated by their distinctive location within the larger social structure. They are "those who *create* and *distribute* culture, that is, the symbolic world of man, including art, science, and religion".[1] Intellectuals thus defined are the core of the broad intellectual group defined by Lipset (1981). In Lipset's schema, intellectuals can be seen as a social group with a core and periphery (Karabel 1996). Those who create or produce culture are considered the "hardcore" of the intelligentsia, such as scholars, authors, artists, and editors. Those who distribute or transmit culture are also in the core but are one step away from the hardcore. Their representative members include teachers and journalists. At the periphery of the intelligentsia are those who apply culture, such as lawyers and teachers in primary and middle schools. In this chapter, intellectuals only refer to those who create and transmit culture, and thus they are the core of the Chinese intelligentsia.

Specifically, intellectuals discussed in this chapter are those who create and transmit a small proportion of culture such as Confucianism. They have expertise and professional knowledge about Confucianism. In anthropologist Katherine Verdery's (1991) words, they are "privileged in forming and transmitting discourses" concerning Confucianism. Different from other social groups, such as entrepreneurs and the ordinary urban middle class, as will be discussed in this chapter and Chap. 5, who have only moderate or even little knowledge concerning Confucianism, intellectuals are the professionals of Confucianism and hold dominant cultural capital in this area.

However, it needs to be pointed out that intellectuals are sometimes also defined by a phenomenological approach which often links intellectuals with some ideological, moral, epistemic, psychological, or even behavioral attributes (Eyerman 1994). For example, Edward Said (1994, p. 11) claimed that intellectuals are those who "publicly raise embarrassing questions, to confront orthodoxy and dogmas". Dickstein (1992, p. 92) described intellectuals by their epistemic qualities, and he argued that most intellectuals "do not qualify to be intellectuals, unless they begin to reflect upon the first principles of what they're doing and on its implications for society at large".

The rationale for defining intellectuals only in the realist-structuralist approach in this chapter is that it fits with the aim of the chapter. This chapter intends to explore the relations between the Chinese state and intellectuals within the context of contemporary Chinese society. Thus, the realist-structuralist definition, which captures intellectuals' place within the larger social structure, is more suitable for these purposes. In addition, the phenomenological approach, given that it usually emphasizes moral commitment as the judging criterion for intellectuals, confines intellectuals into a small group of "genuine" intellectuals and therefore narrows the scope of the inquiry into intellectual-state relations (Eyerman 1994; Karabel 1996).

In addition, intellectuals in this chapter are confined to those who should work in the traditionally defined realm of "society", such as higher educational institutes, research bodies, and media organizations. Public intellectuals with no fixed affiliations are also included, as they are a part of society. Intellectuals in this study do not include professionals who work in any level of the Chinese government, as they are part of the state. Such definition, however, does not imply that the Chinese intellectuals are independent from the state, as most of them still rely on the Chinese state for their livelihood and career development.

4.1.2 Intellectuals' Growing Power and Autonomy in the Post-Mao Era

Intellectuals, in general, are crucial for the CCP's authoritarian rule as they possess specialized knowledge and, more importantly, ideological resources to legitimate or delegitimate the current political system. There is a powerful tradition of intelligentsia's control over state legitimacy in China. During the imperial era, Confucian literati (intellectuals), by virtue of their Confucian knowledge, could even challenge the emperor when they perceived his behavior had deviated from the Confucian ideals of morality, although such power was often heavily circumstanced.[2] Even during the Maoist era, when intellectuals were heavily suppressed and persecuted, "establishment intellectuals" (intellectuals who were trusted by the power elites and assigned to key posts) were still relied upon for building the legitimacy of the socialist system (Gu and Goldman 2004).

During the post-Mao era, especially the post-Deng era, there has been a rapid expansion of the intellectual group. Although it is difficult to assess the number of intellectuals in China today (given that there are many different criteria for defining intellectuals), the increasing number of intellectuals can be seen from the burgeoning number of those who received higher education. In 1999, the number of college students was 4.13 million, but the number jumped to 26.25 million in 2015. There were only 0.23 million postgraduate students in 1999. However, its number reached 1.91 million in 2015, more than eight times larger than in 1999 (National bureau of Statistics of China 2015). Although not all these college students or postgraduates became intellectuals as defined in this chapter, the numbers reveal the growing numbers of those obtaining higher education.

Intellectuals, at the same time, have gained increasing power on the Chinese political stage. This is, in part, due to the rising importance of knowledge and technology in the modernization process. Intellectuals with professional knowledge and expertise are highly valued in various policy-making processes (Feng 2003). In addition, with improving mass communication technology and widening public space, intellectuals, particularly public intellectuals, exert growing influence over public opinion (Goldman 2011).

In parallel, they have also enjoyed considerable autonomy from the Chinese state since China's accelerated marketization after Deng's Southern Tour in 1992. Marketization has opened up more opportunities for intellectuals' career development, and therefore granted intellectuals relative financial autonomy from the state (Gu and Goldman 2004). Some intellectuals, besides holding positions in their work units, find a second or even third job outside academia due to a vibrant market economy (Gu and Goldman 2004). They sell their expertise in the market in exchange of financial returns, which has significantly reduced their dependence on the state. Although most of the intellectuals still belong to the political establishment and benefit from the state in terms of career and material life,

they keep at least some reasonable independence in their ideological outlook, sticking to neoliberal, anti-Mao, and anti-Communist attitudes
(Hao 2012; Cheng 2008).

4.1.3   Intellectuals as Double-Edged Swords for the Party-State's Rule

Chinese intellectuals are both an ally of and a challenger to the Chinese
state. Like intellectuals in most other societies, Chinese intellectuals can
also be viewed as the "dominated fraction of the dominant class" in
Chinese society.[3] As dominant holders of cultural capital (or recourses),
they belong to the elite class and benefit from privileges which non-elite
social classes cannot enjoy. However, as intellectuals do not possess key
political and economic resources, they are also subordinate in relation to
the holders of political and economic capital in society. Their peculiar
social position determines that their relations with the Chinese state are
both cooperative and contentious.

Chinese intellectuals largely support the current regime. They have
their vital interests closely attached with the status quo and rely heavily on
political and economic power to sustain and improve their well-being. The
majority of Chinese intellectuals are employed by various state organs,
such as universities, academic institutes, and policy research organizations
(Gu and Goldman 2004). As cultural elites, they are officially categorized
as "state cadres" (*guojia ganbu*) and entitled to various benefits such as
pensions and free healthcare, which are not enjoyed by subordinate social
groups like workers and migrant laborers. In fact, there has been a long
history of intellectuals being privileged "cultural elites" in Chinese society.
During the imperial era, the Confucian literati (intellectuals) were the only
elite class aside from the monarchy.[4] They were arranged to staff the imperial bureaucratic system, delegated to administrate society, and even
respected as personal counselors for the ruler (Goldman et al. 1987).

In contemporary China, most intellectuals link their personal development with the state's survival and prosperity (Ogden 2004). As Gu (1999)
has noted, even political scientists, sociologists, and economists, who are
most likely to be dissidents against the CCP's rule, usually hope to serve as
advisers to the leadership. Intellectuals are interested in building patron-
client ties with CCP officials because these can bring them honorary
positions in academic and even political institutions, opportunities for
overseas conferences, publications in officially sponsored journals and

books, and increased economic remuneration. Hence, it is natural that Chinese intellectuals usually share with the party-state the same position in reinforcing rather than questioning the existing political order.

Intellectuals, however, also have strong potential to challenge the status quo. This is because they are dominated politically and economically, and their subordinate positions, under certain circumstances, meant that they may oppose the political elite. For example, Chinese intellectuals are restricted in their political activities, and their freedom of speech and associations are also limited (Bonnin and Chevrier 1991). Those who enter the certain "no go" areas might invite suppression of their activities. Even during imperial times, the Confucian literati's rights were circumscribed by emperors, courtiers, and even eunuchs.[5] In the twentieth century, both the Kuomintang (KMT) and the CCP regimes required exclusive loyalty from intellectuals. This reached a climax during the Cultural Revolution period (1966–1976), when any intellectual who dared to criticize the CCP regime even in the slightest way might be imperiled. "Rebellious" intellectuals were either publicly humiliated or sent to labor camps for "re-education"; some were even persecuted to death or driven to suicide (Becker 1998; MacFarquhar and Schoenhals 2006; Thurston 1988). After the economic reforms in the 1980s, though intellectuals were valued and some were even recruited into the bureaucracy (Feng 2003), Chinese intellectuals as a whole, nevertheless, have never enjoyed a dominant position in the ruling class (White 1987). The recent CCP leadership of Jiang Zemin and Hu Jintao detained, put under surveillance, or expelled from the academic establishment those intellectuals who dared to openly express their dissent and criticize party policies (Goodman 2008, p. 332). For example, Jiao Guobiao, a journalism professor at Peking University, and Wang Yi, a law lecturer at Chengdu University, were barred from teaching due to their open criticism against the state. The journal *Zhanlue yu guanli* (Strategy and Management), which was an outlet for extreme liberal intellectuals, was closed down in 2004.

Intellectuals can be serious challengers of political regimes. Many Chinese Intellectuals publicly criticized both the KMT and the CCP for their repressive policies and strongly advocated political reforms (Goldman 1999). They passionately led various political movements like the May Fourth Movement in 1919, the Communist Movement in the 1930s and 1940s, the April Fifth Movement in 1976, and the June Fourth Movement in 1989. The formation of the China Democracy Party[6] in the late 1990s and launch of the Charter 08 in 2008 are recent examples showing intel-lectuals' antagonism towards the party-state.

The focus of the antagonism between intellectuals and the state lies in freedom of expression. For intellectuals, freedom of expression is vital to their career and even life pursuit. To be an intellectual means "make knowledge/value claims, to gain some degree of social recognition for them, and to participate in social relations on the basis of this exchange of claims and recognition" (Verdery 1991, p. 89). Thus, the right to express their views is essential for an intellectual. However, for the CCP, the cur-rent authoritarian power structure does not allow total freedom of expres-sion as such freedom may be used by the state's opposers to erode its ruling legitimacy. Both the KMT and the CCP had experienced strong social upheavals mobilized by opposing intellectuals after the parties relaxed their control over intellectuals' freedom of speech. The most recent example is the June Fourth Movement in 1989, before which the then CCP general secretaries, Zhao Ziyang and Hu Yaobang, had consid-erably relaxed restrictions over intellectuals' freedom of speech (Nathan and Gilley 2002; Nathan and Link 2001).

4.1.4   The CCP: Balancing Co-opting and Coercing Intellectuals

The CCP faces a dilemma. On the one hand, it needs to extend intellectu-als' freedom of expression in order to co-opt them and absorb their con-trolled symbolic resources; however, on the other hand, due to the authoritarian power structure, it is impossible for the CCP to allow total freedom for intellectuals, especially those critical of it. This has become a serious problem especially since the early 1990s when intellectuals have become more powerful and autonomous due to China's intensified mar-ketization and globalization. Whether the CCP could solve the dilemma is vital for the CCP's control over intellectuals and their burgeoning power.

How could the CCP solve the dilemma? Previous literature explained that the CCP tried to reach a balance through a cyclical pattern of restric-tion (*shou*) and relaxation (*fang*). Restriction means "stifling intellectual discourses", while relaxation is "encouraging intellectual creativity". According to Goldman (1993), the party tightens its control (restriction) until intellectuals appear reluctant to produce; it then relaxes its control (relaxation), until its political authority appears threatened.[7] During the intervals of relaxation, the party permitted and even encouraged intellectuals to engage in debates, introduce Western "advanced" theories and criticize the bureaucracy in order to foster economic development. However, when all these debates, discussions of Western thoughts, and criticism entered the "no go" areas such as criticism of the Leninist political system and suggestions of alternatives such as democracy, the regime cracked down with varying intensity (Fewsmith 2001; Goldman 1985, 1993; Hamrin 1987). For example, during the first several years after China's reforms, from 1978 to the early 1980s, the CCP relaxed its control by encouraging debates such as "whether practice is the only criterion for testing truth". However, this was followed by restrictive policies shown by the CCP's "anti-spiritual pollution" campaign against some "excessive" intellectuals in 1983. Later, as a sign of "relaxation", the then CCP General Secretary Hu Yaobang permitted greater freedom for intellectual discussion, but in 1986, the CCP again launched an "anti-bourgeois liberalization" campaign against "subversive" intellectuals. Such cycles continued into the Jiang Zemin era. For instance, in 1997, Jiang's speech at the Central Party School was widely regarded as the beginning of "relaxation", while in late 1999 the CCP's suppressions on democratic activities announced the coming of "restrictions".[8]

However, since Hu Jintao and his team assumed power in 2002, this alternation pattern of relaxation and restriction has become less dominant in the CCP's control of intellectuals, although it still exists.[9] This paper, by examining how the party-state regulated the Confucian revival among intellectuals since the early twenty-first century, finds that a new governing pattern, decentralized responsiveness, has been on the rise. In this decentralized mechanism, the central government acted as a conservative *stabilizer*. It monitored intellectuals by strengthening its official ideologies and setting bottom lines for so-called treacherous intellectuals. The local authorities, on the contrary, acted as active *reformers*. They took measures to encourage intellectuals' work on Confucianism, particularly works that are de-politicized or potentially valuable for local governance. This local promotion not only facilitates those local authorities' co-optation of intellectuals but also strengthens their control of Confucian symbols and beliefs, reducing the possible threats that Confucian intellectuals may pose on the regime. Accordingly, intellectuals also had freedom of expression (on Confucianism) extended. In this way, the decentralized mechanism both expanded intellectuals' freedom and kept the Chinese government's rein over intellectuals. Before coming to the details of this decentralized mechanism, it is necessary to introduce the regeneration of Confucianism among intellectuals as the prelude for the whole story.

4.2   INTELLECTUALS' EFFORTS AT REVIVING CONFUCIANISM

Since the early 1990s, there has been a renewed and sustained interest in Confucianism among intellectuals. Academic papers and conferences concerning Confucianism have grown exponentially (Fig. 4.1). While there were only two research seminars addressing Confucianism in the whole of the 1970s, the number jumped to 34 in the 1980s, 72 in the 1990s, and 97 from 2001 to 2008 (China Confucius Foundation 2009; Liang 2010). Various academic organizations for Confucianism studies were set up. According to one account, before 1990, there were only 14 Confucianism-related organizations established in China, and the number soared to approximately 200 by 2000 (Makeham 2008).

Some have argued that the revival of Confucian academic discourses was underpinned by the Chinese state's support (Meissner 1999; Min & Galikowski 2000). This view might explain intellectuals' interest in Confucianism during the 1980s and much of the 1990s, as the Chinese state did sponsor studies on "New Confucianism" out of its interest in the purported efficacy of "Confucian Capitalism" and "anti-Western" motives after the June Fourth Movement in 1989 (Makeham 2008). However,

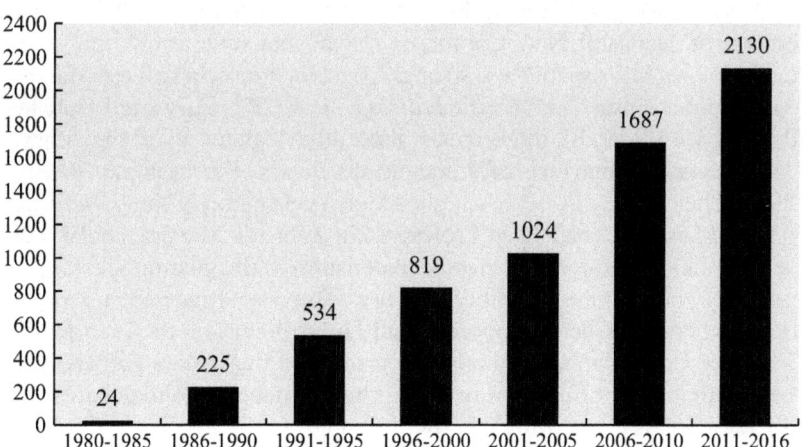

Fig. 4.1   The number of academic articles with "Confucianism" (*ruxue*) in titles from 1980 to 2016 in the CNKI Database. (Source: CNKI—Chinese National Knowledge Infrastructure)

after the late 1990s, the upsurge of intellectual discourses which demanded the restoration of Confucianism in contemporary Chinese society is clearly not what the Chinese state intended. Some of these discourses directly challenged the legitimacy of Marxism and suggested replacing Marxism with Confucianism.

Since early this century, intellectuals have begun to link Confucianism with China's social and political realities, and viewed Confucianism (or certain of its elements) as remedies for social and political anomies unleashed by China's modernization process. Confucian discourses during this period have largely gone beyond academic interpretations of "Confucianism" at large, which was the common pattern during the 1980s and 1990s. Some of the discourses argue for rehabilitation of the Confucian social order and even contain strong political appeal. For example, Ren Jiantao's "Socio-Political Confucianism" (2000), Jiang Qin's "Political Confucianism" (2003),[10] and Kang Xiaoguang's "Confucianism as Regime Legitimacy" (2004a, b)[11] all point to the decayed legitimacy of the official ideology and aim to re-establish political system by extracting Confucian legacies.[12] Cai Degui's "Practical Confucianism" (1996)[13] and Guo Qiyong's "Confucianism as a Lifestyle"[14] argue for the restoration of elements of the Confucian social order to resolve social anomie in Chinese society (Wang 2004).

Among these intellectuals, the most radical are the so-called fourth generation of Mainland New Confucians,[15] who not only firmly oppose the orthodoxy of Marxism but also strongly plead for "replacing official Marxism with Confucianism" or "*Confucianizing* the CCP". They even launched debates with Marxist intellectuals about the legitimacy of the Marxist Materialism's dominance of academic discourses. For example, in April 2004, Chen Ming, one of the so-called fourth generation of New Confucians on the Mainland, challenged Professor Liu Zehua, a Marxist scholar, concerning Liu's argument on Marxist materialism as the guiding ideology for understanding Chinese political history. This also triggered a series of debates between Chen's supporters and Liu's students on the Internet.

These Confucian scholars openly promoted their views and attracted wide public attention. In May 2004, they launched public debates with liberal scholars concerning whether it is appropriate for children to learn Confucian texts. The debate was made in both print and electronic media and lasted for months. The New Confucians also held public forums to promote their Confucian propositions. In July 2004, Jiang Qing held a seminar entitled "The Contemporary Destiny of

Confucianism" ("*ruxue de danggai mingyun*") in Guiyang, Guizhou province. He invited several representatives of "Confucian fundamentalists", such as Chen Ming, Sheng Hong, and Kang Xiaoguang, and media journalists to attend the seminar. The mainstream Chinese media described the seminar as "China's Cultural Conservatism Summit". In addition, Confucian intellectuals gave public lectures promoting their Confucian assertions. One influential lecture was made by Kang Xiaoguang, "Why I Advocate 'Confucianization': Conservative Thoughts about China's Future Political Development" (*wo wenshenme zhuzhang ruhua—guanyu zhongguo weilai zhengzhi de baoshou zhuyi sikao*) in the graduate school of the Chinese Academy of Social Sciences on November 24, 2004. All the activities were high profile, and some of the Confucian intellectuals have large numbers of followers on the Internet.[16]

Confucian intellectuals and their discourses and activities raise a thorny issue for the state. It is true that these intellectuals' discourses are of some value in solving social anomie and maintaining stability. Considering the declining appeal of Marxism and Socialism in Chinese society, it is understandable that the state allows some intellectuals to make attempts to boost traditional culture so as to strengthen nationalism and even possibly map out a new route for rejuvenating its official ideology. However, Confucianism, as has been analyzed in Chap. 1, is fundamentally different from the official ideology. The rapid rise of these Confucian intellectuals and their discourses, once out of control, will become autonomous social forces and constitute threats to the current regime. In addition, as a post-totalitarian state, the CCP regime is simply unable to forgo its ideological legacy, Marxism and Socialism, even though these ideologies are now heavily discredited among the Chinese public (Bell 2008). They still serve as the foundations for the CCP's guiding principles such as "socialism with Chinese characteristics" and "harmonious society". The CCP has also learned from the collapse of the former Soviet Union and Eastern European countries about the huge risks of losing ideological control (Shambaugh 2008). Thus, for the CCP, the old dilemma comes back: how can it control intellectuals and their Confucian discourses while at the same time co-opting them and manipulate their Confucian discourses (which can be viewed as a kind of ideological resource and power) to its own advantage? This time, the CCP did not employ the oscillating policies of relaxation and restriction. Instead, it adopted a decentralized responsiveness mechanism.

4.3   THE CENTRAL STATE: CONSERVATIVE "IDEOLOGICAL STABILIZER"

The central government, in responding to Confucian intellectuals and their discourses, was conservative. Contrary to the popular assumption that the Chinese government is interested in Confucianism,[17] the central government has showed very limited endorsement for intellectuals' studies on Confucianism. In contrast, it strengthened the teaching and researching of Marxism and other official ideologies (Shambaugh 2007). It set bottom lines for critical intellectuals, and any intellectual stepping over these lines would do so at their peril. For the central government, the growing influence of Confucian intellectuals and their academic discourses is not aligned to its interests, as these intellectuals and their Confucian symbols and beliefs may become too powerful to control, thus endangering the state's own efforts to build its preferred symbolic environment.

It is true that certain central leaders, such as President Hu Jintao and Premier Wen Jiabao, had quoted Confucian expressions in their public appearances,[18] but this does not mean the center intends to promote Confucianism, or as some scholars reasoned, intends to make Confucianism a backup or supplement for its official ideology.[19] One needs to differentiate appropriating the charisma of Confucius symbols from promoting Confucianism as an ideology. Furthermore, certain leaders' personal use of some Confucian expressions does not mean the central government has the collective will of raising the banner of Confucianism. In reality, the central government's support for Confucianism is only marginal. A case in point is its very limited funding for academic projects concerning Confucianism, which is shown in the list of the National Fund for Social Sciences (*guojia shehui kexue jijin*, hereafter NFSS). The NFSS is widely recognized as the largest and most influential state support for social research in China and is now regulated by the National Planning Office of Philosophy and Social Sciences (*quanguo zhexue shehui kexue guihua bangongshi*), which is under direct control of the CCP's Central Propaganda Department. Thus, the NFSS's choices of projects should, to a large extent, reflect the central CCP's intention. However, a survey of The Guidance for Applying NFSS (*guojia sheke jijin shenjing zhinan*) from 2006 to 2017 shows that only very few topics concerning Confucianism were on its list.

During the twelve years from 2006 to 2017, there were merely one or two topics directly related to Confucianism out of dozens of topics in the category of philosophy each year.[20] For example, in 2009, only one topic was directly linked to Confucianism.[21] Although there were also topics concerning Chinese traditional culture or "Chinese national spirit", which are arguably connected with Confucianism in one way or another, their number was also very small (see Fig. 4.2).[22] Even in the 2012 NFSS fund for Cultural Studies, which was supposed to be related with Confucianism, there was only one relevant topic, namely, "inheriting excellent traditional Chinese culture", out of a total of 36 topics. Even this topic is only somewhat related to Confucianism.[23] In contrast to the few Confucianism-related topics, topics directly associated with Marxism or other official ideologies almost dominated the entire list.

The center's lack of interest in developing Confucian intellectual discourses was confirmed by my interviews with intellectuals who undertook studies of Confucianism. Even those scholars who study Confucianism under the guidance of Marxism denied that they or their discourses about Confucianism received preferential treatment or attention from the central government. One professor from the Chinese Academy of Social Sciences, who has an established reputation for undertaking Confucianism studies from the Marxist perspective, said,

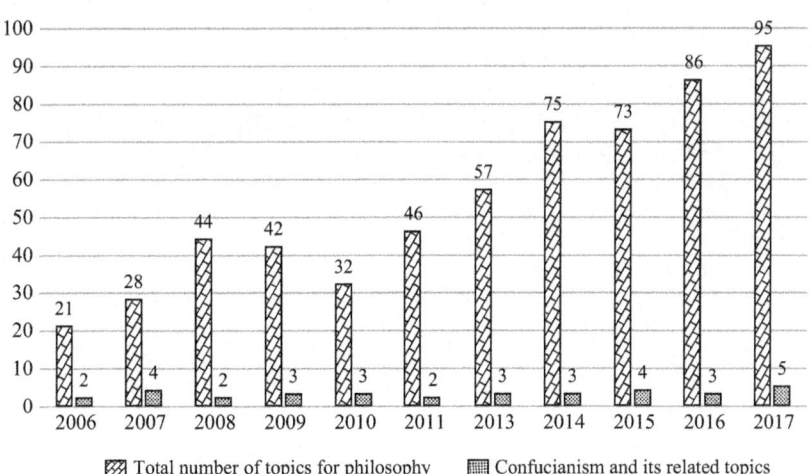

Fig. 4.2 The number of topics for philosophy and confucianism-related topics in NFSS from 2006 to 2017

I do not believe that the central authorities are interested in my works on Confucianism, needless to say my proposals about putting Confucian social order into practice. I do not have much hope for this government. (Interviewee 40)

One of the critical Confucian intellectuals directly claimed, "The CCP Central Propaganda Department was very conservative, and it once even barred me from participating in an academic conference on Confucianism in Nishan, Shandong Province" (Interviewee 41).

In reality, after Hu Jintao and his colleagues assumed power in 2002, the central authorities seldom issued formal documents explicitly endorsing creative intellectual works on Confucianism or encouraging education of Confucianism in higher educational institutions.[24] On the contrary, they were active in promoting education and research in Marxism and other official ideologies among intellectuals. For example, in 2004, the central committee of the CCP and the State Council issued "Opinions on Further Strengthening and Improving University Students' Ideological and Political Education" (*zhonggong zhongyang guowuyuan guanyu jinyibu jiaqiang he gaijin daxuesheng sixiang zhengzhi jiaoyu de yijian*), clearly requesting "intellectuals in the faculty of philosophy and social sciences (in higher educational institutes) should insist on and consolidate the guiding position of 'Marxism' in the ideological sector, and apply the latest theoretical developments of Sinicized Marxism (Marxism combined with Chinese realities) in their teachings". Article 13 in this document also writes:

As a part of academic projects for building and studying Marxist theories, (Intellectuals of Philosophy and Social Sciences) are required to carefully compile textbooks that fully demonstrate Mao Zedong Thought, Deng Xiaoping Theory and theories of "Three Represents" for the teaching of Philosophy, Political Economy, Scientific Socialism, History of the CCP, Political Science, Sociology, Legal Studies, History, Journalism Literature and so on. In all, intellectuals should endeavor to build a disciplinary system of philosophy and social sciences, with Chinese characteristics, Chinese styles and Chinese features which are guided by Marxism. They should also compile corresponding text books along with the disciplinary system.

In 2008, the Ministry of Education further issued "Opinions on Building 'Thought Work' Teaching Faculties in Tertiary Educational Institution" (*guanyu jinyibu jiaqiang gaoxiao sixiang lilun zhengzhike jiaoshi duiwu de yijian*), which required every university directly affiliated with the Ministry of Education to establish a college-level school of Marxism and improve the teaching of Marxism and other official ideologies among university students.[25]

In 2004, the CCP Central Committee issued the "Opinions on Further Developing of Philosophy and the Social Sciences" (*guanyu jinyibu fanrong fazhan zhexue shehui kexue de yijian*), which clearly emphasizes the guiding position of Marxism in researching philosophy and the social sciences. During the same year, the central propaganda department organized a large-scale research project involving the building and developing of Marxist theories among intellectuals.

Besides the fortification of official ideologies, the central government imposed its restrictions on Confucian intellectuals by punishing those who dared to step over its bottom line. The purpose was to repress and censor particular Confucian discourses detrimental to the CCP's rule. What is the bottom line? Most interviewed intellectuals agreed: "challenging the Leninist political structure, the CCP or its leadership especially on public occasions that lay within the 'forbidden zone'".[26] Three of the interviewed intellectuals confessed to being either barred from participating in conferences or delivering public lectures. For one critical intellectual, one of his books could not be published; for another, one of his books had been delayed being published for five years. Unlike the cruel persecutions during the Mao period, the government's repression is now usually directed at a specific work rather than an intellectual's entire career or life work, and with a few important exceptions, attacked intellectuals are not detained, imprisoned, or ostracized, or subjected to disgrace (Goldman 1996)[27]; there is enough evidence to show that the government has increased its use of "soft" strategies of repression and has actually contracted intellectuals' freedom since the late 1990s, especially for the central government (Goldman 2011).

However, it needs to be clarified that not all of the central government is coercive in dealing with the Confucian intellectuals. Two of the interviewed critical intellectuals claimed that different divisions of the central government, in fact, held different attitudes and took different measures towards them. One emphasized that he was just attacked by the most conservative division of the government.

It is just the CCP Central Propaganda Department that is very conservative. Those practical divisions (He means those government branches in charge of practical rather than ideological affairs such as economic or civil administration) are, comparatively speaking, more open-minded. (Interviewee 41)

Another interviewee's words are also illuminating. This interviewee is a critical Confucian scholar, and several of his articles and books were barred from publication in China. I thought he might complain about the central state during my interview. To my surprise, however, he said,

> I think some people in the central state, especially the head (I think he meant former President Hu Jintao and Premier Wen Jiabao), are sympathetic with me. They are also interested in the Confucian revival. But they are still waiting. You know, the central government is always like this. They are waiting for an appropriate chance, just like what they did for economic reforms. They waited until the time riped. ... The central CCP propaganda department is very strong, and that is ... my works got censored. (Interviewee 32)

Their words show two important facts. First, some sections of the central state such as the central CCP propaganda department are conservative, eager to rein in the Confucian scholars and their discourses. This is understandable, given that the central propaganda department is, in fact, a vested interest group whose existence relies on maintaining the official ideology. It benefits from close control over ideologies as this could bring them more power and resources. Second, some other parts of the central state (including the former head and his colleagues) may be interested in the Confucian revival and intend to innovate the decayed official ideology by appropriating some Confucian elements, for the purpose of boosting the regime legitimacy. But they have been ambivalent. It seems very likely that the central government does not have a clear consensus on how to deal with Confucianism and these critical Confucian intellectuals. However, regardless of the internal inconsistency, the center's role in the Confucian revival is more of a stabilizer rather than innovator.

4.4   Local Governments: Active "Ideological Reformers"

Contrary to the central government which acts as a conservative "restriction imposer", local governments took the role of "active reformers". Local authorities were observed, in my fieldwork, as taking active measures to encourage intellectual works on Confucianism, particularly those with potential value for local governance or de-politicized theoretical research. The following section will first elaborate on how and why local authorities promoted intellectual works on Confucianism, and then will proceed with two carefully selected cases to elucidate how these local authorities, by promoting their preferred Confucian academic discourses and activities, actively co-opted intellectuals and manipulated Confucian academic resources to their own advantage. It shows that local authorities' active promotion of Confucianism was sometimes driven by their strong instrumental mentality for career development, which was partly shaped by the decentralized institution.

4.4.1   Local Authorities' Supportive Measures for Studying Confucianism

"Local authorities" in this article refers not only to local government officials but also leaders in public institutions (*shiye danwei*) where "intellectuals" aggregate, such as higher educational institutes, research, and media organizations. In China, public institutions are highly bureaucratized and leaders in these public organizations are usually delegated by different levels of government. For example, the top two leadership positions in higher educational institutes, the president and party secretary, are assigned by the government,[28] and they hold equivalent administrative ranks to local government officials. Thus, they can be viewed as local authorities in tertiary educational institutes (Price 2005).

Local authorities advanced Confucianism and its related intellectual discourses mainly through three approaches. The first approach is to establish an independent or affiliated educational and research organization teaching and researching Confucianism. Since 2000, at least the top Chinese universities have built their Confucianism-related schools or centers, thanks to the support of leaders in these universities (Kang et al. 2010). For example, in 2005, the People's University of China (*zhongguo renmin daxue*, hereafter PUC), with the active support of its president, Ji Baocheng, established a new college teaching and researching national studies including Confucianism (which will be illustrated in the second case study later). In 2006 and 2009, Fudan University and Qinghua University also built their own Confucian studies research centers. Many local tertiary educational institutes followed suit. Many prestigious social science research organizations, such as the Chinese Academy of Social Sciences and Shandong Academy of Social Sciences, also established parallel Confucian studies centers. These institutes, again with support from local leaders, launched new teaching programs aiming at promoting Confucianism, convened Confucianism studies conferences, and published journals and periodicals, all of which have contributed to the development of Confucian discourses. For instance, from 2000 to 2008, there have been more than 97 academic conferences addressing Confucianism, most of which were financed and sponsored by local authorities in higher educational institutes (Wu 2010; *China Yearbook of Confucianism* 2009).

The second approach is local governments' permission for the vigorous growth of Confucian Studies Associations (hereafter CSA; *ruxue yanjiuhui*) established by intellectuals all over China. CSAs are a kind of voluntary civil group formed by intellectuals interested in Confucianism. According to the Chinese regulations concerning civil organizations, these groups need to obtain governmental permission and register in corresponding governmental bureaucratic organizations. Before 2000, there were approximately nine local CSAs such as CSA founded in 1987 in Suzhou, Jiangsu Province (Kang et al. 2010). After 2000, such CSAs sprang up all across China, and until 2016, according to one incomplete list, there were at least 52 locally registered CSAs in more than 20 provinces and municipal cities, such as the China Confucian Businessmen Culture Research Association (established in 2014) and the CSA in Shanghai (established in 2015).[29] Some of the CSAs received government subsidies for their activities.

There are also many underground CSAs to which local governments gave their silent permission. A typical case is "Youth Confucianism Studies Seminar" (*qingnian ruxue luntan* YCSS) initiated and organized by Professor Gan Chunsong (甘春松) from the PUC, and Professor Peng Guoxiang (彭國翔) from Beijing University. YCSS is widely recognized as one of the most active CSAs in Beijing, and it now has over 20 regular members who are all scholars interested in Confucianism. Its activities mainly include monthly meetings discussing and critiquing articles that its members submit (Kang 2008).

The third approach is local authorities' funding for Confucianism-related research projects. For example, the Beijing municipal government has substantially subsidized the compilation of the *Canons of Confucianism* (*ru zang* 儒藏) (Wu 2006a). The total number and specifics of these government-funded projects are difficult to obtain because many local authorities do not (or are not willing to) publicize such data. But during my fieldwork in Beijing, Shandong, and Guangdong, local educational authorities in Qingdao, Jinan, and Shenzhen confessed that they had funded research projects about Confucianism. One of my informants in Qingdao viewed government-funded projects as a major instrument for local governments to influence intellectuals and their work.[30]

4.4.2 Underlying Rationale for Local Governments' Supportive Measures

Most local authorities encouraged Confucian intellectual discourses not because they were interested in Confucianism or because they wanted to go against the central government. Their support was usually based on careful and rational calculations of possible benefits and losses. First, although the center did not support Confucianism, it did not forbid or suppress it, either. Therefore, for the local authorities, there was a "gray area" concerning how to manage these Confucian intellectuals and their discourses. As one local official suggested during the field trip, "as long as local officials did not step over the bottom line set by the central authorities, they were not in conflict with the center".[31] In fact, many local authorities even "created" the center's permission for their measures. For example, as one of my informants revealed to me,

> For locally convened conferences of Confucianism, local authorities usually invited retired officials who had worked in central government such as the Chinese People's Political Consultative Conference or the National People's Congress, to deliver the opening speech at the conference, as a sign of the center's permission and support for the conference. However, in reality, these retired officials often directly told the local authorities and organizing committees that they did not represent the central government but themselves. However, such words, more often than not, did not reach as far as participants of the conference. (Interviewee 16)

Second, local authorities are under pressure to attain achievements in their governance because of the decentralized administrative system. Within this system, local officials have considerable authority within their jurisdictions (Jin et al. 2005; Zheng 2007). This means local authorities can basically take whatever measures they consider as appropriate to manage local affairs. At the same time, they are strongly motivated to make achievements while in office and win higher favorable assessment of their superiors. Given that the center has no clear regulations on the management of Confucianism, some local officials view promoting Confucianism in "proper" ways as an opportunity for contributing to effective local governance. The following two cases will illustrate this in detail.

4.4.3   Case Studies: Local Support for Studying Confucianism

This section contains two case studies: (1) the Beijing municipal government's support for the Oriental Morality Research Institute (*dongfang daode yanjiusuo*, hereafter OMRI) and (2) the establishment of the National Studies College (NSC) in PUC. Selection of these two cases is based on the following considerations. First, local authorities in these two cases are different. The first case concerns local government officials, while the second relates to leaders in higher educational institutes. These are the two major types of local authorities involved in managing intellectuals; thus, the two cases combined are representative in showing how different types of local authorities support and manipulate intellectuals' discourses about Confucianism. Second, intellectuals involved in the two cases are also different. In the first case, the OMRI is only a local research institute funded by a local government, and most staff in this organization are middle or lower level intellectuals; while in the second case, as the PUC is one of China's elite universities, intellectuals in this university belong to the top strata in terms of expertise and prestige. Hence, the combination of the two cases should draw a balanced picture showing how different levels of intellectuals (and their symbolic resources) were co-opted by local authorities.

The two case studies show that while the local officials of the Beijing government preferred intellectual work with instrumental value for local governance, authorities in the PUC encouraged de-politicized and theoretical research about Confucianism. The different preferences, however, were both shaped, to a large extent, by the same instrumental mentality produced by the decentralized institution. The two cases vividly demonstrate how local authorities' instrumental mentality allows sufficient flexibility in co-opting intellectuals of all kinds.

4.4.3.1   Case Study I: Beijing Municipal Government's Support for the OMRI

The OMRI was founded in 1994 and is currently affiliated with the Beijing Youth College of Politics (*Beijing qingnian zhengzhi xueyuan*). It is a research institute funded and regulated by the Beijing Municipal Government (hereafter BMG). According to the OMRI's current directors,[32] the founding of the OMRI was proposed by its former dean, Professor Wang Dianqin (王殿卿), who committed himself to promoting Confucianism, especially Confucian morality. Wang perceived Confucian ethics as an effective cure for the sharp moral decline among youngsters in the early 1990s, which he believed was serious. Wang therefore suggested the then BMG to build the OMRI for promoting Confucian ethics among the populace, especially the youth. The BMG positively responded by granting him financial support, though there were antagonistic voices from some conservative authorities at the beginning.[33]

The OMRI currently has seven full-time faculty members and more than 30 part-time researchers. Its research faculty has produced more than 20 books, published more than 280 articles and reports, finished 23 research projects, and held approximately 30 academic conferences. It has also run the longest series of programs promoting Confucian values (under the cover of "traditional virtues") in China since 1994. According to the former dean of the OMRI, they had over 350,000 students in 2002, and the number had risen to 600,000 by the end of 2004 (Makeham 2008, p. 325).

After its establishment, the BMG continued to support the OMRI through subsidizing its operations[34] and selectively funding its research projects and teaching programs. Among its 23 finished research projects, 16 were funded by the BMG. The BMG also collaborated with the OMRI for a trial program teaching traditional Chinese virtues, which included more than 140,000 students from more than 20 universities and over a hundred primary and secondary schools.

The BMG's support for the OMRI often came with strong instrumental and utilitarian motivations, one of which was to make use of the increasingly popular Confucian symbolic resources for its local governance. For example, the government was apparently more interested in projects that are of pragmatic utility for perpetuating social stability. OMRI has five major branches of Confucianism research: (1) "basic theories of Confucian ethics"; (2) "universal value of Confucian ethics"; (3) "modern transformation of Confucian ethics"; (4) "Confucian ethics and economic globalization"; and (5) "Confucian ethics and youth moral education". The government, however, seemed more interested in the last branch of research, since all of its funding was allocated on research projects in this area. Similarly, some of the OMRI's projects funded by the BMG were related to building family ethics and morality education within local communities and villages.[35] The BMG's instrumental approach to Confucian research was confirmed by my interviewees in other higher educational institutes in Beijing.[36]

The local government's instrumental mentality is easy to explain. It can be attributed to the pressure imposed on them by the Cadre Responsibility System (CRS), which has been fully discussed in the previous chapter. Local officials control substantial resources and power, but they are also under pressure to make full use of these resources so as to obtain higher achievements in their local governance. As a result, local governments such as the BMG tend to maximize the use of their funding for intellectuals' projects, and prefer to subsidize those that can bring tangible benefits for local rule.

This instrumental or utilitarian principle enables local officials to adopt a flexible attitude towards Confucian intellectuals. Even those critical intellectuals who directly challenge Marxism and other official ideologies could sometimes get protection from local authorities, as long as they could benefit the local authorities in some way. The story of one researcher L (whose real name I cannot disclose) in a research institute in Beijing is a case in point.[37] L has long been critical of the official ideology and often expressed his opposition on the Internet under a pseudonym. He built an online forum (*wangshang luntan*) dedicated to discussing Confucianism, together with several other critical Confucian scholars. The forum is successful, attracting a large number of people and L, by actively participating in the forum, has gradually earned his fame online and even within the academic circle of Confucian studies. Some of his online discussions about Confucianism (using a pseudonym) were, in fact, sensitive and sometimes apparently anti-government. But the director of this institute did not show any disapproval of his actions and even commended him for building the online forum when I was there for my interview. Strange as it first seems, the whole story is simple. Although L has made anti-governmental expressions online, he worked hard on the institute's research projects, including those funded by the BMG. He viewed this as his job and believed promoting Confucian ethics as beneficial for society and therefore meaningful. More importantly, his fame earned from the online forum turned out to be an advantage for him to compete for research projects (or other financial resources) from social organizations and even enterprises, which the director was glad to see. The more projects the staff can obtain, the more financial revenues and the higher social reputation will there be for the institute. The director, therefore, turned a blind eye to L's sometimes excessive expressions online and did not report L's "problems" to higher officials. Maybe he reasoned that it was L's outspokenness that helped L to attain his popularity and obtain some of his research projects.

Local authorities' flexible control over critical intellectuals was confirmed by several other interviewees. One of the critical intellectuals whom I interviewed commented that local governments, especially their "practical divisions" (bureaucratic departments which are not closely related with ideology but are more associated with governance of practical affairs such as the local economy) were particularly open to him.[38] The case of another critical intellectual, Jiang Qing (蔣慶), is illustrative. Jiang earned his notoriety as an "anti-Marxist" as early as in 1989 when he published his article "*Zhongguo dalu fuxing Ruxue de xianshi yiyi jiqi mianlin de wenti*" (The Practical Implications and Its Problems of Reviving Confucianism in Mainland China) in the Taiwanese journal *Ehu* (*Legein Society*). However, he has still been invited to lectures, cultural activities, and academic conferences organized by local authorities since that time. For example, he was invited to make a public speech at Xiamen University[39] and during the 2008 Confucius Cultural Festival, which was organized by the local government in Qufu, Shandong Province.[40] These two speeches contained some sensitive messages such as "building a Confucian political system" and adopting Confucianism for political legitimacy. But local authorities did not stop him or censor his speeches afterwards. For local authorities in Qufu, Jiang Qing was a celebrity within at least academic circles. Consequently, his participation in the local Confucius Cultural Festival should draw attention from both academics and the public media, and therefore boost publicity for the Festival. However, it is worth pointing out that even though restrictions upon intellectuals and their discourses at the local level have been greatly relaxed, their freedom was not without limits. Intellectuals' criticisms against the regime cannot be too flagrant. They cannot initiate or participate in any collective action that aims to overthrow the government; or else even the most sympathetic of local authorities will have to send them to the police.

In sum, local authorities' support for Confucian intellectual projects, discourses, and activities, though mostly out of utilitarian purposes, extends certain freedom to these intellectuals. Their support, at least, serves as a positive gesture, symbolizing governmental recognition for the de facto legitimacy of Confucianism in local settings. Intellectuals, thus, obtain both financial and political resources for their work, though their freedom of expression is still limited. For the local authorities, their instrumental promotion of Confucian discourses has not only enabled them to co-opt these intellectuals, but also keep their work within control. For example, intellectuals in the OMRI, by working on the BMG-funded research projects and programs, tied their interests closely with the BMG. Their works produced by the BMG's funding were certainly beneficial for the BMG. In this sense, both the intellectuals and the local government have obtained their needed resources and therefore became mutually empowering.

4.4.3.2 Case Study II: The Establishment of the NSC in the PUC
The NSC was established by the PUC authorities in May 2005.[41] In 2008, NSC had 54 teachers of whom 25 were full-time faculty members as well as over 150 students including both undergraduates and postgraduates.[42] It is the first college-level institute in China that aimed to promote exclusively the teaching and researching of "national studies" (*guoxue*) or sinology. National studies refer to the studies of ancient Chinese civilization which covers a wide variety of subjects, such as ancient Chinese philosophy, religions, history, and architecture (Zhang 2007). Though broad in scope, national studies mainly concentrate on traditional thought such as Confucianism, Taoism, and Buddhism; and due to Confucianism's dominant position in traditional culture, national studies share considerably overlap with Confucianism.

Since the early 1990s, there have been strong voices for the promulgating of national studies among intellectuals. Some intellectuals in Hangzhou University, Wuhan University, and Beijing University had already undertaken small-scale teaching experiments to train students in professional knowledge of national studies long before the establishment of the NSC (Yuan 2005). In 1995, nine intellectuals, most of whom were well-known cultural celebrities, had openly called for the state's support in education of national studies.[43] However, no significant move from the state was seen. Again in 2004, initiated and led by five prominent intellectuals—Xu Jialu (許嘉璐), Ji Xianlin (季羨林), Yang Zhenning (楊振寧), Ren Jiyu (任繼愈), and Wang Meng (王蒙)—72 influential cultural figures jointly signed a "Cultural Declaration in the Year of Jiashen" (*Jiashen wenhua xuanyan*), which strongly appealed for social and state support for protecting "national culture". The building of the NSC is an active response to these voices. After the establishment of the NSC in the PUC, many other universities followed suit. For example, Beijing University and Qinghua University, two of China's most prestigious universities also built equivalent organizations for national studies. This has triggered a "domino effect" on China's other higher educational institutes and research organizations.

The building of the NSC is an important measure that the PUC authorities took to support studies of Confucianism. It privileges intellectuals with better access to academic resources, because as a college, NSC is better situated than "departments" or "research centers" in gaining opportunities for research projects from the university or the state.[44] In 2011 alone, its faculty had ten research projects funded and subsidized by the university and the Beijing municipal government.[45] In addition, with the PUC's backing, the NSC launched two academic journals, the *Journal of National Studies* (*guoxue xuekan*) and *Serindia History and Language Studies* (*xiyu lishi yuyan yanjiu*), which serve as important platforms for academic communications among intellectuals.

The president of the PUC, Ji Baocheng (紀寶成), who was the local authority in this institute, was critical to the establishment of the NSC.[46] He was the one that raised the proposal to create the NSC, and participated in the preparation work. He wrote at least five articles introducing and promoting the NSC in influential newspapers such as the *Nanfang Daily* and *Guangming Daily*, and all my interviewees in the PUC confirmed his role as the founding father for the NSC.[47]

President Ji's enthusiasm for the NSC was partly out of his commitment to traditional Chinese culture. He raised the proposal (bill) to restore traditional festivals as public holidays four times from 2004 to 2007 in the National People's Congress, and his proposal was finally put into practice in 2008 (Pang 2012). More than once he has publicly expressed his apprehension for the decline of traditional culture among the youth, saying,

> Some of our youth are so captivated by the Hollywood movies that they even do not know who is *Qu yuan* or *Si maqian* (the two are important Chinese historical figures). Some of our students can achieve high scores in TOEFL, but they cannot read simple ancient Chinese articles or even write a simple Chinese essay. (Kang 2008, p. 182)

With his overt support, a huge Confucius statue was erected on the campus of the PUC in September 2001, which was unprecedented in Chinese universities after the founding of the PRC. Thanks to his endorsement, in 2002, the PUC built a Confucius Research Institute and Chinese Traditional Culture Research Center (Kang 2008).

Ji's efforts to build the NSC were also partly motivated by the President Responsibility System (hereafter PRS),[48] a decentralized management system adopted in China's tertiary educational institutes. According to Article 39 of the 1998 Higher Education Law, all Chinese tertiary educational institutions should implement the PRS, under which the president has the authority to regulate and, at the same time, be fully responsible for the teaching, researching, and administrative work of the institution.[49] For Ji, he had the authority for institutional reorganization, personnel management, and funding allocation for the building of NSC. But he did so not just for his interest in Confucianism. As president of the PUC, he has managerial responsibility, that is, promoting the PUC's teaching and researching development, or put it directly, lifting the PUC's academic ranking. The establishment of the NSC, apparently, provided a good opportunity for enhancing the university's reputation in the teaching and researching of "national studies", as the NSC is the first of its kind and also biggest in terms of the number of professional staff and students in China. Ji, therefore, had strong incentives to make the NSC a creative exemplar for other universities to follow.[50]

The PUC authorities' control over intellectuals in the NSC and their academic works was different from the BMG's influence on the OMRI. It was much more subtle and implicit. During my fieldwork, I found that the research outputs by the NSC, unlike those in the OMRI, were more theory-based or academic in nature. They usually took a de-politicized approach and focused on historical studies such as specific questions concerning the historical evolution of Confucianism (or other traditional thoughts). For example, all of the 19 research projects finished by the research faculty in the NSC from 2007 to 2012 were about non-politically sensitive issues in Chinese history.[51] Such preferences for non-political and theoretical research can possibly be shaped by two factors. First, the PUC is funded by the Ministry of Education, part of the central government, which, as I have argued previously, is not interested in developing Confucianism as an ideology, not to say subsidizing such research projects. Thus, the NSC faculty had limited choices. Second, the NSC faculty was highly encouraged by the university authorities to produce high-quality research outputs. For the authorities, the more high-quality publications that can be produced, the higher the academic reputation that the PUC would have. For the faculty, non-political, purely academic articles or books had better chances to be published in influential outlets than politically sensitive ones, which can be easily blocked in the reviewing process. In addition, the PUC also tends to subsidize pure academic research. Therefore, most of the scholars in the NSC chose to conduct de-politicized theoretical research. As a result, though the PUC authorities, on the surface, did not intervene in the NSC faculty's research, they, in fact, controlled these intellectuals and their research work by tactically limiting their choices.

In all, the two case studies demonstrate two basic approaches for local authorities to influence these intellectuals' discourses: one is to buy preferred intellectual works using government funding and the other is to divert their discourses from excessive political involvement. They are both used by the two types of authorities, local governments and authorities in research institutes, except that local government officials are more inclined to use the first, while the authorities in research institutes usually prefer the second. This is related to the different power and resources that these authorities control. Local governments usually command financial resources but have limited ways to exert direct control over intellectuals, whereas authorities in institutes have direct control over intellectuals but sometimes insufficient funding. As far as intellectuals are concerned, whether at the elite or lower level, they are all susceptible for the two kinds of control. For example, the faculty in the PUC can also apply for the BMG's projects and those working in the OMRI are also advised to not get deeply involved in political writings.

4.5　Conclusions: Flexible and Balanced Control of Intellectuals

Since the late 1990s, there has been renewed interest in Confucianism among China's intellectuals. They saw the value of Confucianism in solving contemporary Chinese social and political problems caused by modernization and made efforts to revitalize Confucian traditions in the current Chinese social settings. Their public discourses and activities have attracted wide social attention. The Chinese state responded to them through a decentralized mechanism. Specifically, the central government was conservative, offering very limited support and even imposing restrictions on these intellectuals and their discourses. Some local authorities, however, were progressive, and they were seen as actively supporting intellectuals' work and activities on Confucianism. The two case studies show that while local governments were generally interested in intellectual work with instrumental value for local governance such as keeping social stability, local authorities in higher educational institutes tend to encourage intellectuals to produce research work on Confucianism that does not touch on the political order.

The decentralized responsiveness mechanism has a strong institutional basis. The central government, as head of the CCP organization and Chinese bureaucratic system, viewed the dominance of its official ideology as fundamental for its rule. A powerful and influential Confucian ideology is not to its advantage, as it may become a strong competitor for its official ideology. While for local authorities, they tended to be pragmatic about the Confucian revival and saw the potential value in manipulating Confucian beliefs and symbols for their local governance and career development. The local authorities' strong instrumental mentality was mainly shaped by the decentralized institutions which spurred them to make tangible achievements in their management performance.

The decentralized responsiveness has two distinctive features: the first is its flexibility in controlling intellectuals and their discourses, especially at the local level. Local authorities' utilitarian attitude allows them to transcend ideological barriers and even accept critical intellectuals. Whether Confucian intellectuals choose to work with the state, or to stay away from politics, or even to keep criticizing the state (within certain limits), as long as these intellectuals or their discourses are viewed by local authorities as instrumental for their career development (or other benefits), they could possibly get local protection and even preferential treatment. This is also beneficial for the growth of Confucian intellectual discourses and extending Confucian intellectuals' freedom.

The other feature is the balance of coercion and co-optation of Confucian intellectuals. The central government imposes restrictions on the Confucian revival, especially at the national level. In fact, it maintains strong power and resolution to crack down on any non-official ideology which challenges the dominance of its official ideology, just as what it did for the Falun Gong. In this sense, the central government's restrictions on the Confucian revival form a delicate balance with local authorities' utilitarian support for it. In other words, the decentralized mechanism allows the central and local governments to closely complement each other, reaching a somewhat balanced system of flexibility and rigid control. This chapter focuses on intellectuals' discourses of Confucianism. The following chapters will shift to Confucianism in two other social groups: the "Confucian entrepreneur" in private enterprise and urban middle class citizens and their education in Confucianism.

Notes

1. This is a part of Lipset's definition of intellectuals. He defined intellectuals as "all those who create, distribute and apply *culture*, that is, the symbolic world of man, including art, science and religion". See Lipset (1981, p. 333).
2. For a detailed discussion concerning the uneasy alliance between the monarch and Confucian literati, please refer to Levenson's study of the "love-

death" of Confucianism and the monarchy; see Levenson (1968) and Nivison (1959).

3. The phrase "dominated fraction of the dominant class" comes from Bourdieu (1990, p. 145).

4. According to Tu Weiming, Confucian intellectuals in ancient China were not only influential on the political stage but also in the social realm. They also took the function of priests and philosophers in Western society. For details, please see Tu (1993).

5. For a detailed discussion concerning the uneasy alliance between sovereign and Confucian literati, please refer to Levenson (1968) and Nivison (1959).

6. For details about the Chinese Democratic Party, see Wright (2004).

7. According to Goldman (2011), the CCP has adopted this strategy since the early 1950s.

8. For a detailed discussion of the cycles in the 1980s and 1990s, please refer to Ngeow (2007).

9. The recent scholarship tends to argue that the Hu and Wen regime restricted intellectuals' freedom in a consistent manner. See Goldman (2011) and Shambaugh (2007).

10. Jiang Qing's "political Confucianism" advocates creating a Chinese-styled political system based on *gongyang learning*, a kind of Confucianism embodying Confucius' "kingly heart and kingly way" (*wang xin wang dao*).

11. Kang Xiaoguang argues that Confucius's "benevolent governance" should act as the foundation of China's political legitimacy and insists on "Confucianization" as the direction for future political development in China.

12. Unlike Jiang and Kang, Ren does not openly claim the decay of official ideology in his academic works.

13. Cai Degui advocates "Practical Confucianism", which links Confucianism with social development such as rebuilding a Confucian spiritual home for the Chinese people.

14. Guo Qiyong supports a "Life Confucianism" in which Confucianism serves as a way of living for the Chinese people; see Wang (2004).

15. The title was given by Professor Fang Keli (方克力) from the Chinese Academy of Social Science. See Fang (2005). He also named the four representatives of the fourth generation: Chen Ming (陳明), Jiang Qing (蔣慶), Kang Xiaoguang (康曉光), and Shenghong (盛洪).

16. There is a detailed analysis of the so-called cultural conservatism; see Sina.com (2004).

17. Many news reports and journal articles contain this view. For example, Ho (2009), Dotson (2011), Bell (2008).

18. For example, both Premier Wen Jiabao's speech at Harvard in 2003, *ba muguang touxiang zhongguo* (Looking towards China) and President Hu Jintao's 2005 talks for provincial leading cadres, *zai shengbuji zhuyao lingdao ganbu tigao goujian shehui zhuyi hexie shehui nengli zhuanti yantaoban shang de jianghua* (Speech for provincial leading cadres at the seminar of building a harmonious socialist society) directly quoted words from the Confucian classics.

19. For example, according to Richard Baum, "The Confucian idea of a 'mandate of heaven,' where the emperor ruled with a virtually absolute mandate, provided he took care of the people, is very close to the modern-day notion of a benevolent despotism", quoted in Robertson and Liu (2006). There are similar views in China, only such views are expressed indirectly by commenting on the autocratic ROC (Republic of China) dictators' use of Confucian education as a way to promote its authoritarian rule in the ROC; see *Nanfang dushi bao* (2011).

20. Selected topics in the NFSS are classified into different categories such as philosophy, political science, history, and sociology; Confucianism is categorized as part of Chinese philosophy.

21. It is the 18th topic that year, "comparative research on Marxism and Confucianism".

22. For details, please refer to www.npopss-cn.gov.cn/GB/219471/219473/14842789.html

23. For details, please refer to www.npopss-cn.gov.cn/GB/219468/16505661.html

24. Although there are some documents supporting research of "traditional culture", but traditional culture in these documents does not necessarily mean Confucianism.

25. For this piece of information, I would like to thank Professor Peng Guoxiang from Beijing University for pointing it out to me.

26. This view is also shown in Goldman (1996, 1999).

27. In fact, the three interviewed critical intellectuals did not blame the central government during the interview.

28. Specifically, for a hundred plus universities that are affiliated with the central government, their presidents and CCP secretaries are assigned by the Ministry of Education (among these universities, however, approximately ten are directly controlled by the State Council). As for other higher educational institutes, their leaders are appointed by different levels of local government.

29. The full list of CSAs in China is available at the website of "Chinese Contemporary Confucianism" (*zhongguo dangdai ruxue wang*): http://www.cccrx.org/index.php

30. Interviewee 16.

31. Interviewee 19.
32. Interviewee 42 and 43; there are actually two directors in the OMRI. One is the dean and the other is the CCP Secretary there. Both of them agreed to be interviewed.
33. During the early stage of the OMRI, Professor Wang had had experienced delays in publishing his works as well as criticism from one newspaper controlled by the central government. However, since the beginning of the twenty-first century, the OMRI's two leaders said that their research and educational programs had received greater support from the BMG and some social organizations.
34. According to the dean, the BMG allocates some funding for their operational use, but the amount is not enough. Some of their income and operational fees rely on the donation of enterprises and some unofficial organizations. They are now allowed and even encouraged to collaborate with other segments of society.
35. For a detailed list of their research projects, please refer to http://baike.baidu.com/view/1471002.htm
36. Interviewee 41, 48, and 49.
37. In order to protect my informant, I will not provide the name of this institute here.
38. Interviewee 37.
39. For details, please refer to www.chinakongzi.org/rjwh/ddmj/jiangqing/200705/t20070523_2176686.htm
40. For details, please refer to www.scuphilosophy.org/ScholarsLibrary_display.asp?userid=563&art_id=6955
41. The central government gave its permission for the establishment of the NSC. On the day of the opening ceremony, one of the associate heads in the Ministry of Education came and delivered a speech as a sign of the center's approval. However, this approval cannot be exaggerated as the central authorities' support for Confucian studies. The establishment of NSC, to a large extent, remains a conduct of local authorities.
42. For details, please visit its official website: www.guoxuejiaoyu.com/
43. The nine figures are Zhao Puchu (趙朴初), Bing Xin (冰心), Cao Yu (曹禺), Xia Yan (夏衍), Ye Zhishan (葉至善), Qi Gong (啟功), Wu Lengxi (吳冷西), Chen Huangmei (陳荒煤), and Zhang Zhigong (張志公).
44. Interviewee 49.
45. Including one from the NFSS.
46. Ji resigned from the post of president in late 2011.
47. Interviewee 32, 39, and 49.
48. The PRS's full name is "President Responsibility System under the Leadership of the CCP Committee" (*dangwei lingdaoxia de xiaozhang fuzezhi*). The CCP committee here means the grassroots CCP committees

in the tertiary educational institutions. The PRS system has been reshaped again and again since the early 1980s. The Central CCP has issued several major documents to implement the system such as 1985s *Decisions on Reforming the Educational System*; 1990s *Document on Strengthening the Construction of the Party Organization in Higher Educational Institutes*; 1996s *Regulations on the Grass-Roots Organizational Work of the Communist Party of China in Higher Learning Institutes*; and 1998s *Higher Education Law*. For details, please refer to www.ebeijing.gov.cn/Elementals/InBeijing/StudyingInBJ/Laws/t1017526.htm

49. For details, please refer to www.ebeijing.gov.cn/Elementals/InBeijing/StudyingInBJ/Laws/t1017526.htm. For a detailed discussion of the PRS system, please see Law (1995).

50. President Ji himself has never implied that to attain managing achievements was one of his considerations in building the NSC. However, one of my interviewees informed me that the PRS was so significant for officials like Ji that he simply could not ignore this factor when he made his decision to build the NSC.

51. For details, please see http://guoxue.ruc.edu.cn/displaynews.asp?id=682

REFERENCES

Becker, J 1998, *Hungry ghosts: Mao's secret famine*, Henry Holt & Co, New York.

Bell, DA 2008, *China's new Confucianism: Politics and everyday life in a changing society*, Princeton University Press, Princeton.

Bonnin, M & Chevrier, Y 1991, 'The intellectual and the state: social dynamics of intellectual autonomy during the post-Mao era,' *The China Quarterly*, vol. 127, pp. 569–593.

Bourdieu, P 1990, *In other words: essays towards a reflexive sociology*, Stanford University Press, Stanford, CA.

Cai, D 1996, 'Shiyong ruxue chuyi' ('Discussions on the nature of practical Confucianism'), In Cai, D (ed.), *Lu Culture and Confucianism*, Shandong Friendship Press.

Cheng, Y 2008 'Liberalism in Contemporary China: ten years after its 'resurface'', Journal of Contemporary China, vol. 17, no. 55, pp. 383–400.

China Confucius Foundation (*zhongguo kongzi jijinhui*) 2009, *Zhongguo ruxue nianjian* (*China Confucianism Yearbook*), China Confucius Foundation, Jinan, Shandong Province, China.

Dickstein, M 1992, *Double agent: the critic and society*, Oxford University Press, New York.

Dotson, J 2011, 'Confucian revival in the propaganda narratives of the Chinese government', US-China Economic and Security Review Commission staff research report, July 20th.

Eyerman, R 1994, *Between culture and politics: intellectuals in modern society*, Polity Press, Cambridge.

Fang, KL 2005, 'Jiashen zhinian de wenhua fanxi—pin dalu xinruxue fuchu shui-mian he baoshou zhuyi ruhua lun' ('Reflection of cultural development in Jiashen years—comment on the emergence of the mainland new Confucianism and Conservative Confucianization Theory'), *Journal of Sun Yat-Sen University (Social Science Edition)*, no. 6.

Feng, C 2003, 'Shichanghua, quanqiuhua he Zhongguo zhishifenzi de jiaose zhuanhuan' (Marketization, globalization, and role changes of Chinese intel-lectuals), In Zhao B (ed.), *Zhishifenzi yus hehui fazhan (Intellectuals and social development)*, Huaxia chubanshe (Huaxia press), Beijing.

Fewsmith, J 2001, *China since Tiananmen: the politics of transition*, Cambridge University Press, Cambridge.

Goldman, M 1985, 'The zigs and zags in the treatment of intellectuals', *The China Quarterly*, December, no. 104, pp. 709–715.

Goldman, M 1993, 'The intellectuals in the Deng era', In Kau, MY & Marsh, SH (eds.), *China in the era of Deng Xiaoping: a decade of reform*, M.E. Sharpe, Armonk, pp. 285–326.

Goldman, M 1996, 'Politically-engaged intellectuals in the Deng-Jiang era: a changing relationship with the party-state', *The China Quarterly*, March, no. 145, pp. 35–52.

Goldman, M 1999, 'Politically-engaged intellectuals in the 1990s', *The China Quarterly*, September, no. 159.

Goldman, M 2011, 'Role of China's intellectuals in the People's Republic of China', In Kirby, WC (ed.), *The People's Republic of China at 60—an interna-tional assessment*, Harvard University Asia Center, Cambridge.

Goldman, M, Cheek, T & Hamrin, CL (eds.) 1987, *China's intellectuals and the state: in search of a new relationship*, Harvard University Press, Cambridge.

Goodman, D 2008, 'Class, stratum and group: the politics of description and prescription', in *The new rich in China*, Routledge, pp. 52–66.

Gu, EX & Goldman, M 2004, *Chinese intellectuals between state and market*, RoutledgeCurzon, London.

Gu, EX 1999, 'Cultural intellectuals and the politics of the cultural public space', *The Journal of Asian Studies*, vol. 58, no. 2, pp. 389–431.

Hamrin, CL 1987, 'Conclusion: new trends under Deng Xiaoping and his succes-sors', In Goldman, M, Cheek, T & Hamrin, CL (eds.), *China's Intellectuals and the State*, Harvard University Press, Cambridge, pp. 275–304.

Hao, Z 2012. *Intellectuals at a crossroads: the changing politics of China's knowl-edge workers*. SUNY Press.

Ho, N 2009, 'Unlikely bedfellows? Confucius, the CCP and the resurgence of Guoxue', *Harvard International Review*, 26 October.

Jiang, Q 2003, *zhengzhi ruxue—dangdai ruxue de zhuanxiang tezhi yu fazhan (Political Confucianism—the reformation, characteristics and development of contemporary Confucianism)*, Sanlian Bookshop Publishing House, Shanghai.

Jin, HH, Qian, YY & Weingast, B 2005, 'Regional decentralization and fiscal incentives: federalism, Chinese style', *Journal of Public Economics*, vol. 89, pp. 1719–1742.

Kang, XG 2004a, 'Renzheng: quanwei zhuyi guojia de hefaxing sikao' ('Benevolent politics: the legitimacy of authoritarian states'), *Zhanlue yu Guanli* (*Strategy and Management*), no. 2.

Kang, XG 2004b, 'Wo wenshenme zhuzhang ruhua: guanyu zhongguo weilai zhengzhi fazhan de baoshouzhuyi sikao' ('Why I advocates Confucianization: conservative thoughts about China's future political development'), *Yannan shequwang*, December.

Kang, XG 2008, *Zhongguo guilai—Dangdai zhongguo dalu wenhua minzuzhuyi yundong yanjiu* (*Back of China—research on the cultural nationalism movement in contemporary Chinese mainland*), Global Publishing Company, Singapore.

Kang, XG, Wang, J & Liu, SL 2010, *Zhendizhan: Guan yu zhonghua wenhua fuxingde gelanxishi fenxi* (Struggle for cultural hegemony: Gramscian perspectives of revitalizing Chinese traditional culture), shehui kexue wenxian chubanshe (Social Science Literature Press), Beijing.

Karabel, J 1996, "Towards a theory of intellectuals and politics", *Theory and Society*, vol. 25, no. 2.

Law, WW, 1995, 'The role of state in higher education reform in mainland China and Taiwan', *Comparative Education Review*, vol. 39, no. 3, p. 340.

Levenson, JR 1968, *Confucian China and its modern fate: a trilogy*, University of California Press, Berkley.

Liang, C 2010, 'Zhongguo ruxue yundong de fuxing yun qianjing' ('Revival and prospects of Confucianism in China'), *Hangzhou Shifan Daxue Xuebao* (*Journal of Hangzhou Normal University*), no. 2.

Lipset, SM 1981, *Political man* (expanded edition), Johns Hopkins University Press, Baltimore.

Lin, M & Galikowski, M 2000, *The search for modernity: Chinese intellectuals and cultural discourse in the post-Mao era*, Macmillan.

MacFarquhar R & Schoenhals M, 2006, *Mao's last revolution*, Harvard University Press, Cambridge.

Makeham, J 2008, *Lost soul: Confucianism in contemporary Chinese academic discourse*, Harvard University Asia Center, Cambridge, MA and London, England.

Meissner, W 1999, 'New intellectual currents in the People's Republic of China', In Teather, D & Yee, H (eds.), *China in transition: issues and policies*, Palgrave Macmillan.

Nanfang dushi bao (*Nanfang Metropolis Daily*) 2011, 'Minguo chunian guanfang changdao de zunkong dujing' (The promotion of Confucian Classics and reverence of Confucius in the early years of ROC), 30 January, AT06.

Nathan, AJ & Link, P 2001, *The Tiananmen Papers*, Public Affairs.

Nathan, AJ & Gilley, B 2002, *China's new leaders: the secret files*, New York Review of Books.

National Bureau of Statistics of China 2015, China statistical yearbook, Chapter 4, "Population", http://www.stats.gov.cn/tjsj/ndsj/2015/indexch.htm, accessed on June 1st, 2013.

Nivison, DS (ed.) 1959, 'Introduction', in *Confucianism in action*, Stanford University Press, Stanford.

Ngeow, CB 2007, 'Conceptualizing intellectual-state relations in China: with a focus on the contemporary era', *Issues & Studies*, vol. 43, no. 2, pp. 175–216.

Ogden, S 2004, 'From patronage to profits: the changing relationship of Chinese intellectuals with the party-state', In Gu, X & Goldman, M (eds.), *Chinese intellectuals between state and market*, Routledge Curzon, London.

Pang, Q 2012, 'A socio-political approach to the resurgence of traditional culture in contemporary China—a case study of the Chinese government's approval of four traditional Chinese festivals as public holidays', *International Journal of China Studies*, vol. 3, no. 1.

Price, RF 2005, *Education in modern China* [reprinted], Routledge, London.

Ren, J 2000, 'Shehui zhengzhi ruxue de chongjian—guanyu 'rujia ziyouzhuyi'de lilun' qidai' ('The reconstruction of socio-political Confucianism—about 'Confucian liberalism' theory'), *YuanDao*, vol. 7.

Robertson, B & Liu, M (2006), 'Can the sage save China?', *Newsweek*, March 20.

Said, E 1994, *Representations of the intellectual*, Pantheon Books, New York.

Shambaugh, D 2007, 'China's propaganda system: institutions, processes and efficacy', *The China Journal*, vol. 57.

Shambaugh, D 2008, *China's Communist Party: atrophy and adaptation*, Woodrow Wilson Center Press & University of California Press, Washington DC & Berkeley.

Sina.com, 2004, *Wenhua baoshou zhuyi taitou (The rise of the cultural Conservatism)*, viewed on January 30th, 2011, available at http://news.sina.com.cn/c/2005-01-18/11015584894.shtml

Thurston, AF 1988, *Enemies of the people: the ordeal of the intellectuals in China's great cultural revolution*, Harvard University Press, Cambridge.

Tu, WM 1993, *Way, learning, and politics: essays on the Confucian intellectual*, State University of New York Press, Albany.

Verdery, K 1991, *National ideology under socialism: identity and cultural politics in Ceausescu's Romania*, University of California Press, Berkeley, CA.

Wang, D 2004, 'Ruxue shi women de shenghuo fangshi—Guo Qiyong xiansheng fangtanlu' ('Confucianism as our way of living—interviews with Guo Qiyong'), viewed on November 8th, 2011, http://www.confucius2000.com/admin/list.asp?id=2911

White, LT 1987. 'Thought workers in Deng's time', In Goldman, M. (ed.), *China's intellectuals and the state: in search of a new relationship*, Harvard University Press, Cambridge.

Wright, T 2004, 'Intellectuals and the politics of protest: the case of the China democratic party', In Gu, X & Goldman, M (eds.), *Chinese intellectuals between state and market*.

Wu, C 2006a, 'Ruxuede dangdai fuxing jiqi zhexue jingyu' (The revival of Confucianism and its development in philosophy), *Zhongguo zhexue nianjian*

(*China philosophy yearbook*), Zhexue zazhi chubanshe (Philosophy Journal Press), Beijing.

Wu, G 2010, 'Xinshiji ruxue fuxinde shida biaozhi yu zhanwang' ('The ten signs of the revival of Confucianism in the new century and prospects for the future'), viewed on February 21st, 2011, http://www.cssn.cn/news/159326.htm

Wu, J 2006b, *Ziben yuanshi jilei zai zhongguo jiushi guozi de liushi* (*Primitive accumulation of capital and the transfer of state properties into the private sector*), viewed February 8th, 2010, finance.sina.com.cn/review/zlhd/20060208/09322325142.shtml

Yuan, W 2005, 'Ping jibaocheng xiaozhangde chongzhen guoxuelun' ('Comments on President Ji Baocheng's theory of reviving national studies'), *Nanfang dushibao* (*The Southern Metropolis Daily*), viewed on January 12th, 2012, http://www.southcn.com/nfsq/ywhc/ls/200506100291.htm

Zhang, EF 2007, *Guoxue jianshi (Brief history of national studies)*, Chongqing Publishing House, Chongqing.

Zheng, YN 2007, *De facto federalism in China: reforms and dynamics of central-local relations*, World Scientific Publishing, London.

CHAPTER 5

Confucianism with Consent: The Revival of "Confucian Entrepreneur" and the Chinese State's Responses

This chapter explores how the Chinese state has responded to the rise of the "Confucian entrepreneur" among private entrepreneurs since the early 1990s. It is critical because China's private entrepreneurs, whose numbers have grown exponentially since the early 1980s, is a key factor in determining the future of Chinese political institutions. With their ever-increasing economic clout, private entrepreneurs are crucial to the stability of the current political system, as they have both resources and the potential to challenge authoritarian rule (Guo 2003a; White 1994; White et al. 2004; Zheng 2004b).

For Confucianism, its contemporary relevance for the private entrepreneur is the concept of "Confucian entrepreneur" or "Confucian merchant" that arose centuries earlier. This concept, different from intellectual discourses in the previous chapter, is a practical notion that combines Confucianism with business practices. It refers to both a set of Confucian business moral codes and a kind of ideal Confucian businessman who applies Confucian principles in their business practice.

The rise of the Confucian entrepreneur poses challenges to the deficiencies of the official ideology. The enthusiasm to be a "Confucian entrepreneur" showed their growing thirst for social status and ideological affirmation; however, the official ideology has been inadequate in satisfying entrepreneurs' needs, due to its traditional denunciative stance towards the capitalist, even though heavy modifications such as the "Three

© The Author(s) 2019
Q. Pang, *State-Society Relations and Confucian
Revivalism in Contemporary China*,
https://doi.org/10.1007/978-981-10-8312-9_5

Represents" have been made to justify private entrepreneurs' contributions to the Chinese economy.

This chapter comprises five sections. The first and second sections provide the background for the research, introducing the entrepreneur's strained relations with the CCP and their resurgent interest in being a "Confucian entrepreneur", respectively. The third and fourth sections analyze the local and central governments' distinctive policies towards the rise of the Confucian entrepreneur. The last section is the conclusion. I conclude that the CCP has adopted a decentralized response pattern towards the "Confucian entrepreneur". On one hand, local governments actively promote and exploit the honorary title of "Confucian entrepreneur" to satisfy the entrepreneurs' demand for social reputation. On the other hand, however, the central government wants to downplay this demand. As it happens, official support for the Confucian entrepreneur is kept at the local level, and the Chinese government thus achieves its dual aims of both elevating the entrepreneurs' social status and maintaining its autonomy in ideology.

5.1   PRIVATE ENTREPRENEURS AND THEIR STRAINED RELATIONS WITH THE CCP

5.1.1   Private Entrepreneurs' Demand for Higher Social Status

The term "entrepreneur" refers to people who assume the risks of bringing together the means of production, including capital, labor, and materials, and receive reward in profit from the market value of the product (Schumpeter 2008). In the Chinese context, entrepreneurship can take place in both the public sector such as state-owned enterprises (SOEs) and private enterprises. However, the term "entrepreneur" in this chapter only encompasses entrepreneurs in the private sector. This is because SOEs are, in essence, a part of the Chinese state, and managers in SOEs are in fact state bureaucrats. The relation between managers in SOEs and the Chinese state is intrinsically different from that between private entrepreneurs and the state.

China's three decades of rapid economic development has given birth to a bourgeoning legion of private entrepreneurs with tremendous wealth. Since 1978, the private sector has grown at an annual rate of 20%, far above the economy's 8% average growth for the same period (Welborn

2002). In 2015, there were over 19 million private enterprises (*siying qiye*, economic entities that employ at least eight persons) and 51 million individual firms (*getihu*, businesses that employ fewer than eight employees) in China. Their registered capital has approached 140,000 billion RMB (National bureau of Statistics of China 2015). Even by 2007, the private sector has already contributed to 66% of China's GDP and 71% of tax revenue (Zhou 2009).

The rising entrepreneurs, with their ever-growing economic sway, are critical to the CCP's survival during modernization. Samuel Huntington (1970) points out that one of the main threats to an authoritarian regime is the "diversification of the elite resulting from the rise of new groups controlling autonomous source of economic power, that is, from the development of an independently wealthy business and industrial middle class". The history of first-wave democratization, according to Barrington Moore (1966), reveals that early European capitalists' burgeoning wealth independent of the state (or monarch) gave rise to their demand for greater political participation, a process in which democracy arose.[1] According to modernization theory, economic modernization will bring about social and cultural changes, especially value changes in favor of democracy (Diamond 1999; Huntington 1991). The entrepreneurial class, which accumulates enormous wealth and influence, once internalizing democratic values, would act as instrumental supporters for democratic transition.

The CCP has not been blind to such challenges. To overcome this, the CCP leader Jiang Zemin launched the Three Represents theory to win support from the newly affluent capitalist class, despite its apparent deviation from the traditional Marxist and Socialist canons. The Three Represents claims that the CCP represents "the development of advanced social productive forces, the direction of advanced culture, and the fundamental interests of the greatest majority of the people". The theory acknowledges private entrepreneurs as part of "advanced social productive forces", and based on the theory, CCP has selectively incorporated private entrepreneurs into the party organization and created formal and informal institutional nexuses with private enterprises and firms, such as implanting party branches in them (Dickson 2003, 2008; Tsai 2005).[2] Local Chinese state and private entrepreneurs have also developed various informal institutions to accommodate the entrepreneurs' growing demand for favorable economic policies and easy access to political power (Tsai 2005).[3]

However, although such co-optation strategies have enabled the entre-preneurs to enjoy some inclusion in China's political system (Dickson 2008), they have still fallen short of the entrepreneurs' demands for social status and reputation. This is closely related with Marxist tenets, which still serve as the foundation of the CCP's official ideology. The Marxist theory of sur-plus value, a key assumption of the ideology, postulates that "blood-suck-ing" capitalists who own the means of production appropriate the surplus value produced by workers and that workers should unite and rebel against their oppressors. This ideology has depicted entrepreneurs as rapaciously preying on workers, which has seriously eroded private entrepreneurs' social images. Although Jiang's Three Represents tried to justify the existence of entrepreneurs and their contributions to the Chinese economy, which marks redemption of the entrepreneurs, it does not claim that entrepreneurs are honorable, nor would the CCP even dare to claim so. In reality, the Three Represents has instilled much confusion while summoning opposition from the hardliners of the party, who put great pressure on CCP General Secretary Hu Jintao to put an end to the theory or change the direction of ideological propaganda (Heilmann et al. 2004; Holbig and Gilley 2010).

The lack of proper social recognition for private entrepreneurs is poten-tially dangerous for CCP's rule, given that social status is a key component of social influence and mediates many processes in which people are evalu-ated, rewarded, and directed towards power and wealth (Berger and Zelditch 1998; Ridgeway 1998; Webster and Hysom 1998; Zang 2008). In all cultures, individuals, and groups crave respect and recognition (Zang 2008). Lack of social status creates dissatisfaction and resentment among entrepreneurs towards the CCP, especially when they believe that this problem is caused by the current Leninist power structure. As can be seen in Table 5.1, China's economic elites considered their social status as being only at the middle or lower-middle level. On average, their per-ceived social status was only 5.36 across the range from 1 (the highest rank) to 10 (the lowest rank). Given that they actually occupied the high-est economic status in Chinese society, the contrast between their actual economic status and perceived social status is alarming. Research also shows that they believed they should enjoy at least the same social status as state cadres (Lu 2002). For example, when asked about whether "pri-vate entrepreneurs should enjoy the same social and political status as lead-ers in state-owned enterprises", 100% of the surveyed private entrepreneurs agreed or somewhat agreed (Lu 2002). In China, leaders in SOEs, strictly speaking, are government officials; thus, private entrepreneurs' total

Table 5.1 Private entrepreneurs' views of their social and political status

Level	Social status	Political status
1	1.5	1.2
2	3.8	3.4
3	11.6	9.7
4	12.1	10.5
5	27.9	21.9
6	18.2	15.8
7	10.9	10.7
8	8.2	11.0
9	3.9	8.0
10	1.8	7.8

Note: Levels 1–10 in the first column from the left are levels of social and political status, with level 1 being the highest and level 10 being the lowest. The numbers in the second and third columns from the left are percentages

Source: Chinese Private Economy Research Association (zhongguo saying jingji yanjiuhui), Report of The Tenth National Survey for Private Enterprises in 2012 (*2012 nian dijiuci quanguo siying qiyi chouyang diaocha shuju fenxi zonghe baogao*), China industry and Commerce United Publishing House (*zhonghua gongshang lianhe chubanshe*), p. 55

agreement with the previous statement suggests their dissatisfaction about their lower social status than government officials.

Such dissatisfaction may threaten the entrepreneurs' support for the CCP, especially in times of economic difficulties, for the history of the third wave of democracy has shown that once capitalists perceive that the regime is under challenge by broad parts of society, especially during an economic downturn, they may turn from regime support to covert and even overt opposition (Haggard and Kaufman 1995). This dynamic has played out in countries like South Korea, the Philippines, Brazil, and Peru, where businessmen shifted their support from government to the democratic opposition at a critical turning point (Bellin 2000; Huntington 1991). Thus, it is not enough for CCP to just induct the entrepreneurs into the political system. To stabilize its rule, the CCP still needs to fully co-opt entrepreneurs by enhancing their social status.

5.1.2 The CCP's Choice of Handling Entrepreneurs

Although the CCP needs to establish adequate support from the newly rising economic elites by carefully co-opting them, it cannot risk its autonomy by allying too closely with them. To survive, the CCP has to maintain its autonomy, and too close relations with one particular social class will easily lead to "state capture" by this class and result in CCP's loss of support among other social classes. Furthermore, excessive support to the private entrepreneur might possibly lead to their independency from the state, which would threaten CCP's rule in return.[4] Thus, the CCP cannot afford to cede too much social prestige to the entrepreneur, especially at the expense of its own autonomy such as compromising the official ideology or the current Leninist power structure (Evans et al. 1992). For the CCP to maintain its hold over entrepreneurs, it has to strike a balance between the two seemingly paradox tasks: on the one hand, to enhance the social status of entrepreneurs so as to establish their support and, on the other, to keep their social status within a certain level that will not endanger or harm the CCP's power structure. However, how can the CCP achieve this?

This chapter, by carefully examining the Chinese government's response towards the rise of the Confucian entrepreneur among entrepreneurs, reaches the conclusion that the Chinese government has shown its capacity in achieving the balance between co-opting and controlling private entrepreneurs by adopting a decentralized response mechanism. Local Chinese governments, out of their motivation to seek political stability and economic development (so that they could be rewarded with economic bonuses and political promotions), have acted as "catalysts" for the Confucian entrepreneur. They have manipulated the term "Confucian entrepreneur" as a badge of "social reputation" for embracing wealthy and influential entrepreneurs. But the central government, out of their wariness of being compromised by private entrepreneurs and fear of possible ideological competition from Confucianism, shows no overt support for the Confucian entrepreneur agenda. In this way, the local and central Chinese authorities have complemented each other in keeping the promotion of the Confucian entrepreneur at only the local level, effectively confining it within reasonable limits. Hence, the Chinese government, on the one hand, satisfies private entrepreneurs by taking active measures to elevate their social status and, on the other hand, avoids allying so closely as to risk losing mass support. The current Chinese political system, therefore, shows resilience in coping with the entrepreneurs' need for social status. However, before coming to details of how the government manipulated and appropriated the enthusiasm for Confucian entrepreneurship, the following section will introduce what is a Confucian entrepreneur and demonstrate why it is gaining popularity among contemporary Chinese entrepreneurs.

5.2   THE RESURGENCE OF THE "CONFUCIAN ENTREPRENEUR" SINCE THE EARLY 1990s

5.2.1   The Confucian Entrepreneur: History and Socio-cultural Implications

Before introducing the enthusiasm for Confucian entrepreneurism among the contemporary Chinese entrepreneurs, the following section will first define "Confucian entrepreneur" and elaborate its history in China. Confucian entrepreneur, after all, is an ancient concept. The rise of the Confucian entrepreneur in current China, in fact, bears close resemblance with its history. Then, what is a Confucian entrepreneur? Why did it gain ascendency among merchants in the ancient Chinese society?

Confucian entrepreneur (*rushang*, 儒商) literally means an entrepreneur who believes in Confucianism and gives primacy to Confucian principles in their business practice (Cheung and King 2004).[5] Because the Chinese word *shang* (商) refers to both "merchant" and "entrepreneur", the term Confucian entrepreneur in this paper also includes merchants when discussing ancient Confucian entrepreneurs. Thus, a Confucian entrepreneur is a combination of Confucianism and business practice. However, such a fusion had always been regarded as impossible before the Ming dynasty (1368–1644) because Confucianism, while emphasizing on subordinating material interests (*li*, profitableness) to moral principles (*yi*, righteousness), views profit-seeking business activities with contempt. For example, Confucius (551–479 BC) once said, "the gentleman can be reasoned with what is moral. The petty man can be reasoned with what is profitable" (*Analects*, Book 4). In the Neo-Confucianism that developed during the Song dynasty (960–1279), righteousness and profitableness represent two contrasting forces, *li* (principle) and *yu* (desire), and are viewed as irreconcilable.

The intermingling of Confucianism and business, or the emergence of the Confucian entrepreneur, can be attributed to the rise of a merchant class during the late Ming dynasty (1368–1644) and their strong desire for social recognition and political power. During this period, the Chinese economy developed rapidly, culminating in a series of business booms. This attracted a significant number of Confucian students (and scholars) to join the burgeoning cohort of merchants. Another reason for the Confucian students' participation in business, according to Yu, was due to population pressure. During this period, the total population increased from 60 million in the late fourteenth century to 150 million by the late 1600s (Yu 1997b). However, the quota for officials in the Ming dynasty did not rise accordingly. Thus, an increasing number of Confucian students had to relinquish their dreams of becoming scholar officials and seek business opportunities to support themselves due to this limited quota.

This gave rise to a sizable social stratum of educated merchants with at least some Confucian knowledge. Some of them were very successful, accumulating wealth in amounts that could even rival that of the state in the Qing dynasty (Yu 1997a, b). With this ever-growing wealth, this group of merchants became unsatisfied with their social status because in the Ming and Qing dynasty in China, where society was highly Confucian, merchants remained at the bottom of the social hierarchy. In the traditional social ranking, merchants' social status was even lower than that of peasants and workers, and far below that of Confucian scholars who had always been the elite of Chinese society. To achieve honorable social status and win social approval in society, these educated merchants claimed to pursue Confucian ideals by practicing Confucian values in their business activities. They claimed themselves as "scholar-merchants (*shishang*)" or "Confucian merchants". To justify their profit-seeking business activities, they argued that righteousness and profitableness were a duality rather than two diametrically opposed forces (Yu 2004). The implication is that they could be a righteous gentleman, although they undertake business activities which aim at making profits. Thus, the concept of "Confucian entrepreneur" served for the merchants' need for social status as "respectable gentlemen" (*junzi*) in a highly Confucian society.

Besides social recognition for businessmen, being a Confucian entrepreneur also involved adopting a set of Confucian precepts concerning how to deal with people by cultivating appropriate personality traits such as subduing selfish desire, practicing reciprocity, and keeping credibility. As Lufrano (1997) argued, the Confucian entrepreneur was not just followed blindly for vanity. It was of strong instrumental rationality, as in a minimally regulated business world such as the one in late Ming and Qing China where there were few government bureaus established to protect the market order, having a reputation of being a respectable gentleman would help retain and even enlarge one's business by the notion that the merchant is trustworthy and would not cheat his customers by unfair treatment (Lufrano 1997). In addition, it also emphasized some elements of Confucian teaching that were suitable for business such as modesty, affability, and patience. All these are active adaptations of Confucianism for business purposes.[6] Thus, Confucian entrepreneurs and the related

"Confucian business culture" flourished among merchants and entrepreneurs for about several centuries during late imperial China.

5.2.2 The Confucian Entrepreneur Craze Since the Early 1990s

Since the end of the nineteenth century, together with the sharp decline of Confucianism, Confucian entrepreneur also declined. The term "Confucian entrepreneur" had even been suppressed in Mainland China immediately after the founding of the People's Republic of China, which targeted both Confucianism and entrepreneurs as its major enemies. However, after its demise over several decades, the Confucian entrepreneur, interestingly, found its way back to China's newly rising entrepreneurs and experienced an unprecedented revival.

Since the early 1990s, rich businessmen, especially entrepreneurs and senior executives of private corporations, have shown great enthusiasm over the traditional notion of the Confucian entrepreneur. They take a strong interest in ancient Chinese philosophies (which include Confucianism, Taoism, and Chan, a Chinese version of Buddhism), especially Confucianism. For example, Pan Shiyi, chairman of the high-profile SOHO China Corporation, claims himself to be an enthusiastic reader of Chinese ancient philosophy (Hawes 2008). Zhang Ruimin, CEO of the Haier Group, one of China's most successful household appliance manufacturers, boasted of his passion for Chinese philosophy (Cheung 2002). They also endeavor to behave themselves as Confucian entrepreneurs by mastering ancient cultural skills such as composing poetry, practicing Chinese calligraphy and even music. It has become fashionable for economic elites to show off their "cultural achievements" by, for example, reciting sentences from the Confucian classics and playing ancient Chinese musical instruments whenever they are given even half a chance to do so. The recent popularity of high-priced "national studies courses", which target wealthy entrepreneurs and instruct them in the basic principles of Chinese philosophy and cultural skills, is a case to show these entrepreneurs' strong interest in learning to be Confucian in their business practices.[7]

Besides labeling themselves Confucian entrepreneurs, they also take efforts to put Confucian philosophy into their management practices and even request their employees to study Confucianism. Their purpose is to promote so-called enterprise culture (qiye wenhua).[8] For example, Mao Zhongqun, CEO of the Fotile group, one of China's biggest manufacturing enterprises for kitchen appliances, established a Confucian management model in which all employees are required to learn Confucianism and even be assessed by Confucian ethic principles as part of their work performance evaluations. In a word, the status of the Confucian entrepreneur has grown so elevated that Wu Xiaobo (2004), one of China's most famous business commentators, once commented, "No (contemporary) businessman (in China) does not want be labeled as Confucian Entrepreneur".

The Confucian entrepreneur has also become an important agenda for both popular and intellectual discussions since the early 1990s. The 1990s has witnessed a burgeoning number of articles concerning the Confucian entrepreneur in newspapers, magazines, and scholarly journals. Figure 5.1 shows the rising number of academic articles with "Confucian entrepreneur" (*rushang*) in their titles from 1994 to 2016 in the Chinese Academic Journal database (*zhongguo qikan quanwen shujuhu*), one of the biggest Chinese databases in China. There have also been many national and international symposia and conferences on Confucian entrepreneur-related themes during this period (Makeham 2008); various Confucian entrepreneur organizations at both international and local level also grew rapidly, such as the International Association of Confucian Entrepreneurs (*guoji rushang xuehui*) registered in Hong Kong and local organizations such as the Yangzhou Association of Confucian Entrepreneur Studies (*yangzhou rushang yanjiuhui*) in Yangzhou, Jiangsu Province.[9]

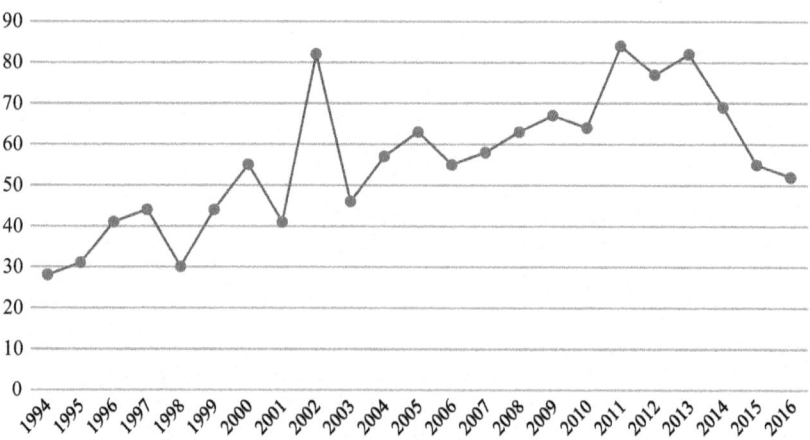

Fig. 5.1 The number of academic articles with "Confucian Entrepreneur" in the title. (Chinese Academic Journal Database 1994–2016)

5.2.3   Socio-economic Causes for the Confucian Entrepreneur Craze

The renewed interest in Confucian entrepreneurship has clear social underpinnings, among which the proliferation of higher-educated private entrepreneurs and their growing need for social recognition are the most important. The rapid increase of highly educated entrepreneurs since the early 1990s is fundamental for the rise of the Confucian entrepreneur, as it produced a large number of private entrepreneurs who may be susceptible to the notion of adopting a Confucian mindset in their business practices. Before the 1990s, China's private entrepreneurs were largely comprised of less-educated "self-made" entrepreneurs who used to be jobless rural youths and retired city workers before they started their own businesses (Li 2001). These people had little idea of "Confucianism" or Confucian entrepreneurship.

However, since the 1990s, a sizable number of educated private entrepreneurs have emerged. Some of these well-educated entrepreneurs are those who resigned from their former collective or state-owned work units and created their own businesses. Some used to be managers of former "state-owned enterprises" (SOEs) and "township and village enterprises" (TVEs), and they became private entrepreneurs during the privatization of the collective and state-owned enterprises in the middle and late 1990s. Some are entrepreneurs who ran technology-intensive enterprises since the late 1990s and are also called "knowledge capitalists" (*zhibenjia*). The rise of educated private entrepreneurs can be seen from Table 5.2. For example, in 1993 only 17.2% of the entrepreneurs had received college-level (including associate degree and bachelor degree) education or higher. However, in 2012, that ratio has jumped to 65.2%.

These educated entrepreneurs, with rapidly increasing wealth, are eager for social recognition. According to the fourth national survey of private entrepreneurs, more than 50% expressed their interest in building their own social image (Lu 2002). Another study by the Chinese Academy of Social Science also confirmed private entrepreneurs' thirst for social respect (Zhang 2002). However, they met similar dilemmas as those of the scholar-merchants of the Ming dynasty. Even though they controlled large sums of economic assets, their social status has not been commensurably high. This can be shown in a survey conducted in five major cities in 1993 in which respondents rated private entrepreneurs as lowest regarding social image and standing though the highest in terms of income and

Table 5.2   The education level of private entrepreneurs (1993–2012)

Year	Primary school and below	Junior middle school	High school (or vocational school)	College (including associate and bachelor degree)	Postgraduate
1993	10.9	36.1	35.9	16.6	0.6
1995	8.5	34.9	38.1	17.6	0.8
1997	6.6	31.5	41.7	19.5	0.7
2000	2.9	19.6	39.2	35	3.4
2002	2.0	17.5	41.9	33.5	4.9
2004	1.7	12.9	33.6	46.1	5.7
2006	1.5	12.6	36.6	44.8	4.5
2008	0.9	8.1	29.3	49.1	12.7
2010	1.2	9.2	28.4	54.2	7.1
2012	1.1	8.2	25.4	57.1	8.1

Source: All-China Federation of Industry and Commerce [*zhonghua quanguo gongshangye lianhehui*] and Chinese Private Economy Research Association [*zhongguo saying jingji yanjiuhui*], *China's yearbook for private economic sector* [*zhongguo siying jingji nianjian*] 2002–2004, 2004–2006, 2008–2010, and 2010–2012. China Industry and Commerce United Publishing House (*zhonghua gongshang lianhe chubanshe*)

earnings (Research Team 1993 cited in Zang 2008). According to research concerning the social prestige attached to different occupations, private entrepreneurs ranked only in the middle, especially in the early and middle 1990s (see Table 5.3), and still lagged behind state officials, particularly professionals and scientists (Xu 2000; Li 2005a, b; Zong 2016). One online discussion can clearly show negative social images and "inferior" social status of private entrepreneurs compared with intellectuals. In 2008, the news that professor Yuan Longping, China's most famous agriculturalist and "father of hybrid rice", had at least six luxury automobiles at his house triggered wide social discussions.[10] Contrary to the strong resentment against rich entrepreneurs who show off their wealth by driving high-class imported BMWs or Mercedes-Benz automobiles, virtually all of the online discussants supported Yuan, claiming he deserved even six private aircraft. While showing their heartfelt appreciations for Yuan and his contributions to China, most discussants expressed strong disapproval towards senior managers and bosses who earned multiples of an average worker's salary, criticizing them as "parasites" on society. The contrast in the public's attitudes towards rich intellectuals and entrepreneurs is illustrative, reflecting the general negative social image they have.

Table 5.3 Prestige scales: occupations in selected survey years

Occupation	1983	1987	1993	1999	2001	2015
Mayor		87.9	81.3	92.9	89.87	
Government minister		82.8	87	91.4	81.1	93.17
Professor	83.8	88.6	87.6	90.1	85.15	84.57
Judge		80.6		88.3		89.09
Court prosecutor			78.4	87.6		
Lawyer		84.2	70.8	86.6	76.12	82.04
Leading cadre in party or government body	68.1	77.7	71.9	85.7	72.41	
Natural scientist	83.8	84.5	75.5	85.3	86.49	83.82
Translator			67.1	84.9		76.77
Social scientist	82.7	83.5	79.2	83.9		
Doctor	86.2	80.9	68.8	83.7	67.04	80.38
Writer	81.7	87.4	67.4	82.5	71.3	
Reporter	81.1	83.2	66.2	81.6	77.32	75
Director or manager of large or medium-size state enterprise		79.4	76.9	81.3	78	87.69
Industrial or commercial administrator/tax officer		68.3	63	81.1	71.58	
Singer			55.1	80.1		81.18
Editor		83	65.2	79.7		
Bank clerk		68.7		79.1		76.4
Private entrepreneur		67.6	58.6	78.6	66.64	78.6
Film or TV actor	57.7		60	78.2	73.43	79.57
Air hostess			56.9	78		
Teacher in public middle or primary school	66.4	70.7	61.4	77.1	79.4	67.2
Policeman	43.8	65.7	66.5	76.2	69.44	78.44
Mechanical engineer			72.4	76		
Director of small state enterprise		73.6		75.9		
Sportsman	62.8		60.4	74.7	68.21	
Accountant in large enterprise	66.4		60.4	73.4	51.54	69.52
Ordinary cadre in party or government body	63	65.5		73.3		
Car driver in party or government body			59.8	70.1	57.11	
Cultural self-employed worker			48.5	68.2		
Political cadre in business unit or institution		63.9	67.6	66.8		
Industrial or commercial self-employed worker		62.2	48.3	65.7	42.67	67.96
Nurse	55.3	66.7	50.2	64.1	53.8	
Hotel cook		43.5	68.8	60.6	43.78	
Taxi driver		66.5	50.4	59.5	42.02	
Postman	46.3	63	42.3	59.1	68.21	
Bus driver	63.2	67.5	50.4	58.5		
Worker in an undertaker's		50.2	27.1	53	37.1	
Shop assistant	42.1	59.9	33.4	50.8	28.62	

(continued)

Table 5.3   (continued)

Occupation	1983	1987	1993	1999	2001	2015
Bus conductor	42.1	53.9	41.5	48.7	32.37	
Worker in large or medium-size stated enterprise		64.8	52.4	47.4		
Sanitary worker	25.9	54.6	28.5	45.5	34.79	
Peasant	57.9	28.2		44.7	31.82	45.86
Worker in town or village enterprise		59.3	43.2	44.3		
Restaurant waiter	39	58	33.2	43.5		
Worker in small stated enterprise		61.4		43.5		
Worker in collective enterprise		59.5	35.9	42.7		
Employees of self-owned laborer			23	37.7		
Housemaid	18.9	49.8	19.1	36.9	9.73	53.6
Sample size	1632	753	3012	2599	6193	986

Note: Numbers show the average prestige ratings for each occupation ranging from 0 to 100
Source: Xu (2000, p. 68), Li (2005b, pp. 83–85), and Zong (2016, pp. 13–14)

Private entrepreneurs' negative imagery can be attributed to an intensive and prevalent social sentiment involving "wealthy people hatred" or "anti-rich" (*choufu*) in contemporary Chinese society, which is clearly shown in the mass media and the Internet. For instance, a search for the word *choufu* on Baidu, China's biggest Internet portal, shows over 4.7 million hits in April 2012. In the public's eyes, entrepreneurs are usually assumed to be bad people without social responsibility, amassing their wealth by immoral means. First of all, these entrepreneurs are widely believed to attain their wealth not by their business acumen, hard work, or willingness to take risks but through immoral or even illegal means such as smuggling, bribing corrupt bureaucrats, evading taxes, speculating, stealing state assets, and various methods of deception (He 2007; Sun 2005; Wu 2006b; Zang 2008). Second, they were regarded as lacking a sense of social responsibility. The rich are often described as selfish and showy, lavishing money on luxury but very stingy on charitable causes. For example, according to the *Nanfang Weekend (South China Weekend)*, the China Charity Federation received only 15% of its donations from domestic donors, in contrast to the 75% from overseas contributors (*Nanfang Weekend*, November 23, 2003).

Whether these images are in accordance with the newly rich entrepreneurs is another matter. The point here is that the entrepreneurs are eager to rid themselves of their perceived image so as to appear capable and socially responsible, hence elevating their social status. However, as has been discussed in the previous section, entrepreneurs cannot rely on the official ideology to win respectable social standing as it is impossible for the CCP to overhaul or inverse its ideology in order to honor the private entrepreneurs, although the CCP has made great modifications such as the Three Represents to justify the contributions of private entrepreneurs. In a word, the entrepreneurs cannot elevate their social status by virtue of state power and its official ideology.

In this context, educated entrepreneurs appropriated the rising enthusiasm for Confucianism among ordinary citizens, especially the reverence towards Confucian scholars who were strong on ethics. Just as their predecessors in the Ming dynasty who claimed themselves as Confucian merchants (which means that they were also Confucian scholars to an extent), some contemporary entrepreneurs also label themselves as Confucian entrepreneurs. They wanted to be viewed as "intellectual" entrepreneurs, who, though engaging in business, still practice intellectual activities and attain Confucian virtues by self-cultivation (Hawes 2008; Zurndorfer 2004). Their purpose is to build the image of a respectable businessman as one who is ethical and who has strong social responsibility.

Their claim to be Confucian entrepreneurs is shown in their frequent attempts to show themselves as cultural connoisseurs, by composing poetry, practicing Chinese calligraphy, especially through quoting traditional Chinese philosophy (Hawes 2008). For example, when Zhang Ruimin, CEO of the Haier Group, one of China's most successful household appliance manufacturers, was interviewed by a journalist who asked him what he considered was the most important thing for a CEO to know, he answered, "I'd say philosophy". He immediately quoted two verses from the *Daodejing*, a Taoist classic (Hawes 2008). As noted by Hawes, the reason why Zhang used the two quotes is that he wanted to be seen not just as a highly successful business manager but also as a deep thinker. Similarly, when Pan Shiyi, Chairman of the SOHO China Corporation, presented himself as an enthusiastic reader of the *Book of Changes*, a Confucian classic, he avowed that he was more than just a money-grubbing capitalist. Such displays of cultural attainments involving Confucian culture mean that they join the ranks of the cultural elite. In other words, "practicing culture", especially ancient Chinese culture, becomes a way of deflecting attention away from their poor social image within society.

To be sure, pursuit of social recognition is not the only motive for the entrepreneurs' interest in being a "Confucian entrepreneur". They are also interested in Confucian business moralities involved in Confucian entrepreneurship such as affability and patience because these old virtues, developed by their predecessors who were also merchants and entrepreneurs, still bear close relevance to contemporary business practice. Some Confucian business ethics have been developed into a so-called Confucian management philosophy (*rujia guanli zhexue*) that has become popular. Many entrepreneurs have actively introduced this philosophy into their management practice.

As has been analyzed previously, entrepreneurs' embrace of Confucianism is the active appropriation of Confucianism to attain higher social status and prestige. However, it is not all for vanity. They are also interested in some of the principles contained in the ancient philosophy which may prove to be beneficial for enterprise management. However, their interest in greater social prestige may be even more complex. Their enthusiasm towards being Confucian entrepreneur does not only show their strong desire for higher social status and influence but also their dissatisfaction with the official ideology because the current official ideology simply cannot privilege them with higher social standing. Therefore, this embrace of Confucianism in their entrepreneurship raises challenges towards the CCP's rule, especially its official ideology.

The following part (Sect. 5.3) of the chapter will first introduce local governments' active response towards these Confucian entrepreneurs, namely, their manipulation of these entrepreneurs to secure local investment. It will then move on to illustrate why local governments are motivated to do so. Section 5.4 shows the center's dampening activities towards the Confucian entrepreneur. Section 5.5 concludes the chapter.

5.3   Local Governments: "Catalysts" for the Rise of the Confucian Entrepreneur

Since the early 2000s, local governments have adopted strategies to respond to entrepreneurs' enthusiasm to adopt Confucianism in various ways, such as promoting various Confucian entrepreneur-related pageants, conferences, and public activities. Their purpose is to elevate these entrepreneurs' social status at least among local social groups. The local governments' motivation for meeting the entrepreneurs' desire for social status is mainly twofold: one is to co-opt private entrepreneurs, who have become an increasingly independent force, and the other is to secure more of their investments in the local economy. Both of these are closely related with the CCP's local cadre responsibility system (CRS) which put local officials' performance in preserving political stability and promoting local economy as the top indicator for assessing their job performance.

It needs to be pointed out that local manipulation of these Confucian entrepreneurs came to the fore with the CCP's launch of the Three Represents campaign in 2001. In reality, during the 1990s, the local governments' attitudes towards the Confucian entrepreneur were indifferent and even suspicious. The reason for the initial suspicion is that local governments were ambivalent about how to properly situate private entrepreneurs in their political and propaganda activities. Private entrepreneurs in orthodox Marxism and Communism are deemed as enemies of the socialist state and therefore should be eliminated; therefore, the local CCP ideological organs were uneasy about the Confucian entrepreneur. However, after the debut of the Three Represents, which justified private entrepreneurs' activities and even saw them being invited to join the CCP, some officials in the ideological organs became less concerned or worried about the Confucian entrepreneur.[11]

After the introduction of the Three Represents in 2001, some local governments were seen as actively promoting the notion of the Confucian entrepreneur. With the local government's backing, various "Confucian entrepreneur pageants" (*rushang pingxuan*, hereafter CEPs) and Confucian entrepreneur conferences (*rushang dahui*, hereafter CECs) were held in cities like Yantai, Shandong Province; Nanchang, Jiangxi Province; and Yangzhou, Jiangsu Province. At this time, over ten registered Confucian entrepreneur associations (CEAs) or Confucian entrepreneur studies associations (CESAs) were also established.

Among the various forms of activities organized and sponsored by local governments, CEPs and CECs (in which senior executives of SOEs could also participate) are the two most commonly adopted. While CEPs are mainly for local entrepreneurs and aim to incorporate their political loyalty, CECs are more for non-local businessmen. In these CEPs and CECs, local governments used the title of "Confucian entrepreneur" as a badge of honor and then conferred it on those entrepreneurs whom they favored and intended to co-opt. But this co-optation was selective because it only targeted upper-level entrepreneurs, especially those with large-scale enterprises, a formula called "grasping the large and releasing the small" (*zhuanda fangxiao*). The underlying rationale is that co-optation of entrepreneurs owning large enterprises is more instrumental to the CCP's rule since it means greater control of various business resources outside the state. And it was only affluent capitalists who could make large-sum investments and bring about large-scale economic growth, which is the top priority of the Chinese government.

5.3.1   Manipulation of CEPs to Co-opt Influential Entrepreneurs

Co-optation of entrepreneurs can be best illustrated by CEPs sponsored by local governments such as the Yangzhou municipal government in Jiangsu Province, Jining municipal government in Shandong Province, and Nanchang in Jiangxi Province. Among them, the CEP in Yangzhou will be chosen for the following case study. The rationale for this selection is that in this case, the Yangzhou government has been more heavily involved than any other local government in other CEPs. Virtually all Yangzhou government branches related to economic affairs have participated in the CEP such as the Industry and Commerce Administration Bureau and Taxation Administration Bureau. The director of the CCP Propaganda Department in Yangzhou was the leader for the Yangzhou CEP organization committee and has directly controlled the whole process.[12] Thus, the Yangzhou CEP case should best represent local government's intentions for holding the CEPs.

The Yangzhou municipal government has held two CEPs, in 2005 and 2010. In 2005, there were 21 entrepreneurs receiving the honor of being deemed a "Confucian entrepreneur" and the number increased to 45 in 2010. In my fieldwork in Yangzhou in 2011, one of the organizers for the two CEPs provided extensive details about the two CEPs, revealing the government's intention of co-opting entrepreneurs. For example, in both of the two CEPs, in order to meet the entrepreneur's strong desire for a good public reputation, the government endeavored to augment the publicity for the CEPs and the winners by heavy media coverage and various kinds of promotion, a strategy called "creating the brand of 'Confucian entrepreneur'" (*dazao rushang pinpai*). As a kind of social reputation, the term "Confucian entrepreneur" has its greatest value when it is recognized by a wide range of audiences. The Yangzhou government, apparently, was aware of this. They spared no effort in enhancing the influence of their CEPs. To begin with, they designed the CEP as a "public election" so as to attract public attention. They promoted the pageant through various government-controlled media outlets, local daily newspapers, television, and Internet websites and invited all Yangzhou citizens to vote for their favored candidates, by online or small message service (SMS) or mailing (concerning the details of the 2005 CEP, please see *Yangzhou rushang yanjiuhui* [Yangzhou Confucian Entrepreneur Studies Association] 2007). Second, the government made carefully designed live TV shows featuring the award ceremony in which winners of the CEP were formally conferred the title of "Confucian entrepreneur" by leaders of the Yangzhou municipal government, including the mayor himself. The live show included songs and dances in praise of the Confucian entrepreneurs' contribution to local society (*Yangzhou rushang yanjiuhui* [Yangzhou Confucian Entrepreneur Studies Association] 2007). Last but not least, following the pageant, the organizing committee continued to publicize the selected Confucian entrepreneurs by exhibiting their photographs in the local communities and compiling their photo albums and biographies for publication (*Yangzhou rushang yanjiuhui* [Yangzhou Confucian Entrepreneur Studies Association] 2007).

The CEP's function as a platform for the Yangzhou government to co-opt favored entrepreneurs can be demonstrated by the selection procedures of the candidates. First, it was the government who nominated candidates. Specifically, all of the 21 and 45 candidates respectively in 2005 and 2010 were selected by the government without any prior public consultation. Although the CEP was open to public voting to elect approximately ten "excellent Confucian entrepreneurs", and thus it seemed to be a contest with winners and losers, one interesting detail betrayed its nature of co-optation rather than competition; that is, no entrepreneur candidate participating in the CEP will fail to obtain the "Confucian entrepreneurs" award. The trick here was that the voting results only determined the ten most "excellent" Confucian entrepreneur awardees among the 21 candidates whom the government had nominated, while the remaining 11 candidates would also be deemed Confucian entrepreneurs. The difference between "excellent" Confucian entrepreneurs and "ordinary" Confucian entrepreneurs was not highlighted or stressed in the awards ceremony. Thus, the CEP became a win-win event for all participating entrepreneurs. After the CEP, the government established further communication mechanisms with the Confucian entrepreneur awardees. According to one informant, those awardees were organized into a club and they met regularly with senior officials such as deputy mayors of the Yangzhou City (interviewee 54).

However, this co-optation was not extended to every entrepreneur. It was selective and only targeted educated business owners with large enterprises who also met certain minimum moral requirements such as "credibility" and "social responsibility". Local governments' preference for entrepreneurs with large enterprises was clearly stated in the official document for the 2010 CEP, which stipulated that one of four criteria for candidature was his/her "business achievement" (*ji*).[13] The document further explains that "business achievement" means "great business performance of his/her enterprises", "his enterprise's business scale, profit, and social contribution should rank highly among those in the same industry in Yangzhou city", and "the enterprise should have made *prominent* (not just great) contributions to the economic development of Yangzhou city". The general profile of elected Confucian entrepreneurs confirmed the government's preference for extremely successful entrepreneurs. For the 2005 CEP, among the 21 Confucian entrepreneurs, six were leaders of the top 32 large-scale industrial enterprises in Yangzhou for 2004. All of these 21 entrepreneurs had owned and managed enterprises with large volumes of production and sales revenue. In terms of sales income, the highest was over 750 million RMB and the lowest was around 50 million.[14] In the 2010 CEP, the scales of the 45 candidates' enterprises, on average, were even bigger that those in 2005.

The government also had a preference for educated entrepreneurs. In the 2005 CEP, all of the participants had received at least an associate degree, and two had a postgraduate education. In 2010, 93.3% had university education and around ten were postgraduates.[15] The co-optation formula is quite similar to the formula for assimilating potential entrepreneurs into the party, which prefers to incorporate young, male, highly educated entrepreneurs who own large-scale enterprises or firms into the party (Dickson 2008). The logic here is that since the government has only limited resources for co-optation, their optimal strategy is to focus on the most influential entrepreneurs who control the greatest resources so as to maximize the positive effect. If an entrepreneur is male and educated, he should have better potential for greater career prospects, which means he could contribute more taxes and provide more job opportunities for local economy.

The government also favored those candidates who meet at least some moral standards, especially "credibility" and "social responsibility", in order to overcome the popular perception of private entrepreneurs' lack of moral scruples and their unlawful conduct. Tax evasion, for example, has deeply troubled the government. As estimated by the Chinese State Council

Development Research Center and the State Administration of Taxation, up to 70% of private entrepreneurs evaded taxes, underpaying by up to 50% (Whiting 2000). Their harsh treatment of workers such as delayed payments resulted in soaring number of strikes, which troubled both local and central governments who are desperate for social stability (Chan 2011). A large number of entrepreneurs' dubious business practices like producing fake or substandard food or medicine have added an extra burden to governments. The CCP now places great stake in private entrepreneurs' lawful and ethnic business behavior for its rule over society.

Co-optation of "virtuous" businessmen who are generally more honest and hold stronger social responsibility than average, according to one of my informants, can also serve as a kind of means to discipline the business behavior of entrepreneurs more generally.[16] The official document for 2010 CEP has put *de* (morality), *cheng* (honesty and credibility), and *ze* (social responsibility) as three major criteria for selecting candidates besides *ji* (business achievements). The document also set concrete measurements of the three criteria. For example, whether the entrepreneur is socially responsible or not should be judged by whether his enterprise has made charity donations and how much it has made; and if one entrepreneur's enterprise has evaded or underpaid taxes, this entrepreneur does not meet the requirement of *cheng*.

In a word, the CEP served as a platform for the local government to incorporate those rich, influential, educated, and socially responsible businessmen by making use of its controlled media and administrative resources. For selected entrepreneurs, they were given not only social status but also political opportunities such as meeting with leaders in the municipal government. The CEP also enabled the local government to reshape the notion of "Confucian entrepreneur" to their advantage. By inserting criteria such as social responsibility in selecting candidates, the government put its favored ethical content into the idea of what was a Confucian entrepreneur.

5.3.2   Exploitation of CECs to Secure Investment

Local governments manipulated the notion of the Confucian entrepreneur in order to win not only entrepreneurs' allegiance but also their personal wealth. Their exploitation of the Confucian entrepreneur was especially explicit when they wanted to solicit investment for the local economy. They simply conferred the honorary title of "Confucian entrepreneur" on wealthy businessmen who could be potential investors. Government-sponsored CECs was a tool for collecting investment to boost economic growth. A case in point is a series of "International Confucian Entrepreneurs Conferences" (*guoji rushang dahui*, hereafter ICEC) sponsored by local governments. This conference was initiated and organized by the International Confucian Entrepreneur Studies Association (*guoji rushang xuehui*), a non-official organization registered in Hong Kong. This conference has been convened six times since 1994. Except for the second event in Malaysia, the remaining five were all based in China, sponsored or supported by different local Chinese governments such as the Haikou municipal government in Hainan Province, Shanghai municipal government, Jining in Shandong Province, and Yangzhou in Jiangsu Province.

These conferences, nominally, were academic symposiums dedicated to intellectual discussions about Confucian entrepreneurship. However, in fact, this was only part of the truth. These conventions had another function. They served as a platform for local government officials to attract investment from participating entrepreneurs who, to be sure, would be awarded with various honors of being deemed "Confucian entrepreneur" in return. Since the third ICEC, the conference was simply divided into two independent sections: academic colloquiums on the "Confucian Entrepreneur" (*rushang luntan*) and business negation forum (*jinmao qiatanhui*). The two were virtually different meetings proceeding at the same time. The academics discussed Confucian entrepreneur-related topics in the colloquium, whereas the rich entrepreneur participants, who were supposed to be involved in the academic discussions, were, in fact, invited by local officials to tour around the local city and be fed with various favorable policies concerning local investment. A case in point is the sixth ICEC. The sponsoring government's aim of attracting investment is clearly shown in its mayor's opening speech in the business negotiation forum. Throughout the whole speech, there is not even a word concerning Confucian entrepreneurs but every aspect about investing in the city, including its prospering economy, refined traditional culture, suitable living environment, new favorable policies, and the government's improved bureaucratic efficiency. The whole speech seemed one long advertisement.[17]

During these conferences, local governments spare no effort to coax entrepreneurs to be honored with the title of "Confucian entrepreneur". During the sixth ICEC, virtually all the participating business representatives, approximately 100 in total, were bestowed honorary Confucian entrepreneur certificates. In fact, in the official documents issued by the government concerning the conferment of a Confucian entrepreneur award, it vaguely writes: "for all participating entrepreneurs, if they could meet the requirements of 'Confucian entrepreneur', they would be given a 'Confucian Entrepreneur' certificate by the organizing committee".[18] But it has never specified what the requirements of the Confucian entrepreneur were, and the result was that every entrepreneur taking part in the conference was awarded with a "Confucian entrepreneur" certificate.

In sum, local governments have actively responded to the entrepreneurs' interest in the "Confucian entrepreneur", by manipulating the value of the Confucian entrepreneur as a highly regarded title to co-opt wealthy and influential entrepreneurs. Their aim is, of course, to improve the social image of the entrepreneurs. Besides the alliance of local governments and entrepreneurs, governments' support of Confucian entrepreneur-related activities also implies that local governments acknowledge the de facto legitimacy of Confucianism in local society. Why would local governments be interested in co-opting entrepreneurs? What has motivated them to do so?

5.3.3   Institutional Motivation for Local Governments

The CRS is the underlying political system that motivates local government to co-opt private entrepreneurs through being awarded the designation of "Confucian entrepreneurs". The current Chinese political system is highly decentralized and is sometimes summarized as Chinese-style federalism (Jin et al. 2005). The CCP rules through the CRS in which the central government, on the one hand, entitles local cadres with considerable authority; and on the other hand, it closely monitors them by the cadre evaluation system (CES). The CES places high priority on political stability and economic achievement; and if local cadres can be positively evaluated by higher officials in these two areas, they will be awarded with economic bonuses and political promotions (Edin 2003; Whiting 2000). Thus, the local government is both credited with discretion to make decisions and motivated by strong incentives to take necessary measures to achieve political stability and economic growth.

To maintain political stability, the local government needs to co-opt entrepreneurs, who have become an increasingly strong and autonomous social force, especially when organized in social groups. As has been analyzed previously, the private sector in China has experienced robust growth and now contributes to almost two-thirds of China's GDP. These private entrepreneurs, with their accumulated wealth, are not satisfied with their comparatively low social status and began to seek social fame. Some of these entrepreneurs began to take interest in Confucianism, form and participate in Confucian entrepreneur associations, which unite these entrepreneurs as an aggregate and autonomous force which might impose challenges to the CCP's rule.

Although it is widely assumed that social groups in China are not autonomous, and even heavily dependent on the state, some organizations do possess considerable de facto autonomy. In fact, there are two basic types of civil organizations. One is top-down mass associations established by the party-state to represent different sectors of society such as All-China Federation of Industry and Commerce (*zhonghua quanguo gongshangye lianhehui*) for entrepreneurs and merchants in the business sector. The second is relatively autonomous non-governmental associations registered with the Ministry of Civil Affairs as "social organizations" like the various Confucian entrepreneur associations (CEAs) in our case. While the first type is "state-oriented organizations", which are closely affiliated with the Chinese government, the second is "society-oriented organizations", which are only loosely connected with the government (Lu 2010).[19] For example, in some of these society-oriented organizations, their directors are taken by retired government officials who normally do not interfere in the internal affairs of the associations unless the associations violate the government's regulations.

Altogether there are over a dozen CEAs in China. They have recruited entrepreneurs who are interested in Confucianism into an autonomous social force. As one example, the Yangzhou Confucian Entrepreneur Studies Association (YCEA) has around 160 members, most of whom are private entrepreneurs and intellectuals. Their honorary head is a retired former deputy mayor, and he seldom imposes any control over their activities. According to one of its vice directors,

> Members of YCEA often meet together and have some sharing activities about Confucian entrepreneurship. Usually the intellectual members go to those entrepreneurs' enterprises and make lectures concerning "Confucian management philosophy" or other ancient philosophies such as Chan Buddhism or Taoism to entrepreneurs and their senior staff. There are also activities among entrepreneurs themselves where they come together to discuss their common interests and concerns, and communication programs between entrepreneurs and intellectuals who will try to provide intellectual support for entrepreneurs and their management practices. (Interviewee 55)

It is these comparatively autonomous CEAs that have pushed for the government's co-optation of private entrepreneurs. According to one of my informants in the YCEA,

> The local government used to be suspicious about private entrepreneurs' joining together and worried that they may organize themselves to challenge the local government once they have some shared complaints concerning government policies. (Interviewee 56)

But later, the organizing committee of the YCEA, especially its director and honorary head (who used to be the city's deputy mayor), successfully convinced the local government that it is to the government's advantage to promote Confucian entrepreneurs because, on the one hand, the government can co-opt these entrepreneurs who might otherwise oppose the government out of grievances over their social status. On the other hand, the government can also make use of the Confucian entrepreneur to discipline entrepreneurs' business behavior.[20] Both help shore-up local stability. The local government accepted this advice. Other local CEAs also took similar efforts to persuade their local governments about the benefits of this co-optation.

Local governments are generally in favor of co-opting private entrepreneurs because after all, political stability is the top priority for local governments. In CCP's cadre evaluation system, political stability is so predominant that it is a "veto" indicator (*yipiao foujue*), which means that if there is one major social uprising (or mass event) in the local area, the local official will be removed from the position or prevented from gaining any further promotion, no matter how well he/she does in other fields such as economic development or urban planning.

Besides political stability, economic development is another priority for the Chinese government. To achieve economic development, investment is the key. Thus, local governments spare no effort to secure investment in local areas, and that is why they conferred the "Confucian entrepreneur" title to entrepreneurs who are willing to make substantial investments. Local governments doing so reaped their reward. For example, during the fourth ICEC, the number of total investments for those participating entrepreneurs was 1.1 billion RMB.[21] The number for the sixth ICEC was at least 3.1 billion RMB (Yang 2008). During the fifth ICEC, the Jining government struck 62 investment deals with conference participants, and the total sum of the investment reached 1390 million US dollars, of which 203 million were from overseas businessmen (most of whom were of Chinese origin).[22] Rumor has it that all top officials in Jining city were promoted after the conference.[23]

5.4   THE CENTRAL GOVERNMENT: "DAMPENER" FOR CONFUCIAN ENTREPRENEUR

5.4.1   The Central Government's Indifference to Confucian Entrepreneurs

The local governments have acted as "catalysts" for Confucian entrepreneurship in Chinese society. However, as has been analyzed previously, due to the authoritarian power structure, it is not in the CCP's interests to accord too much social accolades to private entrepreneurs, as these entrepreneurs, once given lofty social status, might become an independent social force and challenge the CCP's rule. How would the CCP balance the two? During fieldwork, it is found that the central government has taken the role of "dampener", though not necessarily "suppresser", with respect to the Confucian entrepreneur. The central government has not shown any overt support for Confucian entrepreneur in any official document. Even if certain CCP leaders such as Premier Wen Jiabao did mention Confucian entrepreneurs in their public addresses, their intention was to make use of it to discipline entrepreneurs' business behavior rather than promote their social status. For example, Wen made direct reference to the Confucian entrepreneur in his 2011 talk concerning the recent issues about food safety, but his purpose was to explain that entrepreneurs' ethic can be built on traditional Chinese culture such as the Confucian entrepreneur (Wen 2011). In fact, even for the purpose of disciplining entrepreneurs, the central government has not initiated or organized any program that is related with Confucian entrepreneurship.

Although there is some indication that certain sections of the central government such as the Ministry of Commerce may support the Confucian entrepreneur in some way, most of the evidence has turned out to be erroneous. For example, for one Confucian entrepreneur associations, The International Union of Confucian Entrepreneurs (*guoji rushang lianhehui*, IUCE), its current head is the former deputy director of the Ministry of Commerce (*shangyebu*),[24] which seems to suggest the close relations between the Ministry of Commerce and this organization. However, the fact is the former deputy director left his official post in 1998, and thus he could not officially represent the central government when he took the position as head of the IUCE in 2011. Thus, judging by the available evidence such as official policy documents, the central government shows very little formal support for the Confucian entrepreneur.

5.4.2   The Rationale for the Central Government's Dampening Attitudes

The reason for the center's lack of support is twofold. First, the Hu-Wen regime is cautious for granting higher social status to the private entrepreneur. Since Hu Jintao and Wen Jiabao assumed leadership in 2002, they have shifted from Jiang Zemin's pro-elitist route which emphasized urban economic elites to a more populist line, which focuses on the interests of the society at large, especially those disadvantaged in rural areas, at least in the ideological propaganda (Dickson 2004, 2008). Soon after Hu replaced Jiang as party general secretary, he made a subtle reinterpretation of Jiang's Three Represents by shifting the focus of the Three Represents from the first term, "representing the development of the advanced productive force", which was stressed by Jiang and also served as ideological foundation for incorporating private entrepreneurs into the party organization, to the third term, "representing the fundamental interests of the greatest majority of the people" (Hao 2000; Holbig and Gilley 2010; Yue 2003). Later, Hu raised his own ideological formula, the "Harmonious Socialist Society", which emphasizes improving social equity and taking care of disadvantaged social groups. The Hu-Wen regime apparently distanced themselves from Jiang's pro-elite strategy and was wary of trumpeting private entrepreneurs' contributions. The reason for their wariness lies in their fear that private entrepreneurs may become independent enough to challenge the CCP's rule; and more importantly, they also worried that too much privilege given to these economic elites will erode mass support for the CCP due to increasing economic inequality and social tensions between the rich and the poor. In fact, Jiang's Three Represents have already created great controversies both inside and outside the party as many have questioned that Three Represents betrayed the party's nature as vanguard of the working class. In the following year, in order to silence the controversy, Hu had to announce a temporary ban on discussions of the issues in the media, party organizations, and academic circles (Heilmann et al. 2004; Holbig and Gilley 2010).

Another reason for the current regime's aloofness towards the Confucian entrepreneur involves its fear about the possible encroachment of Confucianism into the official ideology. In order to control the private sector, the CCP has built party branches in private enterprises. According to the CCP's regulations, any enterprise with at least three party members should form its own party branch and those with less than three should establish a joint party branch with other enterprises or local business associations. In 2016, there were more than 1.85 million party branches and committees, accounting for 67.9% of the total number of private enterprises that met the conditions for establishing party branches,[25] and the number has been increasing, despite many difficulties in building party branches. However, if one entrepreneur promotes Confucianism in his/her enterprise, for example, by requiring their employees to learn Confucianism, it will create competition with official ideology and therefore party building. As Dickson (2008, p. 131) comments, "one hallmark of a Leninist party is the penetration of both state and society with a network of party cells". Walder (1994) also reasons, monitoring capacity is one of the key elements of a communist system. As it declines, so does the stability of the political system. Thus, the CCP still tries to build party branches even in private enterprises, although its capacity of doing so falls short of the rapid increase in numbers of private and joint ventures. Entrepreneurs' enthusiasm to be Confucian entrepreneurs and their active promotion of Confucian management philosophy among their employees would certainly affect the CCP's party building. Thus, the central government, though it would never suppress the Confucian entrepreneur, is at least not willing to see Confucianism growing too quickly and prominently in the private sector.

5.5   Conclusions

This chapter focuses on the popularity of Confucian entrepreneurship among contemporary private entrepreneurs and examines the state's responses to it. This popularity can be attributed to the emergence of a sizable stratum of educated entrepreneurs since the early 1990s and their strong desire for social status. These rich businessmen, by showing their mastery of traditional philosophy and cultural arts, intend to be viewed as not only materially rich but also culturally sophisticated, thereby gaining social prestige as cultural elites and thus elevating their social status in society.

The comparatively low social status of entrepreneurs has long been a problem besetting the newly rising economic elites, given that social status is an important form of social influence and is also closely related with political power. This poses challenges for the state. Private entrepreneurs, during China's more than 30 years' modernization, have accumulated substantial economic and financial resources which enable them to sponsor ideological discourses such as Confucian entrepreneurship to meet their burgeoning need for social status. This could be detrimental for the party-state's official ideology and the authoritarian power structure, because if the rich business elites cooperate with intellectuals, the combination of the two social forces will be difficult for the state to control.

The chapter finds that in line with its responses to Confucian intellectuals, the Chinese state coped with these private entrepreneurs' enthusiasm over Confucian entrepreneurship by a decentralized response mechanism. Local governments and the central state have very different responses. Some local authorities, out of motivation to seek political stability and economic development (administrative pressure imposed by the decentralized institution), have actively responded to private entrepreneurs' enthusiasm for Confucian entrepreneur. They organized and sponsored various Confucian entrepreneur-related activities among which the CEP and CEC were the most common. The CEPs mainly targeted local entrepreneurs (especially those with large enterprises, higher education, and social responsibility) and co-opted them with social status and political resources. The CECs were intended more for non-local entrepreneurs, particularly those who were willing to invest in a local economy. During both of the two activities, local governments turned the concept of the "Confucian entrepreneur" as an acknowledgment of good social reputation by using their controlled administrative power and resources and then conferred it to entrepreneurs whom they intended to co-opt. By so doing, they also kept their control over the power for interpreting the meaning of Confucian entrepreneurship and thus manipulated this concept to their own advantage. For example, they inserted some elements of "social responsibility" into Confucian entrepreneurship in order to strengthen local economic governance. With these governments' instrumental support, the Confucian entrepreneur as both a social status and an ideology has gained legitimacy at least in these local societies.

The central government, however, out of its wariness of being compromised by private entrepreneurs and fear for possible competition from Confucianism against its official ideology, showed no formal support to

Confucian entrepreneurship. In this way, local and central Chinese governments complemented each other to keep the promotion of the Confucian entrepreneur at only the local level, effectively controlling it within reasonable limits. Thus, the Chinese state, therefore, both co-opted private entrepreneurs and their wealth by taking active measures to elevate their social status and prevented these entrepreneurs from threatening its official ideology and power structure.

In comparison, local governments were seen as more active in supporting Confucian entrepreneurism than Confucian intellectual discourses. Compared with their limited financial subsidies on Confucian intellectual projects, they spent much more financial and human resources to accommodate private entrepreneurs' interest in Confucian entrepreneurism. This is related with the fact that private entrepreneurs command greater economic resources than intellectuals and are more helpful for local officials' career development including their control over local society. In parallel, the central government was also viewed as less stringent in managing Confucian entrepreneurism, as no specific regulations have been issued. This can be attributed to the fact that Confucian entrepreneurism has a small audience and poses comparatively fewer threats to the current regime than the Confucian intellectual discourses.

NOTES

1. A widely quoted phrase of Moore has been, "No bourgeois, no democracy" (1966).
2. Tsai (2005) has argued that entrepreneurs have, in fact, various informal links with the government.
3. Tsai (2005) has a detailed and insightful discussion about the various informal institutional adaptations that the entrepreneurs have developed with the government.
4. In reality, this rationale has long been grasped by the imperial state in the dynastic rule. The imperial state endeavored to reduce or downgrade the social status of merchants so that they had to rely on the state or the bureaucracy.
5. In fact, up till now, there has been no unanimous consensus upon the definition of "Confucian entrepreneur" in the Chinese academic community today. Some believe that all entrepreneurs who exhibit Chinese culture characteristics (whatever that means) should be called "Confucian entrepreneurs" (see Chen 2000).

6. It also reformulated those parts of Confucianism that originally were not closely related to business settings, for example, redefining "righteousness" (*yi*, originally meaning fairness and justice) as "not hurting others for the sake of profit" and "not acting against one's conscience". It ignored those that are not relevant to business, for example, the philosophical discussions of Way (*dao*) or Principle (*li*) in Neo-Confucian philosophy (Cheung 2002, p. 29).

7. These courses usually charge 60,000–500,000 RMB for a year, depending on their content. Their success shows that the Confucian revival is, in part, commercially driven. The rampant commercialism has actively stimulated the consumption of Confucian cultural products, especially among the rich.

8. Concerning entrepreneurs' promotion of Confucianism in enterprises, there are some detailed descriptions in Kang et al. (2010).

9. According to Ge Xin, there were over ten registered Confucian entrepreneur associations in China. For details, please see Ge (2010).

10. For details, please refer to http://news.sina.com.cn/s/p/2008-07-21/080415968573.shtml, http://edu.people.com.cn/GB/88733/115369/8580388.html, and http://bbs1.people.com.cn/postDetail.do?id=87459157

11. Interviewees 54 and 56.

12. Interviewees 54 and 55; the information can also be located in *Yangzhou rushang yanjiuhui* (2007).

13. The rest of the three criteria were *de* (morality), *cheng* (honesty and credibility), and *ze* (social responsibility).

14. For details, see *Yangzhou rushang yanjiuhui* (2007).

15. Information about these candidates and the whole CEP can be found at http://app.longhoo.net/vote/list.php?cid=184

16. Interviewee 56.

17. For details of this speech, see Zhou (2010).

18. The document was provided by interviewee 57.

19. There are approximately two million society-oriented organizations in China, and it accounts for approximately 20% of the total civil organizations.

20. Interviewee 55.

21. For details, please see http://www.gjrsxh.com/Article/ShowInfo.asp?ID=46

22. For details, please see http://www.gjrsxh.com/Article/ShowInfo.asp?ID=105

23. Interviewee 45.

24. This department was later renamed Domestic Trade Department (*guonei maoyi bu*) in 1993.

25. For details, please refer to http://news.12371.cn/2017/06/30/ARTI1498810325807955.shtml

Bellin, E 2000, 'Contingent democrats: industrialists, labor, and democratization in late-developing countries', *World Politics*, vol. 52, no. 2.

Berger, J & Zelditch, M 1998, *Status, power, and legitimacy*, Transaction, New Brunswick.

Chan, A 2011, 'Strikes in China's export industries in comparative perspective', *The China Journal*, vol. 65, January.

Chen, D 2000, 'Rushang jingshen yu 21shiji zhonguo ji dongnanya jingji fazhan yantaohui zongshu' (Review of the Seminar of Confucian entrepreneur spirits and the 21st century China), *Zhonghua Wenhua Luntan (Forum on Chinese Culture)*, Autumn.

Cheung, T & King, AY 2004, 'Righteousness and profitableness: the moral choices of contemporary Confucian entrepreneurs', *Journal of Business Ethics*, vol. 54.

Cheung, T 2002, *rushang yu xiandai shehui: yili guanxi de shehuixue fenxi (Confucian businessman and modern society: the sociological analysis of the relationship between interests and righteousness)*, Nanjing University Press, Nanjing.

Diamond, L 1999, *Developing democracy: toward consolidation*, Johns Hopkins University Press.

Dickson, B 2003, *Red Capitalists in China: the party, private entrepreneurs and prospects for political change*, Cambridge University Press, Cambridge.

Dickson, B 2004, 'Beijing's ambivalent reformers', *Current History*, vol. 103, no. 674, pp. 249–55.

Dickson, B 2008, *Wealth into power: the Communist Party's embrace of China's private sector*, Cambridge University Press, Cambridge.

Edin, M 2003, 'State capacity and local agent control in China: CCP cadre management from a township perspective', *The China Quarterly*, vol. 173, pp. 35–52.

Evans, P, Haggard, S & Kaufman, R 1992, *The state as problem and solution: predation, embedded autonomy, and structural change*, Princeton University Press.

Ge, X 2010, 'Zai dazao rushang de jianan jincheng zhong, wo yuanzuo lazhu zhaoliang manman changlu', In Zhou Xinguo (ed.), *Ruxue yu rushang xinlun (New views concerning Confucianism and Confucian entrepreneur)*, Shehui kexue wenxian chubanshe (Social Science Literature Press).

Guo, BG 2003a, 'Political legitimacy and China's transition', *Journal of Chinese Political Science*, vol. 8, no. 1–2, pp. 1–25.

Guo, X 2003b, *State and society in China's democratic transition: Confucianism, Leninism, and economic development*, Routledge, London.

Haggard, S & Kaufman, RR 1995, *The political economy of democratic transitions*, Princeton University Press, Princeton.

Hao, L (ed.) 2000, *Yi "san ge daibiao" wei gangling quanmian jiaqiang dang de jianshe (Comprehensively Strengthening Party Building with the "Three Represents" as Guiding Principle)*, Dangjian Duwu Chubanshe, Beijing, China.

Hawes, C 2008, 'Corporate CEOs as cultural promoters', In Goodman, D (ed.), *The new rich in China*, Routledge, London.

He, Q 2007, *"Yuanzui" zhi zheng houmian yincang de shehui jinzhang* (*Social tensions as reflected in the debate on "the original sin of the rich"*), viewed February 10th, 2007, http://www.epochtimes.com/b5/7/2/10/nl619404.htm

Heilmann, S, Schulte-Kulkmann, N, & Shih, L 2004, '"Die Farbe der Macht hat sichgeändert": Kontroversen um die Verfassungsreform in der VR China', *China aktuell*, vol. 1, pp. 33–39.

Holbig, H & Gilley, B 2010, 'In search of legitimacy in post-revolutionary China: bringing ideology and governance back in', *Politics & Policy*, vol. 38, no. 3, pp. 395–422.

Huntington, S 1970, 'Social and institutional dynamics of one-party systems', In Huntington, S & Moore, CH (eds.), *Authoritarian politics in modern society: the dynamics of established one-party systems*, Basic Books, New York.

Huntington, SP 1991, *The third wave: democratization in the late twentieth century*, University of Oklahoma Press.

Jin, HH, Qian, YY & Weingast, B 2005, 'Regional decentralization and fiscal incentives: federalism, Chinese style', *Journal of Public Economics*, vol. 89, pp. 1719–1742.

Kang, XG, Wang, J & Liu, SL 2010, *Zhendizhan: Guan yu zhonghua wenhua fuxingde gelanxishi fenxi* (Struggle for cultural hegemony: Gramscian perspectives of revitalizing Chinese traditional culture), shehui kexue wenxian chubanshe (Social Science Literature Press), Beijing.

Li, C, 2005a, 'The new bipartisanship within the Chinese Communist Party', *Orbis*, vol. 49, no. 3, pp. 387–400.

Li, CL, 2005b, 'Danddai Zhongguo shehui de shengwang fenceng: zhiye shengwang yu shehui jingjidiwei zhishu celiang' ("Prestige Stratification in the Contemporary China: Occupational prestige measures and socio-economic index"), Shehuixue yanjiu (Sociology Research), no. 2, pp. 74–101.

Li, C, 2001, 'Diversification of Chinese Entrepreneurs and Cultural Pluralism in the Reform Era, In Hua, SP (ed.), *Chinese Political Culture*, Armonk, New York.

Lu, X 2002, *Research report of the social strata in contemporary China*, Social Science Academic Press, China.

Lu, X 2010, *Dangdai zhongguo shehui jiegou* (*Contemporary Chinese social structure*), Social Science Academic Press, China.

Lufrano, RJ 1997, *Honourable merchants: commerce and self-cultivation in late Imperial China*, University of Hawai'i Press, Honolulu.

Makeham, J 2008, *Lost soul: Confucianism in contemporary Chinese academic discourse*, Harvard University Asia Center, Cambridge, MA and London, England.

Moore, B 1966, *Social origins of dictatorship and democracy: lord and peasant in the making of the modern world*, Beacon Press, Boston.

National Bureau of Statistics of China 2015, China statistical yearbook, Chapter 3, "National Economy", http://www.stats.gov.cn/tjsj/ndsj/2015/indexch.htm, accessed on June 1st, 2013.

Research Team 1993, 'Gaige de shehui chengshouli yanjiu' (A study of the aggregate levels of collective tolerance during market transition), *Guanli Shijie* (*Journal of Management Science*, vol. 5, pp. 189–98.

Ridgeway, CL, 1998, 'How do status beliefs develop?', *American Sociological Review*, vol. 63, no. 3, p. 331–356.

Schumpeter, JA 2008, *Capitalism, socialism and democracy*, Harper Perennial Modern Classics.

Sun, L 2005, *Zhongguo ziben yuanshi jilei de sanzhong leixing ji qi yinfa de wenti* (*Three types of capital accumulation in China and their problems*), viewed on April 7th, 2012, blog.sociology.org.cn/thslping/archive/2005/04/07/1375.aspx

Tsai, KS 2005, *Capitalism without democracy: the private sector in contemporary China*, Cornell University Press.

Walder, AG 1994, 'The decline of Communist power: elements of a theory of institutional change', *Theory and Society*, vol. 23, pp. 297–323.

Webster, M & Hysom, SJ 1998, 'Creating status characteristics', *American Sociological Review*, vol. 63, no. 3, pp. 351–352.

Welborn, JW 2002, 'Review for Kellee S. Tsai's *Back-alley banking: private entrepreneurs in China*', *Cato Journal*, September 22nd.

Wen, J 2011, *Jiangzhenhua chashiqin—tong guowuyuan canshi he zhonggong wenshi yanjiuguan guanyuan zuotan shi de jianghua* (Examine the fact and speak the truth – the talk with counselors of the State Council and librarians in the Central Cultural and History Research Center), viewed on May 13th, 2011, available at http://news.xinhuanet.com/politics/2011-04/17/c_121314799.htm

White, G 1994, 'Democratization and Economic Reform in China', *Australian Journal of Chinese Affairs*, no. 31.

White, G, Howell, J & Shang, X 2004, *In search of civil society: market reform and social change in contemporary China*, Oxford University Press.

Whiting, S 2000, *Power and wealth in rural China: the political economy of institutional change*, Cambridge University Press, Cambridge.

Wu, C 2006a, 'Ruxuede dangdai fuxing jiqi zhexue jingyu' (The revival of Confucianism and its development in philosophy), *Zhongguo zhexue nianjian* (*China philosophy yearbook*), Zhexue zazhi chubanshe (Philosophy Journal Press), Beijing.

Wu, J 2006b, *Ziben yuanshi jilei zai zhongguo jiushi guozi de liushi* (*Primitive accumulation of capital and the transfer of state properties into the private sector*), viewed February 8th, 2010, finance.sina.com.cn/review/zlhd/20060208/09322325142.shtml

Xu, X 2000, 'Cong zhiye pingjia yu zeye quxiang kan Zhongguo shehui jiegou bian-qian' ("Changes in the Chinese social structure as seen from occupational prestige ratings and job preferences"), *Shehuixue yanjiu (Sociology Research)*, no. 3.

Yang, X 2008, 'Shijian shi weidade chuangzao, zuihao de jianyan'(Practice is a great creation, a best test), *Xin Ru Bao (New Confucian Newspaper)*, June 20th.

Yu, S 1997a, 'Special overview: political enthusiasm exists side by side with politi-cal indifference', *Chinese Education and Society*, vol. 30, no. 3, pp. 65–72.

Yu, YS 1997b, 'Business culture and Chinese traditions—toward a study of the evolution of merchant culture in Chinese history', In Wang, G & Wong, SL (eds.), *Dynamic Hong Kong: business and culture*, The Hong Kong University Press, Hongkong.

Yu, YS 2004, *Rujia lunli yun shangren jingshen* (The Confucian ethic and the spirit of businessman), *guangxi shifan daxue chubanshe (guangxi Normal University Press)*, Nanning China.

Yue, QW 2003, *Ru dang xu zhi (What You Have to Know to Join the Party)*, Shanghai Renmin Chubanshe (Shanghai People's Press), Shanghai, China.

Zang, X 2008, 'Market transition, wealth and status claims', In Goodman, DSG (ed.), *The new rich in China: future rulers, present lives*, Routledge, London.

Zhang, H 2002, 'Special report on China's private entrepreneur', In Lu, X (ed.), *Research report of the social strata in contemporary China*, Social Science Academic Press, China.

Zheng, Y 2004a, 'The status of Confucianism in modern Chinese education, 1901–49: a curricular study', In Peterson, G & Lu, Y (eds.), *Education, culture and identity in 20th century China*, Hong Kong University Press, Hong Kong.

Zheng, Y 2004b, *Will China become democratic? elite, class and regime transition*, Eastern Universities Press, Singapore.

Zhou, K 2009, *China's long march to freedom: grassroots modernization*, Transaction Publisher, New Brunswick.

Zhou, X 2010. 'The institutional logic of collusion among local governments in China,' *Modern China*, vol. 36, no. 1, pp. 47–78.

Zong, G 2016, 'Gaige kaifang yilai woguo zhiye shengwang yiji paixu yanjiu' ('Study on Ordination and Changes of the Occupational Prestige Since the Reform and Opening up'), *Beijing gongye daxue xuebao (shehui kexueban) (Journal Of Beijing University Of Technology (Social Sciences Edition))*, April, 2016, pp. 11–17.

Zurndorfer, HT 2004, 'Confusing Confucianism with Capitalism: culture as impediment and/or stimulus to Chinese economic development', paper pre-sented to the Third Global Economic History Network Meeting, Konstanz, Germany, 3–5 June. *2005 Zhongguo siying qiye diaocha baogao (2005 investiga-tion of China's private enterprises)* 2005, viewed on January 13th, 2011, http://www.southcn.com/finance/gdmqgc/gdmqyyrl/200502030218.html

Attenuation, Appropriation, and Adaptation: The Confucian Revival Among the Urban Middle Class and the Chinese State's Responses

This chapter investigates the Chinese state's involvement in the rise of Confucian education among the urban middle class. The urban middle class is a rapidly burgeoning social stratum and it is expected that by 2025 almost half of the Chinese population would be urban middle class (McKinsey Global Institute 2006). This social group, together with its growing economic power and political participation, has become increasingly influential in shaping China's political future. Given the importance of ideology for the CCP's legitimacy, whether the CCP could keep at least some ideological hold over the urban middle class is significant for its rule.

Beginning in the 2000s, Confucianism has experienced a revival among the urban middle class, owing to China's concurrent urbanization and marketization processes. The urban middle class are pragmatic users (or practitioners) of Confucianism. Unlike intellectuals who usually have a thorough understanding of Confucianism and intend to develop it theoretically, the urban middle class, more often than not, have limited knowledge of what Confucianism entails. They are more interested in applying Confucian concepts and principles to solve problems in their family and social life rather than its theoretical underpinnings. For example, they want to seek guidance from Confucianism concerning proper behavior in the constantly changing and ever-materialist society.

This chapter chooses the upswing in Confucian education as a case study to explore the state's response to the Confucian revival among the

© The Author(s) 2019   197
Q. Pang, *State-Society Relations and Confucian
Revivalism in Contemporary China*,
https://doi.org/10.1007/978-981-10-8312-9_6

urban middle class. The rationale for choosing the case is that education is the most popular form of Confucian revival among the urban middle class. Concurrently, education has always been the primary instrument for the CCP to instill its official ideology among its citizens and therefore claim its political legitimacy.

This chapter is organized in the following sequence. The first section will briefly define the urban middle class and review its complex relations with the state. The second section will introduce the Confucian revival among the urban middle class since the early twenty-first century and examine its socio-economic causes. The third section will elaborate on the rationale for choosing urban Confucian education as the main case study. Sections 6.4 and 6.5 will provide a careful examination of how the central and local governments have reacted to Confucian education respectively. The last section is the conclusion.

This chapter argues that the CCP has responded to the popularity in Confucian education using a decentralized method in which the central and local authorities acted in different but complementary ways. The central government, by setting policy parameters confining the autonomous development of Confucianism, acted as a restrictive regulator. Compared with its dealings with intellectuals or private entrepreneurs, it made much more restrictive policy directions for Confucian education among the urban middle class. Local authorities were seen as actively promoting "centrally calibrated" Confucianism in innovative ways, both catering to the middle class's interest in Confucianism and enhancing public acceptance of the official version of Confucianism. In reaching this conclusion, this chapter refutes the common myth that the CCP gives its full support to Confucianism (Dotson 2011; Ho 2009).

6.1   THE URBAN MIDDLE CLASS' MULTIFACETED RELATIONS WITH THE PARTY-STATE

6.1.1   *Who Are the Urban Middle Class?*

The urban middle class in this article refers to people who live in the urban area and rank as the middle or lower middle class in the social strata. Urban middle class is a complex mosaic of social groups, encompassing five clusters of people in terms of occupation: (1) middle- and lower-level professionals and technical personnel, (2) clerks in various organizations,

(3) small private business persons, (4) commercial service workers, and (5) industrial workers. The middle class neither belongs to the elite circle nor the bottom of society. They are not political elites such as political leaders or higher-level state bureaucrats, nor cultural elites like top intellectuals or professionals nor economic elites like entrepreneurs, capitalists, and senior executives of large corporations. However, they are not those at the bottom of society, for example, migrant laborers and the unemployed. The boundary of the "urban middle class" in this book is broad. It contains two different subgroups measured by socio-economic terms: one is the typical urban middle class including professionals and clerks in various organizations, and the other is the lower middle class such as commercial service people and industrial workers.[1]

The reason for combining these two distinctive social segments into one category of "urban middle class" is because it is unnecessary to make differentiations of the two in the study. First, during my fieldwork, I found it difficult to spot the differences in these two groups' interest in Confucianism and their ways of embracing it. There is much overlap between the two groups' attitudes towards and ways of practicing Confucianism. The two groups, as the middle stratum in society, also share similar attitudes towards the current political system though different in degree. For example, both tend to view social stability as fundamental to their interests, although the upper middle class may be more pro-stability than the lower middle class. Accordingly, the Chinese government's attitudes towards them are roughly the same. The Chinese government will not grant them as many social prerogatives as to cultural and economic elites because as a middle social stratum, the two groups hold neither the intellectual power nor the economic resources to win preference from the government. Thus, this chapter does not clearly differentiate between the two social groups and uses "urban middle class" to cover the two.

6.1.2 The Urban Middle Class as Both Ally and Challenger to the CCP

The "urban middle class" is crucial to the CCP's continuing rule, especially in the long term. In 2016, China's urban population reached 792.98 million.[2] In 1979, when China began its modernization, less than 20% of the total population was urban. Now the ratio of the urban population has surged to over 57%, and the growth rate is approximately 3% every year. Within 20 years from 2011 on, the ratio of urban population is expected to reach 75% (Simpson 2012). Among the proliferated urban population, the urban middle class is a major part. The McKinsey Global Institute concluded that there were a total of 100 million Chinese middle-class households in 2009, accounting for 45% of the total urban population. By 2025, the number will have climbed to 612 million, constituting 76% of the urban population (McKinsey Global Institute 2006).[3]

The urban middle class acts as a double-edged sword to the current CCP regime, as it can be both a stabilizing and democratizing force. On the one hand, they tend to be pro-status quo in order to preserve social stability. As beneficiaries of China's economic reforms, they rely heavily on the current political system for their further economic and social development (Lewis and Xue 2003). Since the middle class have accumulated considerable wealth and private property, they have placed great stake in political stability and follow Mencius's dictum that "those with property are inclined to preserve social stability" (*You hengchan zhe you hengxin*; Mencius cited in Li 2010a). It is also argued that China's middle class is only interested in material wealth, not political power, and that they have already struck a deal with the CCP on the unspoken rule (*qian guize*) that the CCP develops the economy in exchange for their support (He 2006).

However, the urban middle class, with increasing consciousness of their political rights, is also seen as a potential challenger to the CCP's rule. According to research conducted by the CASS, they expressed stronger doubt about the official ideology and the current power structure than other social groups (Li et al. 2007). Another study shows that the new middle class are more cynical about policy promises made by the authorities, more demanding about the implementation of government policy, and more troubled by corruption than other social groups (Zhang 2008). A 2008 public survey also revealed that urban residents were far more dissatisfied with the central government's policies on consumer goods, the stock market, and the housing market than those who lived in small towns and rural areas (Li 2010a, b; Yuan and Zhang 2009).

The urban middle class may also turn out to be more enthusiastic in pursuing democracy. There has been much scholarly work arguing that there exists a causal relationship between expansion of the middle class and political democratization. In particular, Lipset (1959, 1963) claimed that a politically moderate and economically self-assured middle class is a crucial prerequisite for democratic transition, as the middle class's professional interests will precipitate growth of civil society and the rule of law, which are key elements of democracy. The middle class will also make use of the mass media whose power is dramatically enhanced by modernization and urbanization to disseminate democratic views and values. Huntington (1968) also believed that the newly rising middle class tends to be idealistic, ambitious, rebellious, and nationalistic in its formative years, although they may grow conservative later. Apart from the literature, historic records from South Korea, Indonesia, and Brazil all confirmed the critical role of the urban middle class in these countries' transitions to democracy (Koo 1991, 2001).

For the CCP, the best strategy to control the urban middle class is to maximize their potential for stability while minimizing their challenges. To ensure the urban middle class's role as "stabilizer", the CCP has carefully avoided hurting their vital interests by preventing economic fluctuations, protecting property rights, and meeting their demands for social improvement such as environmental protection, though in a very limited way; while at the same time, the CCP also spared no effort in shielding them from "excessive political attention" (Hu and Hu 2008).

However, most of the literature concerning the CCP and the urban middle class focuses on socio-economic aspects and ignores the ideological side, that is, how did the CCP try to control ideologies arising from the urban middle class? This is no less consequential to the socio-economic aspect of the question, given that ideologies are fundamental for political legitimacy and, consequently, regime stability. This chapter intends to answer the question by examining how the Chinese state has reacted to rising Confucianism among the urban middle class since the early twenty-first century. The following section will first describe the rise of Confucianism among China's urban middle class and analyze the socio-economic causes. It will then proceed to examine a typical case, the revival of Confucian education among the urban middle class and the state's involvement. Finally, the chapter will conclude with a short summary and discussion.

6.2 Confucian Revival Among the Urban Middle Class

Since early in the twenty-first century, Confucianism has undergone a revival among the urban Chinese public. This is shown in the surging public interest in Confucius and his teachings. The best example is the unprecedented popularity of Professor Yu Dan's TV lectures on Confucianism, entitled *Yu Dan's Reflections on "The Analects"* in 2006.

Her subsequent book based on the scripts of the TV lectures was also warmly received. Within a year, her book had sold four million legal copies across China and an estimated six million pirated ones, remaining at the top of the Chinese bestseller list that year. In the following year, the surging popular demand has given birth to over 100 kinds of books interpreting Confucianism (Chen 2007).

The revival of Confucianism is also shown in the rapidly rising number of children who were sent by their parents to study the Confucian cannons in various "Confucian kindergartens" (*quanrizhi jindian youeryuan*), "Confucian classes" (*dujinban*), and Confucian private schools (*jindian xuetang*) (Fig. 6.1). In Shenzhen alone, a southern coastal city in Guangdong province, there were at least 34 "Confucian classes" and "Confucian private schools" in 2009 (Shi 2010), and their number has risen to at least 40 in 2010.[4] According to one report from the International Confucius Studies Association, children learning the Confucian canons (including those in government-supported Confucian educational programs) amounted to over 10 million (Chen 2007).[5] The report also claimed that besides the 10 million children, there were at least 20 million supporting parents and teachers. In addition, various grassroots social groups that aimed to pro-

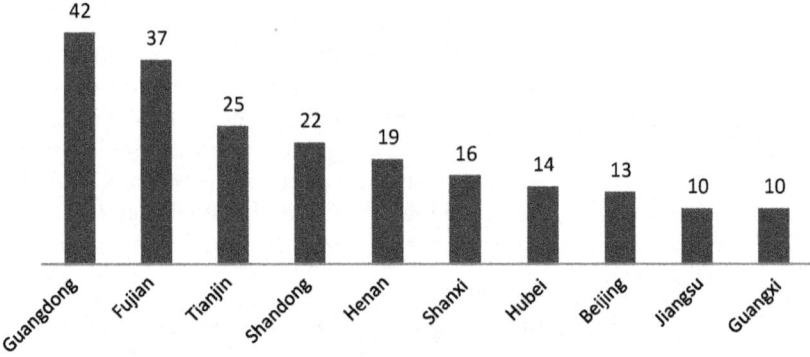

Fig. 6.1 The top ten provinces registering "Confucian Classes" and "Confucian Schools" in 2009. (Note: The number is from Shi Dajian, "Rujing songdu sichao zai minjian shehui xingqi jiqi dongyuan jizhi" (The rise of the trend of reading Confucian classics in the folk society and the mobilization mechanism), 2010, China Doctoral Dissertations Full-text Database, 185. The data may not be complete numbers as quite a few Confucian classes and schools do not get registered in local governments)

mote Confucianism also sprang up, among which *Yidan Xuetang* (*Yidan School*) in Beijing and *Mingde Guoxueguan* (*Mingde National Studies School*) in Tianjin are influential representatives.

There are also dozens of online (virtual) Confucian communities, which attract large numbers of followers. For example, one online Confucian discussion forum, *ruxue lianhe luntan* (Confucianism United Forum) had 11,715 registered members on November 15, 2009. Another similar forum, *Huaxia Fuxin Luntan* (China Revival Forum), had 23,366 registered members on January 19, 2010 (Kang et al. 2010).[6]

The resurgence of Confucianism among the urban middle class can be attributed to the widespread social anomie in urban Chinese society. "Social anomie" refers to an absence or diminution of standards or values (the so-called normlessness) in society (Durkheim 1997). It is closely associated with people's disillusionment with the Marxist and Maoist ideologies, which created an "ideological vacuum", or the so-called crisis of faith among the public.[7] As can be seen from Table 6.1, those who believed that socialism will eventually defeat capitalism are generally in decline within the eight years from 1999 to 2006. Quite a few subsequent studies on university students' job selection criteria also suggest widespread anomie in China, as they consistently show the prevalence of heightened individualism, which is manifested in emphasis on individual happiness and well-being, a stronger sense of independence, but a negligence of other people's interests (Bai 1998; Yu 1997a). It is against the "ideological vacuum" that Confucianism has restaged itself and quickly established itself again in urban Chinese society. During my fieldwork, the most often-heard reason for people to embrace Confucianism was "to calm my mind and get on with my life" (*anshen liming*) when I interviewed those who were interested in Confucianism.[8]

Table 6.1 Survey results on whether Socialism

	1999 (%)	2000 (%)	2001 (%)	2002 (%)	2003 (%)	2004 (%)	2006 (%)
Agree	72.2	65.8	56.9	52.6	47.0	45.5	49.3
Disagree	9.6	10.4	11.5	13.5	13.7	13.8	17.3
Not sure	18.2	23.8	31.6	33.3	38.3	40.7	32.7

Source: 'A longitudinal survey and analysis of the ideological status of the college students in capital of China in the past 10 years' [shinianlai shoudu daxuesheng de sixiangzhuangkuang diaocha yu fenxi] 2009, *Beijing jiaoyu (deyu) (Beijing Education (Moral Education)*, vol. Z1, p. 70)

The social anomie was brought about by profound socio-economic changes, among which China's accelerated urbanization and marketization processes since the early 1980s are the two most important ones. China's transition from rural society to urban society is one major cause for the extensive social anomie among the urban public. Social relations in rural society, according to Tonnies (1887), are based on kinship and tradition. Accordingly, the social bonds in rural society are based on shared moral sentiments and traditions (Durkheim 1984). However, social bonds in urban society are based on specialization and interdependence. Hence, urban people are considerably more autonomous and "self-interested" than rural people and the social ties between urban people are weaker than in rural society. The past 30 years have witnessed accelerated urbanization in China, during which people often felt the old rural social bonds that used to bind them had dissolved, but the new urban social ties have not yet been formed. Thus, many urban settlers began to experience different degrees of "social anomie". One indicator of anomie is the prevalence of depression within Chinese society. According to a 2013 public survey, approximately 90% of the 6027 respondents believed that anxiety had become a social disease (*shehuibing*) in China, among which there were 30.2% and 35.3% of the respondents reporting "extreme" (*feichang jiaolu*) anxiety and "very" (*hen jiaolu*) anxious, respectively.[9] Similarly, other research shows that because of social transition, life satisfaction in China fell from an average of 7.3 in 1990 to 6.5 in 2000, measured on a scale from 1 (low) to 10 (high). The percentage of those who described themselves as "very happy" plummeted from 28% in 1990 to 12% in 2000 (Brockmann et al. 2009).

Market reform since the 1980s is another cause for this social anomie. Before reform, most of the urban population were registered as residents and worked in state-owned enterprises (SOEs). They were highly homogeneous in socio-economic background and shared somewhat similar values concerning social transaction. The social ties were further strengthened by the "work unit" system (*danwei*) in which urban residents were provided with not only permanent working positions but also a "cradle to grave" type of social welfare which covered childcare, education, housing, medical services, and even elder care services. Because the welfare was highly inclusive for employees in one work unit, people who worked in the same work unit formed strong social ties and had close bonds with each other.

However, the market-oriented economic reforms, especially the reforms of SOEs during the 1990s, completely disintegrated the work unit system. Most urban residents now went to the commercial sector to make their living and even bought social services such as medical care and education. By 2007, the private sector had already contributed to 66% of China's GDP (Zhou 2009). According to a survey on college graduates conducted in 2009, it was found that nearly 80% preferred to work in various forms of private market enterprises (Ma and Yue 2011). With the replacement of the work unit system by the market economy, the previous social ties which used to link urban residents have been seriously eroded and social anomie has thus rapidly increased.

The widening social anomie prompted many of the new urban middle class to seek new ideologies or religions to comfort their mind or build inner tranquility amid the rapid social changes. Confucianism, a traditional ideology and a quasi-religion which had influenced Chinese society for over 2000 years, quickly found its way to the urban public. The urban middle class's sustained enthusiasm for Confucianism, however, posed potential threats to the CCP's rule. As has been discussed in the first chapter, Confucianism is different from the official ideology in some fundamental ways, though it also contains some elements that are compatible with the authoritarian power structure. If the massive interest in Confucianism was controlled by autonomous social forces, especially "adversarial" ones, it could become a powerful ideological power challenging and threatening the CCP's rule. How, then, would the CCP deal with the resurgent Confucianism keep it within control?

6.3   CASE STUDY: CONFUCIAN REVIVAL IN URBAN SCHOOL EDUCATION

6.3.1   The Rationale

Among the various forms of Confucian revival in the urban middle class, the revival of Confucianism in school education will be chosen as the case study for the chapter. "School education" in this article refers to precollege-level education covering primary school to high school (or vocational school) level. Most urban children receive at least some school education. This chapter mainly focuses on school education for children from an urban middle-class background, which is usually provided by urban public schools and middle-level private schools.[10] School for the children of the elite and migrant laborers will be excluded in this study because this chapter focuses on urban middle class. Although it is true that some children from cultural or economic elites' families also join public schools or middle-level private schools, the majority of students in these schools are from urban middle-class families.

One reason for choosing urban school education is because education is fundamental to both Confucian revival and CCP's legitimacy. For Confucianism, education is crucial for its dissemination among the populace, whether in the past or at the present. Historically, the spread of Confucianism was primarily achieved through education. Confucius himself was, first and foremost, a teacher, although he was also a philosopher and politician. Among his many posthumous titles, one of the most often used is *xianshi*, meaning "the foremost teacher" (Goldin 2011). Confucius was probably the first to accept disciples from middle- or even lower-middle-ranked families (*youjiao wulei*), a revolutionary measure during his lifetime which laid the foundation for the dissemination of Confucianism across China.

From 154 BC, when Dong Zhongshu advised emperor Han Wu about "revering only Confucianism and dismissing the hundred other schools" (*baichubaijia duzunrushu*),[11] Confucianism dominated Chinese education for more than 2000 years, except for a few short intervals, until 1912 when the Republic of China (ROC) formally abolished teaching Confucianism in schools.[12] Confucian education reached its peak when the Confucian Classics were set as the standard for imperial examinations for selecting bureaucratic administers in AD 605.[13] Historians generally agree that Confucianism has been able to outlive its status as a state quasi-religion and survived persecution, suppression, and revolution because it is sustained not by its social and religious privileges but by its close association with the study and education of ancient classics (Yao 2000).

In the same vein, for the current revival of Confucianism, education is critical. In fact, urban school education is probably the most extensively accepted form for reviving Confucianism among the middle class, involving almost 10 million children and at least 20 million supporting teachers and parents. It is through education as both a means of transmission and a value in its own right that Confucianism has been regenerated in contemporary China. During the twentieth century, Confucianism was forcefully suppressed and receded from China's political and social stage, and was no longer the guiding ideology for social and family life in China. Today, the only space it has regained is in education, both in schools and colleges.

In parallel, for the CCP, education is also crucial to instill the "proper" ideology among its citizens and therefore claim its political legitimacy. In fact, education and the mass media and publications remain the key ideological strongholds over which the CCP can never afford to lose its grip because unlike in liberal democracies in which consent is expressed through an institutionalized system of election, the Chinese political system still relies heavily on mass ideological education and campaigns to obtain and mobilize popular consent for its legitimacy.[14] Since the June Fourth Movement in 1989, CCP leaders have reemphasized the importance of ideological education. Deng Xiaoping (1994), when he reflected on lessons to be learned from the movement, claimed the biggest mistake was in the field of education, in particular ideological and political education. The next cohort of leaders Jiang Zemin and Hu Jintao, following Deng's instruction, launched successive ideological education campaigns among primary, middle, and even college students.

In addition, the state's policies concerning Confucian education in urban public schools is fully representative of its efforts to control the Confucian revival among the urban populace. Local authorities in Qingdao confirmed to me that the policies applicable for local education were more or less the same with the guidelines for public activities related with promoting Confucianism, for example, public lectures on Confucian ethics (*jiangzuo*),[15] special courses on Confucianism run by local community committees (*juweihui*), and courses on Confucianism for the elderly (*laonian xingquban*).[16] This is because all these public activities are finally subject to approval by the local CCP propaganda department who is also responsible for monitoring local education in public schools. Officials in local propaganda departments use similar policy frameworks to "guide" local ideological work, whether in public schools or local communities.[17]

6.3.2   Confucian Education in Urban China

Since the 1990s, there has been a grassroots educational movement aiming to revive Confucianism in Mainland China (for a detailed description of the bottom-up educational movement, please refer to Billioud and Thoraval 2007; Yu 2008), and it has quickly spread to most of the country,[18] especially cities in the rich coastal provinces such as Guangdong,

Fujian, and Shandong (Kang et al. 2010). Grassroots Confucian education mainly takes the form of Confucian classes and Confucian schools
(both of which will be illustrated later), and most are organized primarily
by and for the urban middle class. In Shenzhen alone, a southern coastal
city in Guangdong Province, there were 34 government-registered
Confucian classes and Confucian private schools in 2009 (Shi 2010). All
these based their curricula primarily on the Confucian classics.

"Confucian classes" (*dujingban*) refer to a group of students organized
for the purpose of learning ancient Chinese classics. It usually employs one
or two teachers and recruits children younger than 12 years. Its size ranges
from a few to a few dozen students. Most students come from urban
middle-class families and meet with teachers regularly, usually at the weekend for one or two hours' reading and teaching. Students are sent to these
classes by their parents; and in some classes, parents also participate in the
class activities. Some of the Confucian classes are run by certain social
organizations (e.g. some Buddhist groups) for noncommercial purposes,[19]
but others are purely commercial, such as some training companies in
China. Some of these companies are very successful and have even developed into chain corporations which have more than 30 different local
branches all over China. For example, *Tong Xueguan*, a children's training
organization which was created by an educational corporation in Beijing,
has approximately 32 branches in March 2012.[20] Other similar organizations include *Yansheng jingdian zaojiao zhongxin* in Taiyuan, Shanxi
Province; *Xindongli Jiaoyu jigou* in Wuhan, Hubei Province; and *Juzhai
sishu* in Suzhou, Jiangsu Province.

"Confucian schools" refers to full-time schools specializing in instructing the Chinese classics (*quanrizhi jingdian xuetang*). These schools are
operated by social groups (non-official groups), and most of them are, in
fact, kindergartens which recruit children younger than seven years.
Different from ordinary kindergartens, these schools focus their preschool
education on learning and reciting ancient classics, mainly Confucian
ones. A very small number of Confucian schools target students older than
seven years who are eligible for schooling; these schools, more often than
not, are small scale and adopt old-style teaching methods to instill
Confucian classics to the students. However, this kind of school is, in reality, illegal because it violates the Chinese Compulsory Education Law,
which stipulates that all eligible children should receive an education
which the government prescribes. Thus, a variant of Confucian school
involves those private schools (*minban xuexiao*) that adopt a double-track

system; that is, both normal education as required by the state and Confucian education are conducted in these schools. The only difference between these schools and other government-funded schools is that these schools conduct extra instruction in the Confucian classics, which, in fact, occupies the main part of the curriculum. One example of such schools is the Shiji Xianfeng School in Zhengzhou, Henan Province.[21]

6.4 THE CENTRAL GOVERNMENT'S CONTROL OF CONFUCIANISM IN SCHOOL EDUCATION

The central government is a serious regulator in its control over Confucianism in school education. Though it is only responsible for setting the basic direction and tone for Confucian education like it does for intellectuals and private entrepreneurs, it provides much more restrictive and detailed parameters. It has adopted two main strategies: (1) attenuation—replacing "Confucianism" by an ambiguous notion of "traditional Chinese culture" and (2) appropriation—co-opting particular Confucian elements into the official ideology to achieve its aim of both preventing Confucianism from competing with the official ideology while appropriating certain ingredients of Confucianism to strengthen the official ideology.

6.4.1 Replacing the Term "Confucianism" with "Traditional Chinese Culture"

The central government has responded to the Confucian revival in education, first and foremost, by supplanting the Confucian ideology with "traditional Chinese culture" (*Chuantong zhongguo wenhua*), a term that is deliberately more inclusive and ambiguous than the term "Confucianism". The government has never clearly defined what traditional Chinese culture is in its official documents. However, we can get some idea of its long list by referring to the textbook *Chinese Traditional Culture* issued by the Ministry of Education (Zhu 2010). According to this book, traditional Chinese culture is composed of not only "traditional Chinese thoughts", including Confucianism, Taoism, and Buddhism, but also ancient Chinese architecture, calligraphy, literature, drama, and customs and clothing, to name but a few. Even by this incomplete list, Confucianism can only be counted as *one* minor category of the all-inclusive "traditional Chinese culture", albeit an important one. By diluting Confucianism with the extensive and excursive term "traditional culture", the CCP has managed to limit space for the independent development of Confucianism.

This strategy is clearly shown in the Chinese government's major official documents concerning education and culture, such as the 2001 "Implementing Guidelines Concerning Civil Morality Building" (*gongming daode jianshe shishi gangyao*), the 2004 "Several Opinions Concerning Further Strengthening and Improving Youth Thought and Morality Building by the CCP's Central Committee and State Council" (*zhonggong zhongyang guowuyuan guanyu jinyibu jiaqiang he gaijin weichengnianren sixiangdaode de ruoganyijian*), and the 2006 "The Eleventh Five-Year Plan for Cultural Development, 2006–2010" (*guojia shiyiwu shiqi wenhua fazhan gangyao*, hereafter the 2006 document).

In all these documents, Chinese traditional culture is lauded. The 2006 document, for example, begins by stating:

> Chinese culture, which has over five thousand years of excellence, has greatly contributed to the development of human civilizations. It is the spiritual bond of our nation, the remitting dynamism of our country, and the source of our power in facing various difficulties and challenges.

In Section 30 of the said document, education in "the essences of Chinese traditional culture" was also explicitly emphasized. However, none of the above major documents ever mentions the word "Confucian", "Confucianism", or "Confucius". Rather, expressions which hold some Confucian connotations in these documents are expressions like "traditional culture" (*chuantong wenhua*), "Chinese culture" (*zhonghua wenhua*), and "Chinese traditional culture" (*zhonghua chuantong wenhua*). Even "national studies", which has a comparatively stronger reference to Confucianism, cannot be found in these texts.[22] Traditional culture in these documents, besides, was often vaguely referred to as Chinese calligraphy, painting, some classic arts, poetry, or the classics,[23] rather than Confucianism or its related activities. For instance, in Section 30 of the 2006 document, it clearly stipulates that

> In those primary schools where resources are available, classes in calligraphy, painting and other classical arts should be set and open for the students. At the middle school level, in the course of "Chinese" (*Yuwen*), the proportion of poetry and the classics should be increased. In both primary and middle

school, traditional culture should be incorporated into various disciplines or subjects by connecting traditional culture with their distinctive content.

Such "attenuation" tactic has been carefully implemented in education both at the central and local levels. A typical case at the central level is the 2011 official program titled "Red Scarf National Studies Inheriting and Educating Activities" (*honglingjin guoxue chuancheng jiaoyu huodong*, hereafter "Red Scarf Activities"),[24] which were initiated by the National Children's Work Committee (hereafter NCWC), an important body of the CCP's "ideological work" organ which specifically targets children younger than 14 years.[25] The content of the authorized textbooks for Red Scarf Activities clearly reveals the "attenuating strategy" (Xu 2007). This series of authorized textbooks, containing six volumes for the six different grades in primary schools, were composed of four different parts: the "Precepts", "Ancient Poems", "Ancient Essays", and "National Studies Garden". None of these highlight Confucianism. In fact, only one part, "Ancient Essays", contains some elementary Confucian classics such as *sanzijing* and *dizigui*, but they are so abridged that they cover no more than half of that part. In other sections, such as the "Precepts" and "Ancient Poems", only some scattered and fragmented sentences from the Confucian classics are selected.

However, other forms of traditional culture abound in the book. For example, in the section "National Studies Garden" (*guoxue yuandi*), various traditional arts are covered, such as calligraphy, painting, and even Beijing opera. However, none of them bears direct connections with Confucianism in content. Moreover, this part mainly emphasizes the cultural skills rather than appreciates the content of the paintings or dramas, which might be relevant to Confucianism in one way or another. Thus, in a nutshell, these textbooks put Confucian philosophy in a very subordinate or minor position.

Local educational authorities in Qingdao and Bao'an district, Shenzhen, during our field trip, were all seen as having placed great emphasis on "diversified forms of traditional culture", such as Chinese traditional music and calligraphy.[26] In the Bao'an district, educational authorities even encouraged local schools to develop their own "school-based courses" (*tese xiaoben kecheng*), instructing a certain form of Chinese traditional culture such as Beijing opera.[27] However, none of the schools provides any specialized courses on Confucianism.

It is true that there are some public schools that have put emphasis on Confucian classics, for example, public primary schools in Laixi, Qingdao, require their students to read and even recite the *Three-character Classics* and *Standards for Students*. Such elementary Confucian education is *never* the only and sole part of the traditional culture education in these schools. Compared with the education of other forms of traditional culture such as calligraphy and painting, Confucian education, in fact, is only given limited time and resources in public schools.[28] This is in contrast with some Confucian private schools (which are not government-funded and therefore able to enjoy some degree of autonomy in deciding their own curriculum) which concentrate their education on the reading of Confucian classics.

This attenuating strategy, on the whole, can be seen to be effective as most of the teachers and students interviewed during my fieldwork told me that they did not know much about Confucianism but only the "three-character sentences" embodying the Confucian ethics.[29] This strategy is skillful in that it allows a certain room for Confucianism in public education but denies its full development in such a way that the Chinese government can neither be said to suppress nor promote it.

6.4.2   Co-optation of Preferred Confucian Elements into the Official Ideology

The central government was also observed as selectively drawing elements of Confucianism into its official ideology, notably patriotism and "Socialist Concepts on Honors and Disgraces" (*shehui zhuyi rongruguan*, hereafter SCHD) in education policies. Patriotism and SCHD are two major components of the socialist core value system, which the CCP claimed as "the essence of the Socialist ideology" in its 17th National Congress in 2007.[30] The CCP has carefully selected useful ingredients from the Confucian canons and instilled them among students as an innovative way of promoting nationalism and civic morality. By so doing, the government, on the one hand, takes advantage of the prestige and presumed potency that Confucianism has already acquired among the populace and, on the other hand, deconstructs Confucianism and, more importantly, discards its philosophical premises such as idealism.[31]

6.4.2.1   Co-optation of Confucianism into Patriotism
Confucianism, or more broadly speaking, traditional culture, is compatible with official patriotism in two major ways. First, some Confucian ethics

such as *liguo* (benefitting the country) are in line with this patriotism. Second, instilling traditional culture itself is helpful for cultivating national identity, or the so-called national spirit in CCP jargon. In *Implementing Guidelines for Patriotic Education* (*Aiguo zhuyi jiaoyu shishi gangyao*),[32] a document for the official patriotic education issued by the Central Committee of the CCP, it clearly writes in Section 8 that

> We should carry out education in fine traditional Chinese culture..... The content of traditional culture is not only broad but also profound, comprising not only of achievements in philosophy, social sciences, literature and art, science and technology, but also a noble *national spirit, national integrity and fine morality*.... This rich cultural heritage provides valuable resources for education in *patriotism*.

A recent case of using traditional culture to strengthen patriotism is the official program, Red Scarf Activities, which has been discussed previously. This program, on the surface, claims to educate the young in national studies. In reality, the purpose of the program, as the organizer of the program has bluntly claimed, is to promote patriotism. In the preface that Li Wenge, the associate director of NCWC, wrote for the textbook for the program, he stressed patriotism and "making it the main rhythm of the program" (Xu 2007, p. 2). A survey of the textbooks for the program suggests that patriotism is, indeed, a predominant theme over others such as diligence, credibility, and frugality since the book for patriotism is, by all means, much longer than the others. Chapters related to patriotism are almost double the length of all other chapters (Xu 2007).

The emphasis on patriotism was followed by local educational authorities. For example, in the 2009 *Guidelines for Teaching National Studies* (*guoxue jiaoxue yaoqiu*) issued by the local educational authorities in Bao'an district, Shenzhen, the first and primary teaching objective is "to cultivate the students' *national spirit* for which *patriotism* and the *Zeitgeist* of reform and innovation (*gaige he kaifang de shidai jinshen*) are the two most important ingredients".[33] Official documents in Qingdao contain similar content. The textbooks compiled by the Bao'an Educational Bureau for instructing national studies closely follow the objective, with themes of patriotism always given priority.[34]

6.4.2.2 Co-optation of Confucianism into Civic Morality Education
The CCP has also actively combined Confucianism with civil morality education in schools. After 2006, when the SCHD was issued, an active

alliance between the two was forged. The SCHD is a set of moral concepts developed by the General Secretary of the CCP, Hu Jintao, and is also known as "Eight Virtues and Shames". It encompasses the following list of ethical values: (1) love the country, (2) serve the people, (3) follow science, (4) be diligent, (5) help each other and make no gains at others' expense, (6) be honest and trustworthy, (7) be disciplined and law-abiding, and (8) live plainly and do not wallow in luxuries and pleasures. These eight values largely overlap with the Confucian emphasis on *zhong* (loyalty), *ren* (benevolence), *zhi* (wisdom), *yi* (righteous), *xin* (sincerity and trustworthiness), *li* (propriety and manners), and *jian* (frugality). Some argued that the SCHD was a strong proof for CCP's embrace of Confucianism (Dotson 2011),[35] but this in reality only shows the CCP's appropriation of certain Confucian ethics rather than acceptance of Confucian ideology.

In the 2001 "Implementing Guidelines Concerning Civil Morality Building" document issued by the CCP Central Committee, the use of "traditional fine moralities" (*youxiu chuantong wenhua*) for moral education has already been clearly stated in Section 2, "guiding principles of civic morality building". It states, "We should insist on inheriting the *fine traditional morals* that have been forged in the previous thousands of years by the Chinese nation".

However, this does not mean Confucianism was made dominant in moral education. The use of Confucianism is kept subordinate to the guiding Marxist and socialist ideologies. In moral education practice, Confucianism was often reduced to a set of moral codes in the service of the official moral frameworks, with its philosophical foundations being discarded ruthlessly. A case in point is the moral education program promoted by the OMRI.[36] The "traditional virtues" promoted in the program can be summarized as *bade* (eight virtues): *zhong* (loyalty), *xiao* (filial respect for parents), *cheng* (honesty), *xin* (trustworthiness and credibility), *li* (rituals and respecting others), *yi* (uprightness), *lian* (frugality), and *chi* (sense of shame), a slightly different version of the SCHD. For teachers, their main job was to interpret the eight virtues and instill them among the teachers responsible for moral education in the primary and middle schools. However, the Confucian philosophical underpinnings for these virtues have been largely, if not completely, ignored in the program.[37] Similar educational campaigns have also been launched by some local educational authorities such as those in Nanchang and Shenyang (Lei 2006).[38]

Through this appropriating strategy, Confucianism (or traditional culture) has been employed as an expedient tool for ideological promotion, albeit with appeals that it had "traditional roots". This is not new in Chinese politics. Before 1949, the then ruling Chiang Kai-shek government had also adopted similar strategies in its Confucian-inspired moral education. Emblematic of this are Dai Jitao's theories linking Confucianism and Sun Yat-sen's Three Principles of the People (Zheng 2004a cited in Billioud 2007a). In imperial times, similarly, the state also mastered appropriating skills. They, in regulating popular religious beliefs, appropriated into its official pantheon (like the official ideology today) some popular deities who had already acquired a considerable following. In this way, the state took advantage of popular deities, which after being reshaped and restructured, served for the validation of the state (Shahar and Weller 1996); the CCP seems to be also proficient in this skill.

6.5 LOCAL GOVERNMENTS' ACTIVE PROMOTION OF CONFUCIAN EDUCATION

6.5.1 Local Innovations in Confucian Education

Although the central government has set some parameters for Confucian education, it is the local authorities that are the main agents in deciding relevant policies at the grassroots level. The local authorities, while following the center's "attenuation" and "appropriation" directions, made various innovations concerning Confucian education in their policy-making. Through fieldwork, I discovered that the instruction strategies and methods utilized in educating traditional culture were much more innovative and varied than those used in Confucian private schools (sishu). These innovations, in effect, enhance the public acceptance of the officially approved Confucian education. Thus, local authorities' measures have both accommodated some urban middle class' interest in Confucianism and exploited elements of Confucianism to the CCP's advantage.

In terms of teaching strategies, the locally formulated education of Confucianism (traditional culture) has been deliberately emphasized by local authorities to bear close relevance to students' life. For example, in the official document "Teaching Requirements for National Studies" issued by the Bao'an educational authorities in 2009, it is written clearly:

The teaching of national studies should be guided by Marxism and the Scientific Development Outlook, and *closely connected with students' real life*; and in the teaching practice, various educational reforms should be actively carried out so as to improve the educational quality.

The teaching methods used for Confucian education are also more innovative than those used for conventional ideological education or in private Confucian schools. For example, schools in Xigang, Dalian, were all requested to adopt a special way of reading and singing (*yinsong* and *gechang*) in their instruction of traditional poems and classics (Li 2010a, b). Teachers in Qingdao even combined students' daily morning exercise with Confucian education by creating a special exercise which uses some examples from the *Three-Character Classic* for rhythm. The students, by doing the exercise every morning, can easily remember the content of the *Three-character Classic*.[39] In Shenzhen, teachers adopted ways of debating and drawing cartoons to stimulate the students' interest, and they composed various songs with lyrics chosen from ancient poems for the students to learn.[40] In interviews with local education authorities in Shenzhen, I was told that teachers of national studies were particularly encouraged to develop inventive instructing methods in their classes.[41]

More importantly, local education bureaus have established a series of institutions to ensure the generating and sharing of innovations. The first and foremost of these institutions is the systematic and regular evaluations of the teaching performance of instructing "national studies" for all schools. In some regions, such assessment may take the form of unexpected class visits.[42] "Innovation" is a top criterion of the assessment. Competition is also introduced. Teachers and schools with outstanding performance are awarded with financial prizes. Innovation-sharing is also fostered. "Model teachers" are invited to make teaching demonstrations and share their experience through various channels such as official documents and periodicals disseminated to schools within the jurisdiction of the education bureau. Besides, one informant from local educational bureau in Bao'an reported that:

> We established channels to collect information, especially suggestions from core teachers. For example, we have built a team of part-time liaison officers, who were selected among full-time teachers in all schools, to monitor education in traditional culture and report back peer teachers' suggestions for improving education on regular basis. (Interviewee 10)

By contrast, such innovative efforts were much less visible in the education of official ideologies[43]; still less were seen in Confucian private schools.[44] The teaching methods adopted by Confucian private schools that I observed during fieldwork are quite monotonous. Reading and reciting the Confucian classics was the only major instructing method, although there are different ways of reading these texts such as individual reading, group reading, or reading led by teachers. For example, in the Zhi Qian Confucian School in Taiyuan, Shanxi Province, there are four to six hours' reading for students in the daily class schedule. In another Confucian school in Loudi, Hunan Province, students are requested to read aloud the same passage of a Confucian classic 80 times over four consecutive days.[45]

Local educational authorities discouraged use of these routine methods, as they were worried that these would prove counter-productive. Their intention is to promote innovative Confucian education so as to win recognition from their superintendents. The rote way of teaching may trigger widespread dissatisfaction and opposition from students' parents and prompt superintendents to blame local educational authorities. Thus, the local authorities are strongly motivated to make innovations to their teaching so as to ease possible complaints from students and their parents. Different local authorities even learn from each other to make further improvements. Local educational authorities in the Bao'an district, Shenzhen, said,

> Several official delegates from Liaoning Province have come to visit us. We not only gave them our textbooks but also shared with them our experiences including what to teach and how to teach. We also organized teaching demos for them to watch and participate. They are now trying to emulate us.... . We also organized study tours to learn the experiences of other cities. (Interviewee 7)

It is, however, worth pointing out that these innovations (or adaptations) are made within the official limits which have been specified by the central government because all local education policies are under the auspices of the local CCP's propaganda department. Thus, these local educational officials must conform to the basic principles set by the central authorities, such as the "attenuating and appropriating" strategies elaborated in the preceding sections of this chapter. In this way, the decentralized method of control, while maintaining the center's grip on ideological education, spawns creative adaptations at the local level.

6.5.2   The Institutional Base for Local Government's Innovations

Why are these local authorities interested in making innovations in Confucian education? The CRS can partly explain their efforts. Because of the institution, local educational authorities are given considerable power and authority in managing Confucian education. Since 1978, the central government has begun to relinquish its all-inclusive control and assign more and more responsibility for education management to local officials, especially after May 1985 when the CCP's central Committee issued *The Decision of the Central Committee of the Communist Party of China on the Reform of the Educational Structure* (Fernanda et al. 2002; Mun 2003; Ngok 2006). During fieldwork, it was found that local educational authorities even hold the power to decide whether to insert Confucian education into the public education system or not and the way to conduct this education. Thus, there are striking variances in Confucian education (or education in traditional culture) among different regions in China. For example, in Laixi, Qingdao, as mentioned previously, students in public primary schools are required to read and even recite the *Three-Character Classic* and *Standards for Students*,[46] whereas students in Guangzhou are mostly exempted from such Confucian education. Even in the same city, Shenzhen, for example, education in traditional culture has an imbalanced development in different districts. In the Bao'an district, courses concerning traditional culture are incorporated into the mandatory list of subjects, and various extracurricular activities such as the Beijing opera and Chinese painting are promoted (*Shenzhen Daily*, March, 18 2008), whereas in other districts, such traditional culture education remains only peripheral, with few courses about traditional culture being compulsory or mandatory.

In reality, local educational authorities, especially those at the town (*xian*) or district (*qu*) level, are granted with almost full discretion in making decisions concerning Confucian educational management. This explains why those local innovative measures were usually observed at the town or district level rather than prefecture (*shi*) or province (*sheng*) level. In fact, though there were some authorities at the prefecture level that initiated innovative Confucian education, their efforts were limited. Those at the province level were never found, during my field trip, running any kind of Confucian education. According to one of the informants working at the town level bureaucracy,

Educational authorities at the town or district level, though remaining the lowest in the administrative system, maintain direct authority over local schools about what and how to teach. The authorities at the prefecture level, though higher in administrative ranking, usually do not have direct contact with local schools except through us. The prefectural officials' jobs are to lead (or manage) us, not schools. In fact, it is us who have the direct power to implement new measures among local schools. (Interviewee 10)

Local educational officials are not only positioned to make decisions concerning educational management but also given political and fiscal incentives to improve management because if they are highly evaluated by higher officials,[47] they could be awarded an economic bonus and possible political promotion (Edin 2003; Whiting 2000). Thus, education authorities are deeply motivated to make any necessary innovations so as to win recognitions from their leaders, especially given that Confucian education is their own choice and that they need to be fully responsible for it. During my interview with local educational authorities in Shenzhen, these officials constantly emphasized that their management of Confucian education has been appraised by their superintendents in the educational bureau and the propaganda department of the local CCP branch.[48] They apparently were honored for the commendations from their leaders. In fact, this decentralized system and the CRS mechanism, in fact, have been widely believed to stimulate local initiatives for innovating local governance (Edin 2003; Landry 2008).[49]

6.6   Conclusions: A Balance Between Ideological Stability and Innovations

Since the early years of the twenty-first century, Confucianism has experienced a wide-scaled resurgence among the urban middle class, due to the large-scale social anomie brought about by China's accelerated urbanization and marketization processes. This is critical for the state because the urban middle class, with its burgeoning numbers and growing social and political power, is fundamental for the CCP's rule. This chapter explores how the Chinese state modulated rising Confucian education as a typical case to show how the state has prevented the Confucian revival among urban middle class from turning to an autonomous ideological power that could challenge its rule.

This chapter concludes that the Chinese state, similar to its regulations concerning the Confucian revival among intellectuals and private entrepreneurs, has also responded to the upswing in Confucian education by a decentralized response mechanism, but in a more stringent way. Specifically, the central government sets the broad policy parameters while local governments develop concrete policies. The central government, however, turns out to be much more restrictive in setting the policy directions than its dealings with intellectuals or private entrepreneurs. It adopts "attenuation" and "appropriation" strategies to prevent, or at least minimize, the threats that Confucianism would pose to the official ideology. Local governments, as usual, act as active accommodators. Some promote the "centrally calibrated" Confucianism in innovative ways, which is helpful for enhancing the public acceptance of the official version of Confucianism. Due to the decentralized institutions, most of the innovative measures were initiated at the lowest level of the Chinese administrative system, that is, the educational bureau at the town or district level.

The decentralized mechanism, to some extent, creates a balanced effect between maintaining ideological stability and encouraging innovations. For the central government, its controls on Confucianism enable it to retain its grip over ideological education. It also refuses to promote Confucianism in any heavily centralized mode. In fact, many Confucian proponents, including both academics and prominent social figures, have proposed incorporating Confucian education into the central curricula for all Chinese schools, promoting the Confucian education throughout China. For example, Professor Kang Xiaoguang, once a social-policy adviser to the then Prime Minister Zhu Rongji, has proposed to the Ministry of Education that Confucian education become mandatory for all schoolchildren in China (Robertson and Liu 2006). Professor Li Hanqiu also made similar proposal in the Chinese People's Consultative Conference in 2005 (Anonymous 2005). However, no significant moves have been seen until now.[50]

The center's restrictions on Confucianism, however, do not mean its denial of responsiveness to social needs. By virtue of the decentralized system, the central government gives its consent to local governments for innovative response strategies to the Confucian revival. As has been discussed in previous sections, local authorities are motivated to improve their work performance in order to gain political and economic promotion. Such local responsiveness enables the state to accommodate the Confucian revival among the urban middle class and facilitates its continual negotiation and renegotiation with society, especially at the local level.

Notes

1. The lower middle class overlaps with the meaning of "crowd" or "mass" as defined in previous literature, for example, "crowd" as defined by Thompson (1971) or Canetti (1960). The reason to exclude other disadvantageous social groups such as agricultural laborers and the unemployed, who are also unprivileged, from our study is because Confucianism does not enjoy robust popularity among these classes.
2. For details, please refer to http://www.chyxx.com/industry/201701/489699.html
3. Many empirical studies of China's middle class were made by large multinational corporations for business purposes. Since these companies' research methods may not necessarily meet academic standards, the numbers here can only be used as references for understanding the general picture of the middle class.
4. It is, in fact, difficult to obtain the exact number of these classes and schools, because quite a few do not register with the government. According to a relevant website, their number has risen to at least 40 in 2010. For details, see "Shenzhen Dujing Jiaoyu Jigou Yilan" (A survey of the organizations for reading the Confucian classics in Shenzhen), http://blog.sina.com.cn/s/blog_5d6cf0360100lm4c.html (assessed on January 16, 2011). This list contains 40 organizations including contact persons, telephone numbers, emails, or QQ numbers. I have contacted some of these organizations and confirmed that their information is reliable.
5. Chen did not clearly state how or when this number was calculated.
6. There are approximately 30 influential network communities, among which some well-known ones are *xuxue lianhe luantan* (www.yuandao.com), *huaxia fuxing luntan* (www.hxfx.net/bbs), and *rujiao fuxing luntan* (www.rjfx.net).
7. The "ideological vacuum" has been vividly depicted by Professor He Guanghu from Renming University in Beijing as a "threefold crisis" (*san xin weiji*): "a crisis of confidence" (*xinxin*), "a crisis of trust" (*xinren*), and "a crisis of faith" (*xinyang*).
8. Other scholars have similar findings. For details, please see Billioud and Thoraval (2008).
9. "Dangqian zhongguoren weihe jiaolu? Jiaolu chengdu jihe?" (Why do Chinese feel anxious in Current Day? What are their Anxiety Levels?), Joint research conducted by *Souhuwang* (website of Souhu) and *Renmin luntanwang* (Website of People's Forum) in 2013. For more details, please refer to http://paper.people.com.cn/rmlt/html/2013-03/21/content_1214219.htm?div=-1

10. The research here only focuses on the educational activities in government-funded public schools, as they are the main venues where government policies are meant to be carried out.

11. The proposal was made in his letter to the emperor entitled *"Ju Xianliang Duice"* ("舉賢良對策") in AD 134.

12. In fact, the late Qing court had already formally abrogated Confucian education in 1902. However, it still remained in place until 1912.

13. It mainly includes the Four Books and Five Classics.

14. Regarding the Communist mode of mobilizing popular consent, please refer to Beetham (1991).

15. These lectures are usually given by teachers at local universities who either do them voluntarily or for a small payment. They are usually organized by local Confucian organizations and are subject to the approval of local authorities.

16. During my fieldwork, I found some local communities organizing courses on Confucianism or Chinese traditional philosophy for residents. These courses were usually managed by committees in the local community and also subject to approval by local authorities.

17. Interviewee 8 and 9.

18. Except in Xinjiang and Tibet; this data is from Shi (2010).

19. During my fieldwork, I found that some Buddhist groups were heavily involved in supporting Confucian education. The reason, as explained by one of my interviewees, is that Buddhist groups consider financing such Confucian education a "virtuous act". They viewed it as beneficial for spreading Buddhism among the urban middle class because Buddhism in China, after its more than 2000 years of localization, has now greatly overlapped with Confucianism (Interviewee 16).

20. For details, see www.tongxueguan.com

21. For details about the school, please visit www.xfjy9.com

22. Similar findings have already been noted by other scholars such as Makeham (2008) and Billioud (2007a, b).

23. Although "the classics" may have strong connotations of Confucianism, the documents never clearly denoted the classics as Confucian or Confucianism-related. During fieldwork, I found public schools often included Confucianism, Daoism, Marxism, and some Western classics such as Shakespeare's works in their "classics education".

24. "Red Scarf" is an official symbol of Communism for the Chinese children, whereas "national studies" simply implies traditional Chinese culture with Confucianism at the core. The title means children with communist beliefs studying traditional culture. For a detailed introduction of the activities, please refer to www.gov.cn/jrzg/2011-01/07/content_1780081.htm

25. The NCWC is a branch of the Communist Youth League of China (CYLC). Many current CCP leaders such as former President Hu Jintao and Premier Li Keqiang were former leaders of the CYLC.
26. Interviewees 7 and 9. The information provided by the interviewee can be confirmed by a news report concerning national studies education in the *Shenzhen Daily* (2008).
27. Interviewees 7 and 9; for details of all these schools' activities, please refer to http://bagxt.baoan.net.cn/wz_Class.asp?ClassID=8
28. Interviewee 19.
29. Interviews with teachers and students at No. 5 Middle School and Wudi Silu Primary School, in Qingdao in April 2011 (Interviewees 23, 24, 30, 31).
30. The other components of the core value system are Marxism, "Shared Ideal of Socialism with Chinese Characteristics" *(zhongguo tese shehui zhuyi gongtong lixiang)* and "the zeitgeist of reform and innovation" *(gaige he kaifang de shidai jinshen)*. It is interesting that while Confucianism has actively been restructured and reshaped to be wedged into patriotism and SCHD, no systematic efforts have been observed to connect Confucianism with the other components of the core value system. It may be because there are not many overlaps between Confucianism and the others.
31. For the differences between Confucianism and the official ideology in philosophical founding, see Chap. 1.
32. This regulation was issued on August 23, 1994, and has been used as the basic guidelines for patriotic education until now.
33. This document was given to me by the local educational authorities there. It can be downloaded from http://bagxt.baoan.net.cn/wz_Show.asp?ArticleID=511
34. These books were published by *yuelu shushe* in 2008. For details, see Zhang et al. (2008).
35. For details, see Dotson (2011).
36. For a detailed introduction of the OMRI, see case study one in Chap. 4. The program launched by the OMRI aimed to promulgate Confucian ethics among students and received financial support from the Beijing municipal government and some "relevant departments" within the Ministry of Education. The program involved 373 schools and universities in Beijing, Nanjing, Shandong, Heilongjiang, Chongqing, Sichuan, Shenzhen, Tianjin, Wuhan, and Xian. The information is also available at www.bjypc.edu.cn/dongfang/dongfangdao.htm
37. Interviewees 39, 40, and 41.
38. For an introduction to their specific activities, please refer to www.hgedu.cn/CMS/CMS/zzjg/dyk/lm3/2007-4-13_1176431894737.html
39. The *Qingdao Daily* has a detailed report concerning the creative education of "traditional culture", especially elementary Confucian education, in its A11 section, January 24, 2007.

40. It is based on my fieldwork. *Yangcheng Evening News (yangcheng wanbao)* has a special report introducing the various creative methods used in the education of "national studies" in Bao'an, Shenzhen (Li and Yang 2010).

41. Interview with Shenzhen local official (Interviewee 7).

42. From interviews with teachers in Wudi Silu Primary school in Qingdao (Interviewees 30 and 31).

43. One explanation for the local educational authorities' lack of motivation in providing innovative improvements to the education of official ideologies is that they are simply not given the authority to make any significant change in this field.

44. These Confucian private schools enjoy relative autonomy in their educational management and are not so strictly controlled by local educational authorities as the public schools. What's more, they usually stick to fundamentalist principles, focusing on restoring traditional ways of teaching and learning. They deemed these government innovations as antithetical to their fundamentalist principles and therefore refused to imitate them (Interviewee 16).

45. According to my knowledge, these Confucian schools and classes use this teaching method partly because they are influenced by a Taiwanese educator, Wang Caigui, who postulates that there is no need for a child to understand the classics but just to recite them because children simply cannot comprehend the meaning of those classics until they have enough social experience. Thus, children should just try to recite them without understanding their meaning. See also Kang et al. (2010).

46. There is an official report concerning Confucian education in this county. Please refer to www.cppcc.gov.cn/page.do?pa=2c

47. In the case of the educational authorities at the town (*xian*) or district (*qu*) level, they are subject to the direct leadership of both the propaganda department (*qu/xian xuan chuan bu*) at the same level and the education bureau at the prefecture level (*shi jiaoyu ju*).

48. Interviewee 8.

49. I would like to thank Professor Andrew Nathan for suggesting these publications for me.

50. On the contrary, the indoctrination of official ideologies such as Marxism and "Socialism with Chinese Characteristics" is not only mandatory for all public schools throughout China, but also strictly reinforced. The central authorities do not allow any contravention by local authorities. The centrally made "guidelines" (*jiaoxue dagang*) for teaching official ideologies, which clearly stipulate the content of ideological education in every particular way, do not allow for changes (interview with a local educational official in Qingdao—Interviewee 28).

REFERENCES

Anonymous, 2005, 'Li Hanqiu, chongwen ren yi li zhi xin', viewed on February 3rd, 2011, available at http://www.godpp.gov.cn/lhdbwyhwm/2006-03/03/content_6371545.htm

Bai, L 1998, 'Monetary reward versus the national ideological agenda: career choice among Chinese university students', *Journal of Moral Education*, vol. 27, no. 4, pp. 1–15.

Beetham, D 1991, *The legitimation of power*, Palgrave Macmillan, London.

Billioud, S 2007a, 'Confucianism, 'cultural tradition,' and official discourses at the start of the new century', *China Perspectives*, no. 3.

Billioud, S 2007b, 'Jiaohua: the Confucian revival today as an educative project', *China Perspectives*, no. 4.

Billioud, S & Thoraval, J 2007, 'Jiaohua: the confucian revival in China as an educative project', *China Perspectives*, vol. 2007, no. 2007/4.

Billioud, S & Thoraval, J 2008, 'The contemporary revival of Confucianism, Anshen liming or the religious dimension of Confucianism', *China Perspective*, no. 3.

Brockmann, H, Delhey, J, Welzel, C & Hao, Y 2009, 'The China puzzle: falling happiness in a rising economy', *Journal of Happiness Studies*, vol. 10, no. 4, pp. 387–405.

Canetti, E 1960, *Crowds and Power*, Continuum, New York.

Chen, L 2007, 'Kongzi yu Dangdai zhongguo' (Confucius and contemporary China), *Dushu (Reading)*, no. 11.

Deng, XP 1994, 'Speech to cadres and soldiers of the Beijing Martial Law Corps, Beijing, June 9', In *Selected works of Deng Xiaoping*, vol. 3, Foreign Languages Press, Beijing, p. 297.

Dotson, J 2011, 'Confucian revival in the propaganda narratives of the Chinese government', US-China Economic and Security Review Commission staff research report, July 20th.

Durkheim, E 1984, *The division of labor in society*, Free Press, New York.

Durkheim, E 1997, *Suicide: a study in sociology*, Free Press, New York.

Edin, M 2003, 'State capacity and local agent control in China: CCP cadre management from a township perspective', *The China Quarterly*, vol. 173, pp. 35–52.

Fernanda, A et al, 2002, 'Slouching towards decentralization: consequences of globalization for curricular control in national education systems', *Comparative Educational Review*, vol. 46, no. 1, pp. 66–88.

Goldin, P 2011, *Confucianism*, Acumen Publishing House, Durham, UK.

He, Q 2006, 'The new myth in China: China's rising middle-class will accelerate democratization', *Finance and Culture Weekly*, 8 November.

Ho, N 2009, 'Unlikely bedfellows? Confucius, the CCP and the resurgence of Guoxue', *Harvard International Review*, 26 October.

Hu, L & Hu, A 2008, 'Zhongchan jieceng: Wendingqi haishi xiangfan huo qita' (Middle stratum: a stabilizer, a disrupter, or something else), *Zhengzhixue yanjiu (Political Science Studies)*, no. 2.

Huntington, SP 1968, *Political order in changing societies*, Yale University Press, New Haven and London.

Kang, XG, Wang, J & Liu, SL 2010, *Zhendizhan: Guan yu zhonghua wenhua fuxingde gelanxishi fenxi* (Struggle for cultural hegemony: Gramscian perspectives of revitalizing Chinese traditional culture), shehui kexue wenxian chubanshe (Social Science Literature Press), Beijing.

Koo, H 1991, 'Middle classes, democratization, and class formation: the case of South Korea', *Theory and Society*, vol. 20, August.

Koo, H 2001, *Korean workers: the culture and politics of class formation*, Cornell University Press, Ithaca.

Landry, P 2008, *Decentralized authoritarianism in China: the Communist Party's control of local elites in post-Mao China*, Cambridge University Press, Cambridge.

Lei, J 2006, 'Jia yizuo huayu tongxin de qiaoliang—nanchangshi chushi xiaoxue yi guoxue jingdian kaizhan shehuizhuyi rongruguan jiaoyu' (Building a bridge for educating children—Zhushi Primary School in Nanchang conducted SCHD education through national studies classics), *Jiangxi Jiaoyu (Jiangxi Education)*, no. Z2.

Lewis, JW & Xue, L 2003, 'Social change and political reform in China: meeting the challenge of success', *The China Quarterly*, vol. 176, pp. 926–942.

Li, Y, & Yang, MZ 2010, 'The National Studies Education in Bao'an stays ahead', *Yangcheng Daily*, 9 November 2010.

Li, C 2010a, *China's emerging middle class: beyond economic transformation*, Brookings Institution Press, Washington, DC.

Li, P et al. 2007, *Zhongguo shehui hexie wending baogao (Report on social harmony and conflicts of China)*, Shehuikexue wenxian chubanshe (Social Science Literature Press), Beijing, p. 198.

Li, S 2010b, 'Gaoshang daode: haizimen chengzhang de jinshen liliang' (The fine morality: the spiritual power for the children's growth), *Renmin Jiaoyu (People's Education)*, vol. 615, p. 33–37.

Lipset, SM 1959, 'Some social requisites of democracy: economic development and political legitimacy', *American Political Science Review*, vol. 53, no. 1, pp. 69–105.

Lipset, SM 1963, 'The value patterns of democracy: a case study in comparative analysis', *American Sociological Review*, vol. 28, no. 4, pp. 515–531.

Ma, L & Yue, C 2011, 'Woguo laogongli shichang fenge yu gaoxiao biyesheng jiuye liuxiang yanjiu' (China's labor's market segmentation and the employment of college graduates), *Jiaoyu fazhan yanjiu* (*Research on Education Development*), no. 3.

Makeham, J 2008, *Lost soul: Confucianism in contemporary Chinese academic discourse*, Harvard University Asia Center, Cambridge, MA and London, England.

McKinsey Global Institute 2006, *From "made in China" to "sold in China": the rise of the Chinese urban consumer*, viewed on November, 2011, available at http://www.mckinsey.com/mgi/publications/china_consumer/index.asp

Mun, CT 2003, 'School choice in the People's Republic of China', In Plank, D & Sykes, G (eds.), *Choosing choice: school choices in international perspective*, Teachers College Press, New York.

Ngok, WL 2006, 'The effects of local interpretation of decentralization policy on school autonomy in Guangdong Province of China', In Bjork, C (ed.), *Education decentralization: Asian experience and conceptual contribution*, Springer.

Robertson, B & Liu, M (2006), 'Can the sage save China?', *Newsweek*, March 20.

Shahar, M & Weller, R (eds.) 1996, *Unruly gods: divinity and society in China*, University of Hawaii Press, Honolulu.

Shenzhen Daily, 18 March 2008, 'Beijing Opera Comes to Bao'an' 2008, viewed on May 13th, 2011, available at http://sztqb.sznews.com/html/2008-03/18/content_100999.htm,http://bagxt.baoan.net.cn/wz_Show.asp?ArticleID=1059

Shi, D 2010, 'Rujing songdu sichao zai minjian shehui xingqi jiqi dongyuan jizhi' (The rise of the trend of reading Confucian Classics in the folk society and the mobilization mechanism), China doctoral dissertations full-text database.

Simpson, P 2012, 'China's urban population exceeds rural for first time ever,' viewed on April 28th, 2012, available at http://www.telegraph.co.uk/news/worldnews/asia/china/9020486/Chinas-urban-population-exceeds-rural-for-first-time-ever.html

Thompson, EP 1971, 'The moral economy of the English crowd in the eighteenth century', *Past & Present*, no. 50.

Tonnies, F 1887 (1963), *Community and Society*, translated by Loomis CP, reprint by Harper & Row, New York.

Whiting, S 2000, *Power and wealth in rural China: the political economy of institutional change*, Cambridge University Press, Cambridge.

Xu, F 2007, *Shaoer guoxue duben* (*Children's textbook of national studies*), Jinan daxue chubanshe (Jinan University Press), Guangzhou.

Yao, XZ 2000, *An introduction to Confucianism*, Cambridge University Press, Cambridge.

Yu, S 1997a, 'Special overview: political enthusiasm exists side by side with political indifference', *Chinese Education and Society*, vol. 30, no. 3, pp. 65–72.

Yu, T 2008, 'The revival of Confucianism in Chinese schools: a historical-political review', *Asia Pacific Journal of Education*, vol. 28, no. 2.

Yu, YS 1997b, 'Business culture and Chinese traditions—toward a study of the evolution of merchant culture in Chinese history', In Wang, G & Wong, SL (eds.), *Dynamic Hong Kong: business and culture*, The Hong Kong University Press, Hongkong.

Yuan, Y & Zhang, H 2009, '2008 nian Zhonguo jumin shenghuo zhilian diaocha baogao' (2008 Survey of living standards of Chinese citizens), In Ru, X et al. (eds.), *2009 nian Zhongguo shehui xingshi fenxi yu yuce (Society of China: analysis and forecast for 2009)*, Social Sciences Academic Press, Beijing.

Zhang, et al (eds.) 2008, *Shaoer guoxue duben (Textbook for children reading the Classics)*, Yuelu Shushe press, Changsha.

Zhang, Y 2008, 'Dangdai Zhongguo zhongchan jieceng de zhengzhi taidu' (Political attitudes of the middle stratum in contemporary China), *Zhongguo shehui kexue (Chinese Social Sciences)*, vol. 2, Summer.

Zheng, Y 2004a, 'The status of Confucianism in modern Chinese education, 1901–49: a curricular study', In Peterson, G & Lu, Y (eds.), *Education, culture and identity in 20th century China*, Hong Kong University Press, Hong Kong.

Zheng, Y 2004b, *Will China become democratic? elite, class and regime transition*, Eastern Universities Press, Singapore.

Zhou, K 2009, *China's long march to freedom: grassroots modernization*, Transaction Publisher, New Brunswick.

Zhu, X 2010, *Zhongguo Chuantong Wenhua (The Chinese Traditional Culture)*, People's University Press, Beijing.

CHAPTER 7

Conclusions

7.1 Brief Summary of Major Findings

Whether the Chinese state can effectively control an increasingly powerful and autonomous society produced by China's rapid economic modernization remains a major debate in current research on Chinese politics. This book contributes to a crucial but often neglected aspect of the debate, specifically, whether the Chinese state can properly structure these diversified ideologies and beliefs generated amid a modernizing society. This is significant in that the leading CCP remains a Leninist party which still relies on its official ideology to energize the loyalty of its rank-and-file members. The state, moreover, as a post-totalitarian regime, still resorts to official ideologies to win at least part of its ruling legitimacy among the public. Hence, whether the Chinese state can keep these non-official ideologies and beliefs within its grip remains critical for its control over society.

This book explores the issue by examining an important case, specifically, the state's engagement with the revival of Confucianism in China's urban society. Since the early 2000s, Confucianism has been revived into a vibrant ideology and living tradition among China's urban citizens, particularly intellectuals, private entrepreneurs, and the urban middle class. Together with Liberalism and Socialism, it has now become the most influential ideological current in contemporary China (Tu 2011). Why does Confucianism experience such rapid rejuvenation? What is the role of the state in the Confucian revival? What does the state's involvement in

© The Author(s) 2019
Q. Pang, *State-Society Relations and Confucian Revivalism in Contemporary China*,
https://doi.org/10.1007/978-981-10-8312-9_7

the Confucian revival possibly tell us about the state's capacity in structuring China's symbolic environment? After all, Confucianism, as a non-official ideology, maintains controversial and even has strained relations with the CCP, though some of its tenets are arguably compatible with its authoritarian rule. This book, by exploring the Confucian revival over the past decade and the Chinese state's responses towards it, reaches four major conclusions, which will be briefly summarized as follows.

First, the Confucian resurgence has been mainly brought about by an increasingly active and strong society, which has experienced rapid socio-economic transformation and intended to rebuild part of the social order that has disappeared with modernization through promoting Confucianism. Thus, the Confucian revival has been observed mostly in urban Chinese society, especially social groups emerging and growing amid modernization, for example, the urban middle class and entrepreneurs. These new social forces, out of their rising interest in Confucianism and desire to reestablish social order, seek to renew Confucianism in contemporary Chinese society and sometimes even test the state's authoritarian instincts to their limits. It is true that the Chinese state's softened attitudes towards and even tacit acceptance of Confucianism since the early 1990s is a contributing factor in the current Confucian revival, but it is *not* the decisive determinant.

Second, the Chinese state regulated the Confucian revival through a decentralized responsiveness mechanism. In this mechanism, the state can be viewed as at least two separate power entities, notably the central and subnational levels of government. While the central government has only set some broad policy parameters for regulations, it is the local authorities that have made most of the decisions concerning how to handle the continuing Confucian revival. Local authorities, therefore, have considerable room for policy maneuvers. They sometimes even have full discretion in deciding whether to promote Confucianism or not and in what ways, as long as their measures do not contravene against the center's guidelines. Accordingly, there are great differences in local governments' policies towards Confucianism.

But interestingly, the two power entities' policies are seen as distinctive from and sometimes even contradictory to each other. The central government's policy parameters are coercive in nature and tend to suppress the rapid growth of Confucianism. Local authorities, however, guided by a strong instrumental mentality, are inclined to promote the Confucian revival in order to manipulate it to their own advantage. However, their policies have some variations towards different social constituencies,

Table 7.1 Variations in the central and local governments' responses towards different groups

	The central state's guiding parameters	Local authorities' accommodating support
Urban middle class	The strictest	The least
Intellectuals	Looser than urban public	More than urban public
Private entrepreneurs	The least stringent among the three	Most among the three

namely, intellectuals, private entrepreneurs, and the urban middle class (Table 7.1). Their control of the Confucian revival among the urban middle class is the strictest, with the central government making detailed guidelines and local authorities carefully following them in certain unique ways. Their control of intellectuals and their Confucian discourses are less stringent. The central government does *not* impose specific regulations upon them but draws clear bottom lines to avoid challenges from critical intellectuals and their academic works. Some local authorities are active in co-opting Confucian intellectuals and supporting their work, especially those beneficial for local governance. Their regulations over Confucian entrepreneurs belonging to the business elite are the loosest. The central government does *not* set any explicit policy guidelines or bottom lines. Some local officials were seen as assiduously accommodating to private entrepreneurs' pursuit of Confucian entrepreneur.

The difference in the state's coercion and co-optation of the three social elements may be due to the fact that the Confucian revival among the urban middle class, compared with the other two, affects a much broader segment of society and is therefore regarded as more threatening to the official ideology. Intellectuals' Confucian discourses, however, have a comparatively small audience, and intellectuals hold important ideological resources that the state intends to exploit. Private entrepreneur's interest in Confucian entrepreneur does not directly challenge the official ideology, and the state, especially local officials, has a strong motivation to incorporate these business elites that control substantial economic and financial resources.

Third, the decentralized response mechanism enables the state's control over the Confucian revival to be flexible and balanced. As has been shown in previous chapters, local authorities are given substantial authority in dealing with the Confucian revival, thus allowing local authorities' experiments with

Confucianism in their local policies. Some local officials, due to their own identification with Confucianism and/or motivation for "political promotions", also adopt innovative measures. Local responses towards the Confucian revival, therefore, vary from one place to another, showing the flexibility of the decentralized mechanism. The central government's coercive policies and local authorities' co-opting stance also, to some extent, both preserve the stability of the official ideology and accommodate the growth of Confucian revival. On this score, they have enabled the state to reach a somewhat delicate balance of keeping ideological stability and extending ideological freedom, two seemingly paradoxical trends that in combination serve as the very basis for the CCP's ideological policies. This flexible and balanced control maximizes the state's use of its limited power and resources in controlling society. Besides, it allowed and even encouraged the development of Confucianism all over China, though often in ways that is beneficial for the state. Both intellectuals, entrepreneurs, and the state, therefore, obtain what they want and become mutually empowered during their common efforts in structuring and shaping the Confucian revival.

Last of all, the decentralized response is not a deliberate choice made by certain central authorities but is largely shaped by the Chinese state's own institutions. Local authorities' active responses are underpinned by decentralized political institutions, the CRS in particular. The CRS not only empowers local cadres with substantial authority, but also injects incentives for them to make policy innovations by adopting the CES and introducing competition among cadres at the same level. In parallel, the central government's conservative attitude towards Confucianism also has institutional reasons. As the head of a Leninist party-state, the central government cannot but insist on its official ideology, as the official ideology remains essential to its organizational coherence and solidarity, especially given the historical institutional legacies of the official ideology. This gives proof to the proposition that how the state interacts with society, especially how it coerces and co-opts social forces and its effect are heavily determined by the state's own institutions, particularly those governing internal power distribution and those providing motivation for bureaucrats.[1]

7.2   Theoretical Implications

This study has shed new light on the existing assumptions and theories concerning ideological evolution in China, China's authoritarian resilience, and the Chinese state and society relations.

7.2.1   A New Understanding of Local Governments' Role in Ideological Evolution

To start with, this study refutes the common myth that the Chinese state is ossified in its ideological world, by revealing the ideological reforms and renovations made by subnational Chinese governments. There has been a common assumption that the Chinese state has only made economic reforms without corresponding political, and especially ideological, reforms (Gao 1999; Ho 2004; Palmer 2010; Schuman 2011). However, this is not true. As this study shows, local officials, guided by their strong instrumental and pragmatic mentality, attempt to experiment with using the local Confucian revival to their advantage, albeit within some limits. These scattered and varied local experiments allow and even promote the growth of Confucianism, which has entailed incremental ideological changes in China. Underneath the surface of ideological stagnation at the central level, we have seen vibrant ideological evolution in local settings.

Second, this study reveals local authorities' important role in the reform of ideology in China. Most of the existing literature concerning China's ideological evolution tend to focus on the central government (or the central CCP) and its reformulations of the official ideology (Shambaugh 2008; Holbig 2006, 2009, Holbig & Gilley 2010). This study, however, underscores the importance of local authorities and shows that they have played a growing and sometimes even pioneering role in initiating China's ideological changes. By actively involving and pragmatically responding to rising new ideologies and beliefs, local authorities have also contributed to the transformation of the Chinese ideological landscape. These local-level transformations, though incremental, are significant in shaping China's ideological development.

7.2.2   A New Approach to Explaining the Authoritarian Resilience in China

The decentralized responsiveness model in this study involves a new approach to explaining the resilience of Chinese state's authoritarianism. Most current theories, when accounting for China's authoritarian durability, focus on either the Chinese state's strength in sustaining its organizational stability, or its responsiveness towards changing society. The model discussed in this book, however, combines the two together and emphasizes that a skillfully managed balance of the two is a key for the Chinese state's persistence at least until now.

Existing theories of authoritarian resilience, especially within the Chinese context, usually involve two approaches. The first one tries to explain how the Chinese state endeavors to build itself into a stable and durable organization with strong organizational and administrative capacity. For example, Nathan (2003) argues that the CCP regime has dramatically institutionalized its political leaders' succession, the meritocratic promotion of political elites, and specialization of functional responsibilities. Thus, the CCP regime, in his view, has strengthened its stability and therefore durability. Also, some stress that the CCP has undertaken further measures in revenue collection, regulatory enforcement, and cadre management to strengthen its administrative and organizational capacity, and thus enhanced the Chinese state's internal coherence in implementing policies (Yang 2004; Edin 2003). Shambaugh (2008) also highlights that the CCP has rebuilt itself in ideological and organizational dimensions to keep its internal coherence by learning from the collapse of the USSR and some East European Communist States. A common characteristic of these works is their concentration on how the Chinese state has revitalized itself to become an institutionalized, stable, and coherent bureaucratic organization.

The second approach to explaining Chinese authoritarian durability focuses on the Chinese state's improved responses towards social challenges. For example, Tsang (2009) argues that the CCP has made its Leninist political machinery more resilient by incorporating more consultative channels with the society into the current political system, thus improving its responsiveness to social demands and forming what he called "consultative Leninism". He observes that the Chinese state has initiated governance reforms to better elicit and respond to public opinion in order to preempt public demand for democratization (Tsang 2009). The state has also actively incorporated important social forces such as intellectuals and private entrepreneurs. Since the early 1990s, it has launched a systematic campaign of co-optation to recruit intellectuals and professionals to its fold (Pei 2006; Li 2009). It is also largely successful in preventing private entrepreneurs' organized demands for political change, by forging corporatist links with various business organizations and co-opting entrepreneurs into its organization (Dickson 2003, 2008; Chen and Dickson 2010). The state also refined its repression of the opposition and popular resistance. It has become more selective in using coercion as it has learned from the 1989 experience (Pei 2012, 2006; Dickson 2011; Shambaugh 2000). It has devised a set of strategies to avoid the escalation of parochial social unrest to national movements that threaten the central government, therefore effectively reducing the danger to the whole political system (Cai 2008; O'Brien and Li 2006; Lee 2007). In sum, the literature in this approach tends to focus on the Chinese state's nimble responses to social challenges as a key for its authoritarian resilience.

The two previous approaches explain the Chinese state's durability from the perspective of the state's inward consolidation and outward responsiveness towards society respectively. The decentralized response mechanism in this book, however, demonstrates that another important strength of the state lies in its skillfully balancing the two aspects, that is, its capacity to maintain both its autonomy and responsiveness to society. This is critical because for the Chinese party-state, on the one hand, Leninist though is still the pillar of its rule, and therefore it needs to strengthen the stability of the party organization to ensure its survival; on the other hand, the state also needs to improve its responses to society, or it will soon be engulfed by tremendous societal demands for change. Hence, both are essential for the state's durability.

Similarly, Huntington (1968) also points out that whether a state can survive the pressure of modernization depends on its adaptability to changing society and capacity to maintain its internal coherence.[2] According to Huntington, adaptability means capability to adjust to environmental challenges, especially those from modernizing society. Coherence, on the other hand, refers to consensus within a political organization. Some measure of coherence is essential for any political organization to survive social changes. It is particularly relevant to a Leninist party which rules by strong ideological consensus. But it is not easy to maintain a political organization's internal coherence, particularly in rapidly changing societies, because in such societies, new social forces constantly emerge and demand to participate in politics. In order to cope with the changes, political organizations must expand themselves to co-opt these new groups and actively respond to them. However, rapid expansion in the organizational membership tends to weaken internal coherence, because new social forces bring in new ideas and ways of behaving, and may easily dilute the group coherence that had previously existed. Constant responses towards new social groups' demands may also make the organization lose its autonomy from society. Thus, a proper balance of keeping internal coherence and remaining responsive is vital for the organization's function and stability during rapid social changes.

The decentralized response mechanism shows that the Chinese political institutions, especially decentralized institutions, have some strength in balancing the party-state's adaptability and internal coherence in at least responding to new ideologies and beliefs from society. The two responsibilities, interestingly, are divided between the two major power entities: the central and local government. As has been explained previously, local authorities, on the one hand, have actively responded to the Confucian revival; and on the other, the central government makes restrictive policies to keep it within control, safeguarding the official ideology against serious challenges from Confucianism. Local authorities' adaptive and innovative responses are supported by decentralized institutions such as the CRS which has been widely regarded as motivating local Chinese governments to experiment and innovate in changing economic circumstances (Chen 1993; Montinola et al. 1996; Oi 1992, 1995; Whiting 2000; Xu and Zhuang 1998). But the central government also sets strict institutions to ensure that local authorities would not step over the bottom line or deviate from the center. Though not all members truly believe in the official ideology, the center's insistence upon the official ideology, at least, prevents the rise of ideological chaos and competition from different factions within the party, and therefore avoids serious factional rivalry. In this way, the central and local governments share the responsibilities of adapting to social changes and maintaining internal coherence, reaching a kind of balance between the two.

The importance of balancing internal coherence and responsiveness to society for the CCP can be shown by the Communist regime's setbacks. The June Fourth Movement is a case in point. Before the movement, the CCP, while actively liberalizing the Chinese economy to accommodate current social needs, had also dramatically loosened its control over the official ideology. This, plus the influence of Western Liberalism, gave birth to the rise of the "Right" (who support liberalizing Chinese politics and economy) and correspondingly the strong ideological rivalry between the so-called Left (old Communist ideologues and hard-liners) and Right.[3] This had seriously weakened the ideological consensus within the CCP, and its coherence.[4] Later, their ideological rivalry became one of the catalysts for the June Fourth Movement (Nathan and Gilley 2002; Nathan and Link 2001; Gilley 1998), as the ideological rivalry soon turned into factional struggles within the CCP's ruling elites, which the regime's opponents in the movement also capitalized upon (Nathan and Gilley 2002; Nathan and Link 2001). Thus, when Deng Xiaoping (1994) reflected on what should be learned from the June Fourth Movement, he believed that the CCP's biggest mistake was in its ideological education and control.

The collapse of the Soviet Union and the former Eastern European Communist states also confirms that a prerequisite for the Leninist Party's persistence over socio-economic changes is to retain both its internal coherence and responsiveness towards society. Walder (1994) points out that the sweeping political changes in the Communist world after 1988 originated from "revolutions from within (the parties)", which, step by step, resulted in failure of the Leninist Parties to exercise control within the party-state apparatus. One of the catalysts for this failure was the "ideological revolution" initiated by the USSR's reformist leader Gorbachev. Since 1985, Gorbachev's "New Thinking" or "New Political Thinking", whose core concept is "Socialist pluralism" or "political pluralism", as Gorbachev later accepted, seriously altered the official orthodoxy of Leninism, the ideological consensus of the Communist Party of the Soviet Union (hereafter CPSU) (Brown 1996). This not only eroded the CPSU's coherence but also its autonomy, given that the Leninist orthodoxy had been the ideological foundation on which the higher levels of the CPSU exercised its control over the lower rungs of administration. In fact, in 1985 when Gorbachev initiated political liberalization in the mass media, radical liberal social forces quickly took over the media (Gibbs 1999; Pei 1994). The weakened coherence of the CPSU made it unable to stand up against the impact of the liberal forces, and the USSR soon disintegrated.

Similar cases occurred in the former East European Communist countries. Before their collapse in 1989, the ideological coherence of these Communist states had been so seriously eroded that even members of the state apparatus itself had suffered from a lack of self-confidence about Marxism. The pervasiveness of Western Liberalism generated self-doubt even among the leading members of the *apparatchiki* in these states (Karabel 1996). The resultant ideological chaos and confusion within these states simply dug the grave for the state itself. In fact, it is from the collapse of the USSR and the East European Communist states that the central CCP has learned to resurrect the official ideologies and insist on them coherently within the party-state (Shambaugh 2008).

7.2.3   A New Model of Chinese State-Society Relations

In addition to having implications for the resilience of authoritarianism in China, this research also reveals a different dimension of the relationship between the Chinese state and society, avoiding the traditional "top-down control" and "bottom-up" model. As was pointed out in Chap. 3, most existing literature concerning the Confucian revival employs either the model of state's top-down control over society or society's bottom-up resistance against the state to cover state and society relations. The two models encompasses two basic premises: first, the existence of a single and integrated state performing coherently from top to bottom and a uniform society making one request to state and second, a single-directional communication between the state and society, either top-down or bottom-up. The findings of this study, however, demonstrate that the Chinese state is not an integrated power entity, but a set of scattered power entities with divergent and sometimes even contradictory policy orientations. These different power entities of the state, in the Confucian revival, conduct multilevel and multidirectional interactions with different segments of society that have different requests for the state.

Before coming to the multilevel and multidirectional interactions between the state and society, it needs to be pointed out that the top-down control and bottom-up model have a long history and are powerful paradigms in studying state-society relations, especially the framework of the state's top-down control over society. It has been widely applied in discourses concerning state and society interactions in China.[5] For example, some scholars maintain that the Chinese state has used corporatist strategies to bind social organizations to state patronage and so control their activities (Chan 1993; Saich 1994; Unger and Chan 1995, 1996). Others argue that the Chinese state compartmentalizes social organizations to avoid genuine organizational pluralism (Baum and Shevchenko 1999; White et al. 1996). Some Chinese scholars also adopt this framework in their analysis of emerging Chinese civil society, claiming that there is no independent "civil society" in China, due to the state's predominance in the social arena (Sun 2001; Xiao 2004; Li 2004).

While such models are helpful in understanding the role of state and society in China's social and economic changes, the construction of the Chinese state as "a single actor performing in an integrated manner" may be oversimplified. The state, as has been demonstrated in this study, is comprised of different power entities, including the central and various levels of local governments which hold distinctive attitudes and take divergent policy approaches towards Confucianism. Thus, a single and integrated Chinese state isolated from society may be only an illusion. As Migdal (2001, p. 22) has contended, though in terms of image, a state can be "thought of as a single, centrally motivated actor performing in an integrated manner to rule a clearly defined territory", in practice, it is "a heap of loosely connected parts or fragments, frequently with ill-defined boundaries between them and other groupings inside and outside the official state borders" (p. 22).[6] Various parts of the state have allied with certain social groups, and "such coalitions neutralize the sharp demarcations between the state as preeminent rule *maker* and society as the *recipient* of those rules" (Migdal 2001, p. 20). Thus, there simply is no such a thing as a unified Chinese state.

In addition, as this study shows, there are multilevel interactions between the different levels of state and society (Fig. 7.1). Both the central and subnational governments engage in negotiations with (different segments of) society simultaneously and sometimes in different directions. Thus, there are discrepancies and even contradictions between different levels of government in their interactions with (different elements of) society. The discrepancies are sometimes capitalized by those social elements to their own advantage. For example, intellectuals, entrepreneurs, and the middle-class citizens, as shown in previous chapters, have successfully acquired substantial political support and resources from local authorities for revitalizing Confucianism. Hence, the relationship between state and society is much more complicated than a linear, straightforward top-down or bottom-up process. In reality, state and society are in constant tension with one another and making compromises in their multilevel and multidirectional interactions with each other.

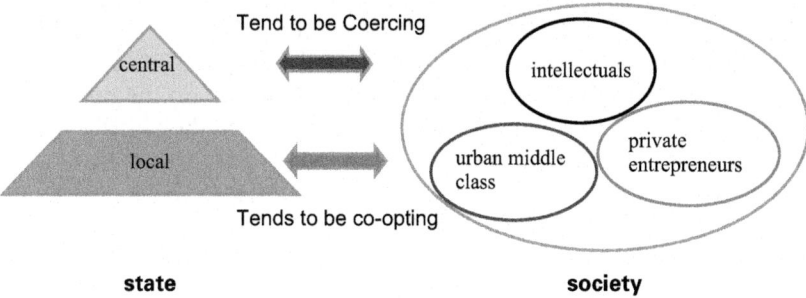

Fig. 7.1   The multileveled and multidirectional relations between state and society

7.3   Directions for Future Research

As China's modernization proceeds, Chinese society will become more heterogeneous, autonomous, and powerful. China's socio-economic structures of society will also continue to experience changes and even major transformations, which, in parallel, will lead to the emergence and vibrancy of various ideologies and beliefs among new social forces. It is thus meaningful to explore how the Chinese state controls society by carefully handling these ideologies. This should better enable us to understand the changes in the relationship between the state and society in China and the resilience of authoritarian government. This research is a preliminary step of a long journey towards a comprehensive understanding of the issue. Future research could proceed in three directions, as sketched below.

The first direction is to extend the research to China's rural and urban lower social groups. Although Confucianism as an ideology has not gained much acceptance among these groups, some Confucian rituals such as ancestral worship have won strong favor with these groups. According to a 2007 survey entitled "The Spiritual Life of Chinese Residents", only 0.2% of respondents identified themselves as "Confucian"[7]; however, 67.6% reported that they venerated their ancestral spirits at their graveside (*shang fen*), which has long been an essential part of Confucian tradition, given that filial piety is one of the Confucian virtues. In comparison, only 6.2% claimed that they attended Christian services, or participated in ritual practices in Buddhist or Taoist temples (or other temples or shrines) (Sun 2009). The resurgence of old Confucian rituals is staggering especially for birth and death in rural areas (Sun 2011). These ancient practices were common in China before the founding of the PRC, but were banned due to the CCP's forceful measures to "uproot old feudal residues" in Chinese society, especially during the Cultural Revolution (1966–1976). With the restoration of the rituals and practices, it remains equally important to examine how the CCP on the one hand allows them to increase social space to grow and on the other hand controls them to avoid their excessive encroachment on the official ideology among its rural cadres (and potential cadres such as rural youth).

Another direction would be to broaden the research to other non-official ideologies such as the New Maoism and Liberalism and even religions like Buddhism, Islam, and Christianity, in order to test the extent to which findings of this study can be generalized to other ideologies and religions. When the CCP responds to the rapid revival of these ideologies and religions, does it adopt the same decentralized response pattern? Or does it react to them in different ways? With findings from such studies, the conclusion of this research can be more solidly grounded. The existing literature provides some clues concerning how the CCP responds to them (Tong 2007; Barmé 2010; Fallman 2010; Qu 2011). However, most of the literature does not proceed from an institutional perspective, for example, how decentralized institutions affect the CCP's handling of these ideologies and religions. There are, in fact, some observations that indicate the CCP's decentralized dealings with these non-official ideologies, such as the resurgence of the New Maoism in Chongqing under the former CCP secretary Bo Xilai and the emergence of Liberalism in Guangdong under Wang Yang, the local CCP secretary. More research, nevertheless, is needed to theorize these empirical findings and test whether the decentralized response pattern summarized in this study can also apply in these cases.

Finally, a possible direction could be shifting from the domestic stage to international arena, examining the Chinese government's employment of Confucianism to gain soft power over overseas audiences. China's modernization process has connected itself closely with other parts of the world. Thus, how the Chinese government is viewed by people in other countries, especially influential ones on the international stage, will also affect the Chinese government's ruling position and therefore China's current political institutions. China has often adapted its public diplomacy strategies by, for example, integrating traditional culture into its overseas propaganda. Though many studies have been done in this area, most focus on exploring the manipulation of, and motivation of the CCP's use of traditional culture. There seems to be a lack of research examining this issue from an institutional perspective. As far as I know, the Chinese state adopts a decentralized partner system in its building and operation of Confucius institutes all over the world. How, then, will the system affect the Chinese state's use of traditional culture in its public diplomacy is an interesting topic, and its findings would also be a worthwhile complement to this study.

NOTES

1. For a clear idea of China's decentralized authoritarian system, see Landry (2008) and Zhou (2014).
2. Huntington (1968) argues that whether a state can endure modernization depends on its levels of institutionalization, which can be defined by its adaptability, complexity, autonomy, and coherence. This section only focuses on adaptability and coherence, because complexity is not related with the

decentralized responses model. Besides, since autonomy and coherence are closely connected with each other, only coherence is discussed here.

3. According to Gilley, even in the summer of 1988, the then Premier Li Peng (Left) launched a withering attack on the rapid economic reform policies of Zhao Ziyang (Right), prefiguring the hard-liner backlash of the following spring. See Gilley (1998).

4. For a detailed discussion about the ideological rivalry between the right and left, please refer to Fewsmith (2001).

5. The framework is not only dominant in analyzing Chinese state-society relations but also for state-society relations in the developing world. For detailed discussions of strong states' top-down control over society in Latin American countries, see O'Donnell (1979), Collier (1979).

6. Though Migdal's 1988 work, *Strong Society and Weak State*, mainly focuses on one dimension of state-society relations, that is, society's influence over states (specifically, how the structure of a society affects its state's capabilities and how societies affect the character and style of states), his state-in-society approach changes the unidirectional "bottom-up" approach and views the state and society as mutually affecting and even integrating with each other.

7. For a detailed explanation of the low rate of self-identification as "Confucian", please see Sun (2009).

References

Baum, R & Shevchenko, A 1999, 'The 'state of the state'', In Goldman, M & MacFarquhar, R (eds.), *The paradox of reform of China's post-Mao reforms*, Harvard University Press, Cambridge, MA.

Barmé, G 2010, 'For truly great men, look to this age alone: was Mao Zedong a new emperor?' in Cheek, T (ed.) *A critical introduction to Mao*, Cambridge University Press.

Brown, A 1996, *The Gorbachev factor*, Oxford University Press, Oxford and New York.

Cai, YS 2008, 'Power structure and regime resilience: contentious politics in China', *British Journal of Political Science*, vol. 38, no. 3.

Chan, A 1993, 'Revolution of corporatism? workers and trade unions in post-Mao China', *Australian Journal of Chinese Affairs*, vol. 29, pp. 31–61.

Chen, P 1993, 'China's challenge to economic orthodoxy: Asian reform as an evolutionary, self-organizing process', *China Economic Review*, vol. 4, no. 2.

Chen, J & Dickson, BJ 2010, *Allies of the state: China's private entrepreneurs and democratic change*, Harvard University Press.

Collier, D 1979, (ed.), *The New Authoritarianism in Latin America*, Princeton University Press, Princeton.

Deng, XP 1994, 'Speech to cadres and soldiers of the Beijing Martial Law Corps, Beijing, June 9', In *Selected works of Deng Xiaoping*, vol. 3, Foreign Languages Press, Beijing, p. 297.

Dickson, B 2003, *Red Capitalists in China: the party, private entrepreneurs and prospects for political change*, Cambridge University Press, Cambridge.

Dickson, B 2008, *Wealth into power: the Communist Party's embrace of China's private sector*, Cambridge University Press, Cambridge.

Dickson, B 2011, 'Sustaining party rule in China', In Brown, NJ (ed.), *The dynamics of democratization: dictatorship, development, and diffusion*, John Hopkins University Press, Baltimore.

Edin, M 2003, 'State capacity and local agent control in China: CCP cadre management from a township perspective', *The China Quarterly*, vol. 173, pp. 35–52.

Fällman, F 2010, 'Useful opium? 'Adapted religion' and 'harmony' in contemporary China', *Journal of Contemporary China*, vol. 19, no. 67, pp. 949–969.

Fewsmith, J 2001, *China since Tiananmen: the politics of transition*, Cambridge University Press, Cambridge.

Gao, SQ 1999, *Two decades of reform in China*, translated and edited by Wang, YL World Scientific, Singapore.

Gibbs, J 1999, *Gorbachev's glasnost: The soviet media in the first phase of perestroika*, Texas A & M University Press, College Station.

Gilley, B 1998, Tiger *on the brink: Jiang Zemin and China's new elite*, University of California Press, p. 106.

Ho, AK 2004, *China's reforms and reformers*, Praeger, Westport, Connecticut.

Holbig, H & Gilley, B 2010, 'In search of legitimacy in post-revolutionary China: bringing ideology and governance back in', *Politics & Policy*, vol. 38, no. 3, pp. 395–422.

Holbig, H 2006, 'Ideological reform and political legitimacy in China: challenges in the post-Jiang Era', In Heberer, T & Schubert, G (eds.), *Regime legitimacy in contemporary China: institutional change and stability*, Routledge, London, pp. 13–34.

Holbig, H 2009, 'Remaking the CCP's ideology: determinants, progress, and limits under Hu Jintao', *Journal of Current Chinese Affairs*, vol. 38, no. 3, pp. 35–61.

Huntington, SP 1968, *Political order in changing societies*, Yale University Press, New Heaven and London.

Karabel, J 1996, "Towards a theory of intellectuals and politics", *Theory and Society*, vol. 25, no. 2.

Landry, P 2008, *Decentralized authoritarianism in China: the Communist Party's control of local elites in post-Mao China*, Cambridge University Press, Cambridge.

Lee, CK 2007, *Against the law: labor protests in China's rustbelt and sunbelt*, University of California Press, Berkeley.

Li, C, 2009, 'The Chinese Communist Party: Recruiting and Controlling the New Elites', *Journal of Current Chinese Affairs*, vol. 38, no. 3, pp. 13–33.

Li, GQ 2004, *Xiandai xingzheng zhong de gongmin canyu (The civil participation in modern public administration)*, The Economic Management Press.

Migdal, J 2001, *State in society: studying how states and societies transform and constitute one another*, Cambridge University Press, Cambridge.

Migdal, JS 1988, *Strong societies and weak states: state-society relations and state capabilities in the Third World*, Princeton University Press, Princeton.

Montinola, G et al, 1996, 'Federalism, Chinese style: the political basis for economic success', *World Politics*, vol. 48, no. 1.

Nathan, AJ & Link, P 2001, *The Tiananmen Papers*, Public Affairs.

Nathan, AJ & Gilley, B 2002, *China's new leaders: the secret files*, New York Review of Books.

Nathan, AJ 2003, 'Authoritarian resilience', *Journal of Democracy*, vol. 14, no. 1, pp. 6–17.

O'Brien, KJ & Li, LJ 2006, *Rightful resistance in rural China*, Cambridge University Press.

O'Donnell, G 1979, 'Tensions in Bureaucratic-Authoritarian State and the question of democracy', In David Collier, D (ed.), *The new authoritarianism in Latin America*, Princeton University Press, Princeton, NJ.

Oi, JC 1992, Fiscal reform and the economic foundations of local state corporatism in China', *World Politics*, vol. 45, no. 1, pp. 99–126.

Oi, JC 1995, 'The role of the local state in China's transitional economy', *The China Quarterly*, vol. 144, pp. 1132–1149.

Palmer, B 2010, 'Is there freedom of speech in China? Only symbolically', *Slate*, October 8th.

Pei, MX 1994, From reform to revolution: the demise of communism in China and the Soviet Union, Harvard University Press.

Pei, MX 2006, *China's trapped transition: the limits of developmental autocracy*, Harvard University Press, Cambridge, MA.

Pei, M 2012, 'Is CCP rule fragile or resilient?' *Journal of Democracy*, vol. 23, no. 1, pp. 27–41.

Qu, H 2011, 'Religious Policy in the People's Republic of China: an alternative perspective', *Journal of Contemporary China*, vol. 20, no. 70.

Saich, T 1994, 'The search for civil society and democracy in China', *Current History*, September, pp. 260–264.

Schuman, M 2011, 'The case for India: free to succeed', *Time*, November 10th.

Shambaugh, D 2000, *The Modern Chinese State*, Cambridge University Press, Cambridge.

Shambaugh, D 2008, *China's Communist Party: atrophy and adaptation*, Woodrow Wilson Center Press & University of California Press, Washington DC & Berkeley.

Sun, A 2009, 'Counting Confucians: who are the Confucians in contemporary East Asia?', *Newsletter of the Institute for Advanced Studies in Humanities and Social Sciences of National Taiwan University*.

Sun, A 2011, 'The revival of Confucian rites in contemporary China', In Yang, FG & Tamney, J (eds.), *Confucianism and spiritual traditions in modern China and beyond*, Brill.

Sun, XL 2001, *Zhongguo xiandaihua jincheng zhong de guojia yu shehui (The Chinese state and society in the process of China's modernization)*, zhongguo shehui kexue chubanshe (China Social Sciences Press).

Tong, JW 2007, *Revenge of the Forbidden City: The suppression of the falungong in China, 1999–2005*, Oxford University Press.

Tsang, S 2009, 'Consultative Leninism: China's new political framework', *Journal of Contemporary China*, vol. 18, no. 62, pp. 865–880.

Tu, WM 2011, 'Confucian Spirituality in Contemporary China', In Yang, FG & Tamney, J (eds.), *Confucianism and spiritual traditions in modern China and beyond*, Brill.

Unger, J & Chan, A 1995, 'China, corporatism, and the East Asian model', *Australian Journal of Chinese Affairs*, vol. 33 (January 1995), pp. 29–53.

Unger, J & Chan, A 1996, 'Corporatism in China; a developmental state in an East Asian context', In McCormick, B & Unger, J (eds.), *China after socialism, In the footsteps of Eastern Europe or East Asia?* M.E. Sharpe, Armonk, NY, pp. 95–129.

Walder, AG 1994, 'The decline of Communist power: elements of a theory of institutional change', *Theory and Society*, vol. 23, pp. 297–323.

White, G, Howell, JA, & Xiaoyuan, S 1996, *In search of civil society: market reform and social change in contemporary China*, OUP Catalogue.

Whiting, S 2000, *Power and wealth in rural China: the political economy of institutional change*, Cambridge University Press, Cambridge.

Xiao, XH 2004, *Gongmin shehui de dansheng (The birth of civil society)*, Sanlian Press, Shanghai.

Xu, CG & Zhuang, JZ 1998, 'Why China grew: the role of decentralization', In Boone, P et al (eds.), *Emerging from communism: lessons from Russia, China, and Eastern Europe*, MIT Press, Cambridge, MA.

Yang, DL 2004, *Remaking the Chinese Leviathan: market transition and the politics of governance in China*, Stanford University Press, Stanford.

Zhou, L 2014. 'Administrative Subcontract (xingzheng fabaozhi),' *Society (shehui)*, vol. 34, no. 6, pp. 1–38.

Appendix 1: List of Formal Interviews

No.	Place	Interviewee's position	Interviewee's institutional type
1.	Guangzhou	Vice president	Middle school
2.	Guangzhou	Teacher	Middle school
3.	Guangzhou	Teacher	Middle school
4.	Guangzhou	President	Primary school
5.	Guangzhou	Director	Government
6.	Shenzhen	Director	Government
7.	Shenzhen	Associate director	Government
8.	Shenzhen	Associate director	Government
9.	Shenzhen	Staff	Government
10.	Shenzhen	Staff	Government
11.	Shenzhen	Vice president	Primary school
12.	Shenzhen	Teacher	Primary school
13.	Shenzhen	Teacher	Primary school
14.	Shenzhen	Dean	Primary school
15.	Shenzhen	Teacher	Primary school
16.	Qingdao	Vice director	Non-governmental organization
17.	Qingdao	Staff	Non-governmental organization
18.	Qingdao	Vice chair	Non-governmental organization
19.	Qingdao	Staff	Non-governmental organization
20.	Qingdao	Journalist	Mass media
21.	Qingdao	Journalist	Mass media
22.	Qingdao	Director	Government
23.	Qingdao	Vice dean	Middle school

(continued)

© The Author(s) 2019
Q. Pang, *State-Society Relations and Confucian Revivalism in Contemporary China*,
https://doi.org/10.1007/978-981-10-8312-9

248   APPENDIX 1: LIST OF FORMAL INTERVIEWS

(continued)

No.	Place	Interviewee's position	Interviewee's institutional type
24.	Qingdao	Teacher	Middle school
25.	Qingdao	Manager	Private enterprise
26.	Qingdao	CEO	Private enterprise
27.	Qingdao	Staff	Private enterprise
28.	Qingdao	Director	Government
29.	Qingdao	Vice director	Government
30.	Qingdao	President	Primary school
31.	Qingdao	Teacher	Primary school
32.	Beijing	Intellectual/researcher	Research
33.	Beijing	Intellectual/researcher	Research
34.	Beijing	Intellectual/researcher	Research
35.	Beijing	Director	Government
36.	Beijing	Intellectual/researcher	Research
37.	Beijing	Intellectual/researcher	Research
38.	Beijing	Intellectual/researcher	Research
39.	Beijing	Intellectual/researcher	Research
40.	Beijing	Intellectual/researcher	Research
41.	Beijing	Intellectual/researcher	Research
42.	Beijing	Intellectual/director	Research
43.	Beijing	Intellectual/vice director	Research
44.	Beijing	Director	Non-governmental organization
45.	Guangzhou	Intellectual/researcher	Research
46.	Guangzhou	Intellectual/researcher	Research
47.	Guangzhou	Intellectual/researcher	Research
48.	Hong Kong	Intellectual/researcher	Research
49.	Hong Kong	Intellectual/researcher	Research
50.	Guangzhou	Director	Non-governmental organization
51.	Guangzhou	Staff	Non-governmental organization
52.	Guangzhou	Staff	Non-governmental organization
53.	Guangzhou	Staff/researcher	Non-governmental organization
54.	Yangzhou	Director	Non-governmental organization
55.	Yangzhou	Vice director	Government
56.	Yangzhou	Dean	Non-governmental organization
57.	Yangzhou	Staff	Non-governmental organization
58.	Yangzhou	Retired associate mayor	Government
59.	Yangzhou	Intellectual/researcher	Research
60.	Yangzhou	Intellectual/researcher	Research

Appendix 2: Map—Location of Informants and Cases

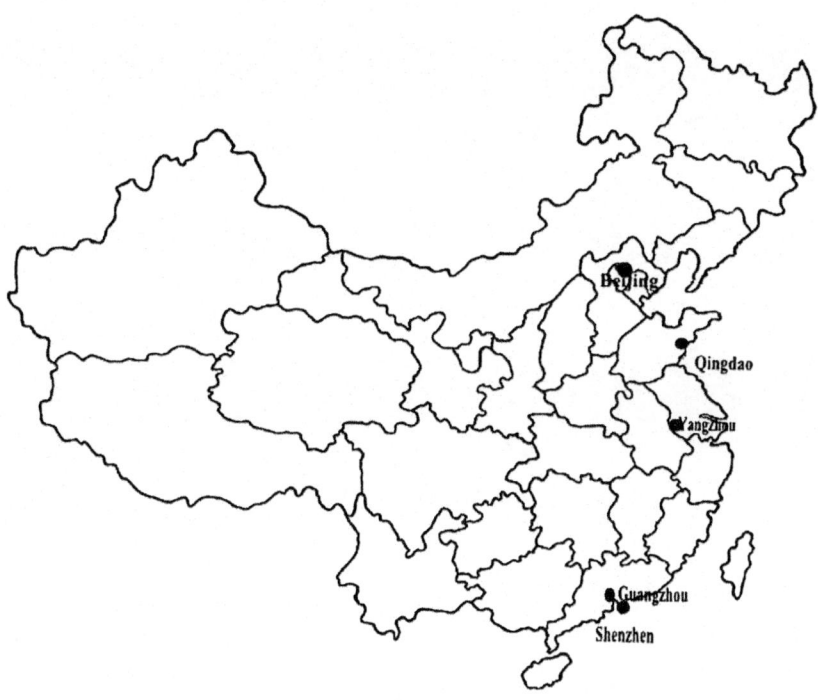

© The Author(s) 2019
Q. Pang, *State-Society Relations and Confucian Revivalism in Contemporary China*,
https://doi.org/10.1007/978-981-10-8312-9

REFERENCES

Ai, J 2008, 'The re-functioning of Confucianism: the mainland Chinese intellectual response since the 1980s', *Issues & Studies*, vol. 44, no. 2, pp. 37–65.

Alagappa, M 1995, *Political legitimacy in Southeast Asia: The quest for moral authority*, Stanford University Press, Stanford, CA.

Almond, G & Verba, S 1989, *The civic culture: political attitudes and democracy in five nations*, Sage, Newbury Park, CA.

Almond, GA & Powell, GB 1966, *Comparative politics: a developmental approach*, Little Brown, Boston.

Alter, P 1994, *Nationalism*, Edward Arnold, New York.

Anagnost, A 1997, *National past-times: narrative, representation, and power in modern China*, Duke University Press, Durham, NC.

Anderson, B 1991, *Imagined communities: reflections on the origin and spread of nationalism*, Verso, London.

Anonymous, 2005, 'Li Hanqiu, chongwen ren yi li zhi xin', viewed on February 3rd, 2011, available at http://www.godpp.gov.cn/lhdbwyhwm/2006-03/03/content_6371545.htm

Arendt, H 1951, *The origins of totalitarianism*, Harcourt, Brace and Co., New York.

Atul, K 2004, *State-directed development, Political power and industrialization in the global periphery*, Cambridge University Press, Cambridge.

Bai, L 1998, 'Monetary reward versus the national ideological agenda: career choice among Chinese university students', *Journal of Moral Education*, vol. 27, no. 4, pp. 1–15.

© The Author(s) 2019
Q. Pang, *State-Society Relations and Confucian Revivalism in Contemporary China*,
https://doi.org/10.1007/978-981-10-8312-9

Barme, G 2000, 'The revolution of resistance', In Perry, E & Selden, M (eds.), *Chinese society: change, conflict and resistance*, Routledge, Taylor & Francis.

Barmé, GR 1995, 'To screw foreigners is patriotic: China's avant-garde nationalists', *The China Journal*, vol. 34, pp. 209–234.

Barmé, GR 2009, 'China's flat earth: history and 8 August 2008', *The China Quarterly*, vol. 197, pp. 64–86.

Baum, R & Shevchenko, A 1999, 'The 'state of the state'', In Goldman, M & MacFarquhar, R (eds.), *The paradox of reform of China's post-Mao reforms*, Harvard University Press, Cambridge, MA.

Becker, J 1998, *Hungry ghosts: Mao's secret famine*, Henry Holt & Co, New York.

Beetham, D 1991, *The legitimation of power*, Palgrave Macmillan, London.

Bell, DA 2008, *China's new Confucianism: Politics and everyday life in a changing society*, Princeton University Press, Princeton.

Bellin, E 2000, 'Contingent democrats: industrialists, labor, and democratization in late-developing countries', *World Politics*, vol. 52, no. 2.

Berger, J & Zelditch, M 1998, *Status, power, and legitimacy*, Transaction, New Brunswick.

Betts, C & Devereux, M 2000, 'International monetary policy coordination and competitive depreciation: a reevaluation', *Journal of Money Credit and Banking*, vol. 32, pp. 722–745.

Billioud, S & Thoraval, J 2008, 'The contemporary revival of Confucianism, Anshen liming or the religious dimension of Confucianism', *China Perspective*, no. 3.

Billioud, S 2007a, 'Confucianism, 'cultural tradition,' and official discourses at the start of the new century', *China Perspectives*, no. 3.

Billioud, S 2007b, 'Jiaohua: the Confucian revival today as an educative project', *China Perspectives*, no. 4.

Bonnin, M & Chevrier, Y 1991, 'The intellectual and the state: social dynamics of intellectual autonomy during the post-Mao era,' *The China Quarterly*, vol. 127, pp. 569–593.

Borcherding, TE 1977, "One Hundred Years of Public Spending." In *Budgets and Bureaucrats: The Sources of Government Growth*, ed. Thomas E. Borcherding. Duke University Press, Durham, NC.

Börzel, TA 2002, *States and regions in the European Union: institutional adaptation in Germany and Spain*, Cambridge University Press, Cambridge.

Bourdieu, P 1990, *In other words: essays towards a reflexive sociology*, Stanford University Press, Stanford, CA.

Bourdieu, P 1991, Language *and symbolic power*, Polity Press, Cambridge.

Bradsher, K 2012, 'Construction and real estate reveal problems in China's economy', *The New York Times*, September 9th.

Breuilly, J 1985, *Nationalism and the State*, University of Chicago Press, Chicago.

Brockmann, H, Delhey, J, Welzel, C & Hao, Y 2009, 'The China puzzle: falling happiness in a rising economy', *Journal of Happiness Studies*, vol. 10, no. 4, pp. 387–405.

Brown, A 1996, *The Gorbachev factor*, Oxford University Press, Oxford and New York.

Brown, K 2012. 'The communist party of China and ideology,' *China: An International Journal*, vol. 10, no. 2, pp. 52–68.

Buchanan, JM 1977, *"Why Does Government Grow?"* In *Budgets and Bureaucrats: The Sources of Government Growth*, ed. Thomas E. Borcherding. Duke University Press, Durham, NC.

Buckley, C 2012, 'China domestic security spending rises to $111 billion', viewed on February 2nd, 2013, available at http://www.reuters.com/article/2012/03/05/us-china-parliament-security-idUSTRE82403J20120305

Burns, J 1978, 'Elections of production team cadres in rural china, 1958–1974,' *The China Quarterly*, vol. 74, pp. 273–296.

Burns, J 1987, 'China's nomenklatura system', *Problems of Communism*, vol. 36, no. 5, pp. 36–51.

Burns, J (ed.) 1989, *The Chinese Communist Party's nomenklatura system: a documentary study of Party control of leadership selection 1979–1984*, M.E. Sharpe, Armonk, NY.

Burns, JP 1994, 'Strengthening central CCP control of leadership selection: The 1990 Nomenklatura', *The China Quarterly*, vol. 138.

Cai, D 1996, 'Shiyong ruxue chuyi' ('Discussions on the nature of practical Confucianism'), In Cai, D (ed.), *Lu Culture and Confucianism*, Shandong Friendship Press.

Cai, D, Mou, Z 1998, 'Ruxue xiandaihua yingxiang Bahai jiqu shenme?' ('What should Confucianism learn from Baha'i?'), *The Journal of Hainan University (Humanities and Social Science Edition)*, no. 3.

Cai, YS 2008, 'Power structure and regime resilience: contentious politics in China', *British Journal of Political Science*, vol. 38, no. 3.

Cai, YS 2010, *Collective resistance in China: why popular protests succeed or fail*, Stanford University Press, Stanford.

Callahan, WA 2010, *China: the pessoptimist nation*, Oxford University Press, Oxford.

Canetti, E 1960, *Crowds and Power*, Continuum, New York.

Carr, CL 1988, 'Coercion and Freedom,' *American Philosophical Quarterly*, vol. 25, pp. 59–67.

Chan, A 1993, 'Revolution of corporatism? workers and trade unions in post-Mao China', *Australian Journal of Chinese Affairs*, vol. 29, pp. 31–61.

Chan, A 2011, 'Strikes in China's export industries in comparative perspective', *The China Journal*, vol. 65, January.

Chan, A Madsen, R & Unger, J 1992, *Chen village under Mao and Deng*, University of California Press, Berkeley.

Chan, H & King, YC 2008, 'Chinese Religion', In Gamer, R *Understanding Contemporary China*, Lynn Reinner, New York.

Chang J 1997, 'The mechanics of state propaganda: the People's Republic of China and the Soviet Union in the 1950s', In Cheek, T & Saich, T (eds.), *New perspectives on state socialism in China*, M. E. Sharpe, Armonk, 1997, pp. 76–124.

Chang, JTH et al, (eds.) 2003, *China's media and entertainment law* (Vol. I), TransAsia Publishing Ltd, Beijing.

Chen, D 2000, 'Rushang jingshen yu 21shiji zhonguo ji dongnanya jingji fazhan yantaohui zongshu' (Review of the Seminar of Confucian entrepreneur spirits and the 21st century China), *Zhonghua Wenhua Luntan (Forum on Chinese Culture)*, Autumn.

Chen, L 2004, *Song Ming li xue (Neo-Confucianism)*, Hua dong shi fan da xue chu ban she (Huadong Normal University Press), Shanghai.

Chen, L 2007, 'Kongzi yu Dangdai zhongguo' (Confucius and contemporary China), *Dushu (Reading)*, no. 11.

Chen, P 1993, 'China's challenge to economic orthodoxy: Asian reform as an evolutionary, self-organizing process', *China Economic Review*, vol. 4, no. 2.

Chen, Y 2012, 'Renewing Confucianism as a living tradition in the 21st century China: reciting Classics, Reviving Academies and restoring rituals', In Giordan, G (ed.), *Mapping religion and spirituality in a post-secular world*, Brill Press.

Cheng, Y 2008 'Liberalism in Contemporary China: ten years after its 'resurface'', Journal of Contemporary China, vol. 17, no. 55, pp. 383–400.

Cheung, T & King, AY 2004, 'Righteousness and profitableness: the moral choices of contemporary Confucian entrepreneurs', *Journal of Business Ethics*, vol. 54.

Cheung, T 2002, *rushang yu xiandai shehui: yili guanxi de shehuixue fenxi (Confucian businessman and modern society: the sociological analysis of the relationship between interests and righteousness)*, Nanjing University Press, Nanjing.

China Confucius Foundation (*zhongguo kongzi jijinhui*) 2009, *Zhongguo ruxue nianjian (China Confucianism Yearbook)*, China Confucius Foundation, Jinan, Shandong Province, China.

Chow, BN 2007, 'Conceptualizing intellectual-state relations in China: with a focus on the contemporary China', *Issues and Studies*, vol. 43, no. 2.

Clegg, SR 1989, *Frameworks of power*, Sage, London.

Cohen, JA, Edwards, RR & Chen, CF (eds.) 1980, *Essays on China's legal tradition*, Princeton University Press, Princeton.

Collier, D 1979, (ed.), *The New Authoritarianism in Latin America*, Princeton University Press, Princeton.

Collier, RB & Collier, D 1991, *Shaping the political arena: critical junctures, the labor movement and regime dynamics in Latin America*, Princeton University Press, Princeton.

Connor, W 1994, *Ethno-nationalism: the quest for understanding*, Princeton University Press, Princeton.

Craig, E 1998, *Routledge encyclopedia of philosophy*, volume 7, Taylor & Francis, London.

Dahl, R 1961, *Who Governs? Democracy and Power in an American City*, Yale University Press, New Haven.

Dahl, R 1963, *Modern Political Analysis*, Prentice-Hall, Englewood Cliffs, NJ.

De Bary, WT 1975, *The unfolding of Neo-Confucianism*, Columbia University Press, New York.

De Bary, WT & Bloom, I 1999, *Sources of Chinese tradition second edition, volume I: from earliest times to 1600*, Columbia University Press, New York.

Dean, JP & Whyte, WF 1969, 'How do you know if the informant is telling the truth?', in McCall, GJ & Simmons JL (eds.), *Issues in participant observation*. Addison-Wesley, MA.

Deng, XP 1994, 'Speech to cadres and soldiers of the Beijing Martial Law Corps, Beijing, June 9', In *Selected works of Deng Xiaoping*, vol. 3, Foreign Languages Press, Beijing, p. 297.

Desmond, K & Lieberman, R 2008, 'Finding the American state: transcending the 'statelessness' account', *Polity*, vol. 40, no. 3, pp. 368–378.

Diamond, L 1999, *Developing democracy: toward consolidation*, Johns Hopkins University Press.

Dickson, B 1997, *Democratization in China and Taiwan: the adaptability of Leninist parties*, Oxford University Press, New York.

Dickson, B 2003, *Red Capitalists in China: the party, private entrepreneurs and prospects for political change*, Cambridge University Press, Cambridge.

Dickson, B 2004, 'Beijing's ambivalent reformers', *Current History*, vol. 103, no. 674, pp. 249–55.

Dickson, B 2008, *Wealth into power: the Communist Party's embrace of China's private sector*, Cambridge University Press, Cambridge.

Dickson, B 2011, 'Sustaining party rule in China', In Brown, NJ (ed.), *The dynamics of democratization: dictatorship, development, and diffusion*, John Hopkins University Press, Baltimore.

Dickstein, M 1992, *Double agent: the critic and society*, Oxford University Press, New York.

Dirlik, A 1995, 'Confucius in the borderlands: global, Capitalism and the reinvention of Confucianism', *Boundary*, vol. 22, no. 3.

Dirlik, A 1997, *The postcolonial aura: Third World criticism in the age of global capitalism*, Westview Press, Boulder, Colo.

Dittmer, L 1987, "Public and Private Interests and the Participatory Ethic in China," in *Citizens and Groups in Contemporary China*, edited by Falkenheim V. C., pp. 18–23, Ann Arbor: Center for Chinese Studies, University of Michigan.

Dotson, J 2011, 'Confucian revival in the propaganda narratives of the Chinese government', US-China Economic and Security Review Commission staff research report, July 20th.

Downing, BM 1992, *The military revolution and political change: origins of democracy and autocracy in early modern Europe*, Princeton University Press, Princeton.

Dryzek, J & Dunleavy, P 2009, *Theories of the democratic state*, Palgrave Macmillan, London.

Durkheim, E 1984, *The division of labor in society*, Free Press, New York.

Durkheim, E 1997, *Suicide: a study in sociology*, Free Press, New York.

Edin, M 2003, 'State capacity and local agent control in China: CCP cadre management from a township perspective', *The China Quarterly*, vol. 173, pp. 35–52.

Eichengreen, B et al, 2012, 'When fast-growing Economies slow down: International evidence and implications for China', *Asian Economic Papers*, MIT Press, vol. 11, no. 1, pp. 42–87.

Elman, B 2000, *A cultural history of civil examinations in late imperial China*, University of California Press, Berkeley and Los Angeles.

Elman, BA 1990, *Classicism, politics, and kinship: the Ch'ang-chou school of new text Confucianism in late imperial China*, University of California Press, Berkeley and Los Angeles.

Esarey, A 2005, 'Cornering the market: state strategies for controlling China's commercial media', *Asian Perspective*, vol. 29, no. 4, pp. 37–83.

Evans, P 1995, *Embedded autonomy: states and industrial transformation*, Princeton University Press, Princeton.

Evans, P 1996, 'Government action, social capital and development: Reviewing the evidence on synergy', *World Development*, vol. 24, no. 6, pp. 1119–1132.

Evans, P et al, 1985, *Bringing the state back in*, Cambridge University Press, Cambridge.

Eyerman, R 1994, *Between culture and politics: intellectuals in modern society*, Polity Press, Cambridge.

Fairbank, JK & Feuerwerker, A 1986, *The Cambridge history of China*, Cambridge University Press, Cambridge.

Fang, KL 1997, *Xiandai xin ruxue yu zhongguo xiandaihua (Contemporary new Confucianism and Chinese modernization)*, Tianjin renmin chubanshe (Tianjin People's Press), Tianjin.

Fang, KL 2005, 'Jiashen zhinian de wenhua fanxi—pin dalu xinruxue fuchu shuimian he baoshou zhuyi ruhua lun' ('Reflection of cultural development in Jiashen years—comment on the emergence of the mainland new Confucianism and Conservative Confucianization Theory'), *Journal of Sun Yat-Sen University (Social Science Edition)*, no. 6.

Fang, M 2011, 'Is Bo & Wang's spat a war over party line?' viewed on December 10th, 2012, available at http://china.dwnews.com/news/2011-07-14/57906363-3.html

Feng, C 2003, 'Shichanghua, quanqiuhua he Zhongguo zhishifenzi de jiaose zhuanhuan' (Marketization, globalization, and role changes of Chinese intellectuals), In Zhao B (ed.), *Zhishifenzi yus hehui fazhan (Intellectuals and social development)*, Huaxia chubanshe (Huaxia press), Beijing.

Feng, CY 2010, 'Charter 08 and China's troubled liberalism', *Asian Times*, viewed on November 3rd, available at http://www.atimes.com/atimes/China/LB26Ad04.html

Fernanda, A et al, 2002, 'Slouching towards decentralization: consequences of globalization for curricular control in national education systems', *Comparative Educational Review*, vol. 46, no. 1, pp. 66–88.

Fewsmith, J 2001, *China since Tiananmen: the politics of transition*, Cambridge University Press, Cambridge.

Fishman, RM 1990, 'Rethinking state and regime: Southern Europe's transition to democracy', *World Politics*, vol. 42, no. 3, pp. 422–440.

Foster, Kenneth W 2001, 'Associations in the embrace of an authoritarian state: state domination of society,' *Studies in Comparative International Development*, vol. 35, no. 4, pp. 84–109.

Foster, KW 2002, 'Embedded within state agencies: Business associations in Yantai', *The China Journal*, vol. 47, pp. 41–65.

Franz, S 1966, *Ideology and organization in communist China*, University of California Press, California.

Fredrik, F 2010, 'Adapted 'religion' and 'harmony' in contemporary China', *Journal of Contemporary China*, vol. 19, no. 67.

Friedman, E et al, 2005, *Revolution, resistance, and reform in village China*, Yale University Press, New Haven.

Friedrich, C & Brzezinski, Z 1956, *Totalitarian dictatorship and autocracy*, Harvard University Press.

Fu, ZY 1993, *Autocratic tradition and Chinese politics*, Cambridge University Press, New York.

Fukuyama, F 2011, *The Origins of political order: from prehuman times to the French revolution*, Farrar, Straus and Giroux, New York.

Gao, SQ 1999, *Two decades of reform in China*, translated and edited by Wang, YL World Scientific, Singapore.

Ge, X 2010, 'Zai dazao rushang de jianan jincheng zhong, wo yuanzuo lazhu zhaoliang manman changlu', In Zhou Xinguo (ed.), *Ruxue yu rushang xinlun (New views concerning Confucianism and Confucian entrepreneur)*, Shehui kexue wenxian chubanshe (Social Science Literature Press).

Geertz, C 1963, 'The integrative revolution: primordial sentiments and civil politics in the new states' In Geertz (ed.), *Old societies and new states*, Free Press, Glencoe.

Gellner, E 2008, *Nations and nationalism*, Cornell University Press.

George AL & Andrew, B 2005, *Case studies and theory development in the social sciences*, MIT Press, Cambridge, MA.

Gerring, J 1997, 'Ideology: a definitional analysis', *Political Research Quarterly*, vol. 50 (December), pp. 957–94.

Gibbs, J 1999, *Gorbachev's glasnost: The soviet media in the first phase of perestroika*, Texas A & M University Press, College Station.

Giddens, A 1979, *Central problems in social theory*, Macmillan, London.

Giddens, A 1981, *A contemporary critique of historical materialism*, Macmillan, London.

Giddens, A 1984, *The constitution of society: outline of the theory of structuration*, Polity Press, Cambridge.

Gilbert, J & Howe, C 1991, 'Beyond 'State vs, Society': theories of the state and new deal agricultural policies', *American Sociological Review*, vol. 56 (April 1991), pp. 204–220.

Gilley, B 1998, Tiger *on the brink: Jiang Zemin and China's new elite*, University of California Press, p. 106.

Gilley, B 2006, 'The meaning and measure of state legitimacy: results for 72 countries', *European Journal of Political Research*, vol. 45, pp. 499–525.

Glahn, RV 1996, *Fountain of fortune: money and monetary policy in China, 1000–1700*, University of California Press, Berkeley.

Gold, TB 1990, "Party-State versus Society in China." In *Building a Nation-State: China at Forty*, edited by Kallgren JK., pp. 125–151. Berkeley: Institute of East Asian Studies, University of California.

Goldin, P 2011, *Confucianism*, Acumen Publishing House, Durham, UK.

Goldman, M & Lee, L (eds.) 2001, *An intellectual history of modern China*, Cambridge University Press, Cambridge.

Goldman, M 1985, 'The zigs and zags in the treatment of intellectuals', *The China Quarterly*, December, no. 104, pp. 709–715.

Goldman, M 1993, 'The intellectuals in the Deng era', In Kau, MY & Marsh, SH (eds.), *China in the era of Deng Xiaoping: a decade of reform*, M.E. Sharpe, Armonk, pp. 285–326.

Goldman, M 1996, 'Politically-engaged intellectuals in the Deng-Jiang era: a changing relationship with the party-state', *The China Quarterly*, March, no. 145, pp. 35–52.

Goldman, M 1999, 'Politically-engaged intellectuals in the 1990s', *The China Quarterly*, September, no. 159.

Goldman, M 2011, 'Role of China's intellectuals in the People's Republic of China', In Kirby, WC (ed.), *The People's Republic of China at 60—an international assessment*, Harvard University Asia Center, Cambridge.

Goldman, M, Cheek, T & Hamrin, CL (eds.) 1987, *China's intellectuals and the state: in search of a new relationship*, Harvard University Press, Cambridge.

Gramsci, A 1971, *The prison notebooks*, Lawrence and Wishart, London.

Greenfeld, L & Martin, ML 1988, *Center: ideas and institutions*, University of Chicago Press, Chicago.

Gu, EX & Goldman, M 2004, *Chinese intellectuals between state and market*, RoutledgeCurzon, London.

Gu, EX 1999, 'Cultural intellectuals and the politics of the cultural public space', *The Journal of Asian Studies*, vol. 58, no. 2, pp. 389–431.

Guang, SJ 1996, 'Cultural collisions foster understanding', *China Daily*, September 2nd, p. 4.

Guo, BG 2003a, 'Political legitimacy and China's transition', *Journal of Chinese Political Science*, vol. 8, no. 1–2, pp. 1–25.

Guo, S 2012, *Chinese politics and government: power, ideology and organization*, Routledge, London and New York.

Guo, X 2003b, *State and society in China's democratic transition: Confucianism, Leninism, and economic development*, Routledge, London.

Guo, YJ 2004, *Cultural nationalism in contemporary China: the search for national identity*, RoutledgeCurzon.

Haggard, S & Kaufman, RR 1995, *The political economy of democratic transitions*, Princeton University Press, Princeton.

Hagopian, F 1994, 'Traditional Politics against State Transformation in Brazil', In Migdal, J, Kohli, A & Shue, V (eds.), *State power and social forces: domination and transformation in the Third World*, Cambridge University Press, Cambridge.

Hall, JA & Ikenberry, GJ 1989, *The state*, University of Minnesota Press, Minneapolis.

Hall, PA 1986, *Governing the Economy: The Politics of State Intervention in Britain and France*, Oxford University Press, New York.

Hall, PA & Taylor, RCR 1996, 'Political science and the three new institutionalisms', *Political Studies*, vol. XLIV, pp. 936–957.

Hamrin, CL 1987, 'Conclusion: new trends under Deng Xiaoping and his successors', In Goldman, M, Cheek, T & Hamrin, CL (eds.), *China's Intellectuals and the State*, Harvard University Press, Cambridge, pp. 275–304.

Hanson, ME 1998, 'Strategies of educational decentralization: key questions and core issues', *Journal of Educational Administration*, vol. 36, no. 2.

Hao, J & Lin, ZM (eds.) 1994, *Changing central–local relations in China: reform and state capacity*, Westview Press, Boulder.

Hao, L (ed.) 2000, *Yi "san ge daibiao" wei gangling quanmian jiaqiang dang de jianshe (Comprehensively Strengthening Party Building with the "Three Represents" as Guiding Principle)*, Dangjian Duwu Chubanshe, Beijing, China.

Hao, Z 2012. *Intellectuals at a crossroads: the changing politics of China's knowledge workers.* SUNY Press.

Harrison, J 1969, *Modern Chinese nationalism*, Anvil, New York.

260   REFERENCES

Hart, D 2002, 'Antoine Louis Claude, Comte Destutt de Tracy (1754–1836): life and works', *The Library of Economics and Liberty*, Liberty Fund, viewed on December, 2012, available at http://www.econlib.org/library/Tracy/DestuttdeTracyBio.html

Hastings, A 1997, *The construction of nationhood: ethnicity, religion and nationalism*, Cambridge University Press, Cambridge.

Hawes, C 2008, 'Corporate CEOs as cultural promoters', In Goodman, D (ed.), *The new rich in China*, Routledge, London.

Hawkins, JN 1998, 'Higher education reform and science and technology in China', In Cummings, W & McGinn, N (eds.), *International Handbook of Education and development: Preparing Schools, Students and Nations for the Twenty-First Century*, Pergamon Press.

Hawkins, JN 2000, 'Centralization, decentralization, recentralization: educational reform in China', *Journal of Educational Administration*, vol. 38, no. 5, pp. 442–454.

Hawkins, JN 2006, 'Walking on three legs: centralization, decentralization, and recentralization in Chinese education', In Bjork C (ed.), *Education decentralization: Asian experience and conceptual contribution*, Springer, pp. 21–46.

Hay, C & Wincott, D 1998, 'Structure, agency and historical institutionalism', *Political Studies*, vol. 46, pp. 951–957.

He, HY 2000, *Dictionary of the political thought of the People's Republic of China*, M.E. Sharpe, Armonk, NY.

He, Q 2006, 'The new myth in China: China's rising middle-class will accelerate democratization', *Finance and Culture Weekly*, 8 November.

He, Q 2007, *"Yuanzui" zhi zheng houmian yincang de shehui jinzhang (Social tensions as reflected in the debate on "the original sin of the rich")*, viewed February 10th, 2007, http://www.epochtimes.com/b5/7/2/10/nl619404.htm

Herder, J 2010, 'Essay on the origin of language', In Barnard, FM (ed.), *Herder on social & political culture*, Cambridge University Press, Cambridge.

Ho, AK 2004, *China's reforms and reformers*, Praeger, Westport, Connecticut.

Ho, N 2009, 'Unlikely bedfellows? Confucius, the CCP and the resurgence of Guoxue', *Harvard International Review*, 26 October.

Ho, S 1994, *Rural China in transition: non-agricultural development in rural Jiangsu, 1978–1990*, Clarendon Press, Oxford.

Ho, PT 1962, *The ladder of success in imperial China: aspects of social mobility, 1368–1911*, Wiley & Sons, New York.

Hobsbawm, EJ 1992a, *Nations and nationalism since 1780*, Cambridge University Press, Cambridge.

Hobsbawm, EJ 1992b, Nations and Nationalism Since 1780: Programme, Myth, Reality, Cambridge University Press.

Holbig, H & Gilley, B 2010, 'In search of legitimacy in post-revolutionary China: bringing ideology and governance back in', *Politics & Policy*, vol. 38, no. 3, pp. 395–422.

Holbig, H 2006, 'Ideological reform and political legitimacy in China: challenges in the post-Jiang Era', In Heberer, T & Schubert, G (eds.), *Regime legitimacy in contemporary China: institutional change and stability*, Routledge, London, pp. 13–34.

Holbig, H 2009, 'Remaking the CCP's ideology: determinants, progress, and limits under Hu Jintao', *Journal of Current Chinese Affairs*, vol. 38, no. 3, pp. 35–61.

Hong 2011, 'Religious policy in the People's Republic of China: an alternative perspective', *Journal of Contemporary China*, vol. 20, no. 70.

Hu, L & Hu, A 2008, 'Zhongchan jieceng: Wendingqi haishi xiangfan huo qita' (Middle stratum: a stabilizer, a disrupter, or something else), *Zhengzhixue yanjiu (Political Science Studies)*, no. 2.

Huang, SC 1999, *Essentials of neo-Confucianism: eight major philosophers of the song and Ming periods*, Greenwood Press, Westport.

Huang, YS 1995, 'Administrative monitoring in China', *The China Quarterly*, vol. 143.

Huberman, BA, Loch, CH & Önçüler, A 2004, 'Status as a valued resource', *Social Psychology Quarterly*, vol. 67, no. 1, p. 103.

Hucker, CO 1975, *China's imperial past: an introduction to Chinese history and culture*, Stanford University Press, Stanford CA.

Hughes, CR 2006, *Chinese nationalism in the global era*, Routledge, London & New York.

Huntington, S 1970, 'Social and institutional dynamics of one-party systems', In Huntington, S & Moore, CH (eds.), *Authoritarian politics in modern society: the dynamics of established one-party systems*, Basic Books, New York.

Huntington, SP 1968, *Political order in changing societies*, Yale University Press, New Heaven and London.

Huntington, SP 1991, *The third wave: democratization in the late twentieth century*, University of Oklahoma Press.

Huntington, SP 1996, *The clash of civilizations and the remaking of world order*, Simon & Schuster, New York.

Hutton, W 2006, *The writing on the wall: why we must embrace China as a partner or face it as an enemy*, Free Press, New York.

Ichisada, M 1981, *China's examination hell: the civil service examinations of imperial China*, Yale University Press, New Haven.

Jacobs, A 2011, 'Confucius statue vanishes near Tiananmen square', *The New York Times*, April 22nd, viewed on May 1st, 2012, available at http://www.nytimes.com/2011/04/23/world/asia/23confucius.html

Jennings, MK 1997, "Political participation in the Chinese countryside", *The American Political Science Review*, vol. 91, no. 2.

Jensen, L 2008, 'politics, history and the state of the States', *Polity*, vol. 40, no. 3.

Jessop, B 1977, "Recent theories of the capitalist state", *Cambridge Journal of Economics*, no. 1, pp. 353–73.

Jessop, B 1982, *The capitalist state: Marxist theories and methods*, Blackwell, Oxford.

Jessop, B 1990, *State theory: putting the capitalist state in its place*, Polity, Cambridge.

Jessop, B 2008, *State power: a strategic-relational approach*, Polity, Cambridge.

Jiang, Q 1989, 'Zhongguo dalu fuxing ruxue de xianshi yiyi jiqi mianlin de wenti (The significance of and obstacles to the revival of Confucianism in mainland China)', *Ehu (Swan Lake)* vol. 170.

Jiang, Q 2003, *zhengzhi ruxue—dangdai ruxue de zhuanxiang tezhi yu fazhan (Political Confucianism—the reformation, characteristics and development of contemporary Confucianism)*, Sanlian Bookshop Publishing House, Shanghai.

Jin, HH, Qian, YY & Weingast, B 2005, 'Regional decentralization and fiscal incentives: federalism, Chinese style', *Journal of Public Economics*, vol. 89, pp. 1719–1742.

Joseph, WA 2010, *Politics in China: an introduction*, Oxford University Press, Oxford & New York.

Kampen, T 2000, *Mao Zedong, Zhou Enlai and the Evolution of the Chinese Communist Leadership*, Nordic Institute of Asian Studies, Copenhagen.

Kang, XG 2004a, 'Renzheng: quanwei zhuyi guojia de hefaxing sikao' ('Benevolent politics: the legitimacy of authoritarian states'), *Zhanlue yu Guanli (Strategy and Management)*, no. 2.

Kang, XG 2004b, 'Wo wenshenme zhuzhang ruhua: guanyu zhongguo weilai zhengzhi fazhan de baoshouzhuyi sikao' ('Why I advocates Confucianization: conservative thoughts about China's future political development'), *Yannan shequwang*, December.

Kang, XG 2005, *Renzheng—Zhongguo zhengzhi fazhan de disantiao daolu (Benevolent politics—the third way for Chinese political development)*, World Science and Technology Press, Singapore.

Kang, XG 2008, *Zhongguo guilai—Dangdai zhongguo dalu wenhua minzuzhuyi yundong yanjiu (Back of China—research on the cultural nationalism movement in contemporary Chinese mainland)*, Global Publishing Company, Singapore.

Kang, XG, Wang, J & Liu, SL 2010, *Zhendizhan: Guan yu zhonghua wenhua fuxingde gelanxishi fenxi* (Struggle for cultural hegemony: Gramscian perspectives of revitalizing Chinese traditional culture), shehui kexue wenxian chubanshe (Social Science Literature Press), Beijing.

Karabel, J 1996, "Towards a theory of intellectuals and politics", *Theory and Society*, vol. 25, no. 2.

Kedourie, E 1985, *Nationalism*, Hutchinson, London.

Kennedy, D 1982, "The States of Decline of the Public-Private Distinction", *University of Pennsylvania Law Review*, no. 130, pp. 1349–1357.

Kennedy, S 2005, *The business of lobbying in China*, Harvard University Press, Cambridge, MA.

Kerry, B, 2012, 'The Communist Party of China and Ideology', *China: An International Journal*, vol. 10, no. 2, pp. 52–68.

Knight, K 2006, 'Transformations of the concept of ideology in the twentieth century', *American Political Science Review*, vol. 100, pp. 619–626.

Koelble, TA 1995, 'The new institutionalism in political science and sociology', *Comparative Politics*, vol. 27, pp. 221–244.

Koo, H 1991, 'Middle classes, democratization, and class formation: the case of South Korea', *Theory and Society*, vol. 20, August.

Koo, H 2001, *Korean workers: the culture and politics of class formation*, Cornell University Press, Ithaca.

Kornhauser, W 1959, *The politics of mass society*, Free Press, Glencoe.

Krasner, SD 1988, 'Sovereignty: an institutional perspective', *Comparative Political Studies*, vol. 21, no. 1, pp. 66–94.

Kriesi, H et al, 1992, 'New social movements and political opportunities in Western Europe', *European Journal of Political Research*, vol. 22, pp. 219–244.

Laliberte, A & Lanteigne, M (ed.) 2008, *The Chinese Party-State in the 21st century: adaptation and the reinvention of legitimacy*, Routledge.

Lam, W 2003, 'Entrepreneurs slowly joining CCP' viewed on June 13th, 2012, available at http://articles.cnn.com/2003-11-11/world/china. bizmen_1_ccp-party-members-businessmen?_s=PM:WORLD

Landry, P 2008, *Decentralized authoritarianism in China: the Communist Party's control of local elites in post-Mao China*, Cambridge University Press, Cambridge.

Larus, EF 2012, *Politics and society in contemporary China*, Lynne Rienner.

Lasswell, HD & Kaplan, A 1950, *Power and society*, Yale University Press, New Haven.

Law, WW, 1995, 'The role of state in higher education reform in mainland China and Taiwan', *Comparative Education Review*, vol. 39, no. 3, p. 340.

Le, QW, 2003, *Ru dang xu zhi (What you have to know to join the party)*, Shanghai Renmin Chubanshe (Shanghai People' Press), Shanghai, China.

Lee, CK 2007, *Against the law: labor protests in China's rustbelt and sunbelt*, University of California Press, Berkeley.

Lee, HY 1991, *From revolutionary cadres to party technocrats in socialist China*, University of California Press, Berkeley.

Lee, WO & Ho, CH 2005, 'Ideological Shifts and Changes in Moral Education Policy in China', *Journal of Moral Education*, vol. 34, no. 4, p. 416.

Lei, J 2006, 'Jia yizuo huayu tongxin de qiaoliang—nanchangshi chushi xiaoxue yi guoxue jingdian kaizhan shehuizhuyi rongruguan jiaoyu' (Building a bridge for educating children—Zhushi Primary School in Nanchang conducted SCHD education through national studies classics), *Jiangxi Jiaoyu* (*Jiangxi Education*), no. Z2.

Lenin, VI 1960, 'The state and revolution', in *Collected Works* 25, Lawrence and Wishart, London.

Levenson, JR 1953, *Liang ch'ich'ao and the mind of modern china*, Harvard University Press, Cambridge, MA.

Levenson, JR 1968, *Confucian China and its modern fate: a trilogy*, University of California Press, Berkley.

Levi, M 1990, 'A logic of institutional change', In Cook, KS & Levi, M (eds.), *The limits of rationality*, University of Chicago Press.

Lewis, JW & Xue, L 2003, 'Social change and political reform in China: meeting the challenge of success', *The China Quarterly*, vol. 176, pp. 926–942.

Li, C, 2005a, 'The new bipartisanship within the Chinese Communist Party', *Orbis*, vol. 49, no. 3, pp. 387–400.

Li, C, 2009, 'The Chinese Communist Party: Recruiting and Controlling the New Elites', *Journal of Current Chinese Affairs*, vol. 38, no. 3, pp. 13–33.

Li Guoqiang, 2004, *Xiandai xingzheng zhong de gongmin canyu (The civil participation in modern public administration)*, The Economic Management Press

Li Xiguang & Liu Kang, 1996, "A look at the coverage of China by the mainstream U.S. media", *Zhongguojizhe (The Chinese Journalist)*, 15 May, pp. 19–23.

Li, Y, & Yang, MZ 2010, 'The National Studies Education in Bao'an stays ahead', *Yangcheng Daily*, 9 November 2010.

Li, C 2005b "Prestige stratification in the contemporary china: occupational prestige measures and socio-economic index" (*dangdai zhongguo de shehui shengwang fengceng*), *Sociological Research (shehuixue yanjiu)*, no. 2, pp. 74–102.

Li, C 2010a, *China's emerging middle class: beyond economic transformation*, Brookings Institution Press, Washington, DC.

Li, C, 2001, 'Diversification of Chinese Entrepreneurs and Cultural Pluralism in the Reform Era, In Hua, SP (ed.), *Chinese Political Culture*, Armonk, New York.

Li, CL, 2005c, 'Danddai Zhongguo shehui de shengwang fenceng: zhiye shengwang yu shehui jingjidiwei zhishu celiang' ("Prestige Stratification in the Contemporary China: Occupational prestige measures and socio-economic index"), *Shehuixue yanjiu (Sociology Research)*, no. 2, pp. 74–101.

Li, CS 1999, 'Ruxue chuangxin yu Makesi zhuyi chuangxin (Innovation of Confucianism and innovation of Marxism)', *Zhexue dongtai (Contemporary Philosophy)*, no. 4, pp. 15–19.

Li, GQ 2004, *Xiandai xingzheng zhong de gongmin canyu (The civil participation in modern public administration)*, The Economic Management Press.

Li, P et al. 2007, *Zhongguo shehui hexie wending baogao (Report on social harmony and conflicts of China)*, Shehuikexue wenxian chubanshe (Social Science Literature Press), Beijing, p. 198.

Li, S 2010b, 'Gaoshang daode: haizimen chengzhang de jinshen liliang' (The fine morality: the spiritual power for the children's growth), *Renmin Jiaoyu (People's Education)*, vol. 615, p. 33–37.

Li, XG & Liu, K 1996, 'A look at the coverage of China by the mainstream US media', *Zhongguojizhe (The Chinese Journalist)*, May 15th.

Li, XG 1998, 'Dangdai Zhongguo wenhua baoshouzhuyide neihan, yiyi yu kunjing (The content, significance and dilemma of contemporary Chinese cultural conservatism)', *Tianjin shehui kexue (Tianjing Social Sciences)*, no. 1.

Liang, C 2010, 'Zhongguo ruxue yundong de fuxing yun qianjing' ('Revival and prospects of Confucianism in China'), *Hangzhou Shifan Daxue Xuebao (Journal of Hangzhou Normal University)*, no. 2.

Lieberthal, K 1995, *Governing China: from revolution through reform*, W. W. Norton, New York.

Lifton, RJ 1961, *Thought reform and the psychology of totalism: a study of "Brainwashing" in China*, Norton, New York.

Lim, L 2012, "In China, a ceaseless quest to silence dissent", viewed on November 30th, 2012, available at http://www.npr.org/2012/10/30/163658996/in-china-a-ceaseless-quest-to-silence-dissent

Lin, JX 2006, 'yetang suowei ertong dujing'(commentary on children reading the Classics), In Hu, XM (ed.), *Dujing: Qimeng haishi mengmei—laizi minjian de shengyin (Reading the Classics: Enlightenment or Obscurantism? Voices from Society)*, Huadong shifan daxue chubanshe (Huadong Normal University Press).

Lin, JY et al, 1998, 'Competition, policy burdens, and state-owned enterprise reform', *The American Economic Review*, vol. 88, pp. 422–427.

Lin, Y 1938, *The Wisdom of Confucius*, Random House, New York.

Linz, JJ & Stepan, A, 1996, *Problems of democratic transition and consolidation: Southern Europe, South America, and post-communist Europe*, John Hopkins University Press.

Lipset, MS 1983, *Political man: the social bases of politics*, Heinemann, London.

Lipset, SM 1959, 'Some social requisites of democracy: economic development and political legitimacy', *American Political Science Review*, vol. 53, no. 1, pp. 69–105.

Littlejohn, RL 2011, *Confucianism: an introduction*, I.B. Tauris, London.

Liu, Q 2006, 'Corporate governance in China: current practices, economic effects and institutional determinants', *CESifo Economic Studies*, pp. 415–453

Lixianghai, 1998, "Dangdai Zhongguo wenhua baoshouzhuyide neihan,yiyi yu kunjing" ("The Content, significance and dilemma of contemporary Chinese cultural conservatism"), *Tianjin shehui kexue (Tianjing Social Sciences)*, no. 1.

Lu, XB & Perry, EJ (ed.) 1997, *Danwei: The changing Chinese workplace in historical and comparative perspective*. M. E. Sharpe, Armonk and London.

Lu, X 2002, *Research report of the social strata in contemporary China*, Social Science Academic Press, China.

Lu, X 2010, *Dangdai zhongguo shehui jiegou* (*Contemporary Chinese social structure*), Social Science Academic Press, China.

Lufrano, RJ 1997, *Honourable merchants: commerce and self-cultivation in late Imperial China*, University of Hawai'i Press, Honolulu.

Lynn TW, 1998, *Unstately power: volume I local causes of China's economic reforms*, M.E. Sharpe, New York.

Ma, JJ, et al, 2009, 'Shinianlai shoudu daxuesheng de sixiangzhuangkuang diaocha yu fenxi' ("A Longitudinal Survey and Analysis of the Ideological Status of the College Students in Capital of China in the Past 10 Years"), Beijing jiaoyu (deyu) (Beijing Education(Moral Education)), vol. Z1, pp. 70–73.

Ma, L & Yue, C 2011, 'Woguo laogongli shichang fenge yu gaoxiao biyesheng jiuye liuxiang yanjiu' (China's labor's market segmentation and the employment of college graduates), *Jiaoyu fazhan yanjiu* (*Research on Education Development*), no. 3.

MacFarquhar R & Schoenhals M, 2006, *Mao's last revolution*, Harvard University Press, Cambridge.

MacPherson, CB, 1973, *Democratic Theory: Essays in Retrieval*, Oxford University Press, Oxford.

Madsen, R 1990, 'The spiritual Crisis of China's intellectuals', In Vogel, E & Davis, D (eds.), *Chinese society on the eve of Tiananmen: the impact of reform*, Harvard University Press, Cambridge.

Makeham, J 2003, *New Confucianism: a critical examination*, Palgrave, New York.

Makeham, J 2008, *Lost soul: Confucianism in contemporary Chinese academic discourse*, Harvard University Asia Center, Cambridge, MA and London, England.

Malloy, JM 1977, *Authoritarianism and corporatism in Latin America*, University of Pittsburgh Press, Pittsburgh.

Manion, M 1985, 'The cadre management system, post-Mao: the appointment, promotion, transfer and removal of Party and state leaders', *The China Quarterly*, vol. 102, pp. 203–233.

Mann, M 1986, *The sources of social power (Volume 1)*, Cambridge University Press, Cambridge.

Mann, M 2012, *The sources of social power: global empires and revolution, 1890–1945*, (*Volume 3*), Cambridge University Press, Cambridge.

Mannheim, K 1943, *Diagnosis of our time*, Routledge and Paul, London.

Mannheim, K 1952, *Essays on the sociology of knowledge*, Routledge & Kegan Paul, New York.

March, JG & Olsen, J 1989, *Rediscovering institutions: the organizational basis of politics*, Free Press, New York.

Marx, K 1973, 'Manifesto of the Communist Party', reprinted in *The revolutions of 1848*, Penguin Books, Harmondsworth.

Marx, K 1979, *A contribution to the critique of political economy*, Progress Publisher.

Mayntz, R & Scharpf, FW 1995, 'Der Ansatz des akteurzentrierten institutionalismus', In Mayntz, R & Scharpf, FW (eds.), *Steuerung und selbstorganisation in staatsnahen sektoren*, Campus, Frankfurt am Main, pp. 39–72.

McCall, GJ 1969, 'Data quality control in participant observation' In McCall, GJ & Simmons, JL (eds.), *Issues in participant observation*. Addison-Wesley, MA.

McCormick, BL 1990, *Political reform in post-Mao China: democracy and bureaucracy in a Leninist state*, University of California Press, Berkeley.

McKinsey Global Institute 2006, *From "made in China" to "sold in China": the rise of the Chinese urban consumer*, viewed on November, 2011, available at http://www.mckinsey.com/mgi/publications/china_consumer/index.asp

McNeill, P & Chapman, S 2005, *Research methods*, Routledge, New York.

Meissner, W 1999, 'New intellectual currents in the People's Republic of China', In Teather, D & Yee, H (eds.), *China in transition: issues and policies*, Palgrave Macmillan.

Meltzer, AH & Richard, SF 1978, "Why Government Grows (and Grows) in a Democracy." *The Public Interest*, no. 52, pp. 111–118.

Merriam, SB 2009, *Qualitative research: a guide to design and implementation*, Jossey-Bass, San Francisco, CA.

Metzger, WP 1949, 'Ideology and the intellectual: a study of Thorstein Veblen', *Philosophy of Science*, vol. 16, no. 2, pp. 125–133.

Michels, R 1962, *Political parties: a sociological study of the oligarchic tendencies of modern democracy*, Free Press, New York.

Migdal, J 2001, *State in society: studying how states and societies transform and constitute one another*, Cambridge University Press, Cambridge.

Migdal, JS 1988, *Strong societies and weak states: state-society relations and state capabilities in the Third World*, Princeton University Press, Princeton.

Migdal, JS, Kohli, A & Shue, V 1994, *State power and social forces: domination and transformation in the Third World*, Cambridge University Press, Cambridge.

Min, L & Galikowski, M 1999, *The search for modernity: Chinese intellectuals and cultural discourse in the post-Mao Era*, St, Martin's Press, New York.

Misra, K 2001, 'Curing the sickness and saving the Party: Neo-Maoism and Neo Conservatism in the 1990s', In Hua, S, (ed.), *Chinese political culture*, M. E. Sharpe, Armonk.

Mok, K 1997, 'Privatization or marketization: educational development in post-Mao China', *International Review of Education*, vol. 43, no. 5–6, pp. 547–567.

Montinola, G et al, 1996, 'Federalism, Chinese style: the political basis for economic success', *World Politics*, vol. 48, no. 1.

Moody, P 1995, Tradition and modernization in China and Japan, Wadsworth Pub. Co., Belmont.

Moody, PR 2007, *Conservative thought in contemporary China*, Lanham, Rowman & Littlefield, MD.

Moore, B 1966, *Social origins of dictatorship and democracy: lord and peasant in the making of the modern world*, Beacon Press, Boston.

Mosca, G 1939, *The ruling class*, Mcgraw Hill, New York.

Mun, CT 2003, 'School choice in the People's Republic of China', In Plank, D & Sykes, G (eds.), *Choosing choice: school choices in international perspective*, Teachers College Press, New York.

Nanfang dushi bao (*Nanfang Metropolis Daily*) 2011, 'Minguo chunian guanfang changdao de zunkong dujing' (The promotion of Confucian Classics and reverence of Confucius in the early years of ROC), 30 January, AT06.

Nanfang Weekend, 2003, '*Nanfang zhoumo* jiang chu fuhao bang yi yulun cu qiyejia dan shehui zeren' (*'Nanfang Weekend* will publish a list of the rich to encourage their willingness to shoulder social responsibilities'), 23 November, viewed on May 13th, 2011, available at news.xinhuanet.com/newmedia/2003-/content_ll83673.htm

Nathan, AJ & Link, P 2001, *The Tiananmen Papers*, Public Affairs.

Nee, V 2006, *China's politicized Capitalism*, Cornell University Press, New York.

Needham, J 1970, *Clerks and craftsmen in China and the West: lectures and addresses on the history of science and technology*, Cambridge University Press, Cambridge.

Nettl, JP 1968, 'The state as a conceptual variable', *World Politics*, vol. 20, pp. 559–592.

Ngok, K 2007, 'Chinese education policy in the context of decentralization and marketization: evolution and implications', *Asia Pacific Education Review*, vol. 8, no. 1, pp. 142–57.

Ngok, WL 2006, 'The effects of local interpretation of decentralization policy on school autonomy in Guangdong Province of China', In Bjork, C (ed.), *Education decentralization: Asian experience and conceptual contribution*, Springer.

Niskanen, WA 1971, *Bureaucracy and representative government*, Aldine-Atherton, Chicago.

Niskanen, WA 1973, *Bureaucracy: servant or master?* , Institute of Economic Affairs, London.

Nivison, DS (ed.) 1959, 'Introduction', in *Confucianism in action*, Stanford University Press, Stanford.

Nordlinger, FA 1981, *On the autonomy of the democratic state*, Harvard University Press, Cambridge, MA.

North, D 1990, *Institutions, institutional change and economic performance*, Cambridge University Press, Cambridge.

North, D 1991, '*Institutions, ideology, and economic performance*', *Cato Journal*, vol. 11, no. 3, pp. 477–488.

Oakes, T 2013. 'Heritage as improvement: Cultural display and contested governance in rural China,' *Modern China*, vol. 39, no. 4, pp. 380–407.

O'Brien, KJ & Li, LJ 2006, *Rightful resistance in rural China*, Cambridge University Press.

O'Brien, KJ 2008, *Popular protest in China*, Harvard University Press, Cambridge.

O'Donnell, G 1979, 'Tensions in Bureaucratic-Authoritarian State and the question of democracy', In David Collier, D (ed.), *The new authoritarianism in Latin America*, Princeton University Press, Princeton, NJ.

Ogden, S 2004, 'From patronage to profits: the changing relationship of Chinese intellectuals with the party-state', In Gu, X & Goldman, M (eds.), *Chinese intellectuals between state and market*, Routledge Curzon, London.

Oi, J 1985, 'Communism and clientelism: rural politics in China', *World Politics*, vol. 37, pp. 238–266.

Oi, J 1989, State and peasant in contemporary China: the political economy of village government, University of California Press, Berkeley.

Oksenberg, M & Tong, J 1991, 'The evolution of central-provincial fiscal relations in China', *The China Quarterly*, vol. 125, pp. 1–32.

Oksenberg, M 1968, 'Occupational groups in Chinese society and the Cultural Revolution,' in Oksenberg, M, Riskin, C, Scalapino, R &Vogel, E (eds), *The Cultural Revolution: 1967 in review*, University of Michigan, Ann Arbor.

Oldstone-Moore, J 2002, *Confucianism: origins, beliefs, practices, holy texts, sacred places*, Oxford University Press, New York.

Oxford Analytica Daily Brief, 2012, 'China's state legitimacy can weather economic slowdown', viewed on October, 2012, available at http://www.oxan.com/Analysis/DailyBrief/Samples/ChinaStateLegitimacy.aspx

Palmer, B 2010, 'Is there freedom of speech in China? Only symbolically', *Slate*, October 8th.

Pang, Q 2012, 'A socio-political approach to the resurgence of traditional culture in contemporary China—a case study of the Chinese government's approval of four traditional Chinese festivals as public holidays', *International Journal of China Studies*, vol. 3, no. 1.

Pang, Q 2014. 'The 'Two Lines Control Model' in China's State and Society Relations: Central State's Management of Confucian Revival in the New Century,' *International Journal of China Studies*, vol. 5, no. 3, p. 627.

Pang, Q 2016. 'Confucian Education in Urban Public Schools: An Ideological Solution to Social Disorder in China's Cities?' *China: An International Journal*, vol. 14, no. 4, pp. 70–94.

Pei, MX 1994, From reform to revolution: the demise of communism in China and the Soviet Union, Harvard University Press.

Pei, MX 2006, *China's trapped transition: the limits of developmental autocracy*, Harvard University Press, Cambridge, MA.

Pennock, JR & Chapman, JW 2009, *Coercion*, Transaction Books, New Jersey.

People's Daily (online English edition), 2003, 'CPC branches in private enterprises' July 1st.

Perry, E & Selden, M 2010, 'Reform, Conflict and Resistance in Contemporary China', *Chinese Society: Change, Conflict and Resistance*, Routledge.

Peter, E 1996, 'Government action, social capital and development: reviewing the evidence on synergy', *World Development*, vol. 24, no. 6, pp. 1119–1132.

Pew Global Center 2012, 'Growing concerns in China about inequality, corruption', viewed on October, 2012, available at http://www.pewglobal. org/2012/10/16/chapter-1-domestic-issues-and-national-problems/

Pierson, C 2011, *The modern state*, Routledge, New York.

Poggi, G 1978, *The development of the modern state: a sociological introduction*. Stanford University Press, Stanford.

Pontussen, J 1995, 'From comparative public policy to political economy: putting institutions in their place and taking interests seriously', *Comparative Political Studies*, vol. 28, pp. 117–147.

Poulantzas, N 1978, *State, power, Socialism*, Verso, London.

Price, RF 2005, *Education in modern China* [reprinted], Routledge, London.

Pye, L 1968, *The spirit of Chinese politics: a psych-cultural study of the authority crisis in political development*, MIT Press, Cambridge.

Qu, H 2011, 'Religious Policy in the People's Republic of China: an alternative perspective', *Journal of Contemporary China*, vol. 20, no. 70.

Reischauer, EO & Fairbank, JK 1962, *East Asia: the great tradition*, Houghton Mifflin, Boston.

Ren, J 2000, 'Shehui zhengzhi ruxue de chongjian—guanyu 'rujia ziyouzhuyi'de lilun' qidai' ('The reconstruction of socio-political Confucianism—about 'Confucian liberalism' theory'), *YuanDao*, vol. 7.

Research Team 1993, 'Gaige de shehui chengshouli yanjiu' (A study of the aggregate levels of collective tolerance during market transition), *Guanli Shijie (Journal of Management Science*, vol. 5, pp. 189–98.

Ridgeway, CL, 1998, 'How do status beliefs develop?', *American Sociological Review*, vol. 63, no. 3, p. 331–356.

Robertson, B & Liu, M (2006), 'Can the sage save China?', *Newsweek*, March 20.

Roucek, JS 1944, 'A history of the concept of ideology', *Journal of the History of Ideas*, vol. 5, no. 4, p. 279.

Saich, T 1994, 'The search for civil society and democracy in China', *Current History*, September, pp. 260–264.

Said, E 1994, *Representations of the intellectual*, Pantheon Books, New York.

Scharpf, F 1997, *Games real actors play, actor-centered institutionalism in policy research*, Westview Press, Boulder/Cumnor Hill.

Schmitter, P 1974, 'Still the century of corporatism?' *Review of Politics*, vol. 36, no. 1.

Schuman, M 2011, 'The case for India: free to succeed', *Time*, November 10th.

Schumpeter, J 1976, *Capitalism, Socialism, and democracy*, Allen & Unwin, London.

Schumpeter, JA 2008, *Capitalism, socialism and democracy*, Harper Perennial Modern Classics.

Schurmann, F, 1966, *Ideology and Organization in Communist China*, University of California Press, Berkeley and Los Angeles.

Scott, A 2010, 'The enforcement approach to coercion,' *Journal of Ethics and Social Philosophy*, vol. 5, pp. 1–31.

Sellers, JM 2010, 'State-Society relations', In Bevir, M (ed.), *Sage handbook of governance*, Sage Publications, London.

Selznick, P 1949, *TVA and the grass roots: a study in the sociology of formal organization*. University of California Press, Berkeley.

Shahar, M & Weller, R (eds.) 1996, *Unruly gods: divinity and society in China*, University of Hawaii Press, Honolulu.

Shambaugh, D 2000, *The Modern Chinese State*, Cambridge University Press, Cambridge.

Shambaugh, D 2007, 'China's propaganda system: institutions, processes and efficacy', *The China Journal*, vol. 57.

Shambaugh, D 2008, *China's Communist Party: atrophy and adaptation*, Woodrow Wilson Center Press & University of California Press, Washington DC & Berkeley.

Shenzhen Daily, 18 March 2008, 'Beijing Opera Comes to Bao'an' 2008, viewed on May 13th, 2011, available at http://sztqb.sznews.com/html/2008-03/18/content_100999.htm, http://bagxt.baoan.net.cn/wz_Show.asp?ArticleID=1059

Shi, D 2010, 'Rujing songdu sichao zai minjian shehui xingqi jiqi dongyuan jizhi' (The rise of the trend of reading Confucian Classics in the folk society and the mobilization mechanism), China doctoral dissertations full-text database.

Shue, V 1988, *The Reach of the State: Sketches of the Chinese Body Politics*, Stanford University Press, Stanford, CA.

Shue, V 2004, 'Legitimacy crisis in China?', In Gries, PH & Rosen, S (eds.), *State and society in 21st-century China: crisis, contention, and legitimation*, Routledge Curzon.

Simpson, P 2012, 'China's urban population exceeds rural for first time ever,' viewed on April 28th, 2012, available at http://www.telegraph.co.uk/news/worldnews/asia/china/9020486/Chinas-urban-population-exceeds-rural-for-first-time-ever.html

Sina.com 2011, 'zaopo buneng dang guoxue', viewed on October, 2012, available at http://news.sina.com.cn/c/2011-03-03/111622045558.shtml

Sina.com, 2004, *Wenhua baoshou zhuyi taitou* (*The rise of the cultural Conservatism*), viewed on January 30th, 2011, available at http://news.sina.com.cn/c/2005-01-18/11015584894.shtml

Skilling, HG 1983, 'Interest groups and Communist politics revisited', *World Politics*, vol. 36, no. 1, pp. 1–27.

Skilling, HG & Griffiths, F (eds.) 1970, *Interest groups in Soviet politics*. Princeton University Press, Princeton.

Skocpol, T 1979, *States and social revolutions*, Cambridge University Press, Cambridge.

Sleeboom-Faulkner, M 2007, *The Chinese academy of social sciences (CASS): shaping the reforms, academia and China (1977–2003)*, Brill Academic Publishers.

Smith, A 1991, *National identity*, Penguin, Harmondsworth.

Smith, A 1998, *Nationalism and modernism: a critical survey of recent theories of nations and nationalism*, Routledge, London.

Smith, A 1999, *Myths and memories of the nation*, Oxford University Press.

Solinger, D 2004, 'The new crowd of the dispossessed: the shift of the urban proletariat from master to mendicant', in Gries, PH & Rosen, S (eds.), *State and society in 21st century China: crisis, contention, and legitimation*, RoutledgeCurzon, New York.

Solomon, R 1971, *Mao's Revolution and the Chinese Political Culture*, University of California Press Berkeley.

Song, ZM 2001, 'Cong pi Kong dao shi Kong de zhuanzhe (From criticizing Confucianism to explaining Confucianism)', *Wen shi zhe (literature History and Philosophy)*, vol. 3, pp. 26–31.

Spencer, P & Wollman, H (eds.) 2005, *Nations and nationalism: a reader*, Rutgers University Press, New Brunswick.

Stake, RE 2010, *Qualitative research: studying how things work*, Guilford Press, New York.

State Administration for Industry and Commerce of the People's Republic of China, 2011, viewed on July 20th, 2011, http://www.chinanews.com/cj/2011/02-04/2827080.shtml

Steven, L 1974, *Power: a radical view*, Macmillan, London.

Strand, D 1990. 'Protest in Beijing: Civil Society and Public Sphere in China,' *Problems of Communism*, vol. 39 (May–June), pp. 1–19.

Sun, A 2009, 'Counting Confucians: who are the Confucians in contemporary East Asia?', *Newsletter of the Institute for Advanced Studies in Humanities and Social Sciences of National Taiwan University*.

Sun, A 2011, 'The revival of Confucian rites in contemporary China', In Yang, FG & Tamney, J (eds.), *Confucianism and spiritual traditions in modern China and beyond*, Brill.

Sun, L 2005, *Zhongguo ziben yuanshi jilei de sanzhong leixing ji qi yinfa de wenti (Three types of capital accumulation in China and their problems)*, viewed on April 7th, 2012, blog.sociology.org.cn/thslping/archive/2005/04/07/1375.aspx

Sun, XL 2001, *Zhongguo xiandaihua jincheng zhong de guojia yu shehui (The Chinese state and society in the process of China's modernization)*, zhongguo shehui kexue chubanshe (China Social Sciences Press).

Sun, Y 1995, *The Chinese reassessment of socialism, 1976–1992*, Princeton University Press, Princeton, New Jersey.

Sun, Y 2014, 'Popular Religion in Zhejiang: Feminization, Bifurcation, and Buddhification,' *Modern China*, vol. 40, no. 5, pp. 455–487.

Sun, Y 2017. 'The Rise of Protestantism in Post-Mao China: State and Religion in Historical Perspective,' *American Journal of Sociology*, vol. 122, no. 6, pp. 1664–1725.

Tang, C 1995, 'Lun Makesi zhuyi yu Zhongguo Ruxue' (On Marxism and Chinese Confucianism), *Renwen zazhi (Journal of Humanities)*, no. 2, pp. 31–4.

Tarrow, S 1994, *Power in movement: collective action, social movements and politics*, Cambridge University Press, Cambridge.

The Wall Street Journal, 'Lardy vs. Pettis: Debating China's economic future', November 7th, 2012.

Thelen, K & Steinmo, S 1992, 'Historical institutionalism in comparative perspective', In Thelen, K & Steinmo, S (eds.), *Structuring politics: historical institutionalism in comparative analysis*, Cambridge University Press, Cambridge.

Thomas, K 2000, *Mao Zedong, Zhou Enlai and the evolution of the Chinese communist leadership*, Nordic Institute of Asian Studies, Copenhagen.

Thompson, EP 1971, 'The moral economy of the English crowd in the eighteenth century', *Past & Present*, no. 50.

Thomson, JJ 1990, *The realm of rights*, Harvard University Press, Cambridge, MA.

Thurston, AF 1988, *Enemies of the people: the ordeal of the intellectuals in China's great cultural revolution*, Harvard University Press, Cambridge.

Tilly, C, 2004, *Social movements, 1768–2004*, Paradigm Publishers, Boulder, CO.

Timothy, B & Frolic, BM 1997, *Civil society in China*, M.E. Sharpe, Armonk, NY.

Tong, J 1989, 'Fiscal reform, elite turnover and central-provincial relations in post-Mao China', *Australian Journal of Chinese Affairs*, vol. 22, pp. 1–28.

Tong, JW 2007, *Revenge of the Forbidden City: The suppression of the falungong in China, 1999–2005*, Oxford University Press.

Tonnies, F 1887 (1963), *Community and Society*, translated by Loomis CP, reprint by Harper & Row, New York.

Townsend, J 1996, 'Chinese nationalism', In Unger, J (ed.), *Chinese nationalism*, M.E. Sharpe, New York.

Truman, DB 1951, *The governmental process: political interests and public opinion*, Alfred A. Knopf, New York.

Tsai, KS 2005, *Capitalism without democracy: the private sector in contemporary China*, Cornell University Press.

Tsang, MC 2003, "School choice in the People's Republic of China", In Plank, D & Sykes, G (eds.), *Choosing choice: school choices in international perspective*, Teachers College Press, New York.

Tu, WM 1985, *Confucian thought: selfhood as creative transformation*, State University of New York Press, Albany.

Tu, WM 1976, *Neo-Confucian thought in action: Wang Yang-ming's youth (1472–1509)*, University of California Press, Berkeley and Los Angeles.

Tu, WM 1989, *Confucianism in historical perspective*, Institute of East Asian Philosophies, Singapore.

Tu, WM 1993, *Way, learning, and politics: essays on the Confucian intellectual*, State University of New York Press, Albany.

Tu, WM 2011, 'Confucian Spirituality in Contemporary China', In Yang, FG & Tamney, J (eds.), *Confucianism and spiritual traditions in modern China and beyond*, Brill.

Tullock, G 1976, *The vote motive*, Princeton University Press, Princeton.

Unger, J & Chan, A 1995, 'China, corporatism, and the East Asian model', *Australian Journal of Chinese Affairs*, vol. 33 (January 1995), pp. 29–53.

Unger, J & Chan, A 1996, 'Corporatism in China; a developmental state in an East Asian context', In McCormick, B & Unger, J (eds.), *China after socialism, In the footsteps of Eastern Europe or East Asia?* M.E. Sharpe, Armonk, NY, pp. 95–129.

Unger, J 2008, *Associations and the Chinese state: Contested spaces*, ME Sharpe.

Van den Berghe, PL 1978, *Race and racism: a comparative perspective*, John Wiley and Sons, New York.

Van Den Berghe, PL 1995, 'Does race matter?', *Nations and Nationalism*, vol. 39, no. 3.

Van Maanen, J 1983, 'The fact and fiction in organizational ethnography', In: Van Maanen, J (ed.), *Qualitative methodology*, Sage, Beverly Hills.

Verdery, K 1991, *National ideology under socialism: identity and cultural politics in Ceausescu's Romania*, University of California Press, Berkeley, CA.

Vogel, EF 1989, *One step ahead in China: Guangdong under reform*, Harvard University Press.

Volker, M & Stehr, N (eds.) 1999, *The sociology of knowledge*, Edward Elgar, Cheltenham, UK.

Walker, KR 1984, 'Chinese agriculture during the period of the readjustment, 1978–83', *The China Quarterly*, vol. 100, pp. 783–812.

Walder, A 1985, *communist neo-traditionalism: work and authority in Chinese industry*, University of California Press, Berkeley.

Walder, A (ed.) 1995, *The waning of the communist state: economic origins of political decline in China and Hungary*, University of California Press, Berkeley.

Walder, AG 1994, 'The decline of Communist power: elements of a theory of institutional change', *Theory and Society*, vol. 23, pp. 297–323.

Waldron, AN 1985, 'Theories of nationalism and historical explanation', *World Politics: A, Quarterly Journal of International Relations*, vol. 37, no. 3, pp. 416–433.

Wang, Jie, 2006, 'chongxin wajue ruxue de dangdai jiazhi' (Re-exploring the contemporary value of Confucianism), *People's Daily* (the theoretical edition),
September 8th.

Wang, Jie, 2007a, 'rujia sixiang yu hexie guannian' (Confucian thoughts and the
idea of Harmony), *zhongguo shekeyuan xuebao (The Journal of Chinese Academy
of Social Science)*, June 26th.

Wang, Jie, 2007b, 'shidai xuyao hongyang he peiyu zhonghua minzu jinshen'
(The need to carry forward and cultivate the Chinese national spirit during our
age), *People's Daily*, March 21st.

Wang, D 2004, 'Ruxue shi women de shenghuo fangshi—Guo Qiyong xiansheng
fangtanlu' ('Confucianism as our way of living—interviews with Guo Qiyong'),
viewed on November 8th, 2011, http://www.confucius2000.com/admin/
list.asp?id=2911

Wang, SG & Hu, AG 2001, *The Chinese economy in crisis: state capacity and tax
reform*, M.E. Sharpe, Armonk, NY.

Wang, SG 1989, *From revolution to involution: state capacity, local power, and
[Un]governability in China*, Manuscript, Yale University, n.d.

Wang, SG 1995, 'The rise of the regions: fiscal reform and the decline of central
state capacity in China', In Andrew GW (ed.), *The waning of the communist
state: economic o of political decline in China and Hungary*, University of
California Press, Berkeley.

Warner, M 2000, *Changing workplace relations in the Chinese economy*, Macmillan
Press, Basingstoke and London.

Wasserstrom, JN & Perry, EJ 1994, *Popular protest and political culture in modern
China*, Westview Press, Boulder.

Weber, M 1958, *From Max Weber: essays in sociology*, translated by Gerth HH &
Mills CW, Routledge.

Weber, M 1963, 'Struggle of monarch & nobility: origin of the *career open to talent*', In Menzel, JM (ed.), *The Chinese civil service: career open to talent?*
D.C. Heath, Boston.

Weber, M 1994, 'The profession and vocation of politics', In Assman, P & Speirs,
R (eds.), *Weber political writings*, Cambridge University Press, Cambridge.

Webster, M & Hysom, SJ 1998, 'Creating status characteristics', *American
Sociological Review*, vol. 63, no. 3, pp. 351–352.

Weiss, L & Hobson, J 1995, *States and economic development: a comparative historical analysis*, Polity Press, Cambridge.

Welborn, JW 2002, 'Review for Kellee S. Tsai's *Back-alley banking: private entrepreneurs in China*', *Cato Journal*, September 22nd.

Wen, J 2011, *Jiangzhenhua chashiqin—tong guowuyuan canshi he zhonggong wenshi yanjiuguan guanyuan zuotan shi de jianghua* (Examine the fact and speak
the truth – the talk with counselors of the State Council and librarians in the
Central Cultural and History Research Center), viewed on May 13th, 2011,

available at http://news.xinhuanet.com/politics/2011-04/17/c_121314799. htm

Weston, TB 2004, 'Society's 'masters' struggle to survive: state workers, joblessness and contention in Post-Deng China', In Gries, PH & Rosen, S (eds.), *State and society in 21st century China: crisis, contention, and legitimation*, RoutledgeCurzon, New York .

Wheatley, A 2008, 'China cannot sustain its model of economic growth', *The New York Times*, February 4th.

White, G 1994, 'Democratization and Economic Reform in China', *Australian Journal of Chinese Affairs*, no. 31.

White, G, Howell, J & Shang, X 2004, *In search of civil society: market reform and social change in contemporary China*, Oxford University Press.

White, G 1993. *Riding the Tiger: The Politics of Economic Reform in Post-Mao China*. Stanford: Stanford University Press.

White, LT 1987. 'Thought workers in Deng's time', In Goldman, M. (ed.), *China's intellectuals and the state: in search of a new relationship*, Harvard University Press, Cambridge.

Whiting, S 2000, *Power and wealth in rural China: the political economy of institutional change*, Cambridge University Press, Cambridge.

Whiting, S 1991, 'The Politics of NGO Development in China,' *Voluntas*, vol. 2, no. 2 (November), pp. 16–48.

Whyte, MK 1992. 'Prospects for Democratization in China,' *Problems of Communism* (May–June), pp. 58–70.

Williams, J 2010. "Attacking Queshan': Popular Culture and the Creation of a Revolutionary Folklore in Southern Henan,' *Modern China*, vol. 36, no. 6, pp. 644–675.

Wittfogel, K 1963 "*The hereditary privilege vs. merit*", In Menzel, JM (ed.), *The Chinese Civil Service: Career Open to Talent?* D.C. Heath, Boston.

Wittfogel, KA 1957, *Oriental despotism, a comparative study of total power*, Yale University Press, New Haven.

Wohlgemuth, M 2002, 'Evolutionary approaches to politics', *Kyklos*, vol. 55, no. 2, pp. 2232–2246.

Wolff, J (ed.) 1987, *Stanford Encyclopedia of Philosophy*, Stanford University.

Wong, C 1991, 'Central–local relations in an era of fiscal decline: the paradox of fiscal decentralization in post-Mao China', *China Quarterly*, vol. 128.

Wong, C 1992, 'Fiscal reform and local industrialization', *Modern China*, vol. 18, no. 2.

Worden, RL, Savada, AM & Dolan, RE 1987, *China: a country study*, US Government Printing Office, Washington.

Wright, AF 1959, *Buddhism in Chinese history*, Stanford University Press, Stanford, CA.

Wright, T 2004, 'Intellectuals and the politics of protest: the case of the China democratic party', In Gu, X & Goldman, M (eds.), *Chinese intellectuals between state and market*.

Wright, T 2010, *Accepting authoritarianism: state-society relations in China's reform era*, Stanford University Press, Stanford.

Wu, C 2006a, 'Ruxuede dangdai fuxing jiqi zhexue jingyu' (The revival of Confucianism and its development in philosophy), *Zhongguo zhexue nianjian* (*China philosophy yearbook*), Zhexue zazhi chubanshe (Philosophy Journal Press), Beijing.

Wu, G 2010, 'Xinshiji ruxue fuxinde shida biaozhi yu zhanwang' ('The ten signs of the revival of Confucianism in the new century and prospects for the future'), viewed on February 21st, 2011, http://www.cssn.cn/news/159326.htm

Wu, J 2006b, *Ziben yuanshi jilei zai zhongguo jiushi guozi de liushi* (*Primitive accumulation of capital and the transfer of state properties into the private sector*), viewed February 8th, 2010, finance.sina.com.cn/review/zlhd/20060208/09322325142.shtml

Wu, S 2015. 'Politicisation and De-Politicisation of Confucianism in Contemporary China: A Review of Intellectuals,' *Issues and Studies*, vol. 51, no. 3, p. 165.

Wu, X 2004, *Beikuaida de shiming (An exaggerated mission)*, Zhejiang Renmin Chubanshe (Zhejiang People's Press), Hangzhou.

Xiang Chunling, 2008, 'rujia wenhua de xiandai yiyi' (The Modern Implications of Confucian Culture), Conference paper in the 2008 Forum for Marxism and Confucianism.

Xiang, CL 2008, *rujia wenhua de xiandai yiyi (The modern implications of Confucian culture)*, In Forum for Marxism and Confucianism, 2008, Beijing.

Xiao, GQ 2008, *zhongguo de da zhuanxing (The great transformation of China)*, Xinxin chubanshe (New Star publishing house).

Xiao, XH 2004, *Gongmin shehui de dansheng (The birth of civil society)*, Sanlian Press, Shanghai.

Xinhua News Agency, 2010, *dangnei tongji zhuanti xinwen fabuhui (The new press for statistics concerning the CCP)*, viewed on October 31st, 2011, available at http://www.xinhuanet.com/zhibo/20100628a/zhibo.htm

Xinhuanet, 2012, 'zhongguo caizheng shouru shoupo shiyiyuan daguan', viewed on February 20th, 2013, available at http://news.xinhuanet.com/fortune/2012-01/20/c_111454601.htm

Xu, CG & Zhuang, JZ 1998, 'Why China grew: the role of decentralization', In Boone, P et al (eds.), *Emerging from communism: lessons from Russia, China, and Eastern Europe*, MIT Press, Cambridge, MA.

Xu, F 2007, *Shaoer guoxue duben (Children's textbook of national studies)*, Jinan daxue chubanshe (Jinan University Press), Guangzhou.

Xu, S 2017. 'Cultivating national identity with traditional culture: China's experiences and paradoxes,' *Discourse: Studies in the Cultural Politics of Education*, 2017, no. 4, pp. 1–14.

Xu, X 2000, 'Cong zhiye pingjia yu zeye quxiang kan Zhongguo shehui jiegou bianqian' ("Changes in the Chinese social structure as seen from occupational prestige ratings and job preferences"), *Shehuixue yanjiu (Sociology Research)*, no. 3.

Xu, Y 2003, *Rural governance and Chinese politics*, China Social Sciences Publishing House Beijing.

Xue, Y 2004, 'zouxiangmengmei de wenhua baoshou zhuyi'(Cultural Conservatism Marching forward to Cultural Obscurantism), *Nangfang Zhoumo (Nanfang Weekend)*, July 8th.

Xue, Y 2007, 'shenme shi mengmei? zaiping dujing' (what is Cultural Obscurantism? Commentary on Reading the Classics), *Lilun Cankao (Theory References)*, no. 7.

Yang, DL 2004, *Remaking the Chinese Leviathan: market transition and the politics of governance in China*, Stanford University Press, Stanford.

Yang, FG & Tamney, J (eds.) 2011, *Confucianism and Spiritual Traditions in Modern China and Beyond*, Brill Academic Publishing house.

Yang, MM 1989. 'Between State and Society: The Construction of Corporateness in a Chinese Socialist Factory,' *Australian Journal of Chinese Affairs*, vol. 22 (July), pp. 31–60.

Yang, X 2008, 'Shijian shi weidade chuangzao, zuihao de jianyan'(Practice is a great creation, a best test), *Xin Ru Bao (New Confucian Newspaper)*, June 20th.

Yangzhou rushang yanjiuhui (Yangzhou Confucian Entrepreneur Studies Association) 2007, *Dangdai rushang fengcai lu (Profiles of contemporary Confucian entrepreneurs)*, Zhongyang wenxian chubanshe (Central Literature Press), Beijing.

Yao, XZ 2000, *An introduction to Confucianism*, Cambridge University Press, Cambridge.

Yep, R 2000. 'The Limitations of Corporatism for Understanding Reforming China: an empirical analysis in a rural county,' *Journal of Contemporary China*, vol. 9, no. 25, pp. 547–566.

Yi, L 1994, *Zhongguo Makesi zhuyi yu xiandai xinrujia (China's Marxism and New Confucianism)*, Liaoning University Press, Shenyang.

Yijie, T 1991, 'Ruxue de xiandaihua wenti' (The question of Confucianism modernization). *Tianjin shehui kexue (Tianjin Social Sciences)*, no. 2, pp. 45–49.

Yin, RK 2004, *The case study anthology*, Sage, London.

Yin, RK 2011, *Applications of case study research*, Sage, London.

Yu, JY 2002, *Contemporary Chinese philosophy*, Blackwell, Oxford.

Yu, S 1997a, 'Special overview: political enthusiasm exists side by side with political indifference', *Chinese Education and Society*, vol. 30, no. 3, pp. 65–72.

Yu, T 2008, 'The revival of Confucianism in Chinese schools: a historical-political review', *Asia Pacific Journal of Education*, vol. 28, no. 2.

Yu, YS 1987, *Zhongguo jinshi zongjiao lunli yu shangren jingshen (Modern Chinese religious philosophy and spirit of Merchantman)*, Lian jing chu ban shi ye gong si, Taipei.

Yu, YS 1997b, 'Business culture and Chinese traditions—toward a study of the evolution of merchant culture in Chinese history', In Wang, G & Wong, SL (eds.), *Dynamic Hong Kong: business and culture*, The Hong Kong University Press, Hongkong.

Yu, YS 2004, *Rujia lunli yun shangren jingshen* (The Confucian ethic and the spirit of businessman), *guangxi shifan daxue chubanshe (guangxi Normal University Press)*, Nanning China.

Yuan, WS, 2006, 'ping dujing' (Commentary on Reading the Classics), In Hu, XM (ed.), *Dujing: Qimeng haishi mengmei—laizi minjian de shengyin (Reading the Classics: Enlightenment or Obscurantism? Voices from Society)*, Huadong shifan daxue chubanshe (Huadong Normal University Press).

Yuan, W 2005, 'Ping jibaocheng xiaozhangde chongzhen guoxuelun' ('Comments on President Ji Baocheng's theory of reviving national studies'), *Nanfang dushibao (The Southern Metropolis Daily)*, viewed on January 12th, 2012, http://www.southcn.com/nfsq/ywhc/ls/200506100291.htm

Yuan, Y & Zhang, H 2009, '2008 nian Zhonguo jumin shenghuo zhilian diaocha baogao' (2008 Survey of living standards of Chinese citizens), In Ru, X et al. (eds.), *2009 nian Zhongguo shehui xingshi fenxi yu yuce (Society of China: analysis and forecast for 2009)*, Social Sciences Academic Press, Beijing.

Yue, QW 2003, *Ru dang xu zhi (What You Have to Know to Join the Party)*, Shanghai Renmin Chubanshe (Shanghai People's Press), Shanghai, China.

Zang, X 2008, 'Market transition, wealth and status claims', In Goodman, DSG (ed.), *The new rich in China: future rulers, present lives*, Routledge, London.

Zeitlin, M 1980, *Classes, class conflict, and the State: empirical studies in class analysis*, Winthrop, Cambridge, MA.

Zhang, EF 2007, *Guoxue jianshi (Brief history of national studies)*, Chongqing Publishing House, Chongqing.

Zhang, et al (eds.) 2008, *Shaoer guoxue duben (Textbook for children reading the Classics)*, Yuelu Shushe press, Changsha.

Zhang, H 2002, 'Special report on China's private entrepreneur', In Lu, X (ed.), *Research report of the social strata in contemporary China*, Social Science Academic Press, China.

Zhang, Y 2008, 'Dangdai Zhongguo zhongchan jieceng de zhengzhi taidu' (Political attitudes of the middle stratum in contemporary China), *Zhongguo shehui kexue (Chinese Social Sciences)*, vol. 2, Summer.

Zhao, S 2016. 'The Ideological Campaign in Xi's China,' *Asian Survey*, vol. 56, no. 6, pp. 1168–1193.

Zhao, SH 1997, 'Chinese intellectuals' quest for national greatness and nationalistic writing in the 1990s', *The China Quarterly*, vol. 152, no. 2.

Zhao, SH 2004, *A nation-state by construction: dynamics of modern Chinese nationalism*, Stanford University Press.

Zheng, Y 2004a, 'The status of Confucianism in modern Chinese education, 1901–49: a curricular study', In Peterson, G & Lu, Y (eds.), *Education, culture and identity in 20th century China*, Hong Kong University Press, Hong Kong.

Zheng, Y 2004b, *Will China become democratic? elite, class and regime transition*, Eastern Universities Press, Singapore.

Zheng, YN 1999, *Discovering Chinese nationalism in China: modernization, identity, and international relations*, Cambridge University Press, New York.

Zheng, YN 2007, *De facto federalism in China: reforms and dynamics of central-local relations*, World Scientific Publishing, London.

Zheng, YN 2010, *The Chinese Communist Party as organizational emperor: culture, reproduction, and transformation*, Routledge, London.

Zhongguo ruxue nianjian (China yearbook of Confucianism) 2009, Zhongguo ruxue nianjian chubanshe (China Confucianism Yearbook Press), Beijing.

Zhongguo siying jingji nianjian 2002 (China's yearbook for private economic sector 2002) 2003. Zhonghua gongshang lianhe chubanshe (Chinese Industrial and Commerce Alliance Press), Beijing, China.

Zhongguo siying jingji nianjian 2008 (China's yearbook for private economic sector 2008) 2009. Zhonghua gongshang lianhe chubanshe (Chinese Industrial and Commerce Alliance Press), Beijing, China.

Zhongguo Tongji Zhaiyao 2010 (*China statistical abstract*), Zhongguo tongji chubanshe (China Statistic Press), Beijing.

Zhou, K 2009, *China's long march to freedom: grassroots modernization*, Transaction Publisher, New Brunswick.

Zhou, L 2014. 'Administrative Subcontract (xingzheng fabaozhi),' *Society (shehui)*, vol. 34, no. 6, pp. 1–38.

Zhou, X 2000. 'Reply: Beyond the debate and toward substantive institutional analysis,' *American Journal of Sociology*, vol. 105, no. 4, pp. 1190–1195.

Zhou, X 2010. 'The institutional logic of collusion among local governments in China,' *Modern China*, vol. 36, no. 1, pp. 47–78.

Zhu, X 2010, *Zhongguo Chuantong Wenhua (The Chinese Traditional Culture)*, People's University Press, Beijing.

Zhuang, Y 1991, 'Dui xiandai xin Ruxue jige wenti de zhenglun:'Xiandai xin Ruxue yu dangdai Zhongguo xueshu taolunhui' guandian jianjie (Debates on several questions of new Confucianism, Symposium on of new Confucianism and contemporary China)', *Xueshuyanjiu (Academic Research)*, no. 2, pp. 24–25, 60.

Zong G, Li P, Sun C 2016a, Research on Occupational Prestige Rank and Its Changes (*gaigekaifang yilai woguo zhiye shengwang paixu paixu ji bianqian yanjiu*), Journal of Beijing Industrial College, (Beijing gongye daxue xuebao), vol. 16, no. 2, pp. 11–17.

Zong, G, Li, PD & Sun, CC, 2016b, 'Gaigekaifang yilai woguo zhiye shengwang paixu ji bianqian yanjiu' ("Study on Ordination and Changes of the Occupational Prestige Since the Reform and Opening-up"), *Beijinggongyedaxue xuebao (Journal of Beijing University of Technology)*, no. 2, pp. 11–17.

Zurndorfer, HT 2004, 'Confusing Confucianism with Capitalism: culture as impediment and/or stimulus to Chinese economic development', paper presented to the Third Global Economic History Network Meeting, Konstanz, Germany, 3–5 June. *2005 Zhongguo siying qiye diaocha baogao (2005 investigation of China's private enterprises)* 2005, viewed on January 13th, 2011, http://www.southcn.com/finance/gdmqgc/gdmqyyrl/200502030218.html

Index[1]

[1] Note: Page numbers followed by 'n' refer to notes.

© The Author(s) 2019
Q. Pang, *State-Society Relations and Confucian
Revivalism in Contemporary China*,
https://doi.org/10.1007/978-981-10-8312-9

Printed by Printforce, the Netherlands